The Roman Empire in Transition and Crisis

The Roman Empire in Transition and Crisis

An Alternative History

Timothy Venning

PEN & SWORD
HISTORY

First published in Great Britain in 2024 by
Pen & Sword History
An imprint of Pen & Sword Books Limited
Yorkshire – Philadelphia

ISBN 978 1 03610 363 7

A CIP catalogue record for this book is
available from the British Library.

Typeset by Mac Style
Printed in the UK by CPI Group (UK) Ltd, Croydon, CR0 4YY.

MIX
Paper | Supporting responsible forestry
FSC® C013604

The Publisher's authorised representative in the EU for product safety is Authorised Rep Compliance Ltd., Ground Floor, 71 Lower Baggot Street, Dublin D02 P593, Ireland.
www.arccompliance.com

For a complete list of Pen & Sword titles please contact

PEN & SWORD BOOKS LIMITED
47 Church Street, Barnsley, South Yorkshire, S70 2AS, England
E-mail: enquiries@pen-and-sword.co.uk
Website: www.pen-and-sword.co.uk
or
PEN AND SWORD BOOKS
1950 Lawrence Road, Havertown, PA 19083, USA
E-mail: uspen-and-sword@casematepublishers.com
Website: www.penandswordbooks.com

Contents

Introduction

The Story So Far…

How the Empire reaches the position which it is in in this timeline by 641, i.e. dominating Europe and the Middle East. A summary of the context of this book, i.e. the changes to real history in my timeline in (i) my Sealion Press internet 'blogs' on AD 180 to 375, Marcus Aurelius to Julian (ii) my Pen and Sword AH Rome book no. 1, AD 375–641.

My altered timeline to this point, in 641, starts with one crucial changed event in the reign of one great Emperor, Marcus Aurelius (r. 161–180): he does not die in the middle of his Danubian campaigns so the Roman absorption of one future hostile power-bloc, the middle Danubian/Bohemian 'German' tribes, is not halted and his incompetent and unstable son Commodus does not succeed him. (This is the start of Edward Gibbon's *Decline and Fall of the Roman Empire* and has long been seen as the end of rule by a line of 'good emperors' and the start of 'decline'.) In Gibbons' words, an age of silver is replaced by an age of iron. In my timeline there is a direct succession from one competent and hard-working emperor, Marcus Aurelius, in 190 (aged 68) to another, i.e. the ageing and irascible but capable general Pertinax (assassinated soon after replacing Commodus in real life 193, but in my version able to rule for a few years, keep Roman occupation of the lands which Marcus annexed in the modern Czach region, and die naturally. He is then succeeded, with a less destructive civil war than in OTL ('our timeline' i.e. reality), by the real-life North African 'hard man' Septimius Severus, despotic and a distrustful outsider to the Italian elite so reliant more on military might than on consent. A succession of minor or major divergences from the real life politico-military crises of the mid-3rd century sees the Empire break up in the 260s (as in OTL) but then be reunited by a series of strong rulers, starting with the OTL reunifier Aurelian – who lasts longer than he did in reality and is not murdered in a plot after a five-year reign.

The new bureaucratic centralized autocracy of Diocletian (to 305) and Constantine 'the Great' (to 340), the first of them a militant and persecuting pagan and the second the creator of a Christian-led Empire, is much as in OTL, but they are ruling a less ravaged and insecure Empire. The persecution of the Christians by Diocletian and company is less harsh and traumatic across the Empire than in OTL due to the earlier downfall of the leading persecutor,

Galerius: the first of several seemingly minor 'butterflies' from the real-life story that have major effects. In this case, the downfall of Galerius means a less intense persecution than in reality, so fewer victims and fewer resulting 'martyr cults' of heroic Christian victims of pagan brutality – a focus for post-pagan popular devotion and local patriotism in and after the Late Empire, so a useful channel to convert the public to Christian worship. There is less bitterness among the surviving Christian 'elite' at the secular, pagan Empire leadership and at those senior Christians who obeyed orders from the State to worship the traditional gods or be killed and at those bishops who meekly surrendered Christian books to be burnt. This lowers the level of inter-Christian feuding in the 4th century, and the level of support by lower-level Christians for anti-pagan hard-liners who want a full purge of pagan shrines and festivals once there are Christians in the Imperial office and the Emperors' Council. These factors are still there, but the 'moderates' who prefer accommodation with the pagan Greco-Roman cultural world and its artefacts are stronger (boosted by a longer reign by and legal protection by pagan emperor Julian, in 360/1–377 not 361–3). More of the pagan world survives into the 6th century and thereafter, with its cults marginalised but rarely banned – and the concept of 'Hellene' i.e. pagan Greek culture does not get a bad name in official and 'high status' cultural circles as it did in OTL Byzantium. My world is as much the heir of the – revered – early Roman emperors, e.g. Augustus, Trajan, and Hadrian – as it is of the Christian world-vision and its rejection of pagan beliefs, with the more monotheistic aspects of pagan Neoplatonism still powerful in intellectual circles and pagan teachers and (secular) schools still active.

Constantine secures the West in 306/312 as in reality, and the East in 324 as ditto. He dies later, in 340 not as in OTL 337, and there is less turbulence and civil war under his sons in the 340s and 350s : but still a civil war in 350–3. As in OTL, the paranoid survivor of Constantine's sons, Constantius II, tries to promote the 'heretic' Arian doctrine and gives power to its bishops and divides the quarelling Christian sects further; he is then overthrown by his young cousin Julian, an idealistic pagan and would-be restorer of the traditional Classical empire and pagan religion

My first Pen and Sword book (AD 375–641), covering the real-life age of the final break-up of the Empire and 'fall' of the West, starts with the reign of the last pagan Emperor, Julian (b 331, r. 360–1 to 363 in real life). An idealist for the Classical era and its culture and religion, a surprisingly good general for his lack of training, and a man determined to reverse the rise of an intolerant monotheism at the heart of the Roman elite. But the heir to a dynasty founded on the alliance with the Catholic Church by his charismatic and long-reigning great-uncle Constantine 'the Great', to which he stood in direct contrast, as well as the leader and beneficiary of a rebellion against his uncle and brother-in-law Constantius II, Constantine's son, in 360–1.

In this version, Julian has sixteen not two years to use his resources and supporters to redress the balance of government in favour of the pagans and hinder Christianity, and he also has the prestige of defeating the Sassanian realm of Persia and annexing Mesopotamia – but he has no heir, as in OTL.

Julian defeats Persia in 363–4 – more luck and more resources than in reality, plus Constantine surviving longer than in OTL to be able to launch his planned invasion of Mesopotamia in 337 and heavily defeat the Sassanian army, acquiring crucial border fortresses so Julian's war can be launched from a more advantageous position with extra aid from Armenian and Arab mercenaries. Julian annexes Mesopotamia with its trade-routes and riches, breaks up Persia into a network of vassal-states supplying him with troops and money, and lasts to 377.

Paganism – i.e. the more important local temples and cults – is revived with Imperial subsidies and (mostly local gentry) priestly recruits, and has a more 'level playing-field' to contest with Christianity on. Julian revives the cultural and educational aspects of paganism and its leading priesthoods' wealthy aristocratic social 'input' to keep a substantial section of society committed to it, and does his best to paint Christianity as unpatriotic, illogical in its divisive theology, and prone to feuding. He also brings supporters of his beliefs into the mainstream of government in both Italy and Constantinople – and in Alexandria (with the main 'Praefecture' over-governorship of North Africa) and Antioch (ditto for the Levant). His work is cut off short but not nearly as soon as in real life – and his military success helps to add to his elite (including military) support and to warn his Christian successors off drastic measures against the pagans. The continued conversions to Christianity are slower in the later 4th century and the great pagan cults last longer. Their aristocratic personnel are less hostile to and divorced from work for the State than in OTL, so the Empire has a broader 'base' of expert officials and slightly better (and less corrupt as not needing to make cash quickly) ministers – a 'tweak' in favour of more competent rule.

There is less of a divergence between the elites in Rome itself and at the Western Court in Mediolanum/Milan than in OTL – and the importance of the 'Julianic' elite to the government in the 370s means that this 'bloc' has to be courted by Julian's Christian successors from 377, Valentinian and Theodosius, more than they needed to do in OTL. This means less aggressive 'Christianizing' legislation – and no mass-closures of temples and cults (or the Olympic Games). Fearing plots, the aggressively Catholic Theodosius has to be more cautious than in real life.

Also, the eclectic Julian does not promote Christianity when he overruns Mesopotamia and western Persia and he allows local Zoroastrianism to continue and co-opts the elites into his army and civil service, so the landed aristocracy and priests are not as anti-Rome as they would be under a Christian empire – though now the Empire has to help its vassal-kings in upland Persia/Media (modern Iran) keep back the raiding Turkic nomads from Central Asia so it has an added security problem. (This will distract even the capable and alert Julian from tackling the hordes of Gothic refugees from the Huns in 376–7 so he is not much better than the real-life sluggish Emperor Valens – Valentinian's brother, ruler of the East, in OTL – in averting disaster).

The Goths migrate West from the Ukraine steppes from the invading Huns and threaten to cross the Danube by force, as in reality. The capable and Christian Valentinian succeeds Julian in 377 (Emperor in 364–75 in OTL) as the latter has lost his last surviving adult male relative, Procopius and Valentinian is the best uncontroversial military leader to hand, and Valentinian fights the Goths in 378 – not his less competent brother Valens as in OTL. (He was ruler of just the West and died in 375, before the war, in OTL.) He wins the equivalent to the battle of Adrianople (but is killed there) so the Goths cannot settle as a semi-autonomous kingdom within Empire as they did in OTL .

Theodosius then succeeds to the East in 379 as the choice of Valentinian's inexperienced elder son Gratian, next ruler of the West, as in OTL, and is a militant Catholic as in OTL, but is too weak to ban paganism as in OTL as Julian has given it stronger hold within the elite and resources and he is too scared of causing a rebellion by its backers; he does defeat the Western emperor Maximus (Gratian's overthrower in 383) in 383–8 as in OTL.

There is no 392 rebellion in the West, so Theodosius has no excuse to shut down pagan worship after this: in OTL the pagan elite of Rome aided the rebels so he repressed them and their religion after his victory in 394.

Theodosius does not die in 395, aged forty-seven, as in OTL so the Empire is not broken up into separate states ruled by his young sons Arcadius (East) and Honorius (West) then, and there is no Gothic attack on Greece either as the Goths are Roman vassal allies north of the lower Danube after losing the 378 confrontation.

Theodosius does not lose Italy to a pagan-led revolt in 392 so he does not purge the pagans, though he restricts their cults and cuts State funding to them; he dies in 407 not 395 and has secured the Rhine frontier plus an allied German protectorate from the Rhine to the Elbe so the great 'barbarian' crossing of the frontier in 408 (OTL406) is of the Elbe not the Rhine. The crossing is impelled both by the Huns' advance and by German land-hunger, as in OTL, and advantage is taken of Theodosius' recent death in my version but of a weak Western regency's government over the past decade in OTL. In my version the West is stronger as it has had no 392–4 civil war and Theodosius (and his predecessors) retained Roman rule of Dacia and Marcomannia/Bohemia so the 'central region' Roman frontier is the Carpathian chain, not crossable rivers all the way from the Channel to the Danube. The German invasions are on a narrower front, and there are no Goths already within the East (Thrace) to weaken it as in OTL.

As a result there is an invasion across the Elbe and then the Rhine which is pushed back by Rome, which it did not do in OTL – though the internal tensions in the Empire then destroy war-winner, Western commander in chief/regent Stilicho (but not his officer-corps as in OTL so the West has a stronger army after this). The uncontrolled German tribal wanderings and disruption within the weakened Western Empire in the 410s to the early 450s are in Germany east of the Rhine, a lightly Romanised 'allied German kingdoms' area, not in the more crucial Rhineland and Gaul to the West – so the effect on the Empire and its revenues is much less.

As a result, the 'arc' of crisis and disruption in the period after Theodosius' death in the West is less, Italy is not touched, there is a stronger Western military leadership able to keep the Germans as semi-subject allies, the coalition that fights Attila the Hun is more heavily weighted in Rome's favour – and the West can recover after the defeat of Attila in 451, which in OTL it does not.

The invasion crises of the late 400s do not involve Alaric the Goth attacking the Empire and ravaging Italy as he is by now a Roman general; he fights for power within the Roman military power-structure, as a semi-autonomous general, gets involved with a revolt by Roman generals on the Rhine to help the regency government out in return for land, and loses. The half-German general Stilicho is regent of the West for his son-in-law Honorius only in 407–12, once Theodosius dies, not in 395–408 as in OTL, and ends up killed in a purge in 412 (not 408 as in OTL) in different circumstances. There is a civil war and a German invasion around 408–12 as in OTL but it has a different trajectory, and the Western Empire holds the Rhine frontier (shakily) and keeps Britain. The civil war is less dangerous as the army in Britain does not get involved, and less of Gaul (and none of Spain) is overrun – so the Vandals do not get into a position ready to invade North Africa and cut off the West's grain-supplies later in the 420s.

After 412 the strongman of the West is Constantius III, the general married to weak emperor Honorius' sister Galla Placidia, as after 410/11 in OTL, but he does not die in 421 but lives until 439 so there is no lapse in central leadership and civil war in the 420s; the Vandals etc. are contained East of the Rhine and do not penetrate to Spain and North Africa as in OTL. The Constantinian regime is stronger than in OTL as well as lasting longer, and integrates more German officers and soldiers into the Roman military 'machine' to help it keep the anti-

Roman tribes beyond the Elbe and the Huns behind them at bay. As there are no German tribal states within the old Roman frontier, the Empire keeps its full 390s-level tax-revenues and can fund a large army – and the lack of real-life ravaging means more agricultural prosperity and more government income.

Constantius III passes on a unified and strong Western Roman army and government to Aetius as chief minister in 439, and the Vandals under Gaiseric are kept back East of the Rhine while Attila the Hun is kept out of Dacia and Hungary by the Roman control of the Carpathians; the Huns can only attack the East, via the Lower Danube.

Attila the Hun is less of a threat to the East or West in the 440s as the Empire holds the Carpathian frontier, but still takes over the lower Danube region; he then heads west via Poland to destroy the Vandal kingdom in the Elbe region and invades the Rhineland in 451. Aetius with a stronger Romano-German force defeats him there, East of the Rhine, and after his death creates a Roman protectorate of his revolted ex-vassals in Poland/W Ukraine. The West is thus militarily stronger than the East, but the latter has been reinforced in the 430s-40s by refugees from Attila so it has a larger army and more tax-revenues. The East is not so dependant on Aspar and other German generals, and the West is dominated militarily by a mixed Romano-German 'high command' under Constantius III and then Aetius (A as strongman and commander in chief to Constantius' and Galla Placidia's weak and immature son Valentinian III). Britain remains Roman, the Saxons are less of a threat, and Ireland is converted by St Patrick as in OTL but as a Roman ploy to Christianise and 'de-fang' the raiding Irish kingdoms and so save on expense on an Irish Sea anti-piracy fleet.

Valentinian III is betrayed as he tries to have Aetius murdered in 454, instead of killing him as in OTL; instead Aetius has the emperor killed in 455 and puts his son Gaudentius on the Western throne as his puppet, married to Valentinian's daughter Placidia. The West is run by a military 'junta' of Aetius and his officers, and after Aetius dies in 469 Gaudentius is murdered for trying to stage a comeback and replaced by the dynamic military commander Majorian (OTL emperor in 457–62). The Romano-German officer corps dominates the Empire and forces the landed aristocracy to pay enough taxes to fund an impressively large army, with the German lands NE of the Rhine as Roman allied vassal-states and the surviving Huns back in the Ukraine as a second-rate raiding threat to the East.

Majorian has no children and is succeeded by the OTL Western Emperor of 467–72 who is slightly altered in name and ability, 'Tiberius II Anthemius', in 488. By this point, due to the Eastern rebellion of 484 and the contentious nature of Zeno's emperorship there in 474–91, the West is the more stable state and is stronger militarily. In this version of events the Rome-allied German states between Rhine and Elbe after Attila's downfall include the refugee Franks and Ostrogoths, and their rulers include the OTL kings Clovis and Theodoric; and their pressure on land in the Lower Saxony region drives some local Saxons as refugees to Britain as 'boat people' in the late 5th century to settle on the 'Saxon Shore' in the south-east.

As Western Emperor from 496, Tiberius' son Titus II (my creation) proceeds to expand the West's trade and military power and incorporates incoming German settlers and soldiers into the Empire, once Romanised, to add to agricultural and military manpower. Some of the OTL late C5th and C6th Germanic kings are among them, with the dynasty of Frankish king Clovis and some of the OTL settlers in Britain, where a part of the Angles from Denmark move after their lands are attacked by the Ostrogothic king Theodoric (in this version settled in N Germany). There is thus an 'Anglian' settlement in E Anglia and Lincs in Britain. The Roman trading allies in the Baltic *include the Geatish king Beowulf (appears in OTL legends). To the South, Roman trade extends over the Sahara to Lake Chad and by sea from Gades (Cadiz) to explore the West African coast and find the Canary Islands, using past Carthaginian exploration records – and there are rumours of America (ignored).

The orthodox/Catholic revolt against Eastern Emperor Anastasius' attempt to enforce a religious compromise with the Monophysites, led by rebel Catholic/ Orthodox 'grip' general Vitalian as in OTL, is used by Emperor Titus of the West to invade and help the Catholic cause, backing up the Pope. Anastasius has to accept a fully Orthodox Church, as in OTL, but in this version Titus makes him agree to himself as co-ruler too; when Anastasius dies in 518 Titus reunifies the Empire. Thus there is no Emperor Justin in the East in 518–27 as in OTL, and his nephew and heir 'Justinian' (born Petrus Sabbatius) appears in this story as a civilian chief minister (Praefect of Constantinople) of the main part of the East to Titus II but not as Emperor. With no Justinian in charge, there is no harsh persecution of non-orthodox Christians or pagans, and there is no 'thought control' of the intellectual atmosphere to marginalise pagan philosophy and drive the pagans out of the University of Athens. There is bureaucratic centralization as in OTL, but under a ruler more sympathetic to paganism and the Classical inheritance and to non-orthodox thinkers – and with no costly wars to reconquer the West and Persia a quiescent vassal state the Empire is less exhausted by oppressive taxation. Titus is prepared to use the Church's 'message' of 'render unto Caesar the things that are Caesar's', i.e. obey the State as long as it does not persecute you; but he is hostile to the basic Christian theological refusal to accept other faiths and keeps a firm grip on the Church's bishops as a supportive department of State with no ideological 'grip' on the policies of the ruler/ministers.

As in OTL the network of archbishops between the 'top level of Pope/ Patriarchs and the 'bottom level' of local bishops in the Church hierarchy mirrors the hierarchy of secular administration – as planned by Constantine 'the Great'. At the top level – secular – Court and ministers in the capital, Rome, and then Praefects in the leading cities of Empire at 'sub-capital' level, i.e. Constantinople, Alexandria, Antioch, Ctesiphon, Trier, Milan/Mediolanum, each controlling the city in question with oversight of surrounding region (the Antioch 'Praefect' heads the regional division of 'Oriens', 'the East' i.e. of the pre-Persian-annexation frontier); then regional 'over-governors' each controlling five or six provinces, termed 'Vicars'; then provincial governors of around sixty small provinces.(This is the basic OTL system set up by Diocletian and Constantine 'the Great', c. 290 to 330.) Religious: Pope in Rome and Patriarchs in Constantinople, Alexandria, Antioch, Jerusalem, Ctesiphon; then medium level of archbishops, one per province; then local bishops in towns and cities. Military: a hierarchy of frontier over-commanders of one or more provinces ('Counts'), some with special 'roving commissions', and one *'dux'* (origin of our 'duke', i.e. 'leader') per province in those provinces needing garrison troops. A 'high command' of the central army ('Comitatus') in Rome, and its regional sub-divisions overseeing a particular frontier.

In this version of events, Titus (d 542) and his dynasty then rule all of the Empire, usually from Rome; the Eastern border is now at the River Oxus and along the approx. modern Iran/Afghanistan border, with the broken-up sub-states of the former Sassanid empire (atomized by Julian in 363–4) under Rome-allied Sassanid princes in Persis, Hycrania and Media – and by this point Rome has taken over Bactria too. Following an Epthalite Huns attempt to install a vassal-state in Sogdiana (north of river Oxus, i.e. approx. Uzbekistan) in the 520s, Rome takes it over to stop attacks on Bactria. The Roman victor is Belisarius, the OTL reconqueror of the West; in this version he is the hero who finishes off the Sassanid state of Sogdiana as a threat to Rome and stabilizes the Eastern frontier.

No 'Plague of Justinian' in this version; a larger population and a more prosperous and confident Empire. With Persia conquered and its resources in Roman hands, there is no massive 'Persia vs Rome' war after 602 as in OTL, and thus no mutual exhaustion of the two Empires as the Arabs unite. In fact the Roman Empire has already used the (real life) war between the Yemeni Arab state in south-west Arabia and Christian Abyssinia/Ethiopia in the 520s to destroy the former and set up a Roman province in Yemen, controlling the trade-route from Egypt via the Red Sea to India. In OTL the Eastern Roman Empire just used Abyssinia to conquer Yemen and keep Christian control of the Red Sea trade route; in this version a stronger Rome has restored the Pharoanic canal from Nile to Red Sea and controls the Red Sea and the port of Aden with a Roman fleet. Rome thence rules south-west Arabia and dominates the local tribes – the war is led by the OTL East Roman general Belisarius instead of him being the 530s Eastern reconqueror of North Africa and Italy.

As a result there is no unification of Arabia by Mohammed and Islam after the 610s, though the Prophet does rule the Mecca/Medina area, the latter is a trading-led ally of the Roman Empire which supplies regular troops to the Empire, and there is no Islamic conquest of the Middle East. Nor is there an Avar tribal conquest of the Balkans, though the Avars do inherit the Huns' role ruling the steppes of the Ukraine. Instead, the warlike Emperor Claudius III completes the conquest of the eastern, vassal states of Persia for the Empire in the 610s and 620s, as a way of preserving the threatened, weak eastern frontier of the Iranian plateau lands on the River Oxus from the arriving Turkic nomads who see the weakly protected but rich lands there as easy prey. Rome reaches the Oxus and annexes ancient Bactria, renewing both the semi-legendary exploits of Alexander 'the Great' and the long-term Achaemenid and Sassanian Persian policy of securing Bactria and the Oxus to 'defend in depth' the lands to the West. Claudius is succeeded by his Iranophile nephew Carus III, a hedonist and tolerant man of culture intoxicated by the ancient culture of the East and caring more about his role as the heir of Darius and Shapur I than as the ruler of the 'less civilised' far West of Europe. But alienation and possible revolt by the European political elite centred on Rome and the Western generals is forestalled by his sudden death in 641 – with no sons to succeed him.

The situation for the Roman Empire as of 641

The above timeline of Book One ends, where this book starts, as the 630s and 640s – in real life the arrival on the scene for the real life Eastern Empire (posing as the full and only 'Roman Empire' after reconquering parts of the West under Justinian, and just having fought off the existential threat of Sassanian Persia in the 620s in a major and exhausting war) of the Arabs. The Prophet has just united Arabia under the banner of Islam and his successors now turn the once-warring and despised, marginal Arab tribes against the exhausted and unprepared Romans – and quickly overrun Syria, Palestine and Egypt plus Iraq and Persia, reducing the Empire to a rump state and ending Roman/Christian rule of all the Mediterranean basin. In my version, this does not happen – the Empire is not exhausted and in a poor state for a major war at this point, aided by the butterflying away by me of a major pandemic in the 540s which cost a massive toll in lives and economic prosperity plus confidence, and instead it has just finished absorbing Persia and has avoided most of the real-life crises of the

C6th and early 7th century. A more generous and inclusive policy towards the Arabs has also enrolled large numbers of their warriors to fight for, not against, the Empire – as with the German tribes in the 4th and C5th centuries. The most controversial if mostly successful emperor of the real C6th, Justinian, has never ruled the Empire – and his intolerant and persecutory version of orthodox Catholic Christianity has not got a grip on the mindset and bureaucracy of Rome either. There is a mixture of a longer-surviving Julian (pagan) and a more politically constrained and cautious Theodosius – the main imperial Catholic creator of stringent laws to 'nudge' ambitious elite personnel to convert to Christianity by imposing financial/legal burdens and exclusion from politics/ government on those who do not, and the man who banned pagan temple cults, sacrifices, and Games and confiscated pagan temple lands and treasures.

As a result, though there are mostly Christian emperors after Julian and most are Catholic with 'heretics' being driven out of office or politically neutered by rebellions, as in OTL, the arc of conversion among the elite and the creation of an elite government/educational culture hostile to the pagan Greek past (as in both the surviving, Catholic post-Roman Western kingdoms and the surviving Eastern Empire in OTL) is much slower and is not fully complete by the 640s. Instead of a raft of legislation inhibiting or banning non-Catholic sects and non-Christian religions there is a degree of toleration in a surviving, Mediterranean-wide Roman Empire; though the 'heretic' Christian sects are still denied any official top jobs, any state-supported churches, or financial support they are not banned from worship and can usually survive 'under the radar'. The State is supportive of the 'glorious' cultural Greco-Roman pagan heritage of the Empire's early centuries so pagan teaching and schools survive. The State's leadership usually also admires the heritage of pagan Athens (and the more disciplined, more politically 'suitable' oligarchic Sparta) and the legend of Alexander as an inspiration for the 'World Empire' and 'World Culture' of Rome – which given its 'miraculous' recovery from break-up in the 3rd century and defeat of Alaric, Attila and company in the 5th century is seen to have Divine support (whether by the Christian God of Constantine or the pagan 'Supreme Being' of Neoplatonist cults favoured by Julian). There is a degree of cultural if not overt religious syncretism in the Empire, which can tolerate 'culturally advanced' Sassanian Persia and its Zoroastrianism if not the less intellectually complex world of 'backward' and 'illiterate' northern Germanic culture and its pagan gods. The Church/intellectual culture is not led in the West by a rigidly orthodox Papacy but by the State under its supreme, Divinely-favoured Emperor. The Christian Church is 'multi-headed' with a series of administratively-supreme 'Patriarchs' under usually firm secular 'guidance' i.e. control – Rome for the Western Mediterranean, Constantinople for the NE

Mediterranean and Balkans, Antioch for the Levant, Egypt and Carthage for Africa, and later on Ctesiphon (the ex-Sassanian capital) for conquered Persia. This is a less theologically rigid version of the OTL 5th and 6th centuries 'frozen in time' by the survival of the era's Roman political structure; under this the subcurrents of intellectual and other cultural developments proceed.

The politico-administrative context is of a surviving Late Roman (4th and 5th centuries) bureaucratic state headed by a large and hierarchical Court, as in both Eastern and Western halves of the Empire then, continuing under a now reunited Empire – but with a strong secular 'lead' to governance instead of the OTL Church domination of divided, non-bureaucratic 'tribal' kingships' by literate elites in the West. It is as if the Eastern Roman/'Byzantine' model of the 6th century was extended to all of the West and to the conquered Sassanian Persian state (and to parts of Arabia, eg the real-life 520s Eastern Roman ally of 'Himyar' i.e. Yemen, as guarding the Red Sea trade-route to India) – but without the culturally exclusive, aggressively orthodox Christian cultural model set up by Justinian in the period 527–65. There is a strong, Imperial-backed cultural and administrative admiration of the – pagan – state and culture of the 'Classical' Early Roman Empire of the period 30 BC–AD 180; the emperors celebrated as models are led by Augustus, Trajan, '(Hellenophile) Hadrian, and (Platonic philosopher) Marcus Aurelius, not the real-life Christianiser Constantine 'the Great'. This was the choice of Julian as emperor in the 360s and 370s, and his model has been kept up since with the OTL orthodox Theodosius 'the Great' less keen on or able to change this – and the Julianic model has been reinforced by (my invention) the domineering, Church-distrusting reunifier Titus II in 496–542. There is a 'state and traditional culture first, religion is an agent of this' model for governance, arguably a Roman equivalent of Chinese 'Legalism' – and a new model of state bureaucratic examinations to funnel the ambitious elite into state service, as in China and influenced by the Romans discovering (vague and not always accurate) details of the latter's polity governance in the C6th. The emperor is usually based in Rome but periodically travels to and resides in the eastern Mediterranean too; and a watchful bureaucratic and military hierarchy balances the power and interests of elites in East and West.

In military terms, the Empire as of 641 encompasses the OTL 'post-Roman' world of the Mediterranean and the Germanic kingdoms, plus a degree of direct or indirect control via military and religious 'missions' over potentially hostile NW neighbours in Ireland and 'Scotland'/Caledonia (converted to Christianity as in OTL in the 5th and 6th centuries) and the trans-Elbe German 'North'. Beyond the Danube, Rome has militarily subdued and either rules or draws mercenaries from semi-autonomous Germanic provinces/kingdoms to the Carpathians – as reconquered or overshadowed by the Empire after the death of Attila in 453 and fall of his empire. In the East, Rome has finally subdued the Sassanians in Iran and Bactria and now rules to the Oxus and the Hindu Kush as the much-trumpeted 'heirs of Alexander' but as a less persecutory Christian state than in OTL tolerates and includes the elite classes of the Persian realm and their culture – while at times 'turbo-charging' conversion by the local Orthodox and Nestorian Christian Churches as the agents of Romanization. The 'One Emperor' of the Roman world cannot govern all of his vast state directly, though he is more mobile and wide-ranging personally than the court-bound majority of OTL Byzantine rulers; but the multiplicity of Roman armies on the frontiers, none large enough to be sure of defeating the central Court army or its own local rivals, and the regular 'changing of the guard' among their commanders to limit local power-bases usually fends off rebellion. The central army is just too powerful, with its inner corps of talented and court-supporting commanders, to make rebellion viable – unless there is a vacancy in control or a disputed succession in Rome. In effect, we have a sort of 'Chinese imperial state under the Western Han or the T'ang', a powerful central government and an ideology of cultural and hopefully political unity, in the Mediterranean/Middle Eastern world – but will this last as long as the Chinese regimes, and like them be able to reunify again if it breaks up?

The basic themes for this book.

The tasks ahead for new rulers lacking the legitimacy of the reunifying 'Anthemian' dynasty after 641 is headed by the need to keep the Empire united and fend off chaos, and rulers have to make a choice of prioritising the 'secular', pagan, Greco-Roman cultural and administrative model of the early Empire (and behind that the Hellenistic world and the example of 'Lord of Asia' Alexander 'the Great') or the new, Christian model favoured by Constantine 'the Great' in the 4th century. The Church is not the mainstay of governance and culture but one among a number of competing sources of support or criticism for the government, though most emperors are orthodox Christians and hanker after 'top-down' hierarchy and stability which the Church can support with its ideology and model of the world reflecting the obedient order of Heaven. Some emperors see the Church as a rival and as an unwelcome cultural and ideological intrusion into the Early Roman 'success story', and they have the model of Julian's defiance of it to call upon as an example; some hanker after cultural syncretism including the non-Christian religions of the Middle East (and later of Asia). This Empire will strive after trade with and exploration in the Indian Ocean world as well as the European and Atlantic regions; and the Scandinavian 'North-West' is seen as a remote and uncivilized, non-Greco-

Roman 'backwater' whose nuisancesome 'pirates' raid Roman lands. As with the OTL early Empire's German foes, reprisal raids on the sources of 'barbarian' attacks, bribing friendly rulers to keep quiet, and hiring local mercenaries to fight their raiding kinsfolk will be the usual Roman riposte – and the 'Viking' threat will often be minimised as a minor nuisance in an unimportant area by elites in Rome who take far more interest in the riches of the East.

But eventually the mixture of rising annoyance about raids and the threat to trade and agriculture alike, played up by the afflicted locals (e.g. pillaged Church monasteries' leaders), will dictate a mood of 'Something Must Be Done' to restore the State's prestige as protector of its citizens, Naval and land expeditions and partial conquest of the Scandinavian region will follow by emperors seeking a new field for glory and for public relations successes. (As with the OTL activities of Trajan in Dacia/Rumania after decades of annoying but not that important raids on the Empire in the 100s.) In real life, the great unifying Christian warlord and statesman and first new 'Emperor' of the Carolingian realm, Charlemagne (crowned emperor by the Pope in 800), is said to have recognized the long-term threat to his citizens from the rising size and boldness of Viking fleets in the 800s but lacked a fleet or the time and ability to so much about it, as he tearfully admitted in his old age. In this world and timeline, the larger and well-resourced Roman fleet can do something about it and does, though its response wavers due to other concerns, and the response is like that towards the real-life Germans in the early Empire – including importing 'tamed' Scandinavian settlers to threatened provinces to boost their defences and their agricultural economies.

We get a 'Viking shore' in the East of 'Britannia', as we acquired a 'Saxon Shore' in the OTL 4th century – and Romans and (real life) Viking warlords fighting over raided and pillaged Ireland and the north of Scotland. We also have the – real life – recruitment of Viking leaders, some of them familiar to history, to the Imperial Guard in Rome (as to the 'Varangian' Guard in Constantinople in OTL), and Viking settlement beyond the reach of Rome in the Slavic settlements of what is to become 'Russia' – including Kiev/Kiyev. But this Empire is also fixated on its Eastern ambitions and the riches and cultural diversity of the East, with a rising arc of trade to India, and the dream of Alexander will draw it East as well as West; and the power of the secular state is usefully greater in the religiously mixed world of Central/South Asia than in the orthodox Christian Mediterranean. The imperial administrative structure's decision-makers are not all zealous orthodox Christians as in the OTL 'Byzantine' Empire, and Buddhism and Zoroastrianism have their attractions to some – and there will be a lack of Imperial support for any moves by orthodox clerics to convert this region.

EMPERORS (with chapter titles for this book, covering 641–950.

The dynasty of reunification: the 'House of Tiberius Anthemius' (i.e. Titus' predecessor, an altered version of the OTL Western emperor of the late 460s).

Titus II 'the Reunifier'	West 496–542 East 515–542
Heraclius (brother)	542–551
Anastasius II (son)	551–559
Nerva II (brother)	559–570
Gallus (son)	570–582
Rillanus (son)	582–590
Carus (brother)	590–615
Claudius III (brother)	615–630
Carus II (nephew; son of Carus)	630–641

Post-Anthemian emperors: subjects of this book.

Leo III (brother-in-law, i.e. brother to wife)	641–642.
Constantine III (elected by Senate)	642–654.
Diomedes I (second son)	654–667.
Constantine IV (son-in-law)	667–680.
Caracalla (son of elder son of Constantine III)	680–709.
Michael I (elder son)	709–717.
Basil I (younger brother)	717–729.

New dynasty: House of Nearonius.

Leo IV (brother-in-law)	729–750.
Probus II (son, married to Basil I's daughter Irene)	750–765.
Probianus (son)	765–767.
Justinian I (brother)	767–797.
Rillanus II (son)	797–812.
Justin (uncle, brother of Justinian)	812–820.

New Dynasty: House of Monachorus.

Constantine V (distant cousin, descended from C III's brother)	820–838.
Irene (widow)	838–846.
Basilicus (younger son of C V, stepson of Irene)	846–860.
Zeno II (son)	860–883, abd.
Probianus II (elder son)	883–892
Aurelianus II (brother)	892–902
Zeno II (father; second reign)	902–912
Honorius II (nephew; son of brother)	912–920
Leo V (brother)	920–927
Constantine VI (son)	927–950

Chapter 1

Aftermath of the Conquest of Eastern Persia: New Dynasty, New Challenges

Leo III (Maussonius) 641–642: The Stop-Gap

Constantine III (Marcellianus) 642 –654: The Lawyer – Bureaucrat

The final years of the previous dynasty since reunification of the Empire in 516/18 had seen unprecedented success and expansion for the Roman Empire, with the final defeat of the state's long-term Sassanid Persian rival and its incorporation into the Empire. The latter now stretched from the Hibernian Sea and the Pillars of Hercules in the West to the Indus and the wilds of Gedrosia (OTL: Seistan, E Iran) in the East, and from the oases of the Garamantes (OTL: southern Libya), the Third Cataract of the Nile, and the port of Aden in the South to the boggy heathland of northern Germany and the shores of the Baltic in the North. But there was always a danger that this vast state would break up into civil war despite the careful divisions of resources (human and material) given to senior civilian and military figures across its many provinces, a strong 'centre' politico-military 'machine' that had a firm grip on the levers of power, and an elite that could operate if there was a weak or under-age ruler. Nor was the system of succession fixed, despite the warnings arising from the disputed successions, poor or controversial rulers, and Imperial Family feuds of the C3rd to the C5th which had helped to keep the Empire on the defensive for much of the time and had divided it for long periods. What if an Emperor turned into a tyrant or a doddering incompetent and his relatives or ambitious generals sought to replace him – and what if such an attempt only partly succeeded and the Empire was divided into mutually hostile states?

Establishing a rule of the current Emperor always having to nominate a clear and hopefully competent heir had been the usual solution, though not written in law and anyway open to challenge if the choice was not accepted by all the elite. Traditionally the army had always favoured 'family loyalty' and a hereditary succession and had challenged capable but unmilitary civilian new rulers in the past. Nor did a genealogical tradition of inheritance by the current ruler's nearest – or nearest adult – male relative guarantee competence or a lack of challenges, eg if the heir was under-age and was catapulted onto the throne unexpectedly before he became adult. A lucky dynasty could avoid this and the Imperial Family of Titus II 'the Reunifier' (ruled in the West from 496 to 542, and in the East from 516/18 to 542) had largely succeeded in that with no accession of an under-age and untried heir. But even the maverick and impulsive Emperor Anastasius II had been faced with an effective (successful) coup by elements of the elite in the name of his sidelined brother and heir Nerva (II) in 559 and had died before he or his allies could try to reverse this, in 590 the more popular but equally unusual young Emperor Rillanus had been assassinated by a lone (?) attacker in the Forum Romanum in broad daylight, and in 615 the middle-aged Emperor Carus (Rillanus' brother and successor) had named his adult and vigorously capable but outspoken brother Claudius (III), not his under-age son Carus II, as his heir and this had been accepted. Had Claudius then had a son and tried to name him not Carus (II) as his own heir, a civil war could have broken out; but he had no son so the original succession-plan of 615 had held.

But now the danger that faced any reliance on succession within a 'legitimate' dynasty had come to pass. The Imperial Family was extinct in the direct male line, though Carus II and Claudius III had both left daughters, the latter's three daughters all being adult and married already. Their husbands (Carus' two teenage daughters once they married the men who their father had assigned to them as fiancés, all of them from major bureaucratic dynasties sympathetic to his 'Alexandrian' Romano-Persian cultural assimilation ideas) could claim the throne as transmitters of the claim to their children. But Carus' wife Julia, still only thirty-five and potentially a major political 'player' behind the scenes given her status as his loyal 'Augusta' with her aristocratic family behind her, was her daughters' guardian. She refused to back the idea floated by some Palace bureaucrats and ministers of getting her eldest daughter Berenice married off quickly to her fiancé Justus Honoratellius – a Cappadocian 'service family' senior finance ministry official and patron of Hellenistic-style poetry and romantic novels, so regarded with suspicion by truculent Italian conservative senators – and putting them on the throne as 'Caran continuation' candidates.

Honoratellius was competent and devoted to Carus' Eastern cultural and geo-strategic interests and had links with families in the Armenian nobility and its generals in the Eastern armies. But he was too controversial as an 'Eastern policies first' man to appeal to the majority of the Senate, not least due to his rumoured sympathy for non-Catholic Christian sects, so his 'forced' appointment might lead to a coup plot in the Western noble elites or the Western armies – or so his enemies in the Roman elite alleged during the secret discussions in the Marble Palace and senatorial mansions that followed Carus' death. None of the (aristocratic military officers) husbands of Claudius' daughters, who some senators and senior figures in the military 'Imperial Comitatus' (central army) headquarters in Rome backed and who were all unimpeachable Catholics and culturally hostile to 'Persian influence', were in Italy at the time, and instead the Senate and ministers eventually agreed to elevate the late emperor Carus' wife Julia's brother Leo Maussonius, aged 43.

Leo had a blameless record of public service, a good military record from his youth serving in Germany and 'Scythia', and known ability as an organiser plus tact and charm, and appointing him brought Empress Julia and her family 'on side'. His more forceful brother Julius was currently Praefect of Constantinople and his cousin Decimus was 'Count of Oriens' (i.e. regional military commander in Syria/Palestine/Armenia) so his appointment would be supported in crucial parts of the East too. As he was a Catholic and sponsor of a new 'Benedictine' monastery in Cisalpine Gaul set up under the auspices of St Benedict's (OTL) monastery of Mount Cassinum, his orthodoxy would bring the 'Chalcedonian' (i.e. Catholic/Orthodox) Patriarchs Sergius of Constantinople, Matthew of Antioch, and Alexander of Ctesiphon and their Church structures 'on side' to support him. This would threaten any dissident military officers in the Persian region who feared being sidelined by a 'West first' regime that they would be excommunicated as 'heretics' if they tried anything subversive. Emperor Leo III was duly acclaimed as Emperor on his arrival in Rome from his current Imperial legal commission work in Cisalpine Gaul on 3 July and was crowned with some haste in St Peter's Basilica by the Pope a week later with minimal ceremony or organization so that there would be no noticeable vacancy in the Imperial office that could spark off a civil war. Though some senior ministers and commanders were nervous that the large army in northern India or the regional command at Ctesiphon, where Carus had been hugely popular, might start a civil war or even accuse the Rome elite of getting rid of the 'Easterner' Emperor nothing happened. The balance of power between the regional armies meant that no ambitious regional command's 'Count' considered it worth risking his career and probably life to tackle the potential unification of several of his rivals' commands against him. The supporters of 'Imperial dynastic legitimacy' were reassured by Empress Julia backing her brother and the implicit possibility that in due course one of her and Carus' daughters and their husband would succeed to the throne. A 'caretaker' Imperial uncle, Claudius III, had succeeded Carus I in 615 while the latter's son Carus (II) was under-age and the 'rightful heir' had taken the throne after him, as promised; so logically once the childless and renownedly 'honourable' legal expert and bureaucrat Leo died the succession would go to the 'rightful heir' again. (In fact, it did not – but this was not known at the time and those of the Empire's elites who did not want Leo on the throne, especially

'Caran' army officers, were too taken aback by the sudden crisis to have any plans in hand for a revolt .) Leo was accepted as Emperor in each province and made all the right public noises about reconciliation and harmony in his first speeches, even releasing the surviving anti-Carus plotters from prison or slavery, but his closeness to the Church (one brother was Archbishop of Dyrrachium in Epirus and a cousin was a senior clerical official running the patriarchal treasury in Constantinople) and public expressions of piety and orthodox beliefs annoyed Carus' more free-thinking cultural allies.

As he dared not rein in Carus' restoration of seized Zoroastrian temple/priestly family lands in Persia for fear of a local army revolt this then annoyed the Church too and led to criticism of his cowardice at a summer 642 Church Council in Rome. Conversely, this cemented the loyalty to the new regime of assorted ex-Sassanian ministers and nobles in the eastern Iranian 'power structures' who had come over to the Roman side to preserve their wealth and influence and needed Roman help to keep Turkic raids back, but feared a new, less pro-tolerance 'fanatic' Christian emperor forcing their conversion. This duly aborted any threat of a 'backlash' rebellion in Claudius III's conquests in the East if and when the new Emperor removed part of the garrisons there and loosened Rome's grip. The Emperor cautiously retained most of Carus' ministers and paid court to his advisers and leading noble courtiers but invited back some of Claudius' military veteran friends too, putting the latter on a special 'Imperial Military Commission' to assist him in deciding military matters as a sort of permanent advisory council. This became a long-term innovation that was kept up for centuries and served as a way for veteran 'duces' and Counts to be recruited to offer expert advice in the capital after their retirement though it was originally intended more as a sop to their pride and suspicion than as a long-term addition to the Empire's policy-making apparatus.

A similar 'conciliate and flatter' policy in legal matters saw a commission of senior, mostly retired lawyers and judges recruited in 642 to advise the Emperor on legal issues and to deal with any serious complaints of bias, corruption or miscarriages of justice across the Empire. The latter proved a surprise – and at the time unintended – route to power for Leo's successor-to-be, the highly respected Apulian lawyer Constantine Marcellianus (born 589) who had been an important young prosecutor with a knack of winning cases in the law-courts of Naples in his twenties, been recruited by a top law firm to assist them in cases in Rome, and had then been chosen by Claudius III in 626 as a proven man of energy and integrity to join one of his commissions into provincial legal misdemeanours. The commission work had highlighted Constantine's mixture of trustability, head for complex detail, encyclopedic knowledge of the law (he reputedly knew all the 'Codex Titi', Titus II's exhaustively comprehensive codification of the Empire's existing laws in one collection of statutes in the 510s–530s, and most of the preceding mid-5th century Eastern Empire's 'Codex Theodosii' off by heart), and complete honesty. In 632 Carus had appointed him as a senior city magistrate in Rome to shake up the often detail-clogged, slow-moving cases there, and now in February 642 he became the most publicly known of the new legal commissioners advising the Emperor and made his mark quickly by using his own experience and his large personal staff of experts (paid for out of his family landed fortune) to identify issues to be tackled. His dislike of the frequent and usually unchecked police habits of beating or starving confessions out of suspects, particularly low-class ones and especially in major Italian cities, and his past investigations of resulting miscarriages of justice had made him popular with the public. As he had successfully urged Leo to reprieve and pardon the majority of the anti-Carus 'civil service plotters' he was approved by the capital's senior bureaucrats. He also notably advised Leo that the role of the Emperor as 'guarantor of justice', the only person who could and would rein in crooked and rich rule-bending 'nobiles' (a legal term for the wealthy and well-born), was crucial to his appeal to the ordinary public and, as Titus II had forseen by his well-publicised legal codification, would put ordinary civilians and soldiers off taking part in rebellions at the behest of the selfish regional 'great men'.

Law was 'the keystone in the arch of governance', as Titus' chief legal adviser Tribonian (OTL figure) had once said – and Leo saw his adviser's proposed strategy as very useful and let him put it to the Imperial Council with his firm support. As Leo was well-meaning but lacked the ability to get a grip on detail or to see the 'big picture' in policy matters unless 'pushed', Constantine, the deputy finance minister Basilius Spartacius, the Praefect of Rome Honorius Lapellius, and the Praetorian Praefect Justus Participianus soon emerged as the effective ruling clique of veteran 'men of business' who directed the Emperor towards what issues needed solving and how to do it. All of them were in their fifties and were former proteges of the blunt, 'no nonsense' military man Claudius III in 615–630 as effective and where necessary ruthless but also immune to pressure or flattery from great nobles or business tycoons.

Under their direction Leo proceeded in early-mid 642 to shake up the public works ministry in Rome to cut out waste and deal with some serious 'double accounting' in the budgets of building companies who were meant to be assisting but were really fleecing major government philanthropic projects. They were to establish a new board of experienced veteran administrators to run the ports of Italy and improve the processing of imports headed for Rome (grain in particular), order the dredging of the silting-up main harbour at Alexandria which Carus II had noted on his tour there but never got round to solving, and also set up a project to improve the safety-measures on roads across the Alps which were prone to winter closure, spring snow avalanches, and summer rockfalls so that hazards could be identified quickly and dealt with and stricken travellers rescued. Until now the Great and Little St Bernard Passes and the Brenner Pass had been so hazardous that many travellers preferred to go via the sea from Massilia to Liguria in the West of the Alps or go round the 'long route' via the Julian Alps and Aquileia in the East and travel and the sending of messages to and from Rome had been frequently disrupted. This was now sorted out by a special 'Board of Alpine Road Travel' led by a high-profile 'Count' (usually a military administrator or engineer) sent from Rome while the efforts of the monks of the wealthy Monastery of St Bernard (founded in the early C6th) on the Great St Bernard Pass, plus their famous rescue-dogs, to guide travellers across the pass, put up weather-hit travelers, and retrieve avalanche-victims were now assisted and replicated by the government although improvements in the roads on these major passes and the installation of a series of 'refuge houses' along them took several decades. All this work commenced under Leo and he accordingly received a good historical reputation, but in fact he initiated very little of it and the 'secret council' of his four leading ministers decided on most of these initiatives and brought him in to rubber-stamp them later.

Leo, who had made a mark in Rome for his extended public games and flattering treatment of the Senate, died unexpectedly when his carriage overturned as he was returning from a public engagement in Narni in Umbria to Rome and was hit by a storm on 18 September 642, aged forty-four, after a reign of little over a year. To prevent the risk of a civil war breaking out with ambitious generals in the outer provinces using their armies to claim the throne the ministers summoned the Senate the following day and held a hasty election-meeting with Praefect Justus warning that if they did not reach a consensus quickly and choose someone credible they faced civil war and probable chaos. Some of the Senate took that as a hint that he expected the throne to go to him and voted accordingly, but he insisted that as he had no children or siblings and his cousins were unknown minor officers his being elected would leave the Empire with another succession-crisis in a decade or two. He could hardly divorce his respected and well-connected upper-class heiress wife, remarry, and have a son once he was on the throne and be sure that he would live until the boy was adult and experienced – and as his wife's sisters and brothers all had large families he might be the one who was infertile. So he proposed Constantine Marcellianus for the throne as the latter was a well-known and popular judge and known for his integrity and he had two adult sons, the elder (Constantine) a respected 'war hero' from the Indus frontier in his early thirties and already married with small children. On 21 September a series of votes for the new sovereign among a variety of candidates, mostly the incumbent ministers and senior senators, ended with a majority consensus for Constantine. The latter was duly proclaimed Emperor Constantine III, aged fifty-three, and with the two next most popular candidates, both former Praefects of Rome now in the Senate, pulling out of the race the others had no option but to give way and the new Emperor wisely conciliated them with senior jobs and sinecures and offered the most truculent of them the chance for his unmarried eldest son to marry Constantine's eldest daughter and become grandfather to future senior Imperial relatives.

The new Pope Theodore, a Greek from Jerusalem with valuable connections in the East, proceeded to crown Constantine on 5 October at another hastily-arranged ceremony and he and the Senate both issued stern statements describing him as the unanimous choice of the traditional leaders of the Empire and reminding all listeners that rebellion was a sin that God would punish and rebels would be declared outlawed and excommunicated. But the backing of the 'comitatus' regiments around Italy and the fears that if one major regional army rose it would not have the backing of others but would be overwhelmed in a concerted action were probably more crucial in causing senior 'Counts' on the Rhine, lower Danube, Nubian, and Persian/Afghan frontiers who had large numbers of war-experienced troops to hand to decide not to risk a rebellion.

Rumours later had it that some ambitious regional Counts (i.e. army commanders of concentrated, experienced regiments, usually on a frontier so with recent military experience if only at catching brigands and infiltrators, as opposed to the provinces' 'duces' who at most had only the garrison troops of one province to hand) had been keeping an eye on the situation carefully at the time of the election, ready to launch a revolt if someone else did so first and the government and its 'comitatus' was thus distracted. These stories may have been true – or invented by the ubiquitous 'spies'/informants of the central command in each frontier region, who kept an eye on the local armies' loyalty – and if so the Empire survived the risk of civil war by luck as much as management. Certainly, the new Emperor had no known close friends or supporters among the regional Counts or the 'duces' as of 642 and many of these men were either the former young officers promoted by Claudius III for competence in serving under him (and as such usually had charisma and skills as commanders) or else were the usual 'career officer' upper-class nobles who habitually chose the army for a career until they inherited their parents' fortunes – and as such had rich families and many friends in the Mediterranean social elites.

But none dared to challenge the new Emperor for whatever reason, probably fear of failure against the large and well-trained central army and the new rulers' ability to shower treasury money on defecting ex-rebels who rallied to the State – and this was also to affect future awkward vacancies of the throne when dynasties ended. In the event, Constantine III, on advice from his 'high command' in Rome, was to adopt the policies of equally unmilitary emperors Rillanus I (an admirer of the war-averse 'people's emperors' Nerva and Hadrian) and Carus I (a cautious bureaucrat) in the 580s and 590s to keep any military figure from building up a 'power-base' in a region that could back him in a revolt. Frequent 'shuffles' of commands so that no frontier region Count and few 'duces' of provinces served in any one post for more than four or five years unless they were exceptionally favoured in and well-known to be loyal to the 'high command' or were the Emperor's own friends. Once a commander was moved he was generally transferred to a new command, of a higher rank and salary if he had done well, usually in the same continent or geographical region (so that he would be familiar with the local hazards of command) but well away from his previous post – and only the more reliable generals were allowed to take their personal staff and their favourite proteges among their junior officers with them. Both well-favoured and 'suspect' commanders were also often moved back to Rome, or to the regional military headquarters for each frontier (eg Constantinople for the Balkans, Black Sea, and western Caucasus, Antioch for Arabia, Alexandria for NE Africa, Ctesiphon for the Persian/Central Asian region, and Trier for Germany and the North Sea), for several years in between frontier commands – and some were brought to ' Comitatus headquarters' in Italy instead.

There were grumbles that the Senate had not chosen a general but at least civilian 'bureaucrat'/lawyer Constantine was not one of Claudius' more aggressive and 'scalp-hunting' legal commissioners. He had a reasonable reputation for letting some of those who his commissions had accused off if the evidence was not strong enough, and in addition his elder son Constantine was currently serving on the lower Danube as a senior aide to the 'Count' there, with a reputation for bravado and coolness under fire in the cavalry campaign which he had joined there in 641 to save a Gothic tribal sub-kingdom in 'Scythia' beyond the river from Avar rebel plunderers. The younger Constantine was known to favour a major campaign to crush the Avars for good so the 'war hawks' in the region and on the 'general staff' in Rome/Mediolanum believed that he should be able to influence his father in favour of a war. He had also served successfully in the Attock region on the upper Indus dealing with tribal raiders in the late 630s and knew the region and its current officers well. As he hastened to Rome to back up his father his superior the 'Count' Sebastian of the lower Danube, a decorated 'war hero' from the Indus valley annexation campaigns in the mid-late 610s and a man with both flair and good aristocratic connections so he could have made a viable bid for the throne, publicly supported Constantine as

Emperor and so squashed the possibility of his own large and war-ready army mutinying against a 'civilian stitch-up' in Rome.

The Empire avoided civil war and the relieved Senate made no protest about the honours and gratuities voted to the regional commanders as a way of paying them off or to the increase in army pay and in subsidies to be spent in aiding veterans to re-settle as farmers and/or traders on retirement. But the shrewd Constantine was aware that he was on shaky political ground as the first Emperor not to be connected to the dynasty of Tiberius Anthemius and Titus II for over 120 years in the East and 150 years in the West and he quickly moved to shore up his position by having the 'Counts' of the Indus region, the Rhine, and the Marcomannian frontier (i.e. the Carpathians) all moved from their posts to honorary service as Imperial military commission members in Rome in the next year and binding Sebastian to him with the Praetorian Praefectship and his son's marriage to one of the Emperor's younger daughters. The Emperor made his past record as a fearless but honest and fair legal inquisitor into a source of strength for his suitability for the Imperial job by issuing speeches and official documents emphasizing the responsibilities of the Emperor to be the 'protector' of his people and his past record in this regard. He also made more of his public speeches than the last four Emperors had done (Carus I had been shy and wary of public exposure, Claudius III brusque and uninterested in the use of rhetoric, Carus II lazy and unwilling to prepare himself to speak formally though lucid in private, and Leo III too busy and cautious) and delivered regular speeches to the Senate and also to meetings of official bodies in Rome, both of professionals (eg lawyers and churchmen) and of businessmen. As he was known to offer the rich no favours and to aid the poor in his courts with free advice and if needed financial assistance the Church under Pope Theodore firmly backed him and soon gave him the titles of 'Protector of the Faith' and 'Protector of the Humble' ('humiliores', i.e. legally the lower social classes) and his even-handedness on matters of religion meant that he did not favour the orthodox at the expense of the minority sects, issuing orders to see that his courts were even-handed on this issue in all the provinces. But he did not waste time and effort coming up with ingenious but controversial new theological formulas to try to reunite the feuding Christian sects either, his efforts in Church matters being limited to seeing that the clergy carried out their duties adequately and did not neglect the poor or embezzle money.

Once the younger Constantine was established in Rome he was made 'Caesar' and provided the charisma that his father lacked, as a golden-haired Adonis with many social skills and a natural charm who drove a four-in-hand chariot around the capital and had as varied a social life with the younger nobility as Carus II had done; his studious and scholarly younger brother Diomedes had reasonable looks but a stammer and stayed in the background as a mathematics student at the Rome university then a trainee in various senior government departments. The 'Caesar' also led the way in preparing a major campaign for 644 to tackle the Avar civil war and in the meantime Roman cavalry aid was sent to the Khazars up the River Don and along the Caspian Sea's West coast from North Adiabene (OTL Azerbaijan). The Emperor proceeded to launch a new initiative to survey and repair the more antiquated and often leaking C1st and C2nd AD aqueducts around the Mediterranean, spurred on by reports of water-shortages in a hot summer in 642 to set up a new and permanent 'Aqueducts Repair Commission' of engineers, architects and bureaucrats in Rome. The work of repairing old aqueducts that had hardly been touched for centuries and were starting to show the signs of age had in fact begun in earthquake-hit Syria as early as the 620s and had been speeded up by Carus II after complaints about it on his Eastern tour. But it was Constantine who systematized it and provided a regular board of supervisors plus extra and guaranteed cash and from 644 there was a special 'Secretary for Aqueducts and Irrigation' added to the list of Imperial ministers, usually a trained engineer and often a military veteran used to providing water for the ever-demanding army on a frontier. The revival and extension of public works in general was a major concern for Constantine and it could also be 'spun' as part of his mantra of the Emperor and his ministers serving the people. Following the initiative on aqueducts he was to proceed to order a major enquiry into the problems of silting-up and lack of adequate maintenance of irrigation in Egypt, where the silt in the main harbour of Alexandria had highlighted the rising problems there, and on their report in 646 order a new board of commissioners to take a force of engineers and labourers to Egypt. They would clear those shallower mouths of the Nile that could be tackled easily and start opening up silted drainage-channels in the agricultural lands on either side of the river, starting with the Fayyum basin in 646–7 and then the Nile delta in 648, the Middle Nile to Abydos in 649–50, and the Upper Nile around Thebes in 651–2. This was advertised in speeches as Imperial, Christian concern for the ordinary tenant-farmers – but raised tax income via production too.

Millions of sesterces were earmarked for the project and in addition a separate board of engineers and force of conscript labourers were sent to Nubia's capital Dongola in 647 to overhaul the irrigation-system in the adjacent area of Nubia, improve agricultural production, and organize the growing of those crops most useful as exports for the Roman 'market' in Egypt. This also served the purpose of extending and advertising the advantages of being a Roman ally to the elite of Nubia, landowners and merchants alike, and brought them to back the pro-Roman alignment without the need for expensive military occupation. From now on the riches that the Nubian elite would gain by exporting to Roman Egypt would tie their government to the Empire and make it unthinkable that any local king, however autonomist in mind, would dare to challenge Rome and so risk having his trade cut off and his elite revolt against him. The success of the top ex-military engineer and irrigation expert Decius Lactantianus as head of the Roman commission in Nubia in 647–9 duly led to him being sent on next to Arabia Petraea (Jordan) to renovate irrigation in the lands East of the Dead Sea and the River Jordan and to extend the reach of viable agricultural estates away from the Jordan valley towards the desert, boosting the role of local provincial capital Philadelphia Ammonitis (Amman) as a trade-centre. This and a simultaneous move to renovate the crumbling irrigation-systems of the upper Orontes valley in Syria, hit by a mixture of earthquake damage and shortage of labour after a plague in 608–10 and never fully restored, caused ambitious farmers and landowners who signed up to receive Imperial funding and hired labourers for the project after 643 to take over land that had recently been annexed unofficially (as unused or under-used) by local nomad Arab tribes for grazing their sheep, goats and camels. Armed clashes followed so there was an unexpected new problem, but as hundreds of armed Arab nomads were called in from further inland by local tribal chiefs and some estates were occupied or burnt the Praefect of 'Oriens' brought troops in to chase the Arabs out. On urgent Imperial orders he avoided an outright war by arranging talks that with a mixture of firmness and bribery persuaded the Arabs not to tackle the new Roman armed guards on the estates but to accept an offer of moving with their flocks to drought-hit lands around Gaza and Pelusium that were now too poor in agricultural yields to sustain crop-farming.

The Arab mercantile oligarchs of Mecca and the mixed theocratic and trading community of Medina, the latter led by the judicious merchant-prince and expert camel-racer chieftain Umar (OTL: Caliph 634–44), assisted the Empire in this arrangement. In return they received land around Gaza and in the arid hills of Judaea for their flocks plus a new 'trade deal' to ship their dates and animals over the Red Sea and along the trade-routes to Nubia. Indeed an imaginative suggestion by the locally expert, Greco-Aramaic governor Aristarchus (of Joppa) of 'Palestine I' (i.e. Judaea and Samaria) even led to a large number of restive Arab tribesmen from the long trade-route across the Hejaz from Mecca to 'Arabia Felix', usually earning cash from brigandage on their settled neighbours in Yemen but reined in by Rome and bored, being moved in the early 650s to Tripolitania. They were to take over drought-hit former agricultural lands inland from Leptis Magna for their flocks and to use their aggression as Roman 'border police' on the trade-route South to Lake Chad. The interest which the practical Constantine III had in expanding trade and increasing revenue was leading to increased Roman trade with the Lake Chad kingdom of Bornu in the 640s and in addition a Roman mercenary expedition to the region in 643–5 to assist their poorly-armed local tribal armies in holding back attacks SW from Darfur by the expelled ex-king of Nubia, Azika. In the late 630s an Arab camel-borne force under their veteran general Khaled (OTL Arab commander) moved in to back this up and defeat the Nubian refugees as they attacked the lakeside trading city of Bornu, then attacking Darfur on their own account to carry off a large quantity of slaves to sell off to the Empire. The policy of using restive and traditionally predatory frontier allies of the Empire as mercenaries to aid trade and assist allies against enemies – and to stop them from attacking the Empire's own citizens in the search for loot and slaves – was also apparent on a smaller scale in Britain. There the allied kingdom of Romano-British warlord Rhydderch 'the Generous' (d 612) (OTL king) on the River Clyde, holding the Western end of the Antonine Wall against the Picts for over 30 years, had fallen into chaos after his death without a son and various pretenders had fought over the throne with the Picts meddling and eventually imposing their own candidate, Rhydderch's cousin Nechtan (OTL), in 620. Claudius III had not bothered to intervene despite appeals from the local 'dux' of Valentia (OTL Lothian) and the 'Count of Britain' as his military priorities were elsewhere and Carus II had only been interested in the 'civilised' East, not a foggy and cold Atlantic island 'backwater'.

But Prince Constantine had served for a year in the garrison on Hadrian's Wall as a trainee cavalry commander and pushed his father into involvement to teach the brigand-like Picts a lesson with the argument that their military threat was now abated as aggressive king Cinioch (OTL) had been overthrown and killed in a coup in 622 and his successor Gartnait had fallen to a local plot in 635. Accordingly in 643 a Roman expedition marched up the east coast of Caledonia from the Firth of Forth to the Moray Firth to defeat the Pictish army in several clashes, the Romans having far greater numbers and in particular cavalry and archers. They set up a chain of forts along the coast from the mouth of the Tay (Septimius Severus' old base at Carpow) to the mouth of the Spey, all of them protected by roving patrols using the old Severan system of roads along the coast that had been kept up (in a patchy state) for trade by the Picts when they were at peace with Rome as required by trade-treaties with the Empire. The local tribesmen either fled into the forests and had their land confiscated for Roman military veterans or accepted that the outnumbered Pictish army, short of cavalry and archers and with virtually no artillery, would never win a battle so they should give up and come to terms with Rome to save their homes. As a result the Empire was finally able to annex the eastern Pictish lowlands and start 'Romanizing' them in a smaller-scale equivalent of the mixed Romano-German social and economic order that had developed in Transrhenus since the later 5th century. Aspirant Roman farmers in the North-West of the Empire, usually military veterans or younger sons who would not inherit farms from their fathers, were short of land and unwilling to tackle the exposed and infertile farmland of Germania Ulterior (OTL East of R Elbe) after the 590s wars, which had left long memories as refugees had spilled over the West of Europe with tales of Langobard savagery.

As a result once the new territory of 'Caledonia Oriens' was safe from Pictish attack by c. 645, with a chain of fortresses shutting the mouths of the Pict-held glens from Loch Lomond north-east along a line to Speymouth with a major military base at the Pass of Killiecrankie, the province could be settled and start to develop with new towns at the mouths of the Tay and Dee. Another permanent Roman base was set up to the West along the coast from the Spey at the mouth of the Ness, formerly the Pictish royal fortress of Dun Padraig and now 'Constantinia Nova' (OTL Inverness). With the Romans able to threaten the Pictish lands to the SW in Moray and to the NW in Caithness from this position the Pictish kingdom was in effect cut in two and was ended as a major power, the Empire forcing the next of their rulers, Talorcan (OTL) in the late 640s (who usefully had a Brittonic-Anglian mother from the Votadini people in Lothian), to submit to sending an annual levy of young warriors to the Roman army so they could be 'Romanised' and persuaded to take up the benefits of 'civilization'. By now the adjoining kingdom of Dalriada, run by king Aedan mac Gabhran (d 598, OTL king of Dalriada in this period)'s family, were mostly Christian under the influence of the monks of Iona, now a venerated 'national' shrine dedicated to the 'Apostle of the Dalriadans' St Columbcille (d 597) (OTL: St Columba), and the menfolk usually served in the Roman army in Britain or Germany for a time as trainee officers and gained a smattering of Roman culture. The Dalriadan kingdom now became Roman allies in 643 to share in the pickings from the defeated Picts, and their Catholic and reasonably statesmanlike king Ferchar 'the Tall' (ruled 642–56 as in OTL), successor of the rash warlord Domnhall (OTL) who had got himself killed in a war in Ireland, preferred trade to Roman troops marching into his lands. In 650 he even visited Rome as a tributary ally to sign a trade-deal with the Emperor and be made 'nobilissimus' and an honorary senator.

The feuding warlords of Ireland were of little interest to a succession of Roman Emperors in the 6th and 7th centuries they no longer raided Britain and Ireland had no towns and little in the way of specialist agricultural produce that could not be found elsewhere. Nor were the nominal 'High Kings' based at the hillfort of Tara much use as vassal allies as they did not have real authority over their sub-kings in the provinces of Meath/Midhe, Leinster, Munster,

Connacht and Ulster. The latter only obeyed the 'High Kings' when it suited them and there was not even a secure succession as two rival lines of the 'Ui Niall' dynasty, one from western Midhe and one from south-west Ulster, ruled at Tara in a rota – punctuated by occasional usurpations and prolonged civil wars. The governor and 'Count' of Britain normally dealt with the local kings rather than their superior in serious negotiations though honorary or trading missions visited Tara from time to time. The only reasonable degree of Roman political influence was on the nearest kingdom to western Britain, Leinster, whose kings were usually granted honorary Roman titles and were given presents on accession but occasional embassies also went to Munster and Ulster, the latter to keep its coastal privateer captains from raiding Britain. The 'Hibernian Sea' fleet had been cut by half after c.580 as raiding in the region decreased, but its admiral – much less important than the North Sea/Channel admiral of the 'Classis Britannia' – from time to time had to negotiate the return of pirated ships or make a naval demonstration off the Leinster coast and some restless young Irish nobles served in his command as trainee captains. But the Church in Britain, mainly the missionary and austerity-loving monks of the Cymric (Welsh) south and west coast (e.g. at the shrine/monastery of St David at Menevia and at Caldey Island) and western Dumnonia (Cornwall), kept up links with the dynamic if feuding Irish Church over the latter's five kingdoms. New bursts of enthusiasm for austere practices like living in island caves, drinking only water and eating grass, and labouring like serfs on the land hit the British monasteries from Ireland from time to time.

The aristocratic higher ranks of the British Church looked down on the rustic Irish abbeys and monasteries as poorly-built dens of eccentrics who had a shaky grasp on theology and dubious practices (such as the wrong sort of monastic tonsure and celebrating Easter on the wrong date). They passed this disdain on to the Papacy which from time to time sent a mission to the Irish archbishopric at Armagh to chivvy its clergy into adopting Roman practices but was ignored. But due to the relative ease and learned 'otium' (dignified, cultured leisure) practiced in most of the small number of British monasteries away from the Cymric coasts and hills some of the more idealistic abbots looked with interest and admiration at the holy hermits of Ireland as an example to follow. In 635 the new bishop of Eburacum (York), an Italian trained in austerity and sackcloth-clad hard labour called Paulinus (OTL Bishop of York in the 620s-30s, sent by the Pope to help convert pagan Northumbria), agreed to let an Irish-influenced missionary monk from Iona in Dalriada called Aedan set up an austere island monastery on the Irish pattern at the island of Lindisfarne up the East coast North of Hadrian's Wall. (Aedan did this in OTL too.) There was a 'demand' for this sort of experiment among earnest young clerics, monks and lay enthusiasts in the see of Eburacum due to its lack of any sense of urgent missionary or monastic commitment. The complacency of its, mostly aristocratic, clerics meant that Paulinus agreed to the proposal made to him to bring in Aedan and some monks from Iona which were put to him by young clerics who had been to Iona in the early 630s, encouraged that at least Aedan spoke Latin and had visited Rome. The new monastery with its sackcloth-clad, vegetarian, hard-labouring monks proved as much of a success as St Benedict had proved in central Italy in the early C6th and was duly given the seal of approval by an archiepiscopal committee that checked its organization and orthodoxy in 637. The 'Iona mission' was later to spread through north-eastern and into central Britain and to lead to other monasteries being founded, including one in the now unused 'Saxon Shore' fortress of Othona in Trinovantia (Bradwell in Essex), and with the émigré Anglian warlord turned NE British stud-farm magnate Aelle (d 615)'s son and successor Eadwine (OTL king of Northumbia), a major supplier of horses to the Roman military cavalry, acting as the mission's main lay funder. A female relative of his, Abbess (St) Hilda (OTL), was later to become the first head of a combined male and female monastery at Streonshalium (Whitby) on the coast near Eburacum, also founding a major girls' school there which made up for a notable lack of female education in Britain and as such attracted funding from the Imperial education ministry.

(In OTL Hild/Hilda is the founding abbess of Whitby monastery/nunnery.)

All of this was, however, very much 'under the radar' and of little import as far as Rome's senior strategic planners were concerned once the new province of 'Caledonia Oriens' had been set up to boost the Emperor's reputation as a conqueror and extender of Rome's imperial 'reach'. Far more important to them was the Roman intervention in the Avar civil war in 644–5 when the 'Caesar' led a force of over 60,000 Roman infantry and cavalry from the lower Danube NE across the steppes to the lower Dnieper. A second army from Cherson (OTL Crimea) marched North under the general Valentinus (OTL Byzantine general), its provincial 'dux' and brother-in-law of the civilian governor there, Heraclius' son Constantine (a learned ex-law-student protégé of the Emperor from the 630s now given major promotion for his brains but hindered by poor health). (In OTL Heraclius was emperor of the Eastern Roman Empire 610–41, and his son Constantine was in 641 but died young.) The Romans and the Khazars moved in on the recent victor of the latest bout of inter-Avar warfare, usurping 'Khagan' Gazan, with the aid of the latter's teenage and more legitimate but inexperienced cousin Barsanes. The Avars for once decided to stand and fight and launched a night-time attack on the 'Caesar's camp with fire-arrows before he could link up with Valentinus. But the prince kept his nerve and ordered half his force to hold the camp perimeter while the others put the fires out and next day the Avars had to retreat instead of being able to sweep into a chaotic and fire-damaged Roman camp. They set fire to the steppes behind them and Constantine and Valentinus had to use their fastest cavalry to catch up the Avar rearguard before it could finish constructing 'pit' traps at the site where they intended to fight the Roman army, driving them in chaos into the forests North of the Dnieper near Kievum, and with the main Avar trap spoiled the tribes soon started to quarrel over the wisdom of hiding in the forests for the winter with their stocks of food and their animals as had been planned. The Romans had brought plenty of food along and all the materials needed for constructing emergency winter camps in case the Avars declined a battle so they did not suffer much in the winer that followed, their scouts on skis keeping the Avar attacks at bay with skilled archery while the main Roman forces 'hunkered down' in their scattered camps. In spring 645 the more daring Avars emerged from the forests to attack the hopefully cold and starving Romans and had a rude awakening to find them well-fed and ready to fight and their horses fully fit too after 'indoor' training in specially-constructed huge tents. The Avars were decimated by Roman archery and artillery in every attack and when a third Roman army arrived up the Dnieper in May 645 they gave up the battle and fled, and as the 'Khagan' was murdered by his relatives who sent his head to the Prince as a peace-offering the 'Khaganate' broke up into chaos and Constantine could impose Barsanes as the new ruler and a Roman puppet in return for him having the aid to defeat his rivals.

The Avars now became Roman allies and had to cede the entire Don valley steppe to the Khazars and also promise to keep three hundred miles North of the Northern entrances to the Crimea and to hand over an annual tribute and a levy of cavalry at Azov. The sons and daughters of many of the Avar nobility were handed over as hostages to Rome and sent to Constantinople to be baptised, educated as Romans, and in many cases found Roman husbands and wives to assist in 'Romanizing' them. In due course they mostly returned home to assist the cause of alliance with Rome and conversion to Christianity there and new hostages took their places. With relative peace restored to the steppes North of the Euxine (for sporadic clashes with the Khazars continued) the 'Caesar' returned to Rome in autumn 645 for a Triumph as 'Avaricus' and in 647–8 was in turn sent to the Caspian as 'Count of the Caucasus' to organize the building of a new frontier wall at the Daryal Pass and turn the tribes of forested and mountainous Daghestan beyond into Roman vassals so that Adiabene (OTL Azerbaijan) was secure from raids. A 'defence in depth' strategy was now set up on the steppes whereby loyal pro-Roman Avar nomad chieftains, visited and given gifts regularly by Roman traders or army officers, supplied horses and military levies to the Empire and in return warned it of any coming trouble from their neighbours. With a large input of Avar steppe horses after 645 to the Roman army's cavalry and its stud-farms (the latter mainly in the Hebrus valley and Thracian plains in the Balkans and in Galatia and Cappadocia in Asia Minor) Rome acquired a distinct advantage over its steppe challengers North of Sogdiana in terms of tough and fast horses and the new and impressive steppe imports also started to appear in Roman chariot-racing teams in Rome, Constantinople, and Antioch. The 'Caesar' had provided a major boost in propaganda as well as military-political terms for his new dynasty and to an extent he now began to overshadow his cautious, unmilitary, and consensual father as he started to develop his own ideas on Rome's imperial mission. His winter-time work at the 'general staff' headquarters and the 'comitatus' bases as he developed into an administrator as well as a general saw him link up to the younger militarists and 'Vergilian' (i.e. Early Empire-style expansionist) enthusiasts that had once congregated around Claudius III. He also added valuable strategic 'input' on using the skilled Avar steppe cavalry as allies, as C5th generals had used Huns.

While Constantine the elder was developing the idea of the Emperor as the benign and hard-working 'first civil servant' and encouraging spending on huge public works projects Constantine the younger was looking ahead to becoming Emperor and turning to the East again, in pursuit of the 'mirage of Alexander the Great' as one of his father's more pacific court poets put it disapprovingly. He was also hoping to use the decline of Abyssinia into a series of post-640 wars between its princes to annex that mountainous Christian land next and move Rome forward as an African power with vast resources of 'uncivilised' and pagan tribes down the East coast beyond the Horn of Africa ready to be Christianised. In 649 the 'Caesar' went on a tour of inspection to Egypt to see how the irrigation-projects and clearance of silted harbours and rivers was getting on and sailed down the Red Sea to Aden to make the first Imperial visit to 'Arabia Felix' and even sail out into the Indian Ocean for a few days on a war-galley. It was said that he had commissioned an armed 'trading' expedition that headed off by sea from Aden a few months later down the African coast to the ports of Mombasa and Zanzibar, currently semi-urbanised settlements of local blacks and post-C6th Arab traders, to explore the possibilities of developing a chain of Roman trading bases and anti-pirate naval settlements there that could muscle in on the trade that Indian and Taprobane (Sri Lanka) merchants were doing there. Certainly some enterprising geographers from the university of Alexandria turned up in Rome in 651 with details of ancient maps from the Ptolemaic era of voyages down the African coast and stories of an earlier naval expedition sent by Xerxes of Persia in the 480s BC and they tried to interest the ministers and the Emperor in exploring this region further. But at this point the 'Caesar' was away from Rome on a year's mission to sort out the increasing threat of the inland, Mauretanian mountain Berber tribes to the drought – and locust-hit farms of Numidia and the Emperor gave them short shrift.

With the agricultural system in the Numidian interior in worse condition than the outlying parts of the Nile valley in Egypt had been earlier the Emperor's main concern was to drive the Berber raiders back and stop the exodus of financially precarious or raid-hit farmers to the coast. But unlike in Egypt there were no nearby rivers to supply water to the region easily and building new aqueducts from the coast was very expensive and it was to Constantine's credit that he did not give up when his son, having driven the tribes back, reported to him in early 652 and he ordered a mass-conscription of peasants in the Carthage coastal region and of farmers' younger sons in Mauretania, Baetica, and Lusitania to go to Numidia and work on the construction of a network of over a dozen new aqueducts which were built to carry water from the coast to the inland plains and hills. This took up much money and was shortly to require a new Imperial commission under a special 'Secretary for North African Agriculture and Irrigation' to supervise it and as it hit the budget the Emperor called off any ideas of expeditions to East Africa that his son was pressing for. The 'Caesar' was angry with his father for lack of 'grand vision' and possibly contemplating stirring up Senate protests about this when he was called upon to deal with an unexpected major pirate raid on Jutland in Dania by aggressive 'jarls' (regional warlords) from the opposite, Norwegian coast of the Skaggerak in summer 653.

The local nobles in mostly mountainous and infertile Norway were more ferocious and competitive than their largely peaceful, forest-dwelling Geatish and Swedish counterparts to the SE but they usually left Rome alone and had not raided Jutland for decades. But a recent storm had wrecked a lot of the Roman Skaggerak fleet while out on manoveures and with dozens of Danish farms burnt and many people carried off as slaves the Empire had to retaliate. Quite apart from the matter of prestige, the great merchants of the North Sea British and Frisian ports were lobbying their governors to warn of the danger of a 'panic' setting in and traders refusing to ship goods overseas in case of Viking pirates swooping on them – and some important Italian merchants had interests in this trade too.

The somnolent commander of the 'Classis Britannia' (British fleet) was an 'old school' aristocratic commander who despised the pagan Norsemen as beneath his notice and spent most of his time womanizing and holding parties for his under-worked and bored officers and the 'duces' of Jutland and Germania Ulterior were ageing men nearing their retirement and uninterested in risky wars so they played down the attacks. But the Emperor had the sense to realise that this sort of challenge could spread if not punished and in spring 654 the 'Caesar' was ordered in at the head of a large fleet, half of it sent from the Mediterranean, and 40,000 troops from all over the Empire. This was to raid and land in Vestfold, the major Norwegian 'jarldom' of the plains around Oslo which had richer agricultural land and a higher density of warriors than most of Norway and had been the origin of most of the raiders of Jutland. The war was successful as Rome had the advantage of numbers and weaponry and in addition the Swedes and Geats sent in expert forest fighters to help track down refugee Norse warriors as their lands could be next to be raided. After most of the main settlements of Vestfold – wooden so easy to burn – had been stormed and sacked in a three-month campaign of systematic ravaging the senior lord of Vestfold, 'king' Halfdan, gave up to save his starving civilians as they hid in the inland forests and his allies in the Trondelag far to the North failed to come to his aid as a Roman fleet from Caledonia appeared off their coasts. Halfdan had to pay compensation, release all his Jutland prisoners, and sign a humiliating treaty of dependence on Rome and annual tribute, and once his nobles and bodyguard had been lined up in front of the 'Caesar' he and they had to shuffle under a yoke in their kilts and then kneel before Constantine to swear allegiance to Rome.

The campaign thus ended with complete Roman success but only in the short term as the disgraced Halfdan was soon deposed by his militant nobles as a 'coward' and replaced by a rebel cousin who ignored the treaty. It also had unintended consequences on the succession in Rome as on the way home the 'Caesar' called in on Britain to 'shake up' the inadequate naval command there and was badly injured in a hunting accident in the woods of Coritania (Lincolnshire) near Lindum (Lincoln) in early October as he fell from his horse and was attacked by a boar. With the 'Caesar' in a coma for weeks with both his legs and assorted ribs broken and then unable to walk for months he was unable to be a viable candidate to be Emperor in an emergency. So when Constantine III died suddenly after falling ill during a strenuous judicial hearing at the Basilica Julia in Rome on 12 December 654, aged sixty-five, the ministers and a picked group of senior generals and senators faced the claims of the 'Caesar's younger brother Diomedes, aged thirty-two and twelve years younger than his brother, that he should succeed as Rome needed an active and fully mentally coherent ruler.

He was known as a capable and cultured administrator and a man of prudent judgement like his father, though until now he had shown little ambition and it was rumoured that his ambitious wife Flavia Neoronia (daughter of a self-made business tycoon from Corcyra in Greece) and her courtier brother Leontius had put him up to it. As there were stories that 'Caesar' Constantine had been having mental blackouts and was unable to concentrate without prompting the majority of ministers decided to pass him over. They also avoided the suggestion of his wife Stateira (a Persian noble lady and daughter and grand-daughter of past governors of 'Persis') that their son Caracalla, named for the Orientophile son of Septimius Severus and aged one, should be Emperor until his father recovered fully with her as regent and then the two should rule together. Traditionalist Roman noble dislike of having a part-Persian emperor may also have played a part in this, but on 14 December Diomedes was duly proclaimed as Emperor and the invalid 'Caesar' did not challenge it and accepted an offer of his son named to succeed the son-less Diomedes though Stateira, pensioned off with her husband to a series of villas in Calabria out of the way of Roman politics, was supposed to be planning a coup within months and later in 655 was sent into exile in Armorica in north-west Gaul on dubious evidence.

Chapter 2

Diomedes 654–667: The Hellenophile.

Younger son of Constantine III; succeeds after his invalid elder brother is passed over.

Constantine IV 667–680: The Cautious Front-Man.

Diomedes' daughter Domitia's husband.

Diomedes, aged thirty-two, was a cultured man and a Hellenist who, though a Catholic Christian, was a follower of the general mindset of Hadrian and believed in a joint Romano-Greek culture of the Classical period which it was his mission – and that of the Emperor 'per se' in view of his role as successor to Augustus – to preserve and amplify. He was not a great speaker or a man of overwhelming confidence and until the 'Caesar's accident he had been in the shadows politically and treated as a second-best 'reserve' by his father. The fact that his beautiful and glamorous wife Flavia had given him confidence and provided them both with a social circle of leading Rome aristocrats to back them was a major reason for his gratitude and resultant granting of a lead role to her as his social 'deputy'. While he was busy with official engagements and business and heading endless Council and sub-committee meetings Flavia was involved in social engagements around Rome and often attended official functions on his behalf. She also took a major role in organizing state patronage for an ever-expanding circle of orphanages, schools for poor children, hospitals, and homes for the indigent elderly that provided a 'safety net' for the deserving poor and looked after those who could not help themselves – mainly in Rome at first but, once Flavia had got her committees of noble ladies and fund-raising organised, across Italy too. Flavia helped to prod her husband to set up a special Imperial 'Secretary', on the Imperial Council, to run the Imperially-sponsored orphanages and to liaise with those run by the Church in Italy and later in the 650s a similar official took over the running of the Imperial hospitals. As the Church eagerly backed her up and the Papacy encouraged its bishops across the West to get local nobles to run provincial equivalents of the Empress' projects she was regarded as being as great a Church ally and as holy and modest as the saintly 'Augusta' Pulcheria had been in the fifth century Eastern Empire. Flavia veered between wearing sumptuous robes and piles of jewellery, some of it imported from the burgeoning diamond-mines of India which were a rising source of Roman fashionable nobles' jewellery in the C7th (mostly via the newly safe Gandhara – Bactria – Persia – Mesopotamia land-routes), to grand parties and receptions and dressing in sackcloth to clean kitchens and schoolroom floors and wash the feet of the poor in her charitable institutions (and the Church's) in Rome and she was assiduous in attending religious services whenever possible and giving generously to shrines. But behind the public face of a virtuous, wool-weaving Roman matron she was ruthless and pragmatic and she made sure that her forgiving husband knew all about the feverishly vengeful but impractical plans that his sister-in-law Stateira made to depose him with her own aristocratic and business allies and former army colleagues of her husband's in the late 650s.

The Praetorian Praefect Decius Decianus (in office 653–69), one of the more long-lasting and capable of her husband's ministers – most of whom he was to choose for their cultured tastes and Hellenist views rather than the ruthless hard work ethic that Constantine III had preferred when he was organizing promotions – and the Rome police chief had similar fear about Stateira. This continued even when her semi-invalid husband, living in precarious health in retirement in the Florentine countryside and trying to get his strength back, had enough of her endless plans and divorced her in 657 before leaving Italy for a Pyrrenean mountain hermitage to train as a monk. In 659 the Empress finally succeeded in having Stateira exposed for encouraging her proteges to murder the Emperor and make her son Caracalla, aged only six but a bright and charming boy who Diomedes had made his heir in 657, the ruler with her as regent. The scandal of exposing Stateira as a would-be coup leader and killer would have been too great so she was allowed to 'retire' to a nunnery in distant Armorica in NW Gaul to live as an honoured guest and lead the local charity fund-raising for new schools (including for girls, a passion of hers) and hospitals and most non-elite Romans thought that she had turned to God like her husband had done. But the court knew the truth and even the easy-going Diomedes had to agree to keep a close police watch on her friends thereafter, taking Caracalla into his own household and bringing him up with his cherished bastard son Petronius (born 647), an equally bright and talented boy who could not be legitimised and made the heir due to the Empress' hatred of him so his father arranged for him to go into the Church. (He ended up as Patriarch of Antioch in 693–722).

The Emperor and Empress only had four daughters and Flavia would have preferred her equally beautiful and vain but less brainy eldest daughter Domitia (born 640) as the heir, but the Emperor was determined that tradition must be upheld and a man must rule so as soon as practicable his daughter must marry a reliable and experienced figure of respectable background and proven competence. Given the popular enthusiasm for his – still invalid but recovering – elder brother as a dashing young officer before his accident, someone with good looks, an easy charm, and a military record would be advisable as a 'front-man' for the civilian ministers and could preside more easily at the annual round of public ceremonies in Rome and on tour across the Empire. But Diomedes was wary of choosing someone from the major landed senatorial dynasties in Italy as they were well-known for their fierce rivalries and if one family was chosen to provide an Emperor their rivals might start plotting and enlist friendly generals to help. His late father Constantine III had spoken to him of the need to keep the well-oiled 'machine' of government working behind a façade of glamour and pomp to keep the public happy and loyal, and had revealed his reluctance to put a capable but uninspiring bureaucrat in charge in case he ended up like the late Emperor Carus I, facing a massive riot from the fickle Roman public. Constantine 's idea had been for a courtly young noble with a degree of shrewdness but without too much originality or fondness for military gambles, and Diomedes was less cautious than that but had agreed that too 'showy' or ambitious a man might bring the risk of disaster.

In 658, Flavia had Domitia married off to a capable and much-admired young officer formerly with the 'Scholae' who had made a name for himself as a charismatic and ingenious garrison-commander at frontier forts in Gandhara, the young Apulian noble Constantine Marcellianus (born 630). Invalided out of the army with a bad leg and now re-trained as a capable and hard-working administrator in the military headquarters in Rome and with a large number of useful rich relatives and ex-officer friends in the Roman social elite to back him up, Constantine was Flavia's candidate to succeed her husband with herself and the party-mad, spendthrift Domitia (who she thought that she had under her thumb) pulling the political strings. But though he was a political novice and not all that fond of 'high politics' either, despising greedy and warfare-shirking political 'fixers', the new 'Caesar' (as of 659) Constantine was quickly taken in hand by Decianus and the rising star of the finance ministry, Xenodorus of Miletus in Ionia (who was to become 'Count of the Sacred Largesses' i.e. finance minister from 660 to 677). They trained him to act as their 'pupil' and acquire the knowledge and skills to contemplate Imperial policy in its wider scope. They also warned Diomedes of the danger of Flavia governing from 'behind the throne' under an inexperienced and politically naïve Emperor Constantine and a spendthrift, glamorous, popular and spendthrift Empress Domitia – who might cripple the military budget given that she was already using up her entire annual allowance on rebuilding mansions and their attendant leisure-facilities in Corcyra and Sicily for her holidays and had spoken of ever grander architectural plans for the capital. Diomedes' favourite architects were by this point in competition to win her contracts and show her and her easily-impressed husband what they could do, with domes and colonnade-supported halls in particular, and they urged Diomedes to see that she was ideal for running the 'public show' aspect of monarchy and would not interfere in politics provided that she got her money. But even the Hellenophile Diomedes, who had his own long-term plans to make Rome look less dowdy compared to Constantinople and to create a network of broad avenues across the city's outer suburbs leading inwards to the inner city of the 'Seven Hills' and the Colosseum Square, was wary that she might cut back on spending on the army and spark off a mutiny or else leave the Empire ill-prepared for a major war. Accordingly, he decreed that the Senate – whose leading and most dignified aristocrats disliked her as a brash and extravagant 'new Messalina' with rather too many adoring young courtiers in her train – should have to approve any new grants of the rank of 'Augusta', knowing that they would not do so to any of the current Imperial womenfolk.

The enthusiastic amateur poet and 'Homer fan' Diomedes, whose proudest creation as Emperor was his new annual 'Homeric Festival' on the ancient Greek poet's alleged home island of Chios where poets (adult and boys) competed to recite both Homer and new poems of their own in his style on Homeric subjects with the Emperor providing prizes and inviting the top winners to court the next winter, was more interested in culture than in politics. He was content to leave the majority of political initiatives and 'big picture' policy drafting to his top half-dozen ministers whose work he then endorsed at Council meetings, though he had the sense to spend money on setting up new committees of experts in each field of governance to be brought to Rome in a new 'round' of searches every three years from among the recommended best personnel in the provincial and Praefectural offices' civil service. But he did take an interest and occasionally the lead in planning Rome's cultural-political role across what was increasingly being known by Greco-Roman university scholars as the 'Universal Oikoumene' (i.e. 'civilised world') and Diomedes either invented or else soon endorsed the new Roman imperial symbol which was adopted in 660 and placed on official flags, tapestries, murals, monuments, and literature – the 'double-headed' eagle, facing both East and West.

The Empire was now symbolically declared to have a combined mission in civilising and bringing order and justice to both East (partially civilised already) and West and this was duly played up in Imperial speeches by the Emperor and

Empress, and though Diomedes was scrupulous in seeing that expenditure on public works projects and charity extended to both regions his own interests were mostly Eastern. As such he even contemplated, but did not carry out, more expansion into India and allowed military planners to 'game-plan' an invasion of the upper Ganges after the great centralising Ganges warlord Harsha died (647) and his empire started to disintegrate. As Harsha, head of the 'Vardhana' dynasts of the upper Ganges plain and based at Kanauj, had had no close family his ex-generals and feudatories were now fighting over his empty throne, disrupting trade and pillaging merchants as well as conscripting civilians for their armies. The situation was little better South of the Narmada river where the Chalukya kings of Vatapi (whose recent warlord Pulakesin had held Harsha back from invading the South) had died too and the capital had been sacked and temporarily occupied by their South-Eastern rivals from Teleganu, the expanding Pallava kingdom. Some local rajahs were so annoyed at the rounds of civil wars and the disruption to trade, which was now booming in Gandhara and on to the main part of the Empire now that the roads were safe West of the Indus, that they wanted and sent embassies to the Empire for Diomedes to invade and restore order as his predecessors had done to the Afghan lands and Gandhara, if not to the rebellion-wracked lower Indus.

The propagandist appeal of Rome as protector of the Buddhist faith from disorder and pillage by civil war or external invaders in Gandhara, which the Empire and its allied Buddhist temple/monastery heads had been putting out since the conquest, had had resonance in the Ganges region too once Harsha's firm and just rule was replaced by chaos. There was a constant local fear of the civil strife encouraging outside predators, most notably the 'Hunnic' (really by this stage more Turkic) nomad tribes in the steppes beyond the Jaxartes who had raided Gandhara and looted cities and monasteries in the pre-Roman conquest period of the mid-late C6th. Only Rome and its strong armies could now protect the Khyber Pass and the Indus crossings from them, so the peace-loving merchant classes and the less 'military' nobles regarded Roman overlordship as less dangerous for them than continuing inter-state wars.. Some small kings in the North-East had even rallied to an affronted T'ang Chinese ambassador to the kingdom of Kanauj, who had had his rich embassy pillaged by warlords on a tour in 652 and had brought in a Tibetan mercenary force to punish the attackers in retaliation.

The Buddhist abbots of the region were particularly vociferous on the need for law and order to help the robbed and exploited rural peasantry, and some great (Roman and local) elite figures in Gandhara responded to their appeals by getting the civilian administration in Taxila to ask for an army to be sent East to 'aid our allies and gain new federate vassals'. But Diomedes was too cautious to turn his private dreams of being the 'New Alexander' (as he called himself) into practice and the most he would do was the symbolic act of visiting the old Macedonian capitals of Pella and Aegae on his Balkan and Thracian tour of 663 and ordering them to be rebuilt as they had been in Alexander's day. A replica of the old 'Argead ' royal palace at Pella where Alexander had grown up was built as one of Diomedes' many imperial estates in Greece, a favourite summer destination of his, and his heir Caracalla was tutored by the best scientists and cultural and political theorists in the Empire in the tradition of Aristotle teaching Alexander. But Diomedes would not put the effort or money required into a major war to conquer India and instead he just ordered all merchants and Church missionaries going there to draw up detailed reports and maps that an invasion could use later.

Meanwhile the growth of the Imperial-monopoly silk industry in Italy, which had been underway for the best part of a century but was now booming thanks to the conspicuous expenditure of the wealthy noble 'set' headed by Empress Flavia and soon joined by her elder daughters, meant that though there was still a substantial 'trade deficit' with the Indian kingdoms and coin was flowing out of the Empire to that region the situation was not as one-sided as in the 5th and 6th centuries. The Emperor showed his own favour for the cultures of the East when he proceeded from his usual early summer stay on his favourite Aegean island of Samos (where he was rebuilding the ancient palace of the famous 6th century-BC pirate king and poetic patron Polycrates, – accurately as possible, in the mid-late 650s as his main summer residence) to Antioch in July 658 and then went on to Mesopotamia for his first grand tour of the ex-Persian domains. Major tented receptions were held for the Persian nobility in Mesopotamia, Persis (at the former royal residences of Susa and Istakr), and Media (where Diomedes had had the one-time palace of the Achaemenid 'Great Kings' and Alexander rebuilt for this visit) in the first Imperial peacetime visit to Persia for centuries. As Diomedes had learnt Persian and wore Persian robes, followed Persian customs, and charmed the nobility with his cultural enthusiasm for Persia – and due to his promise to stop the orthodox Church confiscating ex-Zoroastrian 'fire temple' and priestly lands on various slim excuses – he was a major 'hit' with the nobility and won them over to the Roman imperial 'project' far more than the abrupt and brutal conqueror Claudius III had done in the late 610s. Diomedes went on to Bactria too and held a grand meeting of the local nobility and the military garrisons there with polo-games and races and opened a new bridge over the Oxus. After wintering at Ctesiphon (where he had a new palace built with a Persian-style dome) he returned to Rome by sea in spring 659 and as events turned out never returned to the main part of the East, only reaching Cyprus in 660 and Cappadocia, Pontus, and Armenia on his Asia Minor summer tour of 663. The Emperor had already spent winter 656–7 at Constantinople and most of late spring and early summer 657 in Egypt, where he ordered the partly silted-up main harbour at Alexandria to be cleared and thereafter kept clear by a special Imperial commission for Egyptian irrigation (which was so important for the regions' farmers that it was to acquire its own department and Imperial Secretary under his successor Constantine IV). But otherwise his main summer tours were in Dacia, Illyria and Epirus (661), western Asia Minor (660), North Africa from Leptis Magna and Cyrene west to Carthage (662), and Spain and Numidia/Mauretania (664) and he made a point of spending part of almost every summer at Samos.

He also indulged his love of Hellenic culture in opening a new school of poetry to teach it to (male) teenagers, mainly from the elite, in Rome in 658 and an identical school for the Eastern provinces in Antioch in 661 and in 664 he was to use the love of local epic poetry and pastoral 'love odes' that he had acquired in Persia in 658 to set up a similar school to teach both Hellenic and Persian poetry at Ctesiphon. It was not surprising that he was accused by fuming Christian polemicists by the mid-660s of being a secret pagan though he also paid for new professorial chairs in Church theology and studies of the main Christian sects' history at the universities of Rome, Constantinople, Athens, and Ephesus and he was rather a patron of all 'high' culture and merely opposed to ignorance and philistinism. Nor was he entirely indifferent to the far West, as when the increasing agricultural prosperity of the settled and fertile plains of Jutland and the adjacent Danish islands – now settled by a mixture of Roman, Danish and German small farmers – led to a series of damaging raids by sea by the Norse pirates of Vestfold on the opposite, north side of the Skaggerak in the early 660s Diomedes was more ready to listen to the calls for war and retaliation of the 'high command' in Rome than were the complacent local admirals commanding the Skaggerak and 'Classis Britannia ' fleets who had not seen any warfare for decades and had lazily not bothered to hold naval manoeuvres for years.

The Skaggerak fleet had recently suffered major losses when caught in a storm late in 661 while trying to intercept customs-evading smugglers in the Danish islands so they were short of ships to tackle the raids of 662 and 663 and in the latter dozens of farms were burnt and people carried off to be held to ransom and cattle and pigs stolen to be eaten at pirate feasts by the 'jarls' (nobles) of Vestfold led by their hereditary chief Halfdan, the Empire's old foe. It was the Emperor not the local admirals who insisted that the pirates needed to be taught a sharp lesson that the local forces were inadequate to administer and as a result some 40,000 troops were shipped by a special force of naval vessels from the Mediterranean up to the Skaggerak to be landed in the plains around Oslo in spring 664. They started to systematically ravage and burn them and kill everyone who did not manage to escape with Roman soldiers who were used to woodland fighting and evading ambushes setting out through the forests and along the interconnecting tracks to attack settlements in a methodical pattern, aided by maps provided by traders. Where necessary as when dealing with rebel Germans in the Continental forests for centuries, the Romans started massive forest-fires to 'smoke out' ambushers or clear blocked tracks and lines of wooden fortifications, and Roman galleys rowed up the shallow creeks to bombard coastal settlements with fire-arrows so they did not need to have their ramparts stormed and the lines of waiting, axe-brandishing defenders had to flee the smoke to hide in the woods. Once coastal positions with strategic value had been taken new wooden and earth-ramparted Roman forts were built there, protected by defensive fire-throwing catapults, and landless mainland German tribesmen (often Franks and Langobards) and Danes (often the younger sons of farmers) who had joined the Roman army were installed as garrisons and were promised long-term farms there if they managed to hold onto the properties – which most did.

Some wiser local Norsemen keen to protect their lands were soon giving in ahead of or on the Romans' arrival in their vicinity in force rather than face their villages being burnt down, signing up to become Roman vassal 'federate' troops, and handing over their sons as hostages. As the Romans could not garrison every isolated creekside village or 'hall' the more sensible Roman commanders (some of them ethnically of Germano-British or Danish descent and able to understand the local 'heroic' pagan Norse culture better than haughty Mediterranean officers) accepted these compromises to speed up the war. As long as land was 'neutralised' as a threat and was under Roman 'rule' (even if nominally) the 'high command' usually accepted this as a way of getting 'quick results' to show the Emperor, though some glory-seeking officers grumbled that the generals and bureaucrats at headquarters were spoiling their chances to win awards and good reports for their future careers. Several top ship-plundering local pirate chiefs were reliably said to have paid off arriving Roman commanders with a share of their hidden loot in return for certificates of 'good service and loyalty' that would keep them in possession of their villages and so translated smoothly into being Roman vassals. But it did bring results and diminish the number of minor but time-consuming struggles for control of a mass of long and winding 'fjords' along the mountainous coast SW of the 'South Norwegian Plain'. The Church's demands in Rome that all surrendered Norsemen be forced to convert to Christianity were agreed in principle by the Imperial Council but were not enforced in practice in many areas. Romans and allied Swedes and Geats who traded with the Norse and knew Vestfold were brought in as guides, and with their help those Norse who did not either surrender or stay to fight and be killed as their wooden halls were burnt were tracked into the inland forests and hunted down. In the process the Romans created a new network of (initially earth and gravel not stone) roads along the existing Norse rural trade-tracks to link up their new coastal garrisons and stationed new garrisons in forts on all the major passes. Though Halfdan and his elite warriors managed to flee North over the mountains to the Trondelag the Romans then occupied the plains and coastal creeks/fjords of Vestfold through the winter of 664–5 and spring 665 – and ate up the confiscated food-supplies, reducing the surviving resisting locals to famine.

In 665 the defeated Norse's main jarls and sub-rulers had to come to terms to halt the threat of permanent Roman annexation, and as a result Halfdan and his warriors had to sign a treaty of vassalage, hand over hostages and compensation, release their prisoners, and at a ceremony in front of the Roman commander line up in rags and pass under the yoke in a traditional Roman ceremony of humiliation.

After this the lords of Vestfold did not dare to challenge Rome again for the best part of a century and peace returned to the Skaggerak which continued to host an ever-expanding amount of incoming Roman (mostly from Britain, Gaul, Belgica and the Rhine-mouth) and outgoing local Danish shipping. The most strategic fjords and points on the coast were given to those Norse commanders who had signed up to be Roman vassals, kept in check by a network of garrisons linked by ship patrols to the Roman naval bases in Dania and at the Southern end of the southern Norse plain, and the new (mostly Anglian, German/Frankish, and Danish) farming 'federates' planted on resisting Norse lords' fjords and farms acted as a regional militia to keep the jarls in check. Many of those remaining Norse lords and farmers who kept their lands, indeed, ended up enrolling in the Roman army or navy to have adventure and win loot and prestige over the next century – which was seen by the 'high command' in Rome as a way to tame them, as jobs as mercenaries had 'tamed' the Franks and (most) Vandals. But the temptation for glory-seeking commanders to strike out on their own and not have to obey the 'decadent' and 'unmanly', mostly Mediterranean Roman staff officers at provincial 'ducal' military headquarters was strong, and many also sneaked off for illegal pirate activity in the Northern seas or to become mercenaries in Ireland or the Baltic.

Forbidden to take part in their traditional warfare and raiding by Rome, the enterprising Danish coastal captains were now creating a large-scale maritime trade to export their local corn, cattle, pigs, and meat to the rest of the nearer parts of the Empire and the provincial capitals of Aarhus and Claudianum were already starting to flourish by the 660s. Over the next 50 to 70 years the North Sea was to see a growing trade-boom in which Diomedes' swift suppression of the first Norse threat was surely a contributory factor. The creation of this trade boom also saw new 'entrepots' for the North Sea trade start to spring up spontaneously in Britain – eg the South coast town of Clausentum (Southampton/Bitterne) and the East coast ones of Silvapontum (Woodbridge, Suffolk), Grimsburgum (Grimsby) on the Humber, and Novacastrum (Newcastle) on the Tyne at the East end of Hadrian's Wall, adjacent to the great military base set up on the Wall for the conquest of eastern Caledonia In Belgica, there were the towns of Antuerpium at the mouth of the Scheldt estuary leading up to the rich plains inland, along with the surprising new port of Dordrectium (Dordrecht) in Frisia, near the mouth of the Rhine, which fed the new agricultural region of fertile but flood-prone coastal Frisia where local settlers who had mostly fled from raid-hit Germania Ulterior had settled after 595 and created new coastal farms protected by tall earth walls from the sea.

These decades also saw more intellectual – Christian – culture and more of a vigorous and morally questing Church in the NW of the Empire than the Hellenist Emperor noticed, mostly sparked off by austere and virtue-seeking holy men influenced by monasteries and hermitages in Ireland and western Britain though in the East some influence was also exerted by the 'daughter house' of Iona in 'Votadinia' (or 'Gododdin') North of Hadrian's Wall, the island monastery of Lindisfarne, under St Aedan and his successors. Among their foundations was Iarovium (Jarrow) at the mouth of the Tyne whose 660s founding abbot, the learned Benedict Biscopius (d 690, OTL figure), travelled as far as Rome to acquire copies of many learned books from the Great Library and the library of the Papacy to install at his new monastic library and school at Iarovium. His pupils there included the famous early C8th historian Bedius (OTL the Venerable Bede, historian), who like him was of mixed Anglian and Romano-British ancestry. Bedius indeed put his own 'spin' on his careful and learned study of the history of both his ancestral peoples, writing that it was God's design that the adventurous but pagan Continental farmers and sailors of NW Germany should come to Britain and stir up the 'slothful' locals who had signally failed to repay the Almighty for His gift of their fertile island by playing a leading role in the development of His empire. The German warriors who the great Aetius, 'chosen one of the Lord' in the struggle to defeat the unspeakable Attila the Hun nearly three centuries before, had brought to help the Empire to victory had stayed loyal to Christ and to Caesar since then and had been rewarded with leading roles in the Roman army and navy and widespread lands in eastern Britain – and even the once pagan and fratricidal Irish were developing as a centre of holy monasticism.

In Bedius' view of the Divine purpose it was the duty of the Anglo-Britons to show that they were not sluggards in the work to spread the 'Divine Light' of Faith and Good Works, in which the monasteries of Lindisfarne and Iarovium were leading the way, or the 'awful warning' of the Viking raiders would return to punish them. Bedius was a determinist Christian who deliberately 'talked down' the victories and characters of pre-Christian Roman and German figures and his 'history' of Britain commenced with the conversion to Christianity by Constantine 'the Great' – and ignored pre-Christian Irish and Picts/Dalriadan rulers. Both 'insulted' local aristocrats with pride in their pagan heritage and learned Roman writers in the Augustan pagan traditions of Livy, Vergil, and Horace were hostile to him and his work, which was ignored in fashionable literary circles and at the 'Great Library' in Rome as unsophisticated and too Catholic in its tone – but this militant orthodox Christian interpretation of history was popular in Britain and also in religious circles in Gaul and Spain.

Compared to the vigorous and moralist clergy and monks of western and northern Britain the mostly aristocratic great churchmen of Britain, Gaul and Belgica in the later C7th and early C8th were usually bland and unenterprising careerists who carried out their duties well enough but had no sense of mission and monks seeking spiritual enlightenment and struggle tended to head for the Nand W of Britain or to Ireland. Similarly in Germany the only major centre of education, spiritual struggle and 'searching ', and missionary work was the British foundation at Fulda near the upper Main, founded by the Dumnonian monk (St) Winfrith aka 'Boniface' (OTL figure, 'Apostle of Germany'). But even the most secular and worldly Catholic Roman province was a haven of peace and good government compared to the situation in Rome's local Frankish vassal – state in Transrhenus, the Merovingian kingdom, where after the deaths of the great 'Good King Dagobert' in 649 and his weak but well-meaning son Clovis II (guided by his British/Saxon wife Balthildis) in 662 the latter's sons, the underage Childeric and Theuderic, fell under the control of a succession of feuding nobles as regents and a series of coups and unsavoury murders made the kingdom a 'by-word' for badly governed anarchy. After the brutal but successful stabilization of this by the regent Ebroin in 667 Diomedes was asked to intervene on behalf of a large number of exiled nobles, but he could not be bothered with so 'minor' and uninteresting a dispute among remote 'barbarians' in the 'swamps' of Germany despite Papal advice. The misrule continued until Ebroin was overthrown in 687 by one of the earlier refugees, the wise and shrewd though ruthless Pepin of Heristal who was grandson to king Dagobert's two chief advisers, Pepin of Lamden and Bishop Arnulf. (All OTL figures, really in Gaul.)

Meanwhile the insouciant Emperor proceeded with his plans for another grand tour of the East, the idea for which had come on his 665 tour of the eastern end of the Euxine and the allied kingdom of Iberia (where he visited the old capital of Kutaisi and the new one of Tbilisium, the latter now a major Roman base against raids by mountain tribes). But events forestalled him as in summer 667 his health started to decline after an attack of malaria and a recurrence of this during a short tour of Cisalpine Gaul ended with him collapsing while hunting near Bononia on the way back to Rome in November. On 18 November 667 Diomedes had a seizure in his carriage, apparently after it left the road at speed in a pass in the Apennines (which later conspiracy theorists said had been arranged, either by Stateira's followers or the friends of his wife's secret charioteer lover who was about to be exposed as the father of his youngest daughter), and he died in a local inn to which he was carried a few hours later, aged only fifty.

His wife Flavia and his leading ministers arranged the subsequent senatorial meeting two days later which elected his son-in-law Constantine as the next Emperor, aged thirty-seven, and this was presumed to be a plan to make the latter the Empress' puppet while she ruled from behind the scenes. But the surprises were not yet over as in mid-December, shortly before the new ruler's coronation, the (now Dowager) Empress was suddenly arrested and required to sign a document announcing her retirement from politics as a 'grieving widow' to live a life of holiness and continue her charity-work at a nunnery and girls' school which she had founded in a remote hill town in Marsium, central Italy, and it was apparent that her decision was not entirely voluntary. The new Emperor was not the sort of man to have the nerve and brains to plan this sort of coup and possibly the leading ministers feared that his mother-in-law would interfere with their government, but the way that most of her property and social role was quickly assumed by her supposedly 'unpolitical' but greedy and vain daughter Domitia suggested that she had a leading role in the plot. She certainly took over the social 'lead' in Rome though she did not emulate her mother's aggressive philanthropy and 'image-making' and had little interest in charity-work and she was too lazy and spendthrift to bother with such matters as policy or to influence her husband except to see that her socialite friends' relatives received jobs (mostly sinecures) and imperial presents and she had the ability to spend what she liked on her clothes and parties. To her chagrin, neither her father (to 680) nor her husband would allow her the full legal rank of co-ruler, 'Augusta', that had been held by the great Pulcheria in the 5th century – that would have allowed her to spend money and make appointments as she wished and neither of them (nor the hard-lobbying finance ministry) trusted her commonsense.

Instead, she was able as far as the current ministers would allow to spend increased amounts of cash on her building schemes for her holiday mansions in Sicily, where she created a large Court 'holiday campus' with its own theatres, ball-courts, hippodrome, grass racetrack, and gardens around the Cephalodium suburb of Panormus (Palermo), and on Corcyra and Leucas in the Ionian Islands. She took on her father's role as a major theatrical patron and held a drama festival at her theatre outside Panormus every two summers, with her proteges including the famous Naxian (Aegean) playwright Xenodarus 'the New Anacreon' who in the 670s and 680s wrote a whole cycle of plays about the bloodthirsty intrigues and internecine feuds of the Ptolemaic court (which the Church despised as 'immoral heathen nonsense'). By extension her patronage of a new generation of younger playwrights and help to the 'Euripidean revivalist' multi-millionaire business tycoon Leontius of Chalcedon to set up a drama-school at his Bosphorus mansion kept the 'New Age' of sophisticated psychological drama – based on Hellenistic history not 'immoral and pagan' activities of the sidelined ancient gods – from collapsing for lack of money after the death of the generous Diomedes. The arts, including sculpture and decorative wall-painting, had a lot to thank the Empress Domitia for and the sniffs of the Church (especially the stricter abbots and preachers in Constantinople near her allies' drama-school) about her 'pagan sympathies' were ignored by her husband despite some Catholic nobles plotting to get him to divorce her and replace her with one of their daughters. Probably Constantine, shrewder than he appeared, found it easier to grant her demands for more and more money for her buildings and her theatrical projects and keep her out of politics, while dangling the prospect of divorcing her if evidence of her supposed love-affairs with his socialite noble friends leaked to keep them happy too. Their 'political' marriage may not have had much deep affection but it worked and remained strong with the Imperial couple hailed by the spectacle-loving Rome public at the ever more lavish Games that her proteges organized for an increased sixty or so feast-days every year.

Domitia also passed on her cultured knowledge and enthusiasms to her nephew Caracalla, to whom she sent copies of her favourite works once she discovered his enthusiasm for them, and possibly encouraged him to copy her dislike of Court politics too.; he was more aligned to her cynicism about such goings-on than was his own, intrigue-prone mother Stateira who was rather too open to scheming flatterers. Domitia had the sense to be a munificent patron for Italian and Greek nunneries and Church schools too in order to keep the less judgemental leaders of the Church sympathetic to her. Her Hellenistic cultural interests also led to her proteges searching the archives, private and public, of the former Seleucid and Ptolemaic cities of the Levant for 'lost' plays and poems to bring to Rome for public performance, saving some masterpieces – and incidentally some works of science by Egyptian engineers, doctors, and mathematicians too –from being forgotten. Both Domitia and the third of the Emperor's daughters, Cassia, were by the time that the Emperor died involved with patronizing summer poetry festivals (both for devotional Christian poetry and for traditional 'Horatian'-style 'rural idyll' odes) for well-off literary enthusiasts in Campania and Sicily, along with lobbying the education ministry to see that proper financial provision was made for teaching historic Roman and Greek poetry in all universities across the Mediterranean – Church-funded ones included. The not noticeably strict or moralist contemporary Patriarchs of Constantinople and Antioch, in contrast to their fierce C4th and C5th predecessors as moralist abbots complained, went along with this provided that their bishops' insistence on a ban on 'immoral and obscene' Catullus in all universities with Church funding or trustees was written into law, which the Emperor agreed to in 679 to keep them happy. The political disgrace and effective exile of amateur poetess Domitia after her husband died (see below) was to reduce her ability to act as a patron, or her appeal to festival and school funding-hunters, but Cassia – married off by her brother-in-law to a prominent Constantinopolitan civil servant and later 'logothete' (minister) of aqueducts in the city, Anastasius Assetinius, in 678 – was to remain a major patron of the arts, pagan as well as Christian in inspiration, and leader of the 'Second Capital's social circles well into the C8th. Her own private 'School of Pastoral and Epic Poetry', the 'Vergilianum', on the old Acropolis in Constantinople kept the written arts supplied with new recruits for several centuries to come (though it became more explicitly Christian in its moral tone and more hostile to poems about mythical creatures in the mid-C8th under her grand-daughter St. Flavia's directorship).

Constantine, though competent and a quick learner as he had been as a young officer and also able to inspire loyalty for his honesty, was unimaginative and a complete contrast to his learned, cultured, and innovative predecessor, causing his few ventures into the world of culture in attempts to keep up Diomedes' patronage to lead to disaster and spiteful comments about his clumsiness and lack of knowledge. But he could act as a 'front-man' for his leading ministers and was reliable at carrying out agreed policy though he tended to listen to and weight up advice for too long before making decisions and was prey to those more expert and forceful than himself. Decianus, finance minister Xenodorus, and from 668 to 679 the new 'Master of Offices' and administrative co-ordinator Aurelius Gessianus in effect ran the government for most of the first decade of his reign and were referred to as the 'three-horsed chariot' which the Emperor drove or which rather galloped where they liked and pulled him after them. But he did seek advice from other ministers too if they were experts in particular areas and his choices of new ministers were usually capable if rarely those who he had selected personally from past knowledge rather than had had pushed in front of him by one or other of the three leading officials. He also did much to coax more middle-ranking and ambitious and/or public-spirited nobles from Italy and the neighbouring provinces into government and made it as clear as Constantine III had done that the main aim of a Roman noble should be public service and that brains should be used for the benefit of the Empire. He also continued to encourage nobles and successful businessmen (and the sons of the latter who had money and time on their hands) in the outer provinces, the East in particular, to come to Rome and serve the government or at least do this in their home regions. He continued to bring Easterners into the Senate and was open to advice from the local governors and Praefects in various provinces to reward useful political or social allies with Imperial honours and gifts and to invite them to court, where his wife's skills in organizing huge and lavish parties and dinners were invaluable and she was able to remember hundreds of names at a time without prompting.

But unlike Diomedes he was too cautious and lacking in confidence to risk controversy or, especially, to alarm the Church, and so few people from the frowned-upon Monophysite or Nestorian sects were given any role in government in the East or invited into the Senate – though given the continuing strengths of Zoroastrianism and Mithraism in Persia and Bactria/Sogdiana he had to invite its adherents to work for him or face the alienation of a large section of the nobility there who Diomedes had coaxed to accept and join in the government. He was also interested in improving his subjects' lives as well as the income of the treasury, as prompted by Xenodorus, and as such played a significant role in taking State action once the current problems of ongoing droughts, locusts, crumbling and long-neglected aqueducts and other irrigation-systems, and rising amounts of raiding on farms by restive desert Berbers in Numidia and Mauretania in the 650s – 660s were pointed out to him. With declining income from taxes and agricultural production in inland parts of those provinces a major programme was launched under a special State commission in 669 and funds were allocated to rebuild many aqueducts and improve the silted-up or crumbling-banked drainage systems on farmland. Troops were sent to clear out the raiders and recover their loot but once they had been punished they were offered cash and animals to act as freelance herders and supply meat to the local towns and army garrisons too. Though the programme to restore Numidian and Mauretanian agriculture had been suggested to him by Xenodorus, who was worried at declining revenue and a 'flight from the land', the Emperor did act decisively and see that funds were available on a long-term basis and an extra 'Secretary for North African Irrigation', always a local and usually an ex-army engineer, was added to the Imperial Council to support the one for Egyptian irrigation.

Other irrigation-projects followed in the equally drought-hit farmland on the edges of the deserts in eastern Syria and the Jordan valley in Arabia Petraea in 672, and in 674 the Emperor visited the area in person to check up on progress and chivvy officials into doing better during his main tour of Syria, Phoenicia, and Palestine – where he also opened a new port at Ptolemais (Acre) to handle the growing exports from the Arabia Felix – Hejaz – Mecca – Medina – Petra trade-route. Constantine had inherited ministers and civil servants interested in building up trade via the Indian Ocean – Persian Gulf – Charax – Ctesiphon – Syria trade-route with India from Diomedes. Though the Roman nobility's endless passion for Indian diamonds and other exotic imports was causing a 'trade imbalance' and the export of too much coin to the East the discovery of new metallic mines in Marcomannia and Noricum by army mining-engineers in the mid-660s luckily opened a new way to manufacturing replacement coins within the Empire in the opening years of the Emperor's reign and this did diminish fears of a 'money drain' affecting the economy. Constantine's interest in this was genuine and he had visited mines in Dacia as a young officer, and he duly set up a new 'Secretary for Mines' in 670 to co-ordinate the funding, opening-up, and development of new mines all across the Empire (but in practice mostly in Marcomannia and Noricum). He made sure that the army seconded expert engineers to help with this and the judicial system provided convicts to work the mines, the resulting expansion of the revenue from and job-opportunities available in Marcomannia leading to a mini-'boom' and the development as a major town of the bleak former military base of 'Augusta Prahavorum' (Prague) in the later C7th and early C8th with its citadel re-named the 'Constantinianum' after the Emperor's residence there during his 671 tour of Marcomannia and the upper and middle Danube. Unlike Diomedes the new Emperor had no particular interest in Greece though he did stay at the new palace on Samos a couple of times for the sake of appearances and he also attended the 672 Olympics to give out prizes, using the opportunity to make speeches stressing the importance of physical fitness and military-style training for all young men – his own walking was awkward and limited due to his injuries in the army and he preferred to ride as he had to use a stick for walking. But he did spend winter 669–70 and 671–2 in Constantinople to reassure the citizens and senate that he was as committed to the East as his predecessor and in 672 he crossed Asia Minor and Syria en route to a grand gathering of representatives of the nobility and military forces of the East at Ctesiphon and the opening of another new port at the 'boom city' of Charax (Basra).

He did not visit Persia at all and his other main Eastern trip, to Syria, Phoenicia, Palestine, and Egypt in 674, was his final one to the Levant, and he otherwise mostly carried out tours of the West, including Gaul and the upper Rhine in 673, Spain and Lusitania plus Mauretania in 675, Carthage and Tripolitania followed by Crete and Sicily in 676, and Rhaetia, the entire Rhine down the river as far as Frisia, Belgica, and southern Britain in 677. In 678 Constantine visited the Balkans and Constantinople and went on by sea over the Euxine to pay the first Imperial peacetime visit to Cherson ahead of a visit to Iberia and North Adiabene,. The latter part of his expedition saw the Emperor inaugurate the new city at Bacuvium (Baku) in North Adiabene which Diomedes had ordered to be built in the early 660s to act as a magnet for incoming civilians in a 'boom area' for Caspian Sea trade, the export of furs and horses by the tribes on the steppes to the North, and also the new discovery of petroleum on the salt-flats around the city which could be used for the inflammable liquid needed to fuel the Empire's latest military innovation, 'Greek Fire'. This invention, of projectiles loaded with inflammable liquid (either naptha or petroleum) that could be hurled by catapult or squirted from a tube at enemy troops, cities, or shipping, had been made in the early 670s by a Greco-Syrian scientist working for the army in Mesopotamia, Callincus of Hierapolis (OTL), and had been taken up and tested successfully by the local army and then reported to Rome. But due to bureaucratic conservatism it was only taken up seriously as a major bonus for army and navy alike in the late 670s and now it was demonstrated by Callinicus and his staff to the Emperor near the new 'oil wells' at Bacuvium and the ruler approved of its being adapted for use by not only the army, mainly in attacking obstinate fortresses and burning them down quickly, but by the navy in sinking enemy wooden ships. The conservative naval 'high command' were reluctant to try out anything new and untested and complained that their ships would need to get close to enemy ones to squirt the inflammable liquid onto their decks by tube and that putting large catapults on board ships to fire the liquid in projectiles at a distance would unbalance them. But Constantine for once pressed the issue and in spring 679 a new senior admiral, the 'Great Drungarius' (a Greek title) as the office was now named, was appointed in the person of the youngish and dynamic Achilleus Barsyaticus, a Mesopotamian Greek officer who had sailed on private trading trips to Taprobane and down the East African coast before he joined the navy and who had impressed the senior officers in Rome with his articulate calls for a Roman naval and trading presence in the Indian Ocean as far South as Mombasa and Kilwa.

(In OTL 'Greek Fire' was developed in the Eastern Roman Empire in the 670s and used against invading Arab navies.)

In the event Barsyaticus was to hold office until 702 and remodel the navy to use 'Greek Fire' on its warships by building many new ones that would hold both tubes and catapults and it was due to him that Roman naval supremacy was assured over all its regional seas, albeit at a cost in naval building-programmes that the treasury did not like at all. This was probably Constantine's major military contribution to the Empire though at the time it was less talked-about than his other 'personnel innovation' of 679, the creation of a new 'Ministry of Oriental Trade' to co-ordinate and increase trade with India and think up new exports that Rome could send there to redress the trade-balance. This was thought of by military and literary 'expansionists' as the first step in a campaign that would lead Rome to advance its frontiers into the central lands of India and follow Alexander's route in the hope of going beyond the latter's expedition and over-running the Ganges plains. As the Emperor's only son, the handsome and charismatic Anastasius (born 660),was serving as a junior officer in the army in Bactria it was thought that this campaign might be intended as his route to glory and the throne.

The Emperor had declared that as a faithful and traditionalist follower of the precedents set by Augustus he regarded it as right for age and experience to come ahead of close genealogical birth in the queue for the throne and so his predecessor's elder brother Constantine's son Caracalla (born 653) should come first as his immediate heir, as Augustus had chosen his son-in-law Marcus Agrippa to succeed him not his grandsons in the 20s BC and had then put his wife's elder grandson Germanicus ahead of his heir Tiberius' own son Drusus in the 10s AD. For that matter, Domitia was not over-fond of the rather philistine and sport-obsessed Anastasius, a keen charioteer and runner and very popular with the crowds at the Rome Games (he was not allowed to race his own chariots there but had his private racing-team and spent a lot of money on hiring top charioteers and breeding horses) but barely literate and uninterested in culture. But some partisans of Domitia feared that if Caracalla succeeded then he would see that Anastasius would never get the throne and in addition Caracalla would recall his vengeful mother Stateira from her Armorican exile. The latter was not liked or trusted and might start killing off those who had silenced her in the 650s, so Domitia – normally too fond of parties and her collection of thousands of dresses to care about politics – was persuaded by alarmed nobles who had plotted to ruin Stateira to back Anastasius as the heir in a reconciliation between them in 678. It was unfortunate for them that he was a drunken and rash young womanizer who had none of the equally good-looking and charismatic Caracalla's brains and other talents.

All that Anastasius was good at was gambling and womanizing and he was already a hard-drinking spendthrift in his late teens as he reluctantly did military service, and early in 680 he had to be invalided home to Rome from his new post on the 'comitatus' staff at Ctesiphon with what was officially called a malarial infection but was probably a venereal one given his recent roistering with prostitutes in the Eastern 'capital'. Once he was recovered Anastasius was meant to take up a post on the general staff in Rome and sober up under strict watch by a group of young officers delegated for the task by his worried father. But instead he ended up taking leave of absence that summer without permission to go round the casinos of Baiae in Campania and his huge losses of money there and parties with naked young women led to general scandal and questions by the Church and in the Senate about his suitability to be Emperor – exacerbated by the current ruler having a flare-up of his old leg-injury and being currently bedridden. What exactly was going on in the murky world of court politics and Imperial Family intrigue is unclear except that Constantine most unusually invited the ex-'Caesar' Constantine, now a venerated abbot and holy man in the Pyrenees aged 70, to visit him at his remote Sabine villa as he convalesced in September 680, Caracalla was there and was reconciled with his father who he had not seen for years and had accused of abandoning him for religion, and the Empress Domitia tried to stop the 'summit' and went off to Sicily in a huff after failing.

A few weeks later an allegation of rape at a party by Anastasius and of him beating-up his (upper-class) female victim's brother afterwards were made openly in the Senate by allies of Caracalla's family. (He himself liked Anastasius and was not interested in intrigue so he was unlikely to have been involved.) With the more moralist nobles and Italian clerics calling for the debauched Prince to be struck out of the line of succession the Emperor dithered and apparently had to be stiffened to act by his ministers, but eventually in mid-October Anastasius was arrested at his villa near Paestum, allegedly for his own safety after drunken rampages and attacks on his servants, and was placed under medical restraint and declared to be temporarily 'insane'. The return of the Empress to Rome to try and fail to have him released was followed by a clumsy and failed attempt to poison Caracalla which his doctors detected and foiled. Though it is unclear if Domitia was behind it as she was not usually that drastic firstly she was arrested and then, on 6 December 680, the semi-invalid Constantine abdicated suddenly, aged 50, on the grounds of his ill-health making it difficult to carry out his duties long-term and announced his retirement to his estates in south-eastern Gaul (around Antipolis/Antibes and Nicaea/Nice) to work on his planned books on military strategy.

Chapter 3

Caracalla 680–709: The Showman. Son of the superseded elder son of Constantine III

Caracalla became Emperor at the age of twenty-seven and as he was the 'legitimate' heir to the line of Constantine III and hugely popular as a charismatic young officer there was no question of any dissent or rebellions, especially in the army which still worshipped his father. But the retirement of the ex-Empress Domitia to a remote mansion and estate in western Sicily (not her favourite complex at Cephalodium near Panormus) after an illness, her being kept under guard, and her separation from her now hostile husband caused stories to spread that she had tried to kill Caracalla and the ministers, fearing for long-term instability from the rising Imperial Family feud, had acted to secure the succession and marginalize her. In 683 she was moved to a (fairly lax) nunnery on the Greek island of Paros, supposedly at her own wish, and later took holy orders – which caused more rumours though the abbess was a very rich and poetry-writing aristocratic old friend of hers and rumour had it that she was spending more time partying with local aristocrats and writing poems and plays than praying. Probably her piety did increase later, though, as she was to pay for the building of a large new domed cathedral of the 'Theotokos', the 'Mother of God', on nearby Naxos in the 690s and even went on pilgrimage to Jerusalem – though she was supposed to be kept a close eye on by Imperial police spies and was never to be allowed back to Italy.

Notably though the ex-'Caesar' Constantine attended Caracalla's coronation in January 681 and stayed on in Rome for several months to advise his son on how to be a virtuous and holy ruler the disgraced Stateira was only recalled later for one brief visit to court and was then packed off to live in Sicily in comfortable but politically neutered retirement. The 'insane' and probably alcoholic Anastasius was not recalled at all but ended up (after a year or so in disgraced exile in Epirus under guard) being forcibly made a monk and sent off to a remote monastery in the Jordanian deserts where he had to sober up and follow a rigorous monastic routine under watch by police spies but later became a distinguished and surprisingly capable local abbot in the 700s.

Boosted by his socialite but sensible wife Julia Drusilla, from a super-rich landed Umbrian noble dynasty to which Stateira had arranged an alliance via her son's betrothal to their eldest branch's head's daughter as a child as part of her search for Italian allies, Caracalla now took charge of the Empire with more self-assurance than many people expected given his troubled background. Cut off from his parents as a small child and brought up by courtier guardians selected by his uncle Diomedes plus a formidable array of the Empire's top tutors in many subjects, Caracalla had been shunned by many boys in his court circle as they had been 'warned off' by their parents in case he was exiled or killed off by his uncle to change the succession to his own daughters' lines and Stateira's Persian origins and obsessive intrigues had put other nobles off. So he had not had a normal childhood and as a young adult he had been treated as Constantine IV's presumed heir but still been at risk of displacement by his cousin Anastasius (which the latter's mother Domitia had been known to want to happen) and so been in danger of being ensnared in a fake 'plot' to give an excuse to destroy him. His current friends were mostly fellow-officers from his years as a cadet in the 'Protectores' and after that learning 'on the job' as an assistant and then a full garrison-commander in Dacia, Marcomannia, and Armenia, but he proved less paranoid or open to flatterers than many had expected although he gave his full confidence to few, even those who shared his interests in Hellenic culture and Classical architecture. In this he was a sharp contrast to Diomedes who had had similar cultural interests – and more talent as a poet. Caracalla was more of a mathematician and an amateur architect than a writer and he had a particular fascination with the works and mindset of the famous but obscure C6th BC mathematician, philosopher, and mystic Pythagoras. He was as keen to promote the latter's reputation and keep up studies of him as Julian had been of Plato and indeed proclaimed that Pythagoras, with his belief in the mystic powers of and inner truth of the universe shown by numbers, had been a forerunner of Plato. As Emperor he was soon calling a conference on the works of Pythagoras for 682 at the latter's old base of Sybaris in SE Italy and preparing to attend it himself, while he had works on and by the great thinker dug up in the vaults of the Great Library of Alexandria and copied to be sent to Rome and instituted chairs in the study of Pythagoras at the universities of Rome and Syracuse. (There was already one at Alexandria.) Caracalla also sought to revive the study of the C3rd BC thinker, inventor, and engineer Archimedes of Syracuse and had his works also sought out and brought to Rome for study, but his own specialism lay in architecture. He declared that he would rather have been a Greek architect of the Classical era than Emperor and as it was he would use his position to see that 'ideal' Greek architecture was revived and was used across the Empire.

He was visiting Athens to order the reconstruction 'in situ' of lost Classical-era buildings there as early as spring 681 and he had some major renovations of ancient buildings also carried out at Megara, Corinth, and Argos while assorted venerable statues that Constantine the Great had had carried off to Constantinople were returned, not least the monuments set up a by city-states at the Temple of Apollo at Delphi. But he managed to reassure the prickly and riot-prone citizens of Constantinople of his good intentions with a prolonged stay there with his family from October 681 to May 682 and he not only held lavish public receptions and dinners at the Sacred Palace but built some new pavilions there in the style of a Hellenistic palace and staged elaborate naval games or 'naumachia' in the Bosphorus off the city for which many of the naval personnel and their ships in the Euxine were brought to the city to perform. Caracalla did not forget Rome in his enthusiasm for building either, and his father Constantine – now back in Spain at his abbey in the Pyrenees and engaged in creating a new shrine for the relics of St James the Apostle at a remote site in Galleicia (Galicia) where they had been relocated – had urged him to make an early display of helping the poor to show his priorities. He proceeded to arrange to have many of the overcrowded 'insulae' tenement apartment-blocks in the East of the city, an eyesore for centuries but cheap and convenient for workers, pulled down in a major 'rebuild 'in 682–6 according to plans which he had employed a committee of architects to produce within weeks of his taking the throne.

The 'slums' were replaced by spacious villas, squares, public gardens, and official buildings including a new 'Forum of Caracalla' with its adjoining Basilica and public baths, and the Emperor relocated the majority of the removed inhabitants to new, single-story modest houses with gardens that were built at his expense in a wide arc SE of the old Wall of Aurelian – which had long since been passed by the expansion of Rome into its suburbs but which was now made entirely redundant in this region of the city and pulled down. The strength of Rome was to lie in her soldiers and weaponry – and her united civic spirit – not her walls, as the Emperor declared in an official speech as he commenced the demolition, and in the years to come Caracalla also built a spaciously-planned new suburb with well-spaced houses, squares, gardens, and public buildings in the region North of the main city stretching up to the Milvian Bridge. He incorporated the straggling buildings that were already there, adding a Baths named after his original mentor Diomedes and another named after his father Constantine but not even bothering to include a statue of his disgraced mother at the latter.

Caracalla was the greatest builder in Rome since the time of Constantine and he sought to beautify the city and make it seem more spacious, removing ugly apartment-blocks and slums across the capital, but he also did his best to 'clean up' the badly-planned and rather disorderly C5th AD Imperial 'unofficial capital' of Ravenna, where the marshes inhibited many extensions, and to restore a degree of glamour and prestige to the abandoned C4th and early C5th capital at Mediolanum.

In the East his first major Imperial tour there, by sea to Syria and on by land to Mesopotamia, Media, and Persia, in 683 led to the reconstruction of the Imperial palace at Antioch after another recent earthquake and the building of a large domed hall in the Oriental style there plus the extension of the racecourse and the creation of a luxurious Imperial villa with baths, gardens, a racecourse, and private zoological gardens at Daphne a few miles away. Caracalla was a great huntsman and his visit to the East included massive hunting-parties with the nobility of Syria, Mesopotamia and Persia where he could show off his skills at riding and at despatching wild beasts and back in Italy he became known for the number of hunting-lodges which he built from Apulia via Marsium and Umbria right up to the Alps around Lakes Como and Garda. But though he was able to use this skill to 'bond' with the younger nobility and to show the military that he might not be interested in wars but he was as brilliant and daring rider as any 'macho' officer he avoided the traps of excessive socializing, drinking too much, and becoming obsessed with the races. Although he owned and personally managed a chain of studs across Italy and was keen on importing tough and fast Arab cavalry from Arabia to inter-breed with current Roman cavalry stock and improve their quality he did not let this hobby interfere with his duty to carry out business and he was an assiduous attender of Imperial Council meetings if not as keen on detail and accounts as his predecessor Constantine IV had been.

The only changes that Caracalla, politically cautious given his nerve-wracking youth as a marginal if publicly honoured prince under political suspicion with a disgraced mother, made in the Council in his first year or so in power were minor ones to add some new members in the form of long-term noble and elderly officer allies of his parents (mostly to minor or sinecure posts) as thanks for their long-term support. He also brought in some leading civil servants from long-standing 'Parthian'-era bureaucratic dynasties in Mesopotamia, mixed Greco-Aramaic and Armenian in origin, to join the higher ranks of the bureaucracy – and if talented enough, in due course the ministerial posts – in Rome through the early-mid 680s. This was partly to introduce more men with an 'Eastern' mindset and priorities to the ministerial team's advisers and reassure their connections back in Ctesiphon, Susa, Seleucia, Charax, and Nisibis that they were valued parts of the Empire not just 'tax-fodder' for the distant Rome elite. In due course a number of successful ex-deputy governors of major Persian and Median as well as Mesopotamian cities were to join the ministerial team in Rome, while connections of the Emperor's Persian mother were invited to Court where the Emperor gave them some Household posts (not too many so as not to arouse too much jealousy) and addressed them in the old Iranian court language. Treating the Church as a department of State under his orders and not interested in appeasing hard-line Catholics, he tentatively invited some Nestorians and learned men from other minor Eastern Christian sects to teach at Rome's University or address his private seminars for experts and enthusiasts on Levantine and Persian learning, claiming that the East had provided valuable ideas (e.g. in astronomy and mathematics) to the West and any sensible ruler should be open to the scholarship of all of his subjects, of whatever religion. (They were banned from proselytizing or setting up schools, though.)

Caracalla's careful and methodical creation of a new Imperial Household bureau to run his expanded stud and his recruitment of known experts (some from the racing-world) to staff it showed his potential as a reformer and from 682 he began to add new ministers at the head of new departments to increase funding and concentration on new areas of policy – not sacking any old ministers in important posts to make way for them as he did not want to create enemies. The Imperial Post was 'hived off' from the long-term and initially Julio-Claudian ministry of Imperial correspondence, which was usually run by a long-term career bureaucrat not a great noble, and given its own Secretary and resources and the use of carrier-pigeons was stepped up across the Empire to speed contacts up (it had been in use in Persia since Julian's day and in the Afghan and Indus regions since the 610s conquest). Also a new ministry took over supervising and extending state dockyards to increase merchant shipping as well as naval vessels and speed up trade (and imports of corn to the capital), a ministry was set up to run the Empire's collection of state vehicles to transport goods and personnel on official business and see that they were numerous enough, kept in good condition, and manned properly. The department of the Privy Purse was split up so that the Emperor's estates and mansions/villas/palaces in each part of the Empire were run, funded, and supervised separately by different and regularly refreshed boards of experts under the control of a veteran finance – or Household official. That way the dangers of slack control, local inertia or corrupt dealing, and lack of funding for or repairs of buildings and estate farms could be identified and remedied quickly and it did not all come onto the shoulders of the Secretary of the department, the 'Count of the Res Privatae/Privy Purse'(who had enough to do running the large Imperial Household in Rome and Imperial estates in Italy). Caracalla duly received good notices from his bureaucrats for being able to identify and deal with problems like Constantine III and IV (and being more ruthless and decisive than the latter) though in fact he had been 'tipped off' about the problems in the Household's administration by allies of his family there.

Caracalla also used his own passion for architecture and belief in 'correct' and 'civilised' styles to set up a new school of architecture on the Janiculine Hill in

Rome as early as 682 and brought in architects who shared his Greek classical enthusiasms to teach there. But he did not neglect the newish and Persian-influenced styles of creating large domes and apsidal halls (seen from the C6th, mostly in new churches in the Eastern half of the Empire but also in Rome and Ravenna) either and these were deemed to be suitable for private residences, Imperial villas and palaces included, and also for legal service basilicas and state offices in provincial capitals. The expansion of Caracalla's interests in architecture, especially in Eastern styles, went along with and partly resulted from his own experience of the East following his stay at Constantinople in 681–2, and his tour of Asia Minor and Syria in summer-autumn 682 and winter at Damascus in 682–3. At the latter he held military manoeuvres involving Rome's Arab allies and troops sent up the trade-route from Arabia Felix and he also went on hunting-expeditions with the local nobles and officers.

All this went in step with his planning new villas for himself in the region and he started to plan his 'quirky' new private 'hideaway' villa in the Persian style in the citadel at the top of Mount Silpius in Antioch, to be reached by a grand stairway of a thousand steps from the lower city, dominated by a domed throne-hall, and decorated with eastern mosaics and murals. This was indeed his favourite residence and he usually lived here rather than in the larger palace rebuilt by Diomedes down in the city while attending receptions and the races in Antioch over the next two decades, and he had other villa 'retreats' in the fringes of the Syrian deserts for grand hunting-expeditions along with a new palace built for him at Damascus after his 683–3 stay which also featured an Eastern dome and apsidal halls in the Persian style. In 683 the Emperor returned to Rome and later went on for his first tour of Gaul, where he built a new and 'classical Greek'-style palace on the island citadel in Lutetia (Paris) next to the cathedral of Our Lady and a hunting-lodge in the forests South of the city (i.e. Fontainebleau) which featured exotic Eastern gardens constructed in the Persian style and masses of imported Middle Eastern shrubbery.

So as not to seem to neglect the West and risk military or Church disapproval he also toured the Rhineland that year before a winter in Rome and in 684 visited Spain, in summer 685 he visited Rhaetia and Marcommania to open new civic buildings in Augusta Prahavorum (Prague), and in 686 he visited the middle and lower Danube ahead of another winter at Constantinople. From there he went on by sea to Egypt in spring 687 for six months mostly resident at Alexandria apart from a tour up the Nile to Philae and Aswan and in winter 687–8 he was back at Antioch to use his mountain-top villa there for the first time. A large-scale tour of Mesopotamia, Persia, Media, and Bactria in 688 saw the Emperor hold a local assembly of nobles and military manoeuvres at Balkh and pay the first peacetime Imperial visit to Maracanda and the Oxus and Jaxartes, local

Hunnic and now Turkish chieftains being summoned to an Imperial 'summit' and race-meeting for their horses at Maracanda where Caracalla posed as the 'Lord of the East', using Alexander's title, and used his confidence, cultural openness, and knowledge of local languages to charm his guests and tie their loyalty to Rome. The neglected regions of the NE frontier really seemed to matter as an integral part of the Empire under a Persian-speaking Emperor who loved building Persian-style constructions and spoke warmly of Persian culture. Indeed he even acquired a luxury-loving and spendthrift but luckily 'non-political' Persian mistress, the expert and well-educated 'exotic dancer' Anahitani, who he renamed 'Anastasia' and ended up using as his official hostess on his Bactrian and Sogdian tour as his wife Julia, whose health was delicate and who was not up to rigorous Eastern travel, had stayed behind in Syria to organize local philanthropy and charm the Church with a tour of and gifts to prominent shrines. (She was on pilgrimage to Jerusalem while her husband was in Maracanda.) At first, the Empress' public religiosity countered criticism of his known openness to other beliefs.

The Emperor was not generally unfaithful to his wife or known for his affairs though he had had other women from time to time and the Imperial couple remained on good terms and were back together in public once he returned to Antioch for winter 688–9 and then went on to Rome in spring 689. The Church and court gossips by and large respected his choice of a 'junior consort' (as he styled Anastasia) while the latter was discreet once he reached the West and never appeared in public there. But the fact that he was in effect in possession of two wives and in due course a string of Imperial bastards appeared and were brought up at court and given high rank led to socialite gossip and some angry sermons and writings by moralist Christians, mainly in the West. Though the Emperor did not care what people said about him and did not take it out on the Church it added to his growing distaste for Christian attitudes to sex and encouraged him to start blocking the appointment of moralists who denounced his mistress as bishops. There was no breach with his wife or his two sons, Michael (born 680) and Basil (born 682) who were his acknowledged heirs, though already the prickly and earnest young scholar Michael was acquiring a reputation as a Christian thinker and moralist who wore sackcloth, refused to become a soldier, and preferred studying spiritual to military or administrative works. With Anastasia prudently in the background at court and not given any official duties (but invited to parties by the less judgmental or more toadying aristocrats) the Empress accompanied Caracalla on his official tours of North Africa (from Carthage to Tingis) and Lusitania in 690, Noricum and Illyria in 691, and Greece and the Balkans in 692 and was his official consort for ceremonies and receptions in Constantinople – whose Church's junior ranks had been full of denunciations of the 'Persian prostitute' – in winter 692–3.

The senior hierarchy of the Church in Rome, led by a succession of cautious and 'careerist' Popes appointed by their council of senior clergy and administrators for competence not moral vision and aware of the need not to alienate the fund-giving state, steered clear of criticizing the Emperor for his private life as long as he officially kept his Empress as his 'sole' consort and did not openly flaunt his mistress, which Caracalla in turn accepted. Though they were criticized by assorted religious writers and lower clergy – austere and charismatic abbots and hermits in particular – the latter were usually far from Rome and of little impact except in their won locales. Ironically the revival of passionate Catholic idealism and zeal for austerity and life in tough wilderness monasteries in remote parts of the Spanish peninsula in the late C7th and early C8th, of which the new shrine of St James at Compostellanum in Gallaecia with its rich gifts donated by pilgrims and an aisled C4th-style 'Basilica' cathedral was a symptom as well as a result, had been spearheaded by the Emperor's own father Constantine as he used his private fortune to 'kick-start' the basilica project. It was now turned against his family as holy abbots and hermits accused Caracalla of letting down the Imperial role by lavishing gifts and attention on an 'Eastern whore'. Partly caused by a 'grass-roots' reaction to the plethora of careerist clergy in C7th Spain who carefully avoided antagonizing their lay patrons, even a semi-'pagan' Hellenist Emperor like Diomedes, and to the openness to 'pagan' learning of great bishops cum scholars like Isidore of Sevillanum, this zeal for moral reform was unwelcome to most senior bishops – at least when it threatened to insult the Emperor and hold their own conduct to account. From the early 690s some purges of the more outspoken critics who held office saw assorted abbots and junior clerics sacked or moved to even more remote areas where their raving about corruption and moral turpitude would not be noticed so much, but at least it showed vigour in the Church in contrast to the careerist conformism and lack of zeal in the clergy in Gaul. In Britain, too, this was an era of zealous 'back to the wilderness to live as God intended like St Anthony did' hermits like the famous Cuthbert (d 695) of Lindisfarne in Valentia (OTL St. Cuthbert, d 685). He was a preacher and junior cleric of Anglian blood who lived for 15 years on one of the Farne islands near the Lindisfarne monastery as a hermit with only the seabirds for company but was then made a bishop as the best moral candidate available and reformed the morals and priority of his clergy to help the poor.

The establishment of individual hermitages across the rocky coasts of NE and western Britain in these decades ran parallel to that in Spain but in this case had little to do with disquiet at the hierarchy colluding with an 'immoral'

Emperor and more with disquiet at the comfortable existence available in older monasteries. The latter also tended to have careerist abbots from well-off families who were more interested in learning and in staging sumptuous ceremonies on feast-days than in holiness, and the lowland British Church (more in the South than the North) was thus often at odds with writers in and preachers from Northern/upland monasteries and more vigorously moral 'leaders' among the minor clergy. In this respect, however, the 'wilderness' monasteries of island and mountainsides in western Britain were not all dens of austerity despite some affronted archbishops in Londinium and Eduracum (York) demanding purges of the 'semi-Pelagian heretics' who they saw as 'rooted' in the laxly supervised outer regions (and of which they often conducted harsh visitations). The Demetian island monastery of St Piro at Caldey, famed for its school and its 'outreach' projects of training young men of all classes as priests and sending them to neglected rural parishes across the West of the Empire, was far more tolerant to 'soft' living, complicated and 'artistic' chanted psalms and accompanying music, and monks learning 'pagan' classics than were those on Bardsey in Ordovicia or in the hermitages of the Carvetian 'Fells mountains near Luguvallium (Carlisle). British bishops indignantly denied claims by zealously orthodox Gallic and Hispanic bishops at 'all-Western' Church Councils that they tolerated theologically 'deviant' practices or 'insults' and disobedience towards the higher clergy and the State by their junior personnel; but there were far more austere hermits and sack-clad, grass-eating wandering holy men in Britain and Caledonia than in Gaul where most Churchmen came from the educated landed or urban classes and were comfortable with mixing with the secular elite.

The British monastic establishments also saw a notable influence from Irish monasteries (probably originally brought by wandering Irish clergy and artisans) in the mid-later C7th and the early C8th, as intricate and delicate 'Celtic' forms of decoration to the margins and ornamental chapter-openings of religious books had been a feature of Irish religious literature for generations and now began to appear in those created at British monasteries. The earliest and most notable centre of this in the mid-C7th in Britain had been the Dalriadan-influenced Votadinian island monastery of Lindisfarne, where beautifully-decorated copies of the Bible and the 'Church Fathers' were produced and were exported as gifts to other monasteries and to supportive bishops. But by the later C7th this style of decoration (and the importance of the craftsmen who produced it, who were now valued highly and could be 'exported' too) was seen all over Britain. The popularity of the 'Celtic' decorative styles of what was summarized by one dismissive 'purist' leading Italian late C7th mosaicist as 'whirls and spirals', with humans and animals often represented in an exaggerated and elongated manner, duly spilled over into secular art too as some of these books entered urban public and richer citizens' private libraries, and was to influence murals and mosaics in secular buildings too in the coming century or so – though most richer non-Church patrons tended to keep to established 'Classical' styles of decoration for their homes. The art of Lindisfarne and other 'Iona'-influenced monasteries was at first not seen as a 'serious' and approvable contribution to the Church by many of the higher clergy outside northern and north-western Britain and Caledonia. But the arguments of the initially (and puritanically) disapproving Bishop Cuthbert that it helped to show the mystic beauty of the Christian message and the Universe and so increased appreciation of the benevolence of the Almighty eventually became widely accepted. (The later Emperor Michael, Caracalla's ultra-religious and anti-'sinful extravagance' Christian elder son, was one of the converts to its ideological acceptability.)

The amount of inspiring decorated literary works produced on remote Lindisfarne indeed enabled its humbly-born local Anglian abbot Ceolfrith (OTL figure) to reply forcefully to a sneering aristocratic urban Gallic bishop at the Western Church Council in 693 when asked what his fog – and gale-hit island had ever produced for Christianity in the Empire as a whole apart from self-obsessed and fast-loving 'wilderness' hermits who thought that they were John the Baptist. As the abbot said, the monastery had produced major artistic work on a parallel with the decorative mosaics of important Mediterranean cathedrals that brought the humble and unlearned to Christ and it did more to show the unity and mystic harmony of God's Creation to those who could not understand semantics than any number of learned professors. This intricate decorative work was arguably as important for the newly confident Church in Britain as were the great monastery schools that emerged in the later C7th and C8th, the impressively huge 'basilica-style' monastery abbey churches built in the later C7th at Inis Witrinus (Glastonbury) in Dobunnia and the extended shrine of St Alban at Verulamium (both centres of pilgrimage), and the archiepiscopal cathedrals of St Paul in Londinium and of the Blessed Virgin in Eburacum. Given the mixture of schools, impressive building-work, and artistic innovation, the British Church was indeed more culturally and spiritually vigorous within the Western Church in this period than the Gallic one, despite the latter's antiquity and resources or their huge 'martyrium' shrine complexes that thousands of pilgrims visited every year like that of St Martin at Turones or St Denis outside Lutetia, Earnest critics of the Gallic 'falling-off' from C6th ecclesiastical vigour blamed this on the near-monopoly of major offices in the Church in Gaul by 'slack' aristocrats who had no dynamism or desire to do more than carry on the annual rounds of church ceremonial and elite socialising. The Gallic 'hunting bishops' and those abbots who spent time and money on building up wineries and developing new varieties of vines on their estates came in for a lot of criticism from the more earnest Christian zealots – though the same accusations of worldliness could be levelled at the great abbots of Italy, even at St Benedict's monastic foundation of Mount Cassinum (now more renowned for its school and library than for holy works). There was also more enthusiasm by British than Gallic priests to undertake conversion-work in the 'rough and ready' forested lands of 'ultra-Elbe' Germany and mountainous Norwegia, which was too uncomfortable due to the climate and the lack of amenities to appeal to the usually more easy-going Gallic clergy. Anglian Britons who spoke their ancestral Germanic tongue as well as Latin found it easier to converse with remote German and Norse farmers; many of the new churches and monasteries in these regions from around 660 to 800 were founded by Britons while the equally adventurous and 'challenge-seeking' zealots among the Hispanic clergy sought their 'mission' converting the Berbers in the mountains South of Mauretania. The local Roman authorities in both these regions, short of cash and soldiers, were more than happy to see the wandering Churchmen decrease the local risk of rebellion by winning the obstreperous and barely civilized tribesmen over to peaceful pursuits.

The 'Iona tradition' was more important in Britain than in Gaul or Spain anyway, and as of the 700s some monks continued to go to Ireland to train there and to pick up the notion from their great midlands monasteries (eg Clonmacnois, Clonfert, Durrow, and Seir Kieran) of a 'monastic republic' of semi-autonomous establishments who were more important and more holy than the squabbling, greedy lay elite. Though the senior British clerics looked askance at the Irish Church – and at Iona – for having the wrong tonsures and celebrating religious festivals on the wrong timetable, which the Irish bishops failed to sort out despite plenty of 'nudges' from the Papacy and senior British and Gallic clerics, their juniors did not care about such technicalities. The 'Irish' model was popular enough for some of its supporters to reform and 're-energise' earlier British monasteries, such as Inis Witrinus (OTL: Glastonbury) in Dobunnia, in the later C7th as well as to found new ones like Bardneium in the Fens. A major nunnery, patronised by elite women, was founded by the aristocratic Anglian heiress St. Audreia (OTL St. Audrey/Aetheldreda)

at Elium nearby in the 660s to take advantage of the need to pour resources into an area of low-lying farmland hit by floods and crumbling dykes since the local corn-growing estates declined as the Army in Germania started to rely on corn grown nearer to hand in Frisia around 650–670. This era of monastic and general Christian 'reformism' in the far West coupled with the agricultural trade-boom in the North Sea zone showed that it was not as much of an uninteresting backwater as the Emperor believed. But though some of his ministers noted the local vigour and intellectual and business ferment – and it aided revenue from that region – Caracalla was only focussed on the East, the home of 'civilization' to him, and after his trip to Egypt he became fascinated with the 'benevolent autocracy' of the Pharoahs and their early Ptolemaic heirs and had a number of Egypt's top scholars of this era summoned to Rome to work at the university and advise him. This was mooted publicly as 'tapping into' the advances of Ptolemaic irrigation that could aid irrigation-schemes across the Empire and the surviving papers (or rather papyri) of early Ptolemaic scholars and scientists at the 'Museion' in Alexandria concerning irrigation-projects were brought to Rome, translated into Latin, and used by the Council's irrigation-departments to boost their schemes and improve efficiency and crop-yields, in the West (e.g. Spain) as well as the East. But Caracalla was also interested in the theory of government in the Hellenistic era and in the long-term theory of Pharaonic rule in Egypt and his mid-690s move to bring the few experts in ancient Egyptian hieroglyphs to Rome to translate pre-Ptolemaic palace and temple records in a special private 'Egyptian Studies School' funded by himself led to wits alleging that he fancied himself as a 'Pharoah'.

Caracalla was too cautious to start criticizing the closure of the Egyptian temple cults by his 4th and 5th-century – predecessors but some of his scholars did so and started to attack the Church, alleging that the old Egyptian priestly dynasties had had a family tradition of helping the ordinary citizens but the Church that had taken their lands and riches were corrupt and intolerant careerists. In 698–9 Caracalla was back in Alexandria for the winter and dressed and in effect lived as a 'Ptolemy', having inscriptions put up on public buildings to himself as 'Ptolemy Caracallus' and as heir to Augustus the heir of Cleopatra (VII)'s lover Julius Caesar – and he brought Anastasia along and had her dress up as the moon-goddess Selene at parties while his wife was on a holy sites tour of Palestine. The Emperor was careful to lavish gifts on the usual objects of visiting lay patronage in Egypt like the great and prestigious C4th monasteries of SS Anthony and Pachomius and when he went up the Nile to Dongola in spring 699 for the first Imperial visit to Nubia he also patronized monasteries there. But this and his ostentatious pilgrimage to the monastery of St Catherine on Mount Sinai with his wife to conclude his tour did not assuage moralist criticism of him and his mistress and the latter's being on good social terms with the famously morally relaxed Greco-Egyptian nobility of Alexandria on this tour added to hostility by austere monks and junior clerics to both.

As in the West the Emperor's reaction was to see that moralist 'bigots' were shut out of promotion, which his carefully selected Patriarchs of Alexandria and Jerusalem saw was carried out, but this led to a breach in tone and relations between 'grass-roots' clergy and remote or too-powerful-to-be-purged monasteries and the senior hierarchy. The latter and their supporters were nicknamed the 'Melkites' or (in Greek) 'King's Men' i.e. royal/imperial toadies. The Emperor was also suspicious of the current moves among the more austere and socially 'withdrawn' abbots/monks and clergy of the 'desert fringes' in Syria and Palestine to attack the excessive acquisition and flaunting of wealth by the social elite as a potential return to the embarrassing ravings and anti-Imperial challenges of (St) John 'Chrysostom' in the 5th century and certainly his mistress Anastasia was as much a target of them as Empress Eudoxia had been in the 400s. As a result a number of potential 'troublemakers' were not invited to his special Church Council of the East at Nazareth in 699 which was organized to crack down on 'heresy' and law-breaking 'libellers' and which arranged a purge of troublesome junior clergy and assorted deportations to remote monasteries.

The most learned and innovative of the theologians who were investigated there escaped punishment due to his powerful lay patrons in the local Imperial bureaucracy, however, and indeed came from a long-serving southern Syrian bureaucratic dynasty. This was (St) John of Damascus (OTL figure), a former junior regional bureaucrat turned monk and bishop who was as learned and eclectic in his acquisition of knowledge as Leander of Sevilla, famously learned contemporary cleric, and set up schools for both sexes in his diocese so the Emperor looked on him tolerantly. At this stage John was most famous for his calls for moral reform and less lay-style job-hunting in the 'complacent' Syrian Church. But he was later to take up the cause of defending the expanding and popular (and populist) Eastern devotion to the 'icons' (portraits, usually on wooden panels and richly ornamented thanks to lay supporters' gifts of precious metals, of the saints and the Holy Family) which was being attacked as 'idolatry' by a rival 'wing' of ultra-austere Church reformists. The latter were backed by the banning of any form of portraiture in religious worship or religious buildings by the unusual 'semi-Christian' Arab sect at Mecca and Medina based around the followers of the major early-mid C7th holy man Mohammed ibn Abdallah, who regarded Jesus Christ as a prophet but not the 'Son of God' and their leader as his successor as the 'Seal of the Prophets'. This ultra-austere desert sect with their wandering holy men and inter-tribal mediators apparently had some influence on the 'Iconoclast' beliefs of the austere Levantine reformers of the early C8th but both were shunned by the official Church and did not become 'mainstream'. However they did supply a number of notably austere and rigorously capable desert Arab cavalry and infantry generals to the Empire's armies in the second half of the C7th and well into the C8th. As the Arab officers did not drink alcohol and lived simple lives like ordinary soldiers – and were usually scrupulously honest in their financial dealings out of fear of being sent to Hell when they died – they were spoken well of by their commanders and were not at risk of contempt or mutiny by ill-treated 'other ranks' as were some arrogant aristocratic officers from wealthy Mediterranean or Western European families. They were particularly useful in service in harsh conditions in the East (e.g. in the Hindu Kush or Caucasus garrisons or the Arabian and Nubian deserts) due to their desert or semi-desert upbringing. Arab mercenary troops of archers or camel-riding cavalry were very useful in tackling and hunting down brigands across the East and in protecting the Bactrian and Sogdian frontiers from mobile raiders, and several of their commanders were to end up as 'duces' or frontier Counts in the region or in Garamantia and Nubia in Africa. One impressed general who was an old friend of the Emperor and had served against North Sea Norse pirates called them the 'Norsemen of the Desert', and the nickname stuck. But the ever-anxious bureaucrats of the 'high command' in Rome feared that these independent-minded 'land pirates' feared their God more than they feared the Emperor and were quite capable of turning brigand and setting up secessionist mini-states based on plunder beyond the frontier so they were quite often denied the highest commands. By contrast, some of the more open-minded Mediterranean aristocrats with knowledge of the ancient epics argued that their bravado and reckless fondness for 'one-to-one' duels made them like the ancient heroes of Homer and took to writing admiring poems about the 'simple' and 'pure' life of the desert, where life was lived as in the Heroic Age.

On a more sophisticated and civilian level, the expertise in trading and finance that the upper-class civilian elite of the 'Damascus to Arabia Road' cities had acquired since the Empire took over the Yemen in the C6th helped their more adventurous members (mostly younger sons not in line for major inheritances) to move into administration in the Levantine provinces after c. 650. Most of these were now devout monotheistic 'reformists' too as the ideals and lifestyle of the 'Way of the Prophet' spread, and so were both scrupulously honest and abstainers from alcohol – and in many cases concerned for 'justice' in all matters. They were welcome to the more honest and hard-working elite Roman provincial bureaucrats and magistrates as reliable characters who would not cause a rash of complaints by ill-treated citizens to the central authorities and their roving commissioners/judges. The lack of possessing 'elegant' Latin and/or Greek as linguistic skills by the average Arabic civilian recruit, whose first language was either Arabic or Aramaic, was a problem – though 'greasing palms' or knowing existing senior officials in the lower levels of the bureaucracy usually overcame that as far as job-applications went, and (as with all Roman provincials) fast-rising military 'stars' could usually recommend their friends and relations to the civilian bureaucracy with some success if their commanders helped them. Some senior local bureaucratic 'hirers' did not like 'low-born' applicants and 'peasants' in particular and even passing the Empire-wide annual civil service examinations did not necessarily mean success in getting a significant job or promotion, given local officials' wiles in 'fixing' appointments – a well-connected member of the urban middle classes or the rural landowning families was less likely to be interfered with, as he would probably have friends who could cause trouble for an obstructionist senior bureaucrat or he could get a magistrate or Imperial commissioner interested in his case easier.

But despite these problems for such 'outsiders' as the Arabs (elite or not) getting admission to or promotion in the civil service or other professions – which applied to 'heretic' minority Christian cults and peasants or the urban poor anywhere – a number of determined and reliable Arabs did reach high office in the later C7th and more in the C8th, mainly in the Levant or Mesopotamia. These included several members of the huge 'Banu Ummaya' or Ummayad 'clan' of merchants and judges that dominated the public life of the trading-mart of Mecca – including two governors of Arabia Petraea (OTL: Jordan), Abdal Malichus in the 690s and Hisham in the 720s (OTL : Caliphs), and one of the most influential 'reformist' magistrates in Syria in the early C8th – and the author of major legal commentary books – was one of the Ummayads who had been a star student at the Beyrutus law-school, Umar (OTL: Caliph Umar II).

The principal political influence that some Arab-influenced 'holy' reformers for a 'more just and devout Empire' in the East had was via the Imperial tour of 699, as the Emperor's eldest son Michael, a devout Christian who was already wearing simple tunics not rich robes and living an austere life as a vegetarian, alcohol-shunning faster, accompanied his mother on her Palestine pilgrimage and talked to and was influenced by several radical hermits on this. After the Imperial Family returned to Rome the Prince was to invite one holy man from a Palestinian desert hermitage, the enigmatic skin-clad Father Gregorius, to Rome to advise him and began to establish a small private monastery of reformist monks from all over the Empire – some from Britain and Ireland too, along with Spain – on an estate that his father had given him in Latium with a view to him using it for hunting. The eccentric religious views and friends and the determined opposition to doing any military service by Michael were already causing concern to the army leadership and after the arrival of Father Gregorius and his allies their attacks on military expenditure and war as a 'sin' led to the first moves by angry military men to have Michael barred from the succession. As his party-loving, chariot-racing, womanizing but relatively hard-working younger brother Basil was a conventional young man proud to be a trainee officer he was considered to be a safer potential ruler and was boosted by the Emperor, who as a Hellenist had revived an Empire-wide corps of teenage trainee soldiers who did annual summer military training at camps – the 'Ephebes', named after the Athenian youth corps – as a smallish experimental venture in Italy in the late 680s. He had seen this expand into other regions since, making

Basil 'Princeps Iuventutis' in 701 to lead this organization and head its annual inter-regional Games each September. Basil could be put into the role of next Emperor as a 'safe pair of hands' and Michael be shunted off to a monastery if he was so fond of the religious life and the 'Masters of Infantry and Cavalry' and Praetorian Praefect in Rome actively encouraged this idea, but he refused to go along with it as he had a sense of mission to reform the Empire and rein in its excessive and 'ungodly' militarism and this prospect increasingly alarmed civilian ministers too. The Emperor did not like his elder son's priorities and in addition the naïve Prince was calling Anastasia a 'whore' and calling on her to repent and go into a nunnery but Caracalla was too lazy and crisis-averse to think of disinheriting his heir. After the Empress Julia fell ill of a serious infection caught on a religious shrines tour of North Africa in autumn 702 and died a few months later the political crisis became worse and rumour had it that ambitious – or patriotic? – ministers and top generals were paying the Rome police to investigate the Prince's allies for libellous misdemeanours and other attacks on authority in the hope of getting them banished and/or implicating the Prince.

In the end the new and wily 'Master of Offices' from 701, 'Gallia Narbonensis' bureaucrat Julius Catronius, did more good for domestic stability by using his nunnery-patronising wife as a means to get close to the philanthropic Michael. He persuaded Michael that he could trust the ministers to run the Empire once he was Emperor and should concentrate on setting a good moral example not on causing factional feuds that could lead to the 'sin' of a coup or a civil war. Michael and his close advisers began to develop a concept of the Emperor as 'head of state and of religion' and a worldwide moral leader as the 'Successor of the Apostles', calling on the earlier ideas of Constantine 'the Great' and taking over the role of lecturing the Church on its duty from the Popes and Patriarchs (who would be his agents and deputies). The Emperor would thus return to his old role of Pontifex Maximus/ Chief Priest but as head of the Christian Church and would be deflected from any embarrassing and potentially dangerous political initiatives (for a while anyway). As Michael took up this idea the relieved Caracalla came to rely on the ingenious Catronius as his most useful adviser and soon sacked both the Praefect and the two military 'Masters' in case they should start thinking about a coup. Basil was packed off to military service in Gandhara out of the way in autumn 703 and Michael was encouraged to try to find a suitable and 'holy' bride who could hopefully rein him in from embarrassing confrontations with the elite and counter the social as well as moral reformism of his protégé monks. In spring 704 he was married to an earnest and nunnery-funding heiress from Bergamum in Cisalpine Gaul, Ausonia Ascatellia, who was as devoted to reading the Bible and doing good works as him and liked to wear rags (in private) and do servants' work as a kitchen-maid or serve up food in 'soup kitchens' for the poor to show her godliness but was also a practical organiser of charity-work. The heir's new wife showed a sense of realism and an ability to get on with people that he lacked and also had the tact not to attack Anastasia, even when the Emperor proceeded to scandalise the Church by marrying her in 705, so she was a major asset to the dynasty. But as she was keen on fasting and neglected her health she never conceived children and Basil remained the 'reserve' heir, encouraged by meddling officers to think of removing his brother in the interests of Rome and in the meantime showing his mettle and earning military and public esteem by daring cavalry attacks on brigands in the forests between the Indus and the Beas that kept the 'Silk Road' trade-route open. This led to (technically illegal) small-scale Roman military intervention to prop up friendly and remove unfriendly Indian 'rajahs' whose lands bordered on the Empire in the Punjab and the Thar desert to the South.

Basil had his own ideas about the Empire's Eastern mission in a more belligerent 'arc' of planning than his father's and once he was in a more senior position as an officer on the main Eastern military staff headquarters at Ctesiphon in 705 prevailed on his superiors to send off assorted 'undercover' Roman agents in the form of 'merchants' and 'missionary monks' to the Indian states to assess their geography, resources, and ease of success for an invasion, the latter to be carried out by land via the Indus region rather than by sea as less at risk from storms or uncharted rocks en route. This 'meddling' by Basil was reported to and backed up by the Imperial military planners in Rome who could look ahead to a major campaign once Michael had been removed, voluntarily or not, from the succession or throne and the much more conventional Basil was in charge of affairs – and some expansionist merchant relatives of Anastasia's who had contracts with the HQ in Ctesiphon alerted her so that she could bring her new husband 'on side' for these ideas. The future Emperor was to be lured into agreeing with the plan as it 'would do God's work' by converting the idol-worshipping, polytheistic Hindus.

Caracalla was not prepared to see Michael removed from the succession even if he would be a disaster as Emperor but he was prepared to 'box him in' and came to rely on Catronius to draw up a plan to ensure the smooth running of the state if a religious eccentric was in charge. He was fully conversant with the plan to get Michael to concentrate on 'harmless' matters such as philanthropy and studies of religious doctrine and to leave politics and administration to his ministers. Meanwhile the new Empress induced her husband to spend more time in the East where her role and her past as a professional dancer were not so controversial and from 702 he was rarely in Rome and generally wintered in either Athens or Constantinople, and she took over her predecessor's role as a patroness of Syrian and Palestinian monasteries and sanctuaries as much as was practicable, i.e. avoiding those whose personnel had criticized her, but also set up a new arts-festival in Antioch where not only poetry and song (in Persian and Arabic as well as Greek styles) were patronized and rich prizes in them were competed for but other competitions took place in her own 'discipline', dance, for the first time. It was Anastasia's ambition for the bad reputation among the 'respectable' of society, and especially the Church, of dance and dancers for sleazy immorality to be eased if not erased and for skilled dancers to receive as much acclaim as acrobatic performers in the 'interval' entertainments at the races in the Empire's great cities. She was also keen to rehabilitate Persian dance as a worthy equivalent to the classical dances that had been performed by trained girls and women at temple cults in the Hellenic world until they closed, but her new international school for dancers, opened at Antioch by her as patron during her and her husband's winter 703–4 stay there, though well-funded and full of eager girls and expert teachers, was denounced by quite senior clerics as well as their bigoted juniors as a 'brothel' and was picketed by angry (male) crowds and had its windows smashed and graffiti scrawled on its walls. The Emperor had the riots put down and arrested protesters sent to the slave-mines and Patriarch Patricius of Antioch ended up sacked for refusing to order his clergy to treat the school with respect, but Anastasia stuck to her mission and cunningly arranged for leasing senators to tour the school and see her girls performing graceful dances in modest long gowns in front of and in honour of icons of the Blessed Virgin (with the moves choreographed by a respected church musician of noble connections) and ministering to the local poor at their school 'soup kitchen'.

The majority of senators accepted that the school was respectable after all and the principal and his teachers were mostly modest and devout Christians and the furore slowly died down. But the Persian dance-lessons had to be cancelled as they were 'in honour of pagan gods and performed half-naked' and to satisfy the Church their main dance-teachers had to be whipped in public by monks in front of the new Patriarch to show that they were 'repentant' and thereafter only to teach respectable and fully-clothed stately Sassanid Persian court dances. The survival of the school was a major achievement and tribute to Anastasia's tact and after her husband died her stepsons Michael and Leo were to let her continue running it and funding it – and living in a nearby convent as an honoured guest under a friendly and tolerant abbess – for another 30 years. But in the West the fact that the 'Emperor's whore' was running a school for girl dancers was another reason to condemn him and her and they were known in some monkish circles in Spain and Britain as 'Ahab and Jezebel'. Caracalla himself was furious at the reaction to his wife's school and it helped to sour his view of the Antiochenes so in his last years he spent less time at his mountain-top retreat at Antioch and more in Constantinople, where he had been rebuilding the cathedral church of the Holy Apostles in a domed Eastern style since the 680s. This was also affected by his new enthusiasm for the revivalist 'classical Hellenic' work of the era's greatest dramatist, Philotheus (d 725) from nearby Adrianople, who in the last years of the C7th and the first years of the C8th was producing regular new plays at the dramatic festivals at Pella (Macedonia) and Epidaurus so Caracalla liked to attend these.

The Christian but open-minded Philotheus, son of a renowned Constantinople Hellenistic epic poetry professor, was endeavouring to create a large new 'corpus' of psychological dramas about the 'Iron Age' of the Ancient Greek heroes that updated famous myths but left the old gods and goddesses out so the Church would not be offended. His works that won major competitions – and were then put on at the new playhouse in the Sacred Palace at Constantinople in the winters for the Emperor – included plays on the careers of Theseus and Jason the Argonaut, the Calydonian Boar Hunt, the wars of the Seven Against Thebes and the 'Epogoni' (successors), the Trojan War, the wanderings of Odysseus, and the ancient kings Demophon and Codrus of Athens but also newly-covered stories set in a later era about the first kings of Sparta and its mythical lawgiver Lycurgus. Philotheus also covered the epic and broadly historical stories of the great 'tyrants' – in the sense of autocratic rulers with a reformist mission not just oppressors – Periander of Corinth, Cleisthenes of Sicyon, and Peisistratus of Athens and in the process set rhetorical questions on the methodology and the moral corruptibility of the process of ruling that were still relevant in the C8th AD. This was duly appreciated by the Emperor and the political elites of Greece and Constantinople and led to the Church – pleased to see no 'blasphemous' pagan deities on the stage – treating his work with respect as containing moral lessons and teaching virtue. Philotheus wanted to use his drama to 'move on' from the old classics of C5th BC with their 'deus ex machina' divine interventions and their reliance on the basics of ancient myth and to make use of more recent events and his final works in the early 720s were to focus on the struggles of Greeks and Persians in the early years of Greece's 'Golden Age' and in one play, 'Cincinnatus' (724), even bring a historical Roman hero on the stage.

As Caracalla was keen to back him up the Emperor took up his favourite playwright's idea of a special annual prize at the Pella drama festival for new plays on new, historic subjects dated after the Greek 'Dorian Invasions' of the C12th BC and from 707 the Emperor provided an annual fund to the winner of this prize so that they could both produce more works and if they wished run their own drama-companies. Caracalla made it fashionable for nobles in

Constantinople and Antioch from the late 690s to fund drama-companies and run their own groups of actors named after them as nobles had been funding chariot-racing teams for centuries, and this was also kept up after him by his heir though the latter's belief that theatre had to be 'moral' was more rigidly Christian and he was to spend most of his drama expenditure on vain attempts to locate and help to success dramatists who only wrote about the early Christian heroes, martyrs and bishops in particular. (This led to Michael founding an annual drama festival for Christian-themed plays on Samos from 711 which flopped after his demise and had to be rescued by a rich local abbot and his monastery.) The Empress Ausonia's own drama-festival for plays on the subject of Old Testament subjects, especially the lives of the patriarchs and other events from the Book of Genesis, which commenced in 712 at the monastery of St Demetrius near Thebes in Greece and was transferred to the more conveniently placed Corinth in 720, was a success. That 'strain' of drama did 'take off' and acquire fans in the Christian East though it was still regarded as 'risque' and too much like 'sinful' exhibitionism by over-dressed and made-up men of dubious sexuality in the West, and this revival of drama in both a Hellenic and a more modern Christian context was among Caracalla's legacies to the Empire which showed that he was not just the 'Orientophile playboy' and would-be despot which some critics, especially in Rome which he only set foot in for three months in his last six years in office, called him.

Chapter 4

Michael I 709–717: Saint or 'Heretic'? Basil I, 717–729: The Prudent Military Officer. The Sons of Caracalla

Caracalla died in Antioch, in the older palace by the river Orontes rather than his mountain-top retreat, on 18 June 709 aged fifty-nine after a stroke, having declined into alcoholism in his last couple of years after his health started to decline, his ability to hunt was restricted so he had to shoot wildlife from a chariot, and laziness got the better of him. His elder son Michael was for once with him and was unequivocally given the succession in the hearing of his doctors and chamberlains, who so informed the travelling 'core' of the Emperor's council. So Basil, on an inspection tour of the Marcomannian frontier with other 'comitatus' HQ officers, was unable to mount any coups and a signed message announcing the travelling Council's support for Michael reached Rome by carrier-pigeon before any anti-Michael generals knew what had happened.

The new Emperor was known for his philanthropy and 'common touch' and regularly visited Rome's 'soup kitchens', schools for poor boys, and orphanages to check that their clients were being treated properly not cheated so he was popular in the capital despite his religious oddities. As a result, the cautious Basil, despite regarding him as not strong or ruthless enough, did not risk listening to officer friends who wanted a coup. Basil backed down gracefully and agreed to serve as 'Caesar' provided that he had the right to lead the Emperor's military planning council and the rank of a senior general. Michael dispensed with a grand coronation and just had the unobjectionable and politically cautious bureaucrat Pope Callistus crown him at the end of a special Mass, written for the coronation of Constantine IV, at St Peter's Basilica, wearing a simple white robe over a hairshirt not rich robes and only wearing the invaluable Imperial State Crown (late 6th century) for as long as necessary. He and his wife Ausonia proceeded to sell off a large part of the Palace collections of dresses and jewellery amassed by recent Empresses and their daughters. though especially historic items worn at important occasions were kept on for a 'heritage' display that was put on show in a gallery of the old Palace on the Palatine, and opened to the public for a viewing-fee (the money going to the Empress' charities). The Emperor indeed moved out of the Marble Palace as too expensive and ostentatious and usually lived in a fairly modest villa in the 'Gardens of Carus II' (laid out in the Persian style by that ruler's hired Eastern experts) on the west side of the Janiculine Hill, and with the Empress weaving her own clothes and the Emperor wearing simple tunics and cloaks not robes it was a case of, as an admiring poet from the 'St John Chrysostom Society' of zealous young Christian nobles put it, 'back to Augustus'.

Ausonia required her court ladies to do good works, pray, learn the Bible, and live like nuns or (if married) model Christian wives and all rich and expensive wines were banned at receptions and dinners so in her case it was 'back to Pulcheria'. But apart from her hours of prayer and meditation with her favourite hermits and her endless meetings of the boards that ran her dozens of charities she did take positive initiatives to improve the lives of women rather than just showing off her holiness – and she criticized those toadying noblewomen who emulated her in their lifestyles and joined her prayer-sessions and Bible discussions but did not spend money and time on the poor. Ausonia was a major patron of homes for repentant prostitutes and lobbied hard for a new law that her husband took up and the Senate duly approved making it a criminal offence for a Roman citizen to rape his female slaves or to have their offspring cast out on the streets or sold to 'baby farmers'. She also made it much easier for a female slave to amass money while in service and buy herself out of slavery and set up a special bank – run by the Church – in each province to hold these sums of money for their female owners so that the latter's employers could not embezzle any of it. Women had always been allowed to own property and conduct business in Rome under the post-Constantine (330s ff.) Empire, as confirmed in Titus II's C6th law-code, but now Ausonia had their rights to keep their possessions before marriage separate from those of their husbands if they preferred, and set up boards of 'guardians' (usually clerics and abbesses) to see that this was enforced in each province. She also encouraged women to serve as deaconesses in the Church and make a contribution to running local congregations as well as acting as munificent charity-funders though this was in practice largely sidelined by angry male Church officials as contrary to the wishes of St Paul, and was only acted upon in parts of the West and some more liberal urban Eastern cities (e.g. Antioch and Alexandria but not Constantinople or Jerusalem).

While Ausonia was speaking up for women and unsuccessfully urging her husband and his education ministers to allow girls to attend university – only allowed in practice in Alexandria and then only for the social elite, who had a long Hellenistic tradition of female empowerment – Michael set about his own task of moral reform by giving endless speeches to the Senate about their moral mission and their duty to live up to the strict and just examples set by men like Cincinnatus, Appius Claudius the Elder (4th century BC), Cato the

Elder and Younger, and Cicero. As he also spoke up for the Gracchi and their land-reforms he was accused by some angry nobles behind his back of being a hopeless or dangerous romantic democrat who wanted to undermine the current social order and the very nature of autocracy. His wily and smooth-talking 'Master of Offices' and trusted senior minister Catronius managed to steer Michael away from this sort of reform – at an early date, anyway – with arguments that it all needed the ground to be prepared and public opinion brought in to support it or it would end in disaster and the blood spilt would be on the Emperor's head and a serious 'sin'.

But Michael did go ahead in 710 with a new 'Imperial Land Commission' of reformist and mostly young (and non-noble) lawyers and landholding experts to look into the question of which of the largest current estates in Italy had been gained by strictly legal means and which owed their spread to sharp practice or outright fraud. Those lands identified as being held by 'illegal' means were then listed and on the completion of this task in 714 were sold off at a special series of auctions – with 'first refusal' given to the landless and small farmers and with no large landowner allowed to bid. The alarmed conservative landlords who would be affected tried to bribe the lawyers involved to take their names off the list or if that failed to hold the process up by dubious means and several times the list was stolen or otherwise sabotaged so the schedule fell behind what Michael had envisaged. But the fact that any 'proscribed list' of illegally-held land was drawn up at all and the property involved was sold off to small owners or the landless – with the Imperial Bank granting loans to help their purchases – was a major achievement and it made Michael very popular with small farmers and the more reformist churchmen. The move, though radical, was seen by some approving ministers and clergy as continuing Titus II's emphasis on the Emperor as the protector of ordinary citizens against injustice – now in a more open Christian manner.

Rack-renting by urban or rural landlords was technically banned but this was often evaded and so Michael, aware of this problem for years, had a stronger law drawn up in his first six months as Emperor and vigorously enforced by a special commission which had officials in each province. With his first law-minister or 'Quaestor', the conservative if honest jurist Quintus Dacellius who he had inherited from his father, resigning in protest at this interference in the usual legal processes Michael replaced him with a 'committed' and low-class Christian lawyer from Antioch called Propertius Hadrianus who had a name for offering free legal services to the poor at his law-practice. The latter made sure that the new law was enforced and those who breached it, however rich they were, ended up in court and also were not allowed to hire the Empire's best lawyers to defend them but had to have their lawyers chosen by lot. Breaches of the 'cruelty to slaves' laws were also tightened up by a new law and a new commission in 711–12 and were then enforced in court with 'high-profile' prosecutions. Thanks to Hadrianus' special new body of reformist law commissioners' recommendations the Emperor duly moved on in 714 to have excessive legal fees (which put many poorer citizens off starting legal cases and helped the rich to hire the best lawyers and win in court) banned and a 'sliding schedule' of fixed charges imposed, dependent partly on the gravity of the charge and partly on the means of the litigant as assessed by their tax-records. The leaders of the legal profession in Rome and other major cities were furious and it was rumoured later that Michael's untimely death was due to a 'hit' by criminals hired by the inner circle of Rome's richest lawyers. But for the moment the Emperor could enforce his will and he also had a special 'Slavery Commission' set up in 715, mainly staffed by younger and more moralist churchmen and liberal-minded university academics, to oversee a new law allowing slaves who had done over ten years' domestic service or fifteen years' service as rural labourers to buy themselves out of slavery if they had the financial means (from their salaries or savings, which were now to be held safe for them by a special board of State bankers in each province).

Ultimately Michael wanted to abolish slavery altogether and his hermit adviser Father Gregorius had been urging him to do this as a priority for years and saying that it was his duty to Christ to do this, but the Emperor's special 710 commission into the feasibility of this plus the conditions of rural slavery was hit by delaying tactics by unco-operative slaveholders. After their initial Empire-wide tours and report to him in 715 he had to be content with a 'first step' of legislation to improve conditions of work and a board to enforce this in each province. Even this was highly contentious and added to his enemies and he could not close down the Imperial slave-mines as he had intended to do at the start of his reign as the institutions were needed to abstract metals and ore for the army's and navy's equipment. The armed forces' lobbying power (aided by Basil) was such that a viable alternative means of running the mines had to be found and arranged before the slaves were released – and this solution was repeatedly delayed due to careful non-co-operation by the parties involved.

At least from 713 Michael managed to have the number of crimes punishable by slavery reduced by a half, with the board set up to investigate this filled with moralist clergymen so it was not held up. He also banned the flogging of convicted prostitutes outright and had a new 'Prisons Secretary' appointed with a special staff of committed reformers (mostly churchmen) to investigate and supervise conditions in the Empire's prisons and see that the gaolers were adequately paid and supervised and that poorer convicts did not have to pay for their own food or bedding on pain of being left with minimal amounts of either. All this cost money and led to reductions in the military budget to compensate for the

Emperor's reforms, several regiments of 'limitanei' in each frontier province that was not under demonstrable military threat being cashiered in 711–12 and their men turned into ordinary farmers while a third of the 'Scholae' regiments attendant on the Emperor were sacked in 711 and the 'comitatus' at Ctesiphon was cut by a quarter in 712. But at least Michael did see the point of keeping up the navy in the North Sea to combat the threat of new Norse piracy and in the Indian Ocean to protect merchant-shipping. The Roman supervision by small coastal forts on the Northern shore of the Skaggerak near the Eastern end of the lowlands (OTL: the Oslo area) of the 'federate' Norse chieftains was scaled back under him as a cost-cutting measure, which was later used by antagonistic militarists and Catholic nobles and generals to accuse him of complacency and enabling the more daring and anti-Roman chiefs (mostly younger men who had not experienced war with Rome) to start attacking merchant ships and blame this on 'interlopers' who had supposedly come along the coast from the Trondelag. But at the time Michael was assured by the naval commanders at the North Sea bases in Dania, Frisia, and 'Britain II' (i.e. northern Britannia from Lindum to Hadrian's Wall) that the seas were quiet apart from a few incidents and that the Norse of Vestfold were paying their tribute and sending vassal-troops to the Roman armies and sailors to the navy on schedule. The rich pickings of fully legal trade with the Empire kept most of the local Norse chiefs and merchants (some of them operating as both) 'in line' apart from the occasional tax-dodging. Norse sailors had made considerable contributions to the design of smaller, 'inshore' Roman craft in the North Sea and Hibernian Sea fleets in the past generation, and job opportunities for trade and naval work kept most of the southern Norse loyal for the first half of the eighth century. The worst that could be said of Michael, unlike of his younger brother Basil, was that he did not believe in 'un-Christian' punitive reprisals after the occasional piracy of trading ships or slave-raids on the coast of Dania and Frisia – and after him Basil as Emperor was too busy elsewhere to reply to this as well.

Michael's enthusiasm for trade as a means to enrich the aspirant small traders of the Empire meant that he continued to back the 'Eastern Trade Ministry' secretariat and send out trade-missions to India and Taprobane – and in 714 he sent the Empire's first trading mission to the emerging Hindu-influenced expansionist kingdom of Srivijaya on Sumatra. He was interested in the Eastern religion of Buddhism as a useful and evidently popular source of austere lifestyles, 'godliness', humility, and a desire for social welfare and as such in 715 he invited an early Buddhist mission to convert people in Mesopotamia which was sent by a friendly southern Indian 'rajah' to come on to Rome and teach him its beliefs. But in this he parted company with Father Gregorius who regarded all non-Christians as 'sinners' who had rejected the message of Christ and to the delight of angry spendthrift and law-twisting nobles with slaves and secret bank accounts the arch-preacher and director of the Emperor's conscience then left Rome before the Buddhist monks arrived (for a monastery in Palestine) and never came back, followed by some more conventional but equally bigoted Spanish Catholic monastic advisers of the sovereign. According to informed rumour, Michael was by now uneasy at the luxurious lives of elite bishops and their defence of this – and Gregorius was less keen to antagonise the higher clergy by forbidding this than Michael was.

Michael did not convert to Buddhism but he did invite the mission to arrange for their colleagues in the Deccan in India to send a new mission to Rome to found a 'Theravada' monastery there and this was duly set up in Michael's final months in office in 717. But long before then the Emperor had also managed to alienate the mainstream Catholic theologians as well by his interest in bridging the theological divide between orthodox and Monophysite and his long dabblings in speculative theology, used by Catronius as a way to keep him busy and away from more dangerous political/administrative reform work, now led to him taking up some unusual and not very popular ideas. Back in the later C6th a minor but very learned and unashamedly experimental Egyptian bishop called Theodore had suggested in his writings that the orthodox – Monophysite breach could be healed by being diverted into mutual declarations by both sects of what they had in common and banning any precise speculation on the subject of Christ's human and divine natures (always only one nature, or two fused into one when He was born?). His suggestion had been that it should be decided that Christ had only one 'Will', i.e. direction for His personality, and one 'Energy' however many natures He had originally had and how they related to each other. This solution, known as 'Monotheletism' ('One Will'), had only been taken up by a few theologians in Egypt in the early C7th and had not been accepted by mainstream clerics or thinkers of either persuasion, but now Michael was told about it by his team of theological scholars in winter 711–12 and adopted it as a solution to the problem of the orthodox and the Monophysites both calling the others 'heretics'. Pope Callistus was not sympathetic when the Emperor told him of his solution and said that it was totally contrary to Catholic doctrine and could not be supported by the Church, but when he died in autumn 712 Michael returned to it by having one of the late Bishop Theodore's few supporters in the main ecclesiastical seminary in Rome, Germanus of Dyrrachium who had recently been made bishop of his home town in Epirus, summoned to Rome and invited to become Pope as the Emperor's nominee if he took up the cause and argued for it at the next all-Empire Church Council. The ambitious Germanus agreed and was appointed Pope to general surprise despite his reputation for holiness and learning, but when he brought all of Theodore's works to Rome in an Imperial ship at the Emperor's expense and started to lecture on them as the solution to the long-running theological split and made it clear that he expected his clergy to support him in this he was faced with firstly incredulity and then a 'strike' as virtually nobody took him up on his offer and assorted Italian bishops started to accuse him of 'heresy'. Apparently both lay and religious elite doubters of Michael's priorities saw this as an opportunity to blacken Michael's so far popular public reputation by alleging 'heresy', and so egged him on – but was his brother involved too?

(This religious controversy is invented, but with elements of the real 'Monotheletism' controversy in the Eastern Empire of the mid-C7th and of the real 'Iconoclast Controversy' there which commenced in the OTL 720s.)

After this the Emperor faced a difficult choice of whether to drop the scheme or to press on and to use his so-far-neglected powers of patronage over the Church and enforce a change of doctrine as assorted Emperors had done in the C4th and C5th. But despite the fates and posthumous reputations of 'reformers' backing non-Catholic doctrines (or 'heretics' as the Church now called them) like Constantius II, Theodosius II, Basiliscus, and Anastasius I he pressed on and was backed up not only by assorted bureaucrats, who longed to bring the Church under Imperial control and rein in its 'arrogant' claims to define its own doctrine, but by his brother Basil and some senior ministers and generals who were later supposed to have done this to make him unpopular and so easier to overthrow. To be more charitable both the autocratic Basil and the Praetorian Praefect Andronicus Noractianus believed in the idea of the Emperor controlling the Church as a department of state, which had grown up under the centraliser Claudius III and been boosted by the 'Hellenists' Diomedes and Caracalla. But none of these had been interested in Christian doctrine and Michael's justification for his intervention went back to Constantine 'the Great's actions and was subsequently declared to have been an early step on the road to 'Caesaropapism' i.e. the Emperor acting as Pope and defining doctrine (but as the heir of Constantine, who had presided at the Council of Nicaea, not as the heir of St Peter).

The special Church Council that Michael summoned for spring-summer 713, with representatives from all over the Empire, was carefully prepared for as the Emperor appointed sympathetic bureaucrats (not all of them already in Church service) to take over the Papal administration and set up a new 'Secretariat for Religious Affairs' to assist them – this remained in being after the Church Council as a permanent body with its own, lay minister on the Imperial Council – and the bishops or their substitutes were told when they arrived by a deluge of official documents that the new doctrine of 'Monotheletism' did not contradict either the Council of Nicaea or the Council of Chalcedon. Learned evidence was presented to the Council to that effect and as the leaders of the Monophysite Church in each province where it was in existence arrived in Rome ready for a summons to the Council they received documents assuring them that the new doctrine did not contradict their belief either. But despite Michael's powerful opening speech to the Council calling for reconciliation as their Christian duty few of the bishops responded and they voted not to admit the Monophysites for discussions either, even as 'observers'. As the Pope ignored his fellow-Patriarchs' vetoes on the admission and let the Monophysites come to the Lateran Palace – though not to the same hall – a majority of the bishops walked out of the Council and held a meeting of their own in a church across the Tiber where the Patriarch of Antioch led the way in having a vote passed calling the Pope a 'heretic' and ignoring the Council as illegal, and though they politely declared that Michael had been 'misinformed' rather than that he was a 'heretic' too they voted to burn all of the late Bishop Theodore's works and carried out a bonfire of those that they could find. The Council had to be called off as it did not even have a 'quorum' of delegates left with the legal powers to proceed. Michael did not give up and resorted to a learned study by hired scholars into Theodore's works to prove that they were orthodox, but he faced the opposition of almost the entire Church and his resorting to getting the obedient Pope and the Religious Affairs Secretariat to call in all the Western bishops to the Papal offices and either sign a document backing 'Monotheletism' or hand in their resignations in a long-running process during 714 ended up with over a hundred bishops removed and many refusing to vacate their offices or churches, those in Italy, Britain and Spain in particular though most in Gaul and the Rhineland conformed.

The ex-bishops often called on their congregations to occupy their cathedrals and either the local governors had to bring in the police to evict them and install the new bishops or else they refused to act to 'preserve public order'. With six cathedrals where the new bishops had been installed being then burnt down by 'accident' and very few locals attending the services there the Emperor faced both unpopularity and demands by his ministers, Catronius included, that he give up and restore the Catholic bishops in order to restore order and prevent the danger of some general being inspired by angry Catholic nobles or a sacked bishop to rebel. After an abortive plot in Lower Germany, where an army was being assembled under the 'Master of Infantry' and 'Count' (two separate figures) on the Rhine to invade Transrhenus and stop a civil war in the Frankish kingdom between the pro-Roman illegitimate son (Carolus) and anti-Roman grandson (Grimoald) of the late chief minister Pepin of Heristal (d 714), and the botched attempt to murder the army's commanders in a banquet poisoning by angry Catholic officers Michael was forced with a virtual ultimatum by Basil and his 'high command' in Rome. In order to prevent the 'sin' of a civil war he agreed to hold a new Church Council of the West in 715 to investigate Monotheletism and in the meantime to sack Pope Germanus and allow the bishops of Italy (old and new, Catholic and pro-Imperial) to elect a new leader. This man turned out to be a skilled conciliator and respected theologian who had a reputation for humility and philanthropy, Bishop Gregorius of Bononia, so he was acceptable to Michael. But he also backed the Catholic 'line' to keep the Western Church united and his Church Council duly had to be free of Imperial interference, as pledged by Michael on the Pope's insistence, and declared for Catholicism and condemned 'Monotheletism' and all who supported it.

All the new Western bishops who did not immediately denounce the new doctrine and, if they had previously backed it, do penance and apologise to the Church and their congregations were sacked and some ended up in prison for not vacating their cathedrals and mansions when so ordered. Though about half the sacked Catholic bishops of the pre-713 era did not get their posts back those who were restored were treated as heroes by their congregations and men such as the venerable Archbishop Vilvridus of Eburacum in Britain (OTL St Wilfrid of York d 720), a pugilistic but dedicated missionary who had made his name converting Picts in eastern Caledonia in the 670s-680s, were regarded as more morally deserving than the time-serving and careerist Papacy and its bureaucracy. Some could argue that the result was a victory for democracy in the Church as well as for correct doctrine and the new Pope was able to reassert his leadership of his suspicious and feud-riven Church by patience and goodwill. But the centralization of the Western Church had been shattered by a determined 'grass-roots' stand and the Eastern orthodox Churches had been equally resistant to the Emperor, on a more unanimous level, and had been facing their own mass-sackings so they also now loathed the Emperor.

The latter's reputation with the lay congregations of orthodox/Catholic Christians and with most of the Church was shattered and he was also accused of risking civil war by angry generals and a substantial faction of the Senate. In 715–17 his reign seemed to 'stall' in terms of reform or vigour while Basil proceeded to win plaudits by his deft handling of the Frankish crisis which he took over as the new regional military 'supremo' to evict the 'rebel' Grimoald from Transrhenus and install Carolus (OTL Charles Martel, d 741), a trained Roman officer and a personal friend of his, as the new Frankish chief minister in what was now formally declared to be an 'allied ethnically-defined Roman province' under a hereditary governor from Carolus' family as 'nobilissimus' (with a Merovingian puppet-king who now became a merely honorary figure and was finally pensioned off in 751).

Michael had now lost the backing of the Church and their aristocratic allies in Constantinople and Antioch for his threats of sackings over the 'Monothelete' crisis and the bureaucracy 's leadership all over the Empire regarded him as a dangerous maverick. As his political position declined he was urged by Catronius and others to re-position himself as the embodiment of the Imperial mission to bring justice and efficiency and give the State a moral role – writing off his theological foray as an experiment in reconciliation that had gone wrong and a 'one-off'. At least the Emperor avoided his intended sackings of more ministers for alleged immoral behaviour or piling up fortunes by using their positions to auction off sinecures and grants to supporters while he had been busy with the Church. Instead he let some of his less religiously fanatical 'reformist' proteges, mainly university tutors or court officials, and other guests at his seminars talk him into 'harmless' minor changes to the administration of some larger provincial cities in 716. This would give more 'say' and greater roles to representatives of non-council personnel. These new nominees from professional bodies, eg trades-guilds, business and trader groupings, and professional middle-class careerists (eg headmasters and administrators), were to join the established councillors in cities and towns on councils to represent their own groups and help to run affairs and fund civic projects. It was billed as a return to Ancient-Greek-style local democracy with even some experiments in choosing which councillors ran particular activities or sat on particular boards by lots and in rotation. Planning this and making sure that it ran smoothly kept the Emperor from trying out new religious plans, but he was not to be distracted for long and early in 717 he returned to Church issues to impose a vigorous and earnest new, young secretary for religious affairs, maverick ex-monk turned theologian Honorius of Lerins (the famous and allegedly rather too luxurious and easy-going early C5th monastery and boys' school off the south-eastern Gallic coast near Massilia). Michael backed his plans to remove assorted over-disciplinarian and over-centralising abbots from major monasteries and replace them with younger men who were open to new ideas and new, experimental activities by their monks – initially in the West.

The main ideas of the disillusioned Honorius, based on his own experiences at Lerins, was to remove abbots and their sidekicks in monastic administration who were obsessed with following a fixed routine, accepting established doctrine, parroting out conventional theology, and beating their ideas into their novices and boys at their schools and bring in new and more 'open' senior figures. These would allow experimentation, individuals following an austere life away from the monastic communal life as hermits to perfect their own spiritual life (as in some Eastern monasteries), individual theological and spiritual 'questing', and developing new ideas in communal singing and holy music (as taking place in a few Gallic and Greek monasteries with choirs). This was duly enshrined in Church law by the complaisant Pope Gregorius II and his synod and began to take shape. But the sacking of assorted theologically orthodox and disciplinarian abbots who had poor records for bullying and manipulation of their monks and/or keeping donations of cash for their own use, which began within months as commissioners roamed the West, roused new Church antagonism from powerful figures with important friends in (secular as well as Church) high places. This and the renewal in 717 of Michael's 'Land Commission', this time to investigate land-ownership in southern Gaul and Illyria, resulted in complaints to the Pope and to the Senate and rumours of worried ministers having tried to 'warn off' Michael and being ignored. This all fed into claims of a new plot against him centred in the 'comitatus' at Rome and involving senior aristocratic generals, and when an earthquake hit the towns of the Appenine hills in northern Umbria and Tuscany on 14 December 717 and the news soon reached Rome the Emperor determined to lead the relief-efforts himself and take soldiers from the 'comitatus' up to the devastated area to dig out wrecked houses and save civilian casualties. On the following day he set out in his chariot for the area from Rome and outpaced his escort in his haste, and after he failed to arrive at the first town on his itinerary searchers were sent out and hours later his chariot was found in a gulley at the foot of a slope on an earthquake-hit road which he had apparently taken as a short cut without telling anyone.

The Emperor was lying dead at the roadside but had been stabbed not hit by rocks like his chariot, aged 37, and though nobody was ever indicted for the attack and his brother Basil, who arrived from Naples the next day to take over as Emperor Basil I, declared to the Senate that it had been a mystery attack by opportunistic footpads or interrupted looters of a nearby farm rumour had it that the Emperor had been ambushed – and that the plotters (unidentified) in the 'comitatus' had known his route and sent out ambushers to attack him. Basil refused to hold an enquiry and tried to brush off the incident as the sort of thing that happened in a rough area of the rural Apennines after an earthquake. But he was alleged by some of Michael's distraught supporters to have been behind the 'hit' himself and sermons and literary attacks on him as a 'fratricide' were widespread in 717–18 though they were cracked down on with public floggings and sentences to the mines and exiles.

Basil held a grand state funeral for Michael in the basilica of St Peter in Rome at the end of December and the late Emperor acquired his own cult as a 'martyr' killed by the rich and the 'ungodly' though he was never sanctified despite numerous requests. But the new ruler was left under a cloud over how exactly he had gained the throne and he had to move carefully so he kept on all Michael's ministers into the early 720s and also kept on his projects – though he made sure that the 'Land Commission' did not do anything too radical and the relaxation of monastic communal discipline and sackings of inadequate abbots were also limited in extent. The ex-Empress Ausonia was treated with honour and was made 'Augusta' and given substantial funding for her various philanthropic projects which she continued to run and in 720 she was to retire to one of her villas in Apulia which she set up as her own nunnery with herself as abbess. But the new Empress Serena (born Serena Nearonia, daughter of a venerable Constantinopolitan senator from a major administrative dynasty there) was a much different woman, a beautiful, glamorous and talented socialite who helped her husband by running the main aristocratic salon in the capital. She was also a successful 'fixer' who helped her many friends and proteges to secure court offices and/or funding for pet projects and who was able to charm and lure in support where her abrupt and suspicious husband, a hard-working and competent but not too cultured officer, failed. Serena was also a major cultural patron of music, drama, and literature and patronized Rome's leading cultural salons and she took over the role of the late Emperor Caracalla as a patron of major dramatic festivals and regularly attended them to present prizes, not forgetting in her shrewd way to see that only plays on classical history or mythic themes that avoided mention of the old 'pagan' gods and goddesses won so that the Church was not offended. With Ausonia – on whom she was on good terms – to keep the Christian zealots 'on side' and assure them that Michael's demise had not ended their Imperial patronage the new regime slowly won support and crucially had military backing from the start, not least as Basil was the patron of the 'Ephebic' youths' organization and continued to attend their sports-rallies and to keep on good terms with their provincial organizers.

The regiments cashiered by Michael were reinstated and Rome's expansionist military mission was played up in the Emperor's speeches as he attended military manoeuvres and gave out prizes at military sports-tournaments, along with the Olympic Games in 720 and 724. But Basil was too shrewd to rush into wars whatever his generals wanted and his resumption of Rome's 'outward' mission was kept within tight financial limits, centred on the creation of a new 'Indian Ocean' fleet (in fact just the repositioning of existing anti-piracy Red Sea and Aden naval ships) under a local admiral of Yemeni origin and the building of a naval base on the island of Socotra off the Yemeni coast to control the movement of shipping in and out of the approaches to the Red Sea. This was backed up by a new Roman naval base on the South side of the entrance to the Red Sea, at the ancient Somali port of Mosylon which was now annexed as a Roman possession and a centre for trade with the local ports and tribes. Some Roman naval ships duly ventured down the African coast to Mogadishu, Mombasa, and Kilwa to force these independent commercial ports to become Roman protectorates and their shipping to pay customs-duties to Rome. But that was more for 'show' and for propaganda purposes than a major military move, and Basil also sent a small expedition to Abyssinia in 724 to back up a successful contender for the throne in a civil war and played that up as a major triumph. In fact it was only a minor venture by around 800 infantry and 400 cavalry and the new 'Roman ally' and 'nobilissimus' king of Axum/Abyssinia, Ayasa, was not much use as his drought-hit country was soon too short of cash and food to keep his vassal tribes loyal. In the 730s he was to end up abandoning the old capital of Axum for a more secure hill-town base to the South in the region of Gojjam, leading to the decline and eventual abandonment of the former capital. More useful were the Roman military and naval exploration ventures of the 720s and 730s along the Kenyan coast and South as far as a few hundred miles beyond Kilwa to map the region, find new harbours where 'refuelling stations' could be set up for passing merchant ships, and force the local chiefs to sign up as Roman allies and supply cheap trade-goods and a regular contingent of young men to be trained as Roman warriors in new, predominantly African regiments based in Massawa, Arabia Felix, and the cities of Lower Egypt (reached by the Pharoanic Canal from the Red Sea).

This creation of new black East African infantry regiments was also used to bolster the Roman military presence in Nubia, with the new soldiers used to the hot climate, and to enable better local crackdowns on customs-dodging merchants and peasant-kidnapping slave-traders – and after 15 to 20 years' service those soldiers who wished to return home on the expiry of their service often ended up as culturally Romanised 'agents' back in their tribal lands or East African coastal towns, living in the Roman manner (often with Roman wives) and speaking Latin. This in turn aided a slow 'Romanization' of coastal Kenya in the mid-later C8th and the C9th, while the money and impressive luxuries that the returnees had made in the Empire encouraged other, inland warriors 'on the make' to join the Roman army. If the latter preferred to raid the pro-Roman coast (or kidnap passing Roman merchants for ransom) the Roman-trained coastal ex-soldiers were able to act as a local militia and deal with them. Some of the geographers in Alexandria promoted and assisted and Egyptian traders paid for searches for the fabled 'gold mines' inland of Kilwa or further to the South in the lost 'land of Rhapta' with its jungles from the 720s onwards and Basil apparently hoped to find gold there as he twice sent Imperial Guards officers to command expeditions there, but nothing turned up apart from one blown-off-course naval expedition in the 740s finding the island of Mauritius. The new Roman interest in East Africa and the ocean beyond was partly a practical search for extra troops from a 'virile' source of warlike tribesmen, copying the use of Germans in the C4th onwards and Arabs from the C6th. The military high command used this argument; ministers were more interested in finding gold-mines.

Basil was a capable and shrewd ruler if not congenial or trusting (outside of his own small circle of ex-officers from his youth in the 'Protectores' and in his Indian frontier commands, most of whom he lured to Rome in 717–19 to join his court or take up 'comitatus ' commands). He had the support of the bureaucracy and generals who looked on him as a 'safe pair of hands' so the distrust of Michael's younger admirers in intellectual circles and the hatred of him as a probable regicide and fratricide by the poor did not lead to any serious plots. Once he was more sure of himself he began to make changes in the government and installed new ministers, mostly bureaucratic careerists from the provincial administrations who had been 'examination system' entrants from humble backgrounds and had risen through the ranks by merit or 'gaming the system' so they had no independent allies to rely on and were going to be dependent on him for patronage and hopefully too appreciative of his support to question or undermine him. The bluff and 'brainier-than-he-looked' new 'Master of Cavalry' from 718, Titus Geminius (a typical aristocratic cavalry officer in his sixties with a landed Italian background and a huge moustache) who had once been the young Basil's riding-tutor and had a sister who was a self-promoting but genuinely philanthropic abbess friend of ex-Empress Ausonia, was an invaluable aide to Basil and helped to keep the 'high command' on side. His maxim of 'make your juniors eager to win your praise and let them think that every junior officer potentially carries a general's baton in his knapsack' was also applied by Basil in civilian life as he was keen to get his junior ministers to think that they could be in senior office soon if they impressed him. Unlike the honest but ideological Michael, Basil had the knack of getting people to work for him out of ambition and hopes for their career and he did not care about beliefs or morals as long as someone got the job done, as the number of senior ministers he retained despite their mistresses, 'toy boy' male lovers, or expenses-fiddling showed. He thus had a more stable and coherent government than Michael's with Serena 'talent-spotting' ambitious and/or usefully rich and well-connected nobles at her salon to recommend to him for the appropriate jobs (e.g. as Praefect of Rome and at court).

Basil also kept an eye on and helped the careers of the administrators of the 'Ephebes' and in 720 admitted their head, the annually-changed 'Consul of the Ephebes' (usually a senior administrator of former military experience), to his Imperial Council and gave him access to the 'high command' of the army so the latter could tell him what particular military training they needed in their future soldiers at that point and the 'ephebes' could duly do that sort of exercise. As a muscular former army running and swordsmanship 'star' at inter-regimental competitions Basil also made a point of attending army sports tournaments and dragging senators along too and he stressed the value of physical fitness in his speeches at these occasions, for once sounding like Michael as he denounced drinking too much alcohol and womanizing and declared that no young officer who spent the mornings in bed with a hangover while his subordinates did his duties deserved promotion.

Basil relied on the great minister Catronius for advice on personnel and policy until the latter retired in 721 and was influenced by him to avoid major and especially contentious shifts of policy unless they were essential and had been thoroughly investigated beforehand. When the 'Mastership of Offices' was at last vacant Basil was on his own in controlling policy for a year or two, moving three separate men in and out of the post, until in late 723 he appointed his own brother-in-law Leo Nearonius, the subtle and hard-working Constantinopolitan bureaucrat brother of Empress Serena. Leo had headed the administration in that city since 715 and had risen rapidly through the ranks there in the early-mid 710s as a man who got things done without offending too many of his seniors – and as a smooth operator who had a large family of siblings and cousins in senior roles in the city and neighbouring provinces to back him up. The masterful Leo Nearonius had a grip on minute details of policy and personnel and an appetite for reading and understanding accounts that Basil lacked and he quickly proved essential to his government even if he did bring in some of his own men from the Constantinopolitan administration to the 'Master of Offices' department to aid him and annoyed native Italians there. Soon his Bithynian ex-'boy genius' mathematician turned accountant ally Flavius Paterculus was installed in the finance ministry as assistant to the 'Count of the Sacred Largesses' and in 728 succeeded the latter when he retired, as recommended by Nearonius. The indefatigable Paterculus soon got a grip on the Empire's budget and was to make a major mark in its rationalizing and the removal of anomalies and tax-fiddling under Nearonius as 'Emperor Leo IV' in the 730s and 740s. But for the moment his main innovation was to persuade Basil to stimulate internal trade between provinces by cutting the customs-duties that were paid by traders moving goods from one province to another and by giving a 'tax holiday' to all new shops and trade businesses for their first two years of operation, both carried out in early 729. The lost revenue was recouped by tighter controls on smuggling and evading import-duties on incoming produce on the 'Silk Road' and its maritime equivalent, especially in the Persian Gulf where goods were being landed on the coast of Persis to avoid the customs-houses of Charax in Mesopotamia. More smuggling and customs-evasion was aiding the local Arab rulers of the trading-ports of the Bahrayn peninsula on the Southern coast of the Persian Gulf while traders bringing goods up the Nile via Dongola into Egypt were crossing the deserts to avoid the Roman customs-posts and reaching the Nile, but this was reined in by vigorous action by the local military authorities from the late 720s as recommended to Basil and the 'high command' by military experts who the finance ministry had asked to be called in to compile a report on revenue-losses.

Chapter 5

Leo IV 729–750 (New Dynasty, i.e. Nearonius Family) The Magnificent. Basil's Brother-in-Law

Basil died of an unexpected heart-attack after being taken ill during an audience for local notables in Mediolanum on 25 April 729, aged forty-seven and as he had only four daughters, the eldest (Irene) aged fourteen and too young to marry, the Imperial line was extinct as far as male succession was concerned. The Senate was called upon to conduct an election next day by the Council despite panicking generals on the 'high command' staff asking their seniors to try to insist on a veto by them on anyone inclined to Michael-style religious pacifism or cost-cutting of the military. The compromise candidate as a 'safe pair of hands' and a proven administrator who kept clear of controversy was Leo Nearonius, who unlike some seven or eight senators who put their own names forward was known to the administrative elite and did not have the potential to spring nasty policy surprises on them, so he was chosen as Emperor on the fourth (secret) ballot on 28 April amidst warnings from other ministers that any delay could lead to a military revolt by provincial generals and civil war.

The traumas caused by Michael's land-redistribution plans to the nobility and rich businessmen and by his pacifism to the military also meant that several more imaginative choices of Emperor, among them moderate former advisers to Michael who were still in the senate or buccaneering business tycoons whose wives were friends of Empress Serena, were not backed by enough votes. Once Leo (aged 49) had been elected as Emperor Leo IV the Senate proceeded to set up a formal mechanism for electing Emperors if there was no clear, i.e. adult male relative, heir to a deceased former incumbent – a series of ballots by themselves after consultation with the 'high command' of the military, the ministers, and the Pope. (Suggestions could also be requested by carrier-pigeon from the Praefect of Constantinople and his Patriarch, as nearer than Antioch or Alexandria, and nearer governors, but they would have to be received within a week of dispatch.) Leo was clearly capable and able to win over important members of the elite to back him and he had not put any contentious policies forward as a minister, and his lack of any Imperial blood was made up for as he proceeded to engage his eighteen-year-old son Probus to Princess Irene and so acquired the backing and the social and financial 'clout' of Empress Serena.

As Leo had recently divorced his (first) wife Honoria, Probus' mother, a distant cousin who he had married to acquire her father's business fortune as his heir, and had no Empress the former incumbent took over as his hostess until his remarriage in 733. A reasonably modest coronation at the end of a ceremonial Mass at St Peter's in June reassured the Roman elite that despite his acquisition of lands and mansions as a minister and his fondness for conspicuous consumption Leo was not going to be a politically risky spendthrift who would live as lavishly as Caracalla. Leo was a cultured man interested in Hellenic-style poetry and drama and he kept up his personal connections with and patronage of festivals in both of these arts while he also resumed Caracalla's patronage of the capital's architectural school and dabbled in designing buildings himself, also in the Oriental styles favoured by Caracalla. But he was a devout and orthodox Christian who had made a point of regularly attending extra Masses and debating with theologians in Constantinople and the glowing recommendations he had received from the Church there reassured the Catholic elite in the Western Church that he would not be as much of a 'pagan' cultural sympathizer as Caracalla or Diomedes had been and he would also clearly not risk political turmoil by playing at theological reconciliation by 'fiat' like Michael had done.

Leo already had his own private theological – mostly orthodox – library and a seminar for important theologians visiting Rome had been part of his patronage as a minister for years. He now continued this as Emperor and held debates in the Marble Palace, his main residence, but made it clear that he was doing so as a devout son of the Catholic Church and he was notably dubious about the sort of fanatically austere 'show-offs' who had flourished under Michael, preferring all hermits and preachers to be respectful to the authority of their local clergy. He and his soon-to-be second wife, the leading aristocratic Roman heiress Flavia Raupilla (who he was to divorce too, in 739), were both notably hostile to the rising group of mostly Levantine religious thinkers who were arguing that the current fashion for using religious portraits of the saints and the Virgin and Child – 'icons' – as aides to devotion, putting them up in churches, and parading them in religious processions amounted to 'idolatry' and thus needed to be banned or it would bring God's wrath on the Empire. Quite apart from the influence of austere Palestinian and Syrian desert monks and hermits who had always condemned any form of 'show' or use of wealth in devotion as immoral there was a new and popular sect of extremist rejectors of 'idolatry' to be reckoned with in the region in the form of the skin – or rag-wearing austere desert holy men following the beliefs of the charismatic 'fringe' early-mid 7th-century Arab holy man Mohammed ibn Abdallah of Mecca, not a Christian himself but influenced by Old Testament prophets' works and with Christian admirers and followers.

These 'semi-Christian' groups of hermits, who lived in separate and usually remote communities practicing various forms of mysticism and calling for the rich to give up their wealth to help the poor, pray and fast, and reject all 'sin', were against any form of pictorial representation of holy figures or God. They were very popular among the lower classes and the opponents of 'secularist' rich and well-connected clergy in early-mid 8th Syria and the desert fringes, and (mostly) young urban men and intellectuals seeking 'enlightenment' and a 'more godly lifestyle' had settled among and learnt from them for decades and were now starting to influence the ongoing intellectual 'scene' in major Eastern cities, especially Antioch. One group of them had hailed the 'holy' Emperor Michael as their hero and on his suspicious death had declared him a 'martyr' and their inspiration – for which they had been excommunicated and finally driven out of the Church by an Eastern Church Council in 720 on Basil's orders. Now they chose to take the impressive natural phenomenon of a major eruption of the island volcano of Thera in the Aegean in 726 (OTL event) as a sign of God's wrath at 'idolatry', especially worship of icons, and to declare that more disasters would follow unless the people and the Church reformed. This 'Iconoclast' movement was seen as a threat by the Church as its leaders started to encourage disobedience to 'unholy' bishops and as a result in 730 the new Emperor was asked by a visiting panel of Syrian and Palestinian bishops to Rome to make sure that the doctrine and its practitioners were banned and driven underground to avoid more trouble. The devout Leo had used icons as an aide to devotion himself and his own theological 'trusties' all assured them that worshipping with them was not the same as worshipping them so he agreed with the delegation. In spring 732 a co-ordinated set of Church Councils in the West and the great Eastern Patriarchates (Constantinople, Antioch, Alexanadria, and Ctesiphon) all investigated and condemned the 'Iconoclasts' and those summoned to give evidence in the sect's favour were either tricked into making inflammatory and theologically unsound declarations which could be written down and condemned or were accused of sedition and insulting the senior clergy.

Once the offensive doctrine had been condemned and any clergy supporting it listed by local Church commissioners and lined up to be ordered to publicly repent or be sacked the Emperor and Pope Gregorius wrote off the matter as 'solved'. But in fact resistance to the resultant sackings spread in Syria and Palestine in the mid-730s and was to lead to armed resistance as sacked clerics or monks regained their official residences by force, backed by mobs of pious peasants or Arab nomads, and by 737 the government was having to intervene after worrying police reports and send in troops to regain order. When in 738 a large 'Iconoclast' gathering on the Mount of Olives in Jerusalem led to rioters disrupting the official celebrations and seizing icons for destruction the city faced days of rioting and had to be retaken by soldiers sent in from the desert frontier garrisons around Philadelphia Ammonitis (Amman). In the meantime Leo, whose overall policies centred on avoiding controversy so his creating – or speeding up? – a clash between the authorities and the 'Iconoclasts' was rather ironic – concentrated on building up his dynasty's acceptability. As he tried to make himself better known outside the capital and Constantinople he made a series of Imperial tours each summer from May to September and so was in Gaul in 730, Spain and Lusitania in 731, North Africa from Carthage east to Alexandria in 732, Syria and Asia Minor in 733, Greece and Illyria in 734, Noricum, Pannonia and Dacia in 735, Rhaetia and the Rhineland in 736, and Syria, Armenia, Colchis, Adiabene, Media and upper Mesopotamia in 737. Apart from winter 733–4 at Constantinople he spent every winter in Rome and he was careful to take a senior committee of ministers on tour with him but to keep in touch with Rome by carrier-pigeons and fast horseborne 'post'. He made minimal changes to the list of ministers for his first decade after his initial reshuffling of Basil's advisers in 730 but ensured that nobles, hereditary bureaucratic 'dynasties', and 'new men' from the provinces were all represented in the great offices and that he and his successive wives kept the Italian nobility 'on side' with grand receptions and parties and a judicious distribution of honours and gifts.

Leo did not have any military connections, though he quickly put his son Probus in the 'Protectores' for a military cadet's education and then posted him to Dacia to acquire military experience and skills on the frontier. There, the declining kingdom of the Langobards under the Catholic dynasty of Grimoald was breaking up into factional feuds between powerful barons, each based in a separate regional fief centred on a wooden-palisaded hall in the lands between Oder and Bug, and the Church was the main source of stability as the agricultural land was left deserted by peasants fleeing the civil wars to settle in either Roman 'Germania Ulterior' or the lands along the upper Dnieper to the East. The influx of farmers and their womenfolk seeking peace and quiet from marauding barons and pillaging bandits was aiding the restoration of prosperity. A degree of small-scale urbanization to the Roman lands East of the Elbe that had been wrecked in the 590s were now resumed, and they were producing corn and animals to be exported South up the Elbe to Marcomannia or North from Baltic fishing-ports in the Wends' tribal territory to Dania by Romano-Danish trading vessels. In Langobardia itself the Church was clinging desperately to its Roman links and regular visits by Roman clerics and missionaries to secure a degree of exemption from the general robbery and muggings for its fortified, stone or wooden churches and monastic complexes by warning the laity that any attacks on the 'People of God' would bring the vengeance of God in the long term and Roman soldiers in the short term. As the land-seeking and agriculturally energetic but decentralized and leaderless Slavs moved into the empty farms to take the better land from c.700 and fought or bought off the local Langobard lords and bandits the 'German' land became more 'Slav'. The Roman-educated clerics (often taught at new schools run by the Church in Marcomannia, especially a seminary at Augusta Prahavorum opened in 692) had to learn Slavic to understand and minister to them, and the Roman expeditions that increasingly had to intervene to prop up the less vicious or destructive barons and keep the Church from attack included some after 734 by Prince Probus who thus acquired a good reputation as an active and generous protector of the ordinary people.

This, played up in his reports to the 'high command' in Rome and 'doctored' in suitably heroic terminology to be read in the Senate or posted up in the Forum Romanum, made him extremely popular and his wedding to Princess Irene, in an interval between his military 'tours of duty' in Dacia in summer 738, was a major social and political occasion for the elite of the capital and invitees from all over the Empire. The careful 'spin' by the government of how the Empire was wisely but firmly keeping the 'northern brigands' under control did a lot to build up a reputation for Leo IV as a wise and careful ruler who was determined to assert Roman power and push a Christian mission of Rome as the guarantor of peace and justice. Similar 'spin' was put on another and more difficult campaign at the opposite end of the Empire where in 732 the continuing and annoying attacks by Arab and African nomads from the region of Darfur to the west, ruled by refugees from the Roman-seized lands of Alwa in southern Sudan, on the peaceful agricultural lands of the upper Nile around Quartuma (Khartoum) and Dongola led to a reprisal expedition. In this 25,000 Roman, East African, and Arabian peninsula Arab troops, some on camels and others on horses, went marching or riding across the bleak Sahel 'no man's land' from the upper Nile to Darfur to burn the offenders' tented homes and kill all who did not escape into the forests to the South.

This expedition was commanded by the veteran Mauretanian frontier commander and bandit-chaser Quintus Pachomianus, a swashbuckling Italian aristocrat with a Numidian mother who was renowned for his daring escapades in catching brigands and had learnt how to be a desert tracker as an adventurous teenager when his 'heretic'-supporting father had been exiled for five years to his Numidian estates in the 690s. But its other most famous commander was the veteran Frankish officer Carolus from the Frankish Transrhenus kingdom, now usually its governor for Rome but bored and seeking military thrills, who led a solid 'square' of Frankish infantry to hold back a horde of camel-borne Darfur raiders in the opening battle of the campaign and by his heroic 'stand' for five hours gave Pachomianus with the main army time to come to his vanguard's rescue and catch the exhausted attackers resting in a 'wadi' between charges and slaughter them. The battle made Carolus 'the Hammer' (so-called from his axe-wielding demolition of his foes in battle) (OTL :Charles 'Martel', chief minister/commander and regent of Francia) a general famous throughout the Empire as the campaign was being played up by the capital's propaganda machine and the 'Acta Diurna' (the daily news-summaries put up in the Forum) as a great struggle of civilization against the heathen savages of the African interior.

Once the bandits had been destroyed and Darfur laid waste Pachomianus acted on orders sent from Rome beforehand to see that the raids did not recur by setting up a chain of fortresses, initially built in local mud-brick and staffed by around 8,000 tough Romans from the Mauretanian frontier of his own choice plus around 1,000 young and land-hungry Arab camel-riding warriors. They were to protect an incoming population of landless settlers from the cramped Nile valley who now began to set up a system of Romanised 'desert fringe' agriculture, growing dates and herding animals as the crop-yield was poor. It was decades before the local trade-route to Lake Chad brought any degree of revenue from Darfur to Rome and the new addition to the province of Upper Nubia to its East never really paid for itself or had major towns, but it did settle down and cease to be a home of brigands attacking Roman lands and the new acquisition was played up at Rome as Leo's great addition to the Empire, a sign of his success as a wise military leader, and a crucial link in the chain of Roman military and trading centres that was bringing the Empire into central Africa – where it was now able to send troops from Darfur to prop up friendly rulers around Lake Chad.

This also stimulated the creation of a regular slave-trade for enterprising Mediterranean and Egyptian traders to import captured or sold black tribesmen – starting with the 10,000 or so enslaved Darfurian warriors deported by the Empire to Nubia as slaves after the war to clear the region of dissidents – from the Empire's allied kingdoms of the Sahel, especially Bornu on Lake Chad, to Nubia and Egypt to work as agricultural labourers on the great corn – and cotton-growing 'latifundiae' set up along the river since Rome's annexation of the Dongola/Makuria region and then Alwa. This trade duly boomed in the mid-late 8th century with a slump in the price of slaves after the 732 war due to their availability but recovery later. The Christian Church elite in Dongola and Alwa, a mixture of pre-annexation locals and incoming upwardly mobile Egyptians and directed by the Patriarchate in Alexandria, were anyway hostile to the Darfurians and assorted black tribes further west and south-west due to their past raids on monasteries, farms, and churches in pre-annexation Nubia and regarded them as ethnically inferior 'savages'. So there was little or no local Church opposition to the growth of slavery and this came to aid the 'boom' in wealthy landed estates in Nubia after peace returned – and eventually the trickle of slaves down the Nile also affected Egyptian agriculture too as slave-owning entrepreneurs undercut independent small farmers and bought up their lands. In the long term this aided the decline of small farmers and thus of the latter's younger sons going into the Roman army in Egypt, with 'professional' middle-class urbanites (more likely to be able to afford to train and serve as officers) replacing them and the 'limitanei' forces in both Egypt and Nubia declining as opposed to 'elite' regiments – but this was a long-term problem.

War-victor Leo had now established himself as a successful and patriotic Emperor to please the elite in Rome and reassure the army 'high command', and as he lavished money on chariot-races for the populace in the capital when he was there and introduced a dozen or so more race-days to the annual Circus Maximus calendar he was able to fend off any lingering suspicion by the poor that he was as much of a greedy and self-serving careerist nobleman as 'fratricide' Basil I. His son's marriage to the daughter of the revered if unofficial 'martyr' Emperor Michael also helped, and his defence of the right to worship/revere icons was appreciated by the ordinary citizens of the West in general as they were increasingly fond of parading these painted images of the saints and the Virgin and Child at religious ceremonies and bowing and offering candles to them in church. By now the long-established central and eastern Mediterranean cultural habit of having mosaics or (in less expensive churches) murals of the Holy Family, Christ in glory and a retinue of angels like the Emperor and his court, or the great figures of the Old Testament in churches as an aid to devotion – or to present a coherent story of the Bible to the unlettered – had been taken up across most of the West, though not in the poorer and more puritanical churches of Britain and the Rhineland/Germany. Nobles and other patrons of churches were vying to show their holiness and obtain posthumous redemption from God for their sins by providing the money to decorate churches and monasteries, and so the 'Iconoclasts' in the East were seen as a threat to all this and the Emperor's firm stand against them was appreciated. Indeed, the 'iconodule' Leo and his latest wife Flavia provided their own cash to have churches in Rome, Ravenna, Mediolanum, and other major cities in Italy decorated with icons and new mosaics in the 730s and 740s as a deliberate act of challenge to the 'heretics' and the current Popes Gregorius III (in office 733–42) and Anthemius II (in office 742–50) were 'iconodules' who paid for the decoration of St Peter's Basilica in Rome with new mosaics and icons. In 736–8 Leo provocatively had the grand gateway of the Marble Palace, his main residence, rebuilt as a replica of the 6th-century 'Chalce' gatehouse to the Sacred Palace in Constantinople and had a huge mosaic of Christ in glory receiving the Emperor Constantine 'the Great' in Heaven erected there above the main gate – partly to make himself feel at home as a Constantinopolitan and partly as a gesture to the immanent (739) all-Empire Church Council in Rome whose delegates would visit the Palace.

The Council was mainly held to draw up and confirm new canons of ecclesiastical discipline and to reaffirm that 'Monotheletism', which was gaining support from academics in some Eastern universities as a way of having Monophysites admitted to public life and funding, was 'heretical'. But it also condemned Iconoclasm too and reaffirmed that all attacks on Church property in the Empire by zealous 'anti-idolatry' campaigners were to be punished severely and the perpetrattors forced to pay for repairing the damage. The edicts of the Council were to be rigorously enforced to restore order and extra police and troops were drafted into Syria, Palestine, and certain cities in Mesopotamia and coastal Asia Minor to force the dilatory local authorities to act and to round up suspects, and as a result some ugly clashes took place as arrested wreckers or rioters were put on trial and their supporters tried to storm courtrooms or prisons in the early 740s. Militant monks and armed peasants joined by Arab tribesmen took over Damascus and sacked the governor's palace and several leading churches in early 741 in retaliation for a round of convictions and similar attacks and violent arson took place across Syria and parts of inland Palestine. The police and troops in Jerusalem were cut off in the city by rioters for several weeks and barricading themselves in their new fortress while mobs 'cleansed' the churches of icons and whitewashed paintings of religious subjects as directed by self-proclaimed 'holy men'. This 'mob rule' by the self-styled 'sons of John the Baptist' in spring 742 led to martial law and mass repression in Palestine and the sentencing of several thousand arrested rioters to penal labour, often in chain gangs on government –owned landed estates or building projects in the cities of Caesarea Philippi, Ptolemais, and Joppa. The countryside of Galilee was in some areas virtually cleared of 'Iconoclast'-supporting militant, millenarian peasants and their Arab horse-breeding or camel-herding allies as local landowners hastened to provide the government with lists of 'subversives' who were often people refusing to pay higher rents or do labour on their private fields. As a result much land was either swept clear of small farmers (owners or tenants) in favour of imported labourers, some of them slaves and all of them worse treated by their landlords, or else was sold off to rich entrepreneurs who could sense a bargain and now became absentee landlords there.

Some of these were indeed Jews from the commercial classes of Mesopotamia, grown rich from the booming Indian trade, and so there was a degree of revival of Jewish ownership of land – and later of settlement by less wealthy tenants – in Galilee as a result of the 740s Iconoclast riots and also a large number of Arab tribes who had backed the riots, out of idealism or out of a 'get rich quick' interest in loot, were removed from marginal lands in eastern Syria and Transjordan. New, usually Greco-Aramaic tenant farmers were moved in and started to breed their own animals or else to try to revive declining local irrigation – the latter needing government aid which the relevant ministry in Rome provided from 745. The trouble also spread to poorer districts of Constantinople where opinion was more evenly divided between those who believed in icons as a way to show your devotion and so win Divine favour and those who believed that they were idolatrous and had to be destroyed to avoid Divine wrath, with a plague in the city in 742 being blamed by the rival groups on either icons or iconoclasts major clashes followed in spring-summer 743 as the Iconoclasts tried to forcibly 'cleanse' churches by whitewashing icons and mosaics or smashing the former. Religious and secular statues were also attacked as 'blasphemous' and some of the Ancient Greek artwork set up around the Augusteum square by the Sacred Palace, Senate House, and cathedral of Hagia Sophia (by Constantine in the late 320s) was smashed along with statues up the 'Mese' avenue to the West at the Forum of Constantine. This led to Patriarch Anastasius having all the rioters he and his officials could find tried and dealt with for 'blasphemy' and attacking Church property by his courts as the civil government was too scared (possibly of working-class Iconoclast soldiers) to be firm.

A renewed outbreak of rioting after a series of harsh sentences of rioters in May 743 ended with Hagia Sophia itself on fire and its grand basilica-like rectangular 'hall' roof falling in, and as a result of this vandalism in his own city the Emperor took a hand and declared that the old cathedral, erected after similar riots in the 400s, was too small and old-fashioned and needed to be replaced by a modern building. As fond of Eastern styles of architecture as Caracalla had been but usually more cautious about the cost, he now commissioned a grand competition to find a suitable architect and announced that he would fund the rebuilding himself. A new, 'Hellenist' Praefect with architectural pretensions and former service in Persia (Leontius Basilicus) was appointed to oversee the work and to demolish the rest of the roofless cathedral, and as the Emperor had the final say in the competition the winning design was submitted by a skilled ex-military engineer called Andronicus of Miletus (d 770) who had moved on from designing army camps and 'Ephebic' training-facilities under Basil I to building civic baths and council office complexes in Syria and Cappadocia. The winning design was for a huge, square building with a central dome and two supporting (East and West) semi-domes plus a grand square courtyard to the West and a colonnade onto the Augusteum square to the South, and the main dome was to be the highest and largest in the entire Empire and to dwarf the city of Constantinople's skyline, sitting on top of the final hill before the Bosphorus and visible for many miles by sea and land. The cost and engineering problems would be huge, but Leo was enthralled and put Andronicus in the Senate as his first 'consul of the architects' (from now on a regular title for the Emperor's chosen head of and advisor on the architectural profession). All the money and manpower that he would need were guaranteed – an action that probably hastened the retirement of the cautious 'Count of the Sacred Largesses' Decimus Quartinus (in office 736–43) who was already having to cope with the restructuring of agriculture in Nubia and Syria/Palestine/Arabia Petraea (Transjordan) and the annexation of Darfur.

The Emperor installed his obedient and more free-handed 'Count of the Privy Purse' Archelaus Archetinius, in charge of his private spending, to run the finance ministry instead and provide all the cash that was needed for Hagia Sophia. The project became the 'signature' one of his reign, much criticized for waste and extravagance by sections of the Western nobility and intellectuals but approved of by the Church, and to keep an eye on it Leo spent the winters of 744–5 and 746–7 in Constantinople and called in there too en route to Syria and Mesopotamia on his next grand Eastern tour in spring 748, spending notably less time in the West than before and having no more tours of the main provinces of the Empire West of Italy. In winter 745–6 he was in Rome but otherwise in these years he was mostly on tour in Greece, Asia Minor, Sicily, North Africa (Carthage in summer 745 and Alexandria to Thebes in Egypt in summer 746), and the Balkans. This led to grumbles that this Easterner would rather centre the Empire in that region just like Caracalla had done, but he did not neglect the army and was careful to attend military manoeuvres most years and to create well-funded new regiments (or 'tagmata', a Greek term reflecting the fact that Greek was his own 'home' language). These provided more jobs for aspirant young aristocrats and served to add new cavalry 'wings' to the armies of the lower Danube, Armenia/Iberia/Colchis, Mesopotamia, and Egypt/Nubia staffed largely by local nobles. Leo visited the central and lower Danube as well as Thrace and Macedonia on his Balkan tour in summer 747 and although he normally avoided the more cold and bleak climates of the Empire he made his way with a large entourage as far north as Augusta Prahavorum to open new civic buildings there and meet the vassal king (Ardaric III) of the Langobards and most of the Church leadership of his kingdom. But by this point his latest divorce and his remarriage in 741 to Maria Raupenia, the twenty-two-year-old greedy and party-obsessed socialite daughter of a major bureaucratic 'fixer' ex-colleague of his from Constantinople, was undermining his reputation as she was much his junior and more venal and demanding than his previous wives and even his complaisant Church supporters were uncomfortable at his domestic life – which the presence of several bastard sons and daughters of his from 720s liaisons at his court exacerbated.

Maria was a cunning as well as spendthrift young woman and she was careful to be publicly philanthropic and to appear in modest attire at religious festivals and church services, be seen giving out prizes and free clothes at Italian schools for the poor and orphanages, and to spend money on hospitals, homes for the elderly, and free educational grants for brainy poor boys and girls in Rome and other leading Italian cities. But she was still disliked by the majority of the local nobility as an interloper and was widely attacked by intellectuals as a brainless social climber and by 'off message' Churchmen as a 'whore' and Prince Probus and his wife would have nothing to do with her and were said to have asked the Emperor to get rid of her to no avail. As the Emperor aged he came more under the influence of his final wife and began to make questionable appointments, most notably of various relatives of hers to court offices and a protégé and alleged former love of hers as Praefect of Antioch. But this rarely affected governance and his development of the idea of the Emperor as a majestic embodiment of the state and leader of an impressive round of annual ceremonial and official receptions and parties, much criticized by younger and 'Hellenic republican' enthusiasts at Rome, Syracuse, and Athens universities, had credible roots in the approaches to ruling of Theodosius I and II rather than being just a sign of ageing megalomaniac pomposity as was claimed by his foes. His tame historian of the history of ceremonial and its statecraft uses in ancient Egypt, Babylonia, Achaemenid and Sassanid Persia, and Diocletian's and Constantine I's Rome, learned and multi-lingual Gaius Capellanius from Bononia (son of a headmaster there), was encouraged by Leo to complete his magisterial work on ceremony – aided by a team of scholars paid for by the Emperor – as early as the late 730s. He became 'Consul for Statecraft' and a professor at Rome's University as an Imperial protégé, and by Leo's final years was drawing up an exhaustive 'Book of Ceremonial' based on 5th-century procedure at the Sacred Palace at Constantinople that Leo intended to be his template for the annual rituals and other ceremonial occasions at his Marble Palace in Rome. An enlarged Palace staff with their duties and even their official robes on all occasions prescribed by the 'Book' and 5th-century – Constantinopolitan court practice was put into motion to enact Leo's and Capellanius' vision of the Court as the 'Mirror of Heaven' and an inspiration to its humble and obedient citizens. Those few learned intellectual or well-informed ministerial Romand who were aware of court ritual and theory in contemporary T'ang China at their court in Chang'an found similarities between them and wondered if the tales of the Chinese court delivered by a (very rare) Chinese embassy to the Emperor in Alexandria in spring 746 had gone to Leo's head and he fancied himself as the 'Son of Heaven' like the Chinese Emperor, but his arguments had valid if not exactly Augustan reasoning and some saw a parallel with Constantine 'the Great' in his final years.

Leo certainly now spent more time in Constantine 's great re-foundation city on the Bosphorus than in Rome and from autumn 748 he was based at the Sacred Palace virtually permanently. But this was probably more a matter of supervising his great project of Hagia Sophia and he proclaimed that the huge cathedral, whose dome reflected Heaven in a way that the basilica-like aisled hall of St Peter's in Rome could not, was the architectural equivalent of his 'Book of Ceremonies' – based ceremonial in creating an image of Heaven for the public to look up to and to visually display Rome's mission of glory and stability. This political reasoning was understood if not fully approved of by his heir and his ministers, but tolerating Empress Maria's increasingly brazen larceny and her looting of Imperial jewellery, robes, and estates for her private funds and enjoyment was resented across the political spectrum and even mentioned by the Church leadership – awkwardly – to the Emperor. After she ordered her husband, successfully, to quash legal proceedings against various corrupt members of her large personal court in spring 749 the minister for legal affairs ('Quaestor') resigned. Leo replaced him with his wife's lawyer and shrugged off the resignation of three more ministers, reputedly scared by his wife's threat to leave him if he did not stand up to his 'servants', and his final triumph of the ceremonial opening of the semi-complete Hagia Sophia that September enabled him to boast in his formal speech that 'I have outdone Soloman' – i.e. in the building of a new 'Temple' – though in fact only the main dome, not its side-domes, was complete and the whole building was not finished until 761. (The OTL new cathedral of Hagia Sophia to this plan, and the Emperor's boasts about it, were in fact by Justinian in the 6th century.)

The eight-hour ceremony with its thousands of lay and Church guests and subsequent banquet and firework-display was a triumph of Imperial glory worthy of a Chinese Emperor and the 'Eastern capital' had now acquired its 'signature' greatest building, the largest church in the Empire. But already the generals and ministers gathered for the ceremony were using the time to plot against the Empress, who appeared at the service of dedication dripping with jewels, and only two weeks later a delegation of senior army and navy commanders were led by Prince Probus to the Emperor's apartments at the Sacred Palace and presented him with an order to sign arresting his wife on pain of his being declared insane by his doctors and locked up in one of his local villas if he did not give in. A long list of the Empress' corrupt practices was presented to Leo and apparently he wept when he read it and ended up apologising to his son and calling for his sword so he could kill his wife in person. But even putting her on trial would have been deeply embarrassing so in the end she was merely confined to her apartments 'ill' and later removed to a remote villa up the coast of the Euxine at Mesembria, *en route* to a nunnery in the remote Balkan Range mountains where she had spent a lot of money on a private retreat for hunting but this now served as a luxury prison for her. In March 750 she was divorced and all her assets were seized and her court was broken up and many of its personnel put on trial and sent to prison. Though Leo IV lived until a seizure finished him off on 8 October 750, aged seventy, he was a broken husk of a man who spent most of his time hidden from the public and he did not even have the pride and dedication to keep to his planned ceremonial 'round' but left most of it to his son, now co-emperor as of 12 February, with the Empress' role going to Irene. The senior Emperor left his Eastern court for a supposedly short-term restorative tour of the Aegean in June 750 and settled on the island of Naxos where he ended up falling ill and dying at a villa which had been seized from his wife earlier. With his reputation ruined by the scandals that had brought his final marriage to an end all his solid successes were less remembered than his doting on Maria and his tolerance of her greed as Probus II succeeded to the throne aged 39 and by the latter's marriage his three sons (Probianus, Justinian, and Justin) restored the line of Caracalla and ultimately of Constantine III to the Imperial (i.e. Marble) Palace in Rome .

Chapter 6

Probus II 750–765: The Military Hero. Leo IV's Son

Probus was seen by the relieved lay, Church, and military elite as a man who would keep up the late Emperor's more stabilizing policies and was not averse to his 'hard line' autocratic attitude to dissent either but was not as spendthrift or as open to disabling and embarrassing female influence, and indeed the new Empress Irene was a shrewd and sensible operator who had a considerable degree of 'behind the scenes' influence herself but in a much more acceptable way than Leo's increasingly wayward choice of wives – and she was also capable of handling a large budget sensibly and appearing glamorous in rich robes and jewels without overspending or overstepping the mark of accepted' upper-class taste. Irene was also a major and plausible patroness of Catholic nunneries, schools, hospitals, and homes for elderly people and went on pilgrimages every year without this appearing to be too obviously just 'spin' and she evidently did care for the poorer classes and had a sense of Christian mission, distributing aid to the poor in person after various famines and after the serious eruption of Mount Etna and earthquakes in Sicily in 752, and unlike Leo's later wives she boosted rather than undermined her husband's popularity and also saw that once her sons were old enough they joined her on pilgrimages and relief-missions to learn that not all the Empire's citizens lived in comfort and splendour like the palace aristocrats that surrounded the Imperial Family. Meanwhile Probus, a military man by training and inclination but aware of what was expected of the Emperor, spent this first months in power 'reading himself in' with discussions with the senior ministers and bureaucrats plus a wide circle of Italian nobles who had experience of government and organized a finance ministry overhaul of Leo's recent budgets in great detail, and once he had all the facts at hand he proceeded to cut back court expenditure by around 15 per cent and sack a lot of supernumerary officials with little to do, led by almost all of ex-Empress Maria's relatives and proteges, and also sacked all those ministers who had not kept a grip on spending and appointments in the 740s but had exploited Leo's growing carelessness by corruption, waste, or selling off offices and grants to a mixture of their own friends and anyone who would pay 'up front'.

Unlike Michael's reign in 709–17 there was no ostentatious and narrow-minded (though undoubtably moral) round of appointments of virtuous and the provably 'holy' or temptation-free 'outsiders' from the usual elite and most of Probus' choices were both competent and fully experienced, often as deputy ministers or as long-term administrators, and as most were aged in their fifties and sixties and had worked in government long enough to know exactly how the administration ran this new regime was known as the 'government of the greybeards'. The 'Master of Offices' in 751–6 and 756–9, Cassius Conginius and Demetrius Agronopilus, were both aged in their late sixties at appointment and the 'Counts of Sacred Largesses' in 751–6 and 756–62, Leo Graecinus and Titus Jasperianus, were both in their mid-sixties at appointment and had previously worked in Basil I's household so the Empress knew them from girlhood. But all four were highly competent and Probus also made some unexpected promotions of unknown but recommended provincials from as far afield as Britain, Dacia, Egypt, and Mesopotamia to ministerial rank after sifting through his local administrators' reports on capable junior or middling officials in their regions. His Praefects of Rome were all staid and respectable – and Catholic – elderly nobles who had either a long family pedigree linked back to the emerging Catholic 'new men' service nobility in Rome/Mediolanum/Ravenna of the 4th and early 5th centuries or had a family tradition of civil service work for over a century in Rome. The same applied to most of the holders of the senior administrative or honorary posts governing the capital while in Constantinople – which he did not forget despite mostly living in Rome – he reverted to the use of the main administrative 'service nobility' of the 7th and early 8th centuries and sidelined ex-Empress Maria's 'pushy' allies, most of whom the older nobility had looked down on, so in some respectable quarters he was preferred as a ruler to Leo despite Leo's expenditure on that city.

Probus also resorted carefully to the use of the 'old' service nobility of the 4th to the 7th centuries in his choice of senior post-holders in the civic governments of Antioch and Alexandria and in the provincial governments of Syria and Egypt. He imported some of the most successful office-holders there to work for him in Rome from the mid-750s, not 'rocking the boat' by reaching out to the minority religious sects, but in these cases he also brought in more of the older, Seleucid (Syria) and Early Empire and Ptolemaic (Egypt) administrative dynasties. In Mesopotamia he was as careful to bring the non-Greek landed and administrative dynasties into office-holding as Diomedes and Caracalla had done. The 'pool' of local (well-educated elite) talent used for the administrations of these key provinces were now extended as a deliberate policy, using men of wealth who had an interest in keeping stability – and aligning them as well as the landed nobility to the central government as the source of wealth. This –

probably deliberately – undercut any autonomist urges that a would-be rebel could use. All round the Emperor's policy in choosing who was to help him govern and how was one of co-operation with the existing elites and stressing stability not experiment, but he did keep up the overall 'arc' of Leo's new propaganda campaign on using the Imperial office as the symbol of divinely-backed concord and unity and of making the Imperial office and court reflect the order of Heaven. This was stressed in 'official' creations of new mosaics and murals in churches, especially in major cities, that showed the Emperor and court in their full glory with Christ and the angels and saints – which 'tapped into' the current fashion for icons and subtly made the Emperor a sort of object of worship or at least veneration, as Leo had intended. The actual amount of expenditure and ceremonial at court was cut back but it remained formal and full of the ritual and dignity that the 'Book of Ceremonies' had prescribed. The Emperor continued to lead ceremonies in and around Rome and co-operated fully in this with the Church, whose officials were often in attendance on him to stress its support for him, in return for him fully and explicitly backing the 'Iconodules'. He had no interest in the theological issues. But as a matter of 'power' he arranged for the law ministry to fall on the Eastern 'Iconoclast' rioters and saboteurs with the full vigour of Roman justice and send hundreds of protesters and 'subversive' speakers and writers to do slave-labour in the mines every year until the continuing but declining protests in the Levant were reduced to minor levels.

The creation by Probus of an overall official policy of caution and reassurance to elites also applied to his own past area of specialist concern, the military, where contrary to expectations he did not insist on putting in his 'own men' in senior command in 750 once he had sacked Leo's equivocating Praetorian Praefect. He chose to appoint a mixture of long-term dynastic stalwarts and 'career officers' who had not served in command positions on the frontiers for several decades but had progressed through 'HQ' administrative roles, and the generals who had helped him to face down Leo and Maria in 749–50 were not noticeably rewarded in promotion but had assorted grants and sinecures put their way and mostly ended up in the Senate within a decade. Probus kept a grip on military policy himself but did not immediately risk any rise in expenditure by risky ventures as he had to cut back civil spending after Leo's vast projects and was reassuring his civilian administrators by retrenchment. So when the last king of the Merovingian dynasty presiding over their kingdom in Transrhenus, Childeric IV – more of an honorary figurehead than a real ruler – was pushed aside by his chief minister Pepin 'the Short (d 768), son and successor of Basil I's friend and ally the Roman general Carolus 'the Hammer', in 751 this was done by agreement with Probus after an embassy to his court by Pepin. The latter was made 'Consul of the Franks' and given a seat in the Senate. (These are all OTL Frankish figures of this era.) Pepin's religious-minded younger brother Carloman, currently a respected monk and amateur theological writer at the monastery of St Benedict at Montus Cassinum in central Italy into which Pepin had pushed him into entering in 743 when Carolus died, was an acquaintance of the philanthropic and shrine-visiting Empress Irene. She visited his monastery from time to time and she probably approached her husband ahead of the embassy after a 'tip-off' by Carloman, and Probus avoided the temptation to fully annex the province as a normal Roman region under a normal governor sent from Rome though from now on Roman officials played a greater role there, usually using the regional title of 'counts' (i.e. local governors) and with some ethnic connection to the Franks to reassure this proud and 'touchy' autonomist people. Probus also avoided the temptation to finish off the declining Langobard kingdom (S of the Baltic) and annex it to the Empire though in 753 he received the vigorous new king, Liutprand (OTL Lombard King, but in Italy), in Rome and told him firmly that in return for military and economic aid he was expected to do what the Emperor said and assist Rome by keeping his plundering sub-rulers and barons under control.

As the Slav settlers continued to occupy more of the semi-fertile agricultural lands and timber-trade-centre forests west of the river Bug the kingdom was slowly transformed into a predominantly ethnically Slav one. The area loyal to and paying taxes/troops to the Langobard king was reduced to a 'core' around the Vistula. East of the Bug and the Pripyat Marshes were more Slav lands in the forests North of Kievum and to the south and south-east the steppes were ruled by the Empire's Khazar allies who supplied Rome with regular timber and furs down the Dnieper and Don to their Euxine ports, along with sporadic contributions of horse-borne troops to Roman campaigns. Unlike the 'barbarian'-despising Leo Probus was as interested in the steppes as military planners were and kept an eye on politics and inter-tribal rivalries among the Khazars and he also gave money and men to the Church in Constantinople as it launched an orthodox missionary venture there in the early 750s, invited by the current 'Khagan' who was considering moving his people away from 'primitive' animism to a more sophisticated, monotheistic religion. The Khagan invited Roman orthodox Christian, 'renegade' Monophysite Christian, and Jewish representatives to his court to put their religions' viewpoints to his nobles. If there was actually any formal debate between the religions as alleged by later Roman literary sources this was inconclusive, but the representatives of the Jewish faith had most success in converting locals around the Khazar capital of Itil on the lower Volga. Allegedly the Roman faith was feared by most nobles as bringing political subordination to Rome – and in the coming decades the

Empire's Jewish business communities in Constantinople and Ctesiphon built up close links with co-religionists at Itil and made large profits out of the Khazar fur-trade that financed their setting up new banks and export-businesses. To a certain degree Roman traders made purchases of land too, as some of the older landed nobility in inland Asia Minor began to move their assets from a region afflicted by serious droughts to better irrigated coastal regions in Lydia, Ionia, Caria, and Cilicia. But if the Khazars were wary of Roman influence they at least remained loyal allies and kept the latest incoming migrant tribes in the lower Don and later the lower Dnieper regions, the Magyars, under control as vassals and forbade them to annoy the Empire by raiding to the lower Danube. With the settled Swedes across the Baltic in Scandinavia (who by c. 740 had annexed the Geatish kingdom in Scania) continued to keep the peace with Rome and supply it with timber and mercenaries the only Northern neighbours who were giving the new regime of Probus concern were the Western Turkic confederation in the lands north of the Oxus and Jaxartes.

The lack of interest in or military expenditure on this region under Michael I (who had deplored the brutal Roman conquest of Sogdiana in any case and so annoyed his frontier commanders there that revolt was frequently threatened under his regime), the more financially generous but preoccupied Basil I, and the 'barbarian-despising Leo IV had left the frontier garrisons on the Jaxartes in a poor position. In 747 a local incursion over the Jaxartes by a major grouping of restive, land-seeking Turks in flight from their 'Khagan', head of the main Western Turkic confederation of (Chinese ally) Turkestan, had led to a general abandonment of the river frontier by the Romans to save their stronger and closer-linked forts around Maracanda. As Leo had not bothered to intervene it was left to Probus in 750–1 to order in 25,000 troops from Mesopotamia, 10,000 from Bactria, and 5,000 from Kabul and Gandhara (which could not spare garrisons so easily) to reconquer the Jaxartes valley, the force being led by veteran ex-'*dux*' of Sogdiana Justus Julianus who Leo had sacked in 742 for alleged rudeness at a party about his private life. The Turks, a mixture of several tribes not used to fighting as one coherent unit and apparently minus one of their best warlords who the Romans had bribed to withdraw from their army beforehand, were defeated in an open cavalry clash as the outnumbered Romans fired projectiles full of 'Greek Fire' into their ranks and fled north over the Jaxartes. The Romans then proceeded to retake the lost forts one by one and put in stronger garrisons, armed with 'Greek Fire' and heavy artillery and with larger storehouses built to keep extra supplies in case of siege. These were to be inter-connected by a roaming force of 8,000 cavalry 'limitanei' plus 2000 hired Arab nomad archers sent by the allied mercantile regime at Mecca and some 1,500 local pro-Roman Turks from tribes in the Kara Kum deserts to the south-west on the lower Oxus who already paid tribute to the Empire. But the Emperor did not order any crossing of the Jaxartes to punish the main Western Turkic realm for defying his orders to send him tribute and mercenary help to put down the incursion. Probably the Turks would have been in more hostile mode and could even have aided the 'rebel' Turkic 'squatters' in Transoxiana if they had not been too busy in their own revolt against their regional overlords, the T'ang of China.

The regional Chinese garrisons in the Tarim basin East of the Dzungarian Gates pass in the Pamir Mountains, the westernmost province of the huge Chinese Empire as the 'Protectorate-General of the West' based at Turfan and Kashgar plus other lesser oasis towns, had been exercising suzerainty over the Turks around Lake Balkhash since the 650s. Their Khagans were forced to supply tribute and troops to China as the Khazars did to Rome. But now in 751 the power of the distant T'ang Emperor (currently Hsuan Tsung, as grandiose a ruler as Leo IV had been in Rome) was declining and the Western Turks had cast off their vassalage, and while Rome was reconquering Transoxiana they were defeating an invading Chinese army at the 'Battle of the Talas River' (exact site unknown) and sending the T'ang troops back in disorder east of the Pamirs. The end of Chinese rule in the steppes West of the Pamirs after a century left the field open for Rome and there was later criticism of Probus for not taking this opportunity to force vassalage on the Turks – or split up their confederation and keep rival rulers at each other's throats. Supposedly he could have taken over the role previously held by China or even to advance his frontier to the Dzungarian Gates pass and penned the Chinese in (and secured the customs-dues of that crucial trade-route 'bottleneck'). But at the time he was not keen to risk defeat or spend extra cash and instead the Roman frontier was fixed at the Jaxartes again and the Empire did not seek to meddle in the fluid inter-tribal wars among rival bands of Turks as long as they all steered clear of raiding Roman territory. The danger of a Chinese revival was avoided as in 756 Emperor Hsuan Tsung (like Leo IV, with a controversial wife and restive generals) was to be temporarily overthrown and his dynasty's power permanently damaged by the huge rebellion of his chief Turkish general, An Lu-Shan. As far as Probus was concerned the restoration of the Jaxartes frontier was his sole goal in the 751 war and any steppe campaign would require too much risk and too many resources, and instead he just played up the war as bringing the work of Claudius III in the East to a logical conclusion and ordered his generals in Sogdiana to keep the Jaxartes garrisons at full strength from now on.

Instead the Emperor concentrated his military efforts on targets that were easier to tackle, and as the situation in Caledonia in Britain – a far smaller and easier 'front' for his army – presented opportunities he made the most of the threat posed to Rome there by the warlord Aengus of the Picts (OTL). In the early 730s this charismatic warlord had finally revived his kingdom, deprived of its richer lowlands in the east from Forth to Spey by the Empire, by using Irish and Orkney mercenaries to take on and defeat his rivals in Dalriada – to whose throne he had a claim via his mother – after their wise, Romanophile king Selbach of Lorne (ruled 695 – 726, as in OTL) abdicated to become a monk. The 'civilized' and learned Selbach, who had been in exile in southern Britain as a youth after a previous round of civil strife in Dalriada and had learnt Latin and studied the law in Britain's only legal school in Verulamium, had allied himself to the Empire and its Church and even ordered the Church of Dalriada (centred on the island monastery of Iona) to abandon its 'Celtic' Irish Church customs for those of Rome and to celebrate Easter on the Roman date, drawing up the first written law-code for Dalriada. He had created a small mercantile town next to his main hillfort at Dunadd, but civil war had followed his abdication and departure first for Rome as a pilgrim and then to Ireland as a monk and Aengus the Pict had taken over his throne and imposed a Pictish-Dalriadan union. This had given him the troops needed to dominate western Caledonia and raid the Roman-allied kingdom of Strathclyde for two decades. Leo IV had ignored local Roman commanders' requests for a campaign to rein the Picts in as they were a minor irritant unworthy of his attentions in his mind, but now in 752 Probus decided to 'pick on' the Picts and secure a useful victory. Accordingly 20,000 troops were despatched to Britain and the Hibernian Sea fleet was ordered to land a refugee Dalriadan prince who had been living in exile in Gaul since the early 730s, Aed 'the Fair' (OTL figure), in Dalriada to start a rebellion aided by Roman troops.

While this revolt was tying down the Picts in Dalriada and Roman ships loaded with 'Greek Fire' were keeping Aengus' troops back from attacking the rebel positions on Loch Linnhe the main Roman army, led by 'Count of Britain' Aulus Varianus, marched up the Tay into the heartland of Pictland. He drove off Pictish skirmishers to secure the passes over the Cairngorms, his Alpine and Pyrenean skirmishers scrambling up steep slopes to push the Picts off their ridges, and a major battle at Inverlochy at the head of Loch Linnhe saw the Picts defeated in open combat as they tried to stop their realm being cut in two by one Roman 'push' north-east from Dunadd and another south-west from Loch Ness. In the meantime more Romans had pushed into the wilderness of the Ross and Caithness moorlands and driven the local, northern Picts back into hiding in the bogs and pine-woods. With all of Pictland except the higher mountains occupied the defeated Aengus chose to flee to Ireland and his lords had to come to terms to save their people from starving.

This time the Romans had come to stay and the entire south-east of the Pictish realm, lying on the Southern side of the Loch Ness – Loch Linnhe corridor, was annexed to the Empire and a 'rump' Pictish state was only allowed to keep the lands of Ross and Caithness. These were either too mountainous or too full of desolate moorland to be worth conquering and in any case did not support much of a population, and as Dalriada was restored under Aed 'the Fair' as a Roman vassal the Empire set up a new road lined with forts to keep control of the eastern coast route north from Inverness to the headland of 'Orca' (as in the geographer Ptolemy's 2nd century AD map of Britain, opposite Orkney). Probus could and did claim 'Caledonia capta est' and put that on his coins. As 'Caledonicus' he visited Britain to receive the submission of assorted Pictish chiefs in 753, heading North as far as 'Severiana' (Perth) on the Tay in the first Imperial visit to Caledonia for centuries. With about a third of the Pictish population of the annexed area deported to southern Britain and Gaul and new settlers, many of them continental Germans or Danes, introduced to farm the more valuable agricultural land along the Loch Ness – Loch Linnhe corridor most of the desolate uplands were turned over to breeding tough mountain sheep and goats. Enterprising farmers – some from southern Britain and others from the Alpine mountain provinces – were brought in to set up large new sheep – and goat-'ranches' which exported their produce in annual 'droves' to markets in the Caledonian lowlands around the Clyde and Forth estuaries.

The mostly bleak and inhospitable Pictish kingdom was not much of an economic gain for the Empire and compared to the rest of Britain it did not develop usefully large towns for centuries while allied Dalriada was too small and too poorly populated to give much in tribute or mercenary troops. But Imperial propaganda still claimed that Probus had completed the work that Julius Caesar had begun in 55 BC and the Emperor finished his British trip, which also saw him and his wife visit the shrines at Verulamium (to St Alban), Caerleon (to SS Aaron and Julius), Menevia (to St David), and Lindisfarne (to St Cuthbertus), with a naval tour round the north of the island. This enabled him to land on the Outer Hebrides and attend a 'summit' with the 'High King' Domnhall of Ireland (OTL figure) on the island of Iona at the shrine of St Columcille. The Empire and its Church now made the Abbot of Iona the 'Bishop of the Isles' and the Churches of Dalriada and Pictland were made part of that of Britain, governed by the archbishop/'metropolitan' of Eburacum. With the British military problem seemingly sorted out Probus faced cost-cutting requests from his 'high command' s accountants to rationalize the no-longer-needed British military establishment and abolish the 'Countship' of Britain and the Hibernian Sea fleet. He prudently decided that they might yet be needed to deal with pirates – not least the continuing threat from bored and land-hungry Norse warlords – so he merely cut the British military command from 18,000 troops (the equivalent of three and a half legions) to 14,000 and cut a quarter of the Hibernian Sea fleet. The 'Classis Britannia' fleet in the North Sea, protector of the local mercantile shipping and trade 'boom' from Britain to Frisia and the Danish lands, was not cut at all though most of the 'Saxon Shore' forts had been 'stood down' by c. 720 as major barracks and were now kept as at most minor naval bases. After a winter at Lutetia (Paris) in Gaul Probus went on for an inspection tour of Jutland and the Danish islands, a 'first' for an Emperor, in spring 754 and opened new civic buildings in the Danish islands' provincial capital, Claudiana (Copenhagen), before inaugurating the new anti-pirate fortress and naval base at Elsinorium nearby on the Sound.

A 'summit' with the king of the Swedes to sign a new trade-treaty was followed by the first Imperial naval cruise on the Baltic and Probus visited and ordered the annexation and settling by armed 'limitanei' of the island of Bornholm. This was done so that Rome could control the amber-trade to the Lithuanian coast and impose new customs-duties on it. Then in another 'first' while his wife and court travelled back by sea to the Rhine and up the river to Basilium he led his troops on a military crossing of the allied Langobardic kingdom to call in on his vassal king Liutprand at the fortress-town of Varsavia (Warsaw) on the middle Vistula and celebrate their alliance with a week of feasts. There were also elaborate performances of grand Germanic oral heroic poetry (which led to an interest in this little-known cultural art-form by some of the more open-minded courtiers in his entourage and speculation about what sort of parallel poems had been recited about early Roman heroes in the early Republican era). Compared to Leo IV with his almost total and culturally snobbish ignorance about the Far North Probus was almost, as one court poet called him, the 'Caesar of the North' and 'Voyager to Ultimate Thule' who was bringing the fur-wearing Northern tribes into the embrace of Roman civilization. But once he had established his reputation in 751–4 as a great warlord and an intrepid voyager he seems to have given up on his early enthusiasm for travel and (cheap and easy) annexations. From 755 he restricted his tours to the Mediterranean with one to Spain and Lusitania in 756, one to North Africa from Tingis to Carthage in 757, one to Egypt and Cyrene in 758, one to Palestine involving a pilgrimage to Jerusalem, Bethlehem and Galilee in 759, one to Constantinople and Asia Minor in 760 ending with attending the year's Olympics in late August, one to northern Greece, Thrace, and Macedonia in 761, and one to Illyria, Dalmatia, and inland to Noricum and Pannonia in 762.

In the winters Probus was following a (less ostentatious or expensive) version of Leo's annual round of ceremonial in Rome and in the autumns he generally visited either southern Gaul (where he had hunting-trips to the Narbo Martius and Nemausus areas), northern Italy, or Sicily for the hunting. But he kept up his full routine of Imperial business when he was not in Rome by having papers sent to him by fast horseback postal relays and indeed he maintained a close eye on the task of improving communications in general to bring the Empire closer together and keep Rome informed of developments across its realm. He installed a new 'Minister for Roads' with a specialist department to keep up regular road – and bridge-repairs and experimenting in the late 750s with a system of signals involving flashing lights from fires on hilltop stations along the main routes to the north to bring urgent messages from the Carpathian, Oder, and lower Danube frontiers to Rome so that any 'barbarian' raids or other crises would be quickly announced to the 'high command' and to himself. The Empire's unity was seen as dependant on fast links across its length – not new, but now prioritised by a restless itinerant ruler.

As his confidence in his ability to arrange governance how he thought fit without the danger of revolt began to grow after his military successes Probus showed signs of wanting to tinker with the system that he had inherited. He took an interest in making the organs of government more effective rather than just using them as a useful 'career pathway' for the elites to win the latter's support, and he held a series of seminars in 762–3 in Rome and at his holiday villas with leading administrative figures, private advisers, and university academics on potential changes. The examinations-sytem was seen by some of the more 'pro-autocracy' and 'pro-efficiency' academics who he called in as crucial to reform, in providing a pathway to success and reward for ambitious men of humble background who had no family hereditary 'stake' in seeing that things did not change and injustices or other failings were not remedied. In this instance there was direct evidence of some Chinese 'input' as some traders and geographers who had travelled on expeditions along the 'Silk Route' to T'ang China were among those who the Emperor consulted. Ironically the seemingly impressive and responsive bureaucratic monolith of T'ang dynastic power was being overturned – temporarily but with a lasting lack of confidence – in this period in China itself by the sort of over-mighty military figures and proud 'war winners' with their own loyal armies that Rome had tamed centuries before. But it was China's pre-756 glory that was presented by its impressed visitors to Probus and apparently he confirmed that he was interested in securing as stable a regime for the Roman Empire but without the sort of swollen ceremonial and unwieldy, cost-consuming court – or trend for flattering glorification of the Emperor regardless of his personal failings – that his father had sought to create. Leo had let his greedy last wife and her cronies leech off the state and that was unacceptable to the more moral and restrained Probus quite apart from the 'good example' of a virtuous and philanthropic Empress which his wife was setting successfully. As a result of these discussions Probus began to replace some 'old nobility' ministers who were seen as complacent and non-responsive (though capable of keeping the current government functioning well) in 764–5 with younger men from 'self-made' provincial backgrounds.

The 'greybeards' who had dominated the 750s as a force for stability had served the Empire well after a period of crisis in the mid-late 740s but now Probus wanted to try out some initiatives and to bring in tougher operatives who had had to fight hard and show what they could do to get to senior office. To help this he arranged for his new 'deputy Master of the Offices' in charge of the examinations-system, self-made former Mesopotamian peasant Procles Aristarchus (who had a Greek farmer father and an Arab mother from an nomad family), and a commission of younger bureaucrats selected by the latter to look at overhauling the examinations' line of questions and marking-system to aid the progress of brainy and flexible but less educated applicants. The idea was to downgrade the importance of questions based on the 'classics' of Roman and Ancient Greek literature and increase the amount of questions where a good memory and an ability to think and respond to unusual circumstances of problems would be displayed. Though in the event some offended civil servants who put a knowledge of the classics first as necessary to display your 'civilised standards' and cultural prowess managed to hold up the implementation of the new examinations-questions this did come into effect in the early 770s and boosted the number of non-elite entrants to and victors of the examinations, catapulting a greater proportion of those of humble origins into good civil service jobs (and on to senior rank by the 790s).

This conscious move to extend meritocracy and create new bureaucratic dynasties of loyal and capable civil servants and senior office-holders was played up as the Emperor's duty to God and to his people to utilize their talents and not just look to the selfish and indulgent 'old' aristocracy for support. But he also carefully cultivated the latter in practice with his 'inclusive' and increasingly large hunting-parties for regional aristocrats on his tours and in particular on his visits to southern Gaul, northern Italy, and Sicily. His use of supportive Catholic propaganda on his coinage and in speeches and books by pro-Imperial academics (usually members of his state commissions) led to a degree of reconciliation with the aggressively moralistic and 'anti-wealth' Church preachers, monks, and hermits and secular intellectuals who had backed Michael I and their heirs – who had regarded the indulgent, jewel-dripping Leo IV and his wives with horror. Indeed, the Emperor and his education ministers and advisers even formed a tacit alliance with and occasionally used some mid-century 'revivalist' academics in Athens, Ephesus and Alexandria universities. These thinkers were now studying the advantages of 'benevolent autocracy' Greek monarchy as manifested by the Seleucids and early Ptolemies in the 3rd and early 2nd centuries BC, and leading Ptolemaic enthusiast thinker and analyst Xenocrates of Hermoupolis (Egypt) ended up in the mid-late 750s as a tutor to Probus' three sons and a professor of government at Rome University despite his dubious attitude to the Catholic Church.

Probus also turned out to be as keen as his father on using the Church to bolster the 'mythos' of Imperial power and majesty, albeit in a more responsible and less personally irresponsible way. With a view to a permanent and stable 'system' he made sure that suitably pro-autocracy tutors were selected for the 'secondary' education of his three sons and impressed on them that the Imperial power was the keystone of good government and order as prescribed by God, and that it was to be used wisely but not challenged. All three boys were to receive an intensive and comprehensive education in the basics of both culture and government and were to be brought up to be pious but not aggressively orthodox Catholics and to put morals ahead of self-enjoyment. From their late teens they also received military training and were put into the 'protectores' officer-cadet corps and were then sent off on military work as junior officers on the frontiers not allowed to go to university. The second and third sons, Justinian (born 742) and Justin (born 744), were tough and good at athletics and shared their father's expertise at riding and hunting and lapped up this sort of life, away from responsibility in learning how to govern wisely for a few years and surrounded by noisy and boorish young officers. But the awkward and rather withdrawn eldest son, Probianus (born 740), would rather have been a monk and was in uncertain health so the wisdom of sending him off to the Carpathians as a frontier officer was dubious. Probus insisted that that was his destiny as the heir and he must be presented as a successful and committed military enthusiast and a 'leader of men' as he himself had been.

In the end Probianus ended up with a severe respiratory infection after being caught in a snowstorm in the mountains in winter 763–4 and had to be sent back to Rome in a litter as an invalid and the exasperated Emperor was not at all pleased and started to take it out on him as a weakling who had made his health worse by his fasting with his monk advisers. With Probianus not being made 'Caesar' as planned and being forced to marry a suitable beautiful and confident multi-millionaire Illyrian heiress of the Emperor's choice (Aurelia Draupenia) in spring 764, not his own choice of a more low-born and plain amateur Christian devotional poetess from a business background called Caecilia, the antagonism of Emperor and heir of the later 740s was replayed but without the latter having any military interests or support. Probianus was bullied unmercifully by his father, forced to accompany him to the summer's hunting-parties in Cisalpine Gaul to 'bond' with the nobility, and then sent off on another tour of duty as an officer to the distant frontiers of Sogdiana. There were rumours that Probus was thinking of disinheriting his heir as unable to stand or fit into the role of an Emperor or else intended to 'hedge him in' with strong and assertive ministers and senior nobles and generals who would make sure that he acted as a 'front man' and carried on his father's policies rather than initiating his own – which he had shown no signs of having anyway.

The Emperor could indeed end up as a ceremonial figure not a practical chief executive and some of Probus' advisers argued that this would avoid the risk of a feeble or incompetent ruler and thus stop the main danger facing a hereditary monarchy. Alternatively some of the current Emperor's experts on Hellenistic monarchy argued that if Ptolemy I, seen as one of the greatest and wisest of rulers of that era, could 'cut out' his unstable eldest son Ptolemy Ceraunus from the succession then Probus could do the same and 'hereditary' succession need not mean primogeniture. Rumours spread in 764–5 that the ambitious Prince Justinian's glamorous and ambitious teenage wife Maria Eucheria (who he had married in 761 when he was nineteen and she was seventeen) and some of her male kinsmen were trying to encourage the Prince, loyal to his brother but a far better and more enthusiastic huntsman and officer, to get his father to make him heir and Probianus to become a bishop (clerics who had married before ordination did not definitively have to get rid of their wives though the Western Church preferred this). But in the event the situation was changed suddenly on 12 July 765 as Probus was killed in a freak hunting-accident in the Po valley as he was thrown from his horse as a boar charged him and was impaled on the boar's tusks. The Emperor was fatally wounded and died within hours, aged fifty-four, and by agreement of the Council Probianus was proclaimed Emperor, aged twenty-five, and recalled by urgent carrier-pigeon message from his 'HQ' post at Maracanda in Sogdiana. The question now faced the Empire – how would a system modified by a tough, dynamic, restless traveller and military hero fare when a physically weak and unmilitary heir succeeded him? Would the new ruler be up to the task – or would his seemingly more physically suitable younger brothers end up removing him? Would this even end in civil war, as more than one anxious minister had privately feared as Probianus' character and weak health became apparent?

Chapter 7

Probianus 765–767: The Would-Be Monk. Justinian I 767–797: Ambitious For Glory. The Elder Two Sons of Probus

Some generals and aristocrats would have preferred to proclaim Justinian as Emperor, but Empress Irene refused to see her eldest son disinherited and brought Pope Stephen in to back her. It was also feared that even if Probianus was not the sort to start a civil war and commit the 'sin' of causing lots of bloodshed by his ambition the generals in Sogdiana, led by the hard-headed and ruthless 'Count of the Oxus' Aufidius Geminius, would have no hesitation in doing so. Justinian, currently serving in Dacia, did not object, and he was given the rank of 'Caesar' to keep him happy and indeed arrived in Rome long before his brother and led the senate and ministers loyally until Probianus arrived in his capital, held up by illness and exhaustion at Dara on the Euphrates for several weeks and by storms at sea in Antioch for a month, at the end of October 765.

The new Emperor, backed up by his devout and determined wife and by Irene, was able to make a good start as ruler despite fears among the largely hostile senior bureaucrats that he would turn out like Michael I. He affirmed to the Senate on his arrival in Rome that he had no intention of stepping back from the duties required of him from his position due to his health or his strong morals and that indeed it was his responsibility to govern and carry out the role that God had placed him in. He dispensed with a grand coronation and was crowned at the end of an elaborate but not over-ceremonial Mass as Michael had been, and in the weeks that followed he took stock of his father's and the Imperial Council's written advice on the role of the Emperor and proceeded to pardon most of the exiled or enslaved 'Iconoclasts'. But he made it clear that no breaches of the peace would be tolerated and that he would keep up all his father's and grandfather's police and military patrols across the affected regions. Resultant militant riots in 766 and 767 were duly put down across Syria and Palestine with firmness but not excessive brutality and indeed Probianus had sent out special commissions of Rome jurists and advisory senators with legal experience to investigate and purge the police and military in these regions of the sort of thuggish junior officers who were likely to over-react and/or were bigotedly orthodox and the sort of senior officers likely to back brutality. He also undertook to keep the judiciary and prison service acting within the Law and renewed Michael's efforts to set up a permanent mechanism of Imperially-funded inspectors of the Empire's lawcourts and prisons and roving commissions that would 'audit' the work of both in each province. This was however done with more caution and by more emollient and experienced characters than the usually young idealists who Michael had appointed and Probianus was alert to the dangers of lowly-paid officials accepting bribes or extorting money from prisoners and legal appellants. So he made sure that the relevant people were paid properly, a new 'Quaestor' with decades of experience as an inspector called Lucius Quintanius (in office 766–88) being appointed to oversee all this with vigour and being kept on as a public relations gesture by Probianus' successor.

Also, from 766 a new commission chosen by Quintanius sought to improve the quality of men appointed as magistrates so that lax, biased, or bribe-seeking careerists or men who just had generations of judges and lawyers in their families and entered the profession as a part-time career to boost their pay and their social reputation were reduced in numbers in the legal profession. More 'outsiders' were promoted, but this required greater supervision by the provincial governments and the Law Ministry in Rome than before and there was still a major risk of lax supervision from the 'centre' which the tireless Quintianus spent his career battling – giving credit for his determination to carry on and tackle the corrupt and the useless by his sovereign's inspiration to him. The Emperor thus became linked in the public mind from his early speeches and actions with the causes of legal reform and incorrupt justice and was later nicknamed 'The Just'. This and his wife's personal philanthropy, in the revered tradition of the late Empress Ausonia, meant that although he was notably hostile to any notion of the military as a fulfilling career for the responsible citizen – and he rarely attended any military parades or manoeuvres – he avoided the outright antagonism that Michael I had done.

With Justinian now resident in Rome and taking on the Imperial role as a military patron and enthusiast and Prince Justin serving as a talented if somewhat boorish young commander on the Sogdian frontier, battling raiding Turks, the Imperial Family did not split up into fratricidal feuding and rival courts as some had predicted. Probianus proceeded in 766–7 to relaunch – cautiously – a theological examination of how to lure moderate but resolutely anti-'idolatry' 'Iconoclast' thinkers into accepting that venerating icons was not the same as worshipping them. But events now took another unexpected turn as on 14 April 767, after a reign of less than two years and after less than eighteen months in Rome, Probianus succumbed to a fit after a banquet at the Marble Palace to greet a delegation of visiting mildly pro-'Iconoclast' Eastern clergy, aged only twenty-seven. There were the inevitable rumours of poison and it was supposed by many of the religiously-minded that some extremist Catholics or 'Iconodules' had poisoned the Emperor to stop him halting any further purges of their enemies. But despite the resultant riots the new Emperor Justinian, aged twenty-five, held a swift autopsy that concluded that the Emperor had had an allergic reaction to some over-honeyed food and the Empress, who promptly retired to a nunnery in the Apennines and wore sackcloth for the rest of her life, and Dowager Empress Irene accepted the verdict. If there was foul play, it was never proven.

Probianus and Aurelia had had no children so there was no question of Justinian superseding a boy heir, and indeed he and his own wife Maria Eucheria had so far produced only (three) daughters and were to produce three more in the 770s. Unease about the succession began to appear in political circles given the debaucherous and prostitute-fancying Justin's failure to marry and the moral quality (or rather lack thereof) of those women with whom he was seen when he was off duty in Rome in between his successive frontier postings. But at least Justinian was a more emollient and less sternly moral figure than Probianus and he had many young and hunting-mad aristocrats among his friends so he was seen as more friendly to the traditional elites than his brother had been. He had the shrewdness to keep up all of his brother's legal reforms and to back Quintianus, who was made consul in 770 as a mark of esteem, to the hilt and indeed a whole new body of capable and earnest, hard-working youngish provincial lawyers and law lecturers from around the Mediterranean came to staff the Imperial department of law in the late 760s and 770s. They were to run the roving commissions of legal inspectors across the Empire, even tackling the long-neglected problem of aristocrat-run justice in the staunchly traditionalist Eastern provinces of the former Sassanid lands and semi-'feudal' Gandhara with its Hindu 'high caste' lawyers and judges. Landed nobles' relatives as judges, who had a tendency to acquit them, were thus reduced.

The Emperor himself might be a military officer at heart and he was not as interested in intellectual matters as his late brother had been but he understood the value of having a solid bloc of persuasive intellectuals on his side. In that vein he sought to get his old tutor Justus Olivianus, a C4th and C5th Neoplatonist expert from the university of Athens and a former monk/teacher at the monastery of St Basil of Caesarea (who had been educated at Athens university when it was the Platonic 'Academy'), to collect all the relevant writings of his studied era on the unifying role of the Emperor as symbol and upholder of Divinely-mandated world order. Plato's and Plotinus' world-view was thus shown as agreeing with that of the 'deeper' Christian thinkers. Olivianus had been telling his students at the Caesarea monastery's school – one of the best in the whole of Asia Minor – for decades about how Plato had really been close to being a Christian without knowing it, at least in his understanding of how God had ordered the universe, and that his concept of the 'Divine Light' was reflected in the New Testament with the angels as the equivalent of Plato's 'higher spirits' or 'gods'. Had mentioned this both to his Imperial pupils – of whom only Probianus had really understood it – and in seminars and lectures in Rome while he had been teaching the princes. Now in 768 Justinian called him back to the capital to work on a grand overall theory of the mystic unity and Divinely-organised workings of the Universe and to bring Plato, Plotinus, and Christian thinkers like Origen together in one theory that could be taught at Roman universities – and glorify the Imperial office in the process. As 'Consul of the Philosophers' Olivianus did his best to oblige and in the next two decades managed to bring some elements of these writers' work together and create a learned commentary of the 'true' theory that he maintained they had all been aiming at and had dimly or partially seen. His sovereign thus hoped to reconcile Catholics and Platonists.

This 'Imperial Christian Platonism' and its author's great work the 'Philosophical Digest ' was to be taught at Rome University by Olivianus himself, by then in his late seventies and early eighties, in the final decade of the Emperor's reign from 787. It then passed on to a group of his students who Justinian gave Imperially-subsidised chairs in Philosophy both there (three chairs) and Athens (two chairs) and was to add a new dimension to Romano-Greek philosophy. But the way that Olivianus fitted – or, his enemies said, forcibly crowbarred –the role and symbolic importance of the Emperor, the 'Thirteenth Apostle', into the new theories and gave the 'Heir of Augustus' a major role in his world-view was not to the taste of all those intellectual Platonic or Origenist thinkers who conceded that Olivianus had made some useful contributions. Nor did 'hard-line' Platonists concede that Plato had done more than foreshadow some elements of Christianity and they insisted that he would have been horrified – and so would Plotinus have been – to find the theory of a 'Son of God' come to save Mankind linked to his own view of how the universe worked. There were to be more Catholics who accepted that Plato and his chief disciple and commentator Aristotle could and should be taught at universities to elucidate the Christian theology of the universe than Platonists who accepted any link between Plato and men like Origen. In the long run Justinian's plan to intellectually 'enrol' Plato and the university Platonists across the Empire to boost his view of the significance and centrality of the Imperial office and increase such intellectuals' loyalty and usefulness to the State did 'work' in that Plato (and Aristotle) became more widely taught in Christian schools and universities. In addition Olivianus' exalted view of the value of academics and their theories to the State rubbed off on not only the Emperor but some of his ministers as he held forth to the court and Council at receptions and banquets as Justinian's intellectual mentor. This in turn encouraged both Justinian and later on his son Rillanus to boost spending on the university system and on the whole concept of intellectual research. It was to lead to the emergence of intensive study of nature and its phenomena (as studied earlier by Aristotle) as a sideline to philosophical studies at the University of Rome in the 800s and 810s by the generation of Olivianus' students. Without Olivianus' presence at court and his passion for intellectual study and its uses to the State, would Rillanus have been creating a special 'Department of Scientific Learning' at Rome University and endowing six chairs in it, plus three more in Aristotleian studies at Athens University and two at Syracuse?

But for the moment in Justinian's reign the question of Imperial sponsorship of serious new intellectual study was limited to what he saw as the 'useful' work on Plato and Plotinus. In that pursuit he endowed two new chairs of studies on Plato and two on Plotinus at Rome University in 773 and 776, two on Plato and one on Plotinus and one on Aristotle at Syracuse University in 775–7, two on Plato (but none on Plotinus as the orthodox Church disliked him as an anti-Christian pagan) at the University of Constantinople in 775, and two on Plato and one on the 'local' Origen at the University of Antioch in 776–8. Justinian also expanded his planned educational sponsorship to organise local funding and help his plans, suggested by Olivianus, to set up a more specifically Christian and theology-led new university at Carthage and this duly opened after some delays in 780. But though there was enough interest among the more liberal 'cultured' nobility and teachers there to set up a university and to feature Platonic studies as one of its main academic courses there was even more hostility there to teaching Plotinus and at this establishment orthodox Christian theology was to the forefront. This was necessitated by the amount of funding and practical help in finding and paying tutors that came from the intellectually distinguished but narrow-minded North African Church, a bastion against pagan persecution and 'Donatist' and 'Pelagian' heretics alike. As the uncompromising fifth century Catholic apologist Bishop/St Augustine of Hippo was the region's most distinguished scholar among the venerated 'Church Fathers' and the equally anti-heretic earlier Bishop/St Tertullian was rated as second to him it was their works that dominated the curriculum at Carthage University. They each had two chairs of theology set aside for experts on their work, which even the disapproving Olivianus (a major critic of Augustine) had to accept after the creation of a chair for Plotinus' studies had to be abandoned with the Church threatening to boycott the institution and local preachers threatening riots if any 'pagans' were promoted. A similar 'godly' and hard-line approach met attempts to force chairs of 'Plotinus studies' on the Catholic-led universities of Sevilla Augusta in Spain and Lugdunum in Gaul, but the education ministry's successive ministers and their senior advisers insisted to the angry Justinian that they needed to keep the Church 'sweet' to keep up funding and a large number of distinguished monastic scholars could fill vacant teaching posts at these and other universities so the Emperor had to give way. It was however a major achievement to move the study of Plato into the mainstream of academic teaching in predominantly Christian universities and have a degree of – grudging – reconciliation between his followers and the majority of Christian academics. This was in due course to move studies of the natural world via Aristotle's work too, and the Emperor reaped the benefits of being thought of as a major patron of and inspiration for studies in serious intellectual learning and became known, slightly inaccurately, as a man of wide and well-thought-through learning.

His own interests and passions lay more in the military field, and here too he used his powers of patronage and organization to push through major advances as he sought to get the 'high command' to take a coherent view of and create an over-arching strategy for the frontiers and Rome's neighbours in both East and West. He created an enlarged 'Military Strategy Centre' at the headquarters of the 'Comitatus' where, as at a university, learned experts could draw up policy documents for study, advise the Empire's leadership, and educate the next generation. Senior and retired officers from all over the Empire were called in to work there when it opened in 772. Olivianus the ex-Imperial tutor directed planning in the world of philosophical studies and wrote the essential 'handbooks' himself. One of the senior officers who had taught the Emperor strategy at the 'Protectores' cadet-school and later assisted him as an adviser on his early tours of duty in the Carpathians and Iberia, Sosibius Patrenius, was now called in to draw up the definitive written guide to Roman 'grand strategy'. Many shorter handbooks had been written over the centuries on how to handle Rome's neighbours and enemies in particular regions and books of military strategy for battles and campaigns (regular and guerilla) were two a denarius. But now Patrenius used his thirty years of experience across the Empire and his knowledge of others' books on the subject to draw up a grand overall guide, the 'Imperial Strategy Digest' or 'Strategium Imperium'. When this was complete in 786 (aided by a team of assistants who the author rarely mentioned and apparently kept short of their due money as well) it became essential reading at the new Strategy Centre where it author was the 'Consul for Military Strategy', director of studies, and chief setter of examination questions which naturally centred on his own work. His role was to be savaged as being more one of self-promotion using others' theories which he then passed off as his own than a genuine achievement in later decades and the Centre had to be overhauled and most of its personnel replaced for inadequacy or corrupt practices after he retired in 795. But the institution's achievement in focussing military minds on broad questions of strategy and in piling up valuable information in one place were undoubted and, for example, the details of how Rome had handled Attila the Hun and the Avars were to be invaluable in later centuries in handling the dangerous nomad menaces of the Turks and the Mongols.

In the meantime Justinian ensured that the military and navy received their full budgets and extra pay and resources throughout his reign after the alarms that there had been under Probianus about them being cut back or sidelined. The only later complaints that were made about his own overall strategy – with the benefit of hindsight – was that he underestimated the threat of the land-hungry Norsemen, whose population was outstripping their resources and who even by his accession were starting to launch regular raids on the Pictish-settled Shetlands and Orkneys north of Britain to steal sheep, cattle, and pigs and collect slaves every summer. This was not Roman territory so Justinian was not interested and where his father Probus had made a naval circumnavigation of the region he did not even visit Britain and had no interest in Ireland either (largely as it had few towns and no powerful or dangerous rulers). Through the 770s his concentration of military resources on the Continent led him to cut back the Hibernian Sea fleet and not bother about the Norsemen in their fearsome 'longships' attacking trading-vessels (mostly Dalriadan or Irish) off the Northern coasts of Britain. But he did keep up the 'Classis Britannia' in the North Sea to protect the Britain-Frisia-Jutland-Claudiana trade-route and the Norsemen very rarely dared to attack Roman ships there even in the 790s.

Many Norsemen in their richer Southern lands in Vestfold were content to make money out of trading legally with the Empire and those hereditary chiefs who had been supposed to pay tribute every year to the Emperor and on accession swear allegiance to Rome, since the mid-7th century-wars, kept this up. The complacent or nervous local Roman naval commanders in the eastern North Sea and Skaggerak had rarely if ever seen action in their careers and feared being sacked if a war started and their ships were unable to catch the smaller and faster Norse sailing ships (which could be rowed out of range if the wind fell, unlike most sailed Romans warships). They were happy to reassure the Emperor that all 'pirate' activity in Britain, Caledonia, and Ireland came from the far north in Trondelag and the Norse chiefs of the Vestfold region had no connection to this. This was generally true, though many of these men quietly let their restless juniors join in pirate expeditions and looked the other way in return for a share of the loot. Some more capable and thoughtful junior Roman commanders obtained permission from headquarters in Rome to hire local Norse sailors who knew the Norse coasts well to help with anti-piracy patrols off the Vestfold coasts in the 780s and 790s – their ships had 'Greek Fire' so the pirates would not dare attack them – and they spotted rather too many pirates off the coast, some towing captured Roman vessels, for coincidence. But their superiors sat on the reports, and as the Emperor and his ministers were more interested in stopping piracy by Arab 'dhows' off the Arabian coast near the mouth of the Red Sea (where shipping to and from India was also attacked in the later C8th) and sent any new Roman war-galleys that were built to hunt down pirates there the North Sea problem was neglected.

The military enthusiast Emperor was concerned that not enough ordinary young Roman citizens were volunteering for the army and that it would soon run the risk of being over-dependant on border-settled or allied peoples like the Germans and the steppe nomads as it had been in the 3rd and 4th centuries. The inhabitants of 'secure' Mediterranean (and now Rhine, Danube and Mesopotamian) 'inner' provinces could become soft and decadent as the more austere Christian preachers and hermits of all religious sects were forever saying. Accordingly his early consultations with his senior military staff and advisers saw him pressing for a Roman Republic-style army of 'citizen legionaries' and a form of conscription. As the settled conditions in the inner provinces were now enabling greater agricultural prosperity and larger families surviving on small farms and in urban areas he was able to argue that a larger army and diverting many young men to the army – at least for a few years – would not adversely affect the economy. As a result the 'Ephebic' corps was extended in provinces across the Empire in the late 760s as a first move to enlarge the army by giving military training to youths aged from fifteen to eighteen. Annual inter-provincial 'Ephebic Games', already present in some provinces that had an active corps, were extended across the Empire and even introduced to regions where athletics were little known and were regarded as a bizarre Greek habit, such as Persia and the Arab provinces. But as the Persian young nobility were mostly fond of riding and hunting and the younger and non-urban Arabs were interested in archery and racing camels these were introduced to the 'ephebic' corps in those regions as an alternative to Greek-style athletics, boxing, and wrestling. The Emperor had been a top runner and wrestler in his squadron of the Rome 'ephebic' corps (mostly filled with young nobles and the sons of civil servants) in the 750s as a boy and he was genuinely interested in the corps as a force for moral good and companionship, as was his superbly fit and horse-mad brother Justin. With the new 'Consul of the Ephebes', as the head of the organization was renamed in 768, given extra resources and a Senate seat the corps took an increasingly important role in military training and boys from it could be 'fast-tracked' into the officer-corps.

The Emperor also attended its athletics-contests and presented prizes whenever possible during his overseas tours and when in Rome, and this enthusiasm of his served as a 'dry run' for his plan for conscription of a variable number of youths from each province for the army at the age of eighteen which was finally launched in 778. Until then there had been a degree of conscription of younger sons of farming families in rural regions across most of the Empire, varying in intensity and rigour according to whether it was wartime, whether the army was short of troops, or the Emperor or the 'high command' was pressing for the implementation of the law (which was widely evaded). Also families had been able to buy their younger sons out of service and pay for the recruitment of a hired soldier from elsewhere, often a landless frontier or urban volunteer whose training costs and initial pay would be met by the 'exemption tax' payment; but now this system was tightened up and applied to urban areas too.

The Emperor personally wanted to end exemptions except in cases of family hardship or emergency while the treasury wanted to keep it up as a useful source of income, and in practice the exemption payments continued (behind Justinian's back) for rather more young men than he intended. The number of actual conscripted recruits varied from province to province and was often disguised by calling the paid replacements for exempted recruits 'conscripts' and hiding the pay they received from the exempted candidate's family in the records – the Empire's bureaucracy was just not efficient enough to ensure that the law was followed universally. But the number of military recruits from within the Empire's inner provinces rose and the number of 'border' recruits from the families of military 'limitanei' and from allied states beyond the frontier fell after 780. The experience of being trained and living as a Roman soldier with exactly the same clothing, weapons, training, and lifestyle across the Empire from Britain to Gandhara and from Cherson to Nubia served to draw recruits together and, in the words of one admiring Military Strategy Centre analyst in 802, served as a 'melting-pot' to turn disparate races from disparate social and religious backgrounds into men with one cultural 'conditioning' and loyalty. The Roman army had been doing this for a thousand years but this was now to be extended to a wider group of men from a wider background and made more of a force for 'Romanization'. The size of the army was also increased as intended by the Emperor and 'high command', from around 230,000 troops (about half of them part-time frontier farmers as 'limitanei') to around 270,000,. But due to the small number of actual wars to fight many of the new soldiers ended up serving for only five to eight years in garrisons or mobile units on the frontiers – or in smaller numbers keeping order within the Empire. Thereafter they were part-time farmers who were only 'called up' to take part in garrison-duty in cases of war or when the usual garrison-troops were called off for service elsewhere in the Empire in an emergency. This reform to the army went in tandem with a revival of a militantly moralistic and patriotic enthusiasm for the 'heroic' past and moral leadership of great figures in Roman history, both in textbooks for teaching in schools and in the subjects to be used for poetry and plays performed at court, in the late 760s to early 790s as required by the Emperor's express wishes. With him encouraging and giving prizes at poetry and drama festivals for 'patriotic' poems and plays that encouraged the right patriotic attitudes and inspired the Empire's youth any poets and playwrights quickly latched on to the idea of what would win them financial and honorary prizes and produced these 'to order'.

The era was to see the production of a whole semi-Homeric epic poetry 'cycle' (minus the Greek gods, in order not to offend the Church) by the leading Anatolian poet Achistratus of Magnesia about the Punic Wars from 264 to 146 BC. These showed Rome's heroic struggle against the cruel, corrupt, autocratic, and child-sacrificing Carthaginians, from his 'Regulus' (performed at Rome's annual poetry festival before the Emperor in 772 and winning the 'epic poetry' crown) to his 'Scipio Aemilianus at Carthage' at the same festival in 792 (which also won) via a series of works on the three Punic wars which heroified Rome's leading generals especially the Scipio family, Livius and Claudius the winners of the Metaurus battle in 207 BC, and Marcellus the conqueror of Carthage. He also produced other works for festivals around the Empire about the Macedonian-defeating and Seleucid-defeating general Flaminius and the Roman defeat of Mithradates VI of Pontus by Sulla in the 80s BC. But he had to be more careful with these subjects as the Greeks and Pontics were now close Roman cultural allies of long standing who did not all denounce their past anti-Roman leaders and Sulla the 'tyrant' with his proscriptions was still a controversial figure in Rome. Other poets played up the work and heroic military records of Marius (also controversial as a demagogic 'tyrant' and killer), Pompey, and Julius Caesar and as Augustus was not a great general they played up his wise leadership and political skills instead. Despite his desire for order and a rigorously patriotic 'line' in the literary arts Justinian had the breadth of view not to object (publicly) about works celebrating the First Emperor's defeated and alcoholic rival Mark Antony or Julius Caesar's austere and unbending republican rival Cato the Younger. But he drew the line at any works that gave a flattering view of Pompey's war against Caesar in 49–48 BC and his view of 'acceptable' works on Pompey were limited to his wars against Rome's enemies.

In the case of drama, too, the Emperor rarely rewarded works that did not fit the given 'line' that plays on the Late Republic had to stress the glory of the old days of virtue and stern and incorruptible moral leadership in the 4th to 2nd centuries BC and stress that greed and ambition by amoral mavericks ruined that in the chaos of the late 2nd and 1st century BC but that Augustus wisely reunified the Empire and its people and reined in its feuding elite. The main playwright to meet these criteria and win a string of major awards under

Justinian was the ultra-patriotic but politically careful Dionysius Marcellinus. He was author of the (annual) Rome drama-festival-winning plays 'Scipio Africanus At Bay' (against his malicious detractors in the 180s BC) (winner 772), 'Cato the Elder' (775), 'Camillus' (776), 'Regulus' (always an Imperial favourite for his self-sacrifice) (777), 'Marcus Livius Drusus and the Allies (779), 'Cicero and the Catilinarian Conspiracy' (780), 'Cicero Versus Clodius' (Clodius was a favourite 'bogey-man' of the Emperor's as a violent and crooked demagogue) (783), 'Octavian and Antony' (786), 'Cincinnatus' (787), 'Agrippa and Julia' (790), 'Appius Claudius and Pyrrhus' (792), and 'Popilius Guides the Ptolemies' (795). The Emperor set up a special 'Commission for Drama' in 770 to advise him on the promotion of patriotic drama and how to encourage others to fund drama-festivals and give generously in terms of financial awards and valuable prizes for winners. He was probably inspired by his own lessons as a boy on the drama-festivals and patriotic drama-productions of ancient Athens. Ahead of his own personal presidency of and presentation of prizes at the Athens 'City Dionysia' festival of 769, *en route* to a tour of the Aegean and Asia Minor and then residence in winter 769–70 at Constantinople, he arranged for a new annual drama festival for the Western provinces to be held each summer at Arelate in the Rhone delta in southern Gaul. But given the staunchly Catholic locale and culture most of its plays were to be on Christian subjects and glorifying the Catholic Emperors Constantine 'the Great', Theodosius I, and Marcian and Pulcheria were to be favourite subjects. Culturally, non-Christian subjects were 'safer' for writers to choose in the Hellenic East with more secular schools.

Under Justinian provincial aristocrats and munificent businessmen across the Empire were to be encouraged to take up patronage of poetry and drama festivals and new ones sprung into life, not least in Egypt and Syria where the Ptolemaic and Seleucid pasts were honoured. Though the drama revival was largely restricted to the Mediterranean region the revival of heroic poetry fitted in with the local enthusiasm for bardic recitation glorifying great heroes and past dynasts by the Arabs and Persians. Some major new poets emerged in Persia and the Arabian peninsula, mostly heroifying the safely long-distant Achaemenid era in the former and the inter-tribal wars of the Early Roman era in the latter. (Justinian had any plays about the 3rd century AD anti-Roman rebel queen Zenobia banned, but allowed others about the pro-Roman dynasts of the allied kingdom of Petra and about the Hasmonean dynasty in Judaea.) Meanwhile the Emperor, with Justin as 'Caesar' and as his heir until he had a son, sought to provide his own example of heroic Roman military action to inspire his people and bring in extra army recruits. Though he carefully spent his first few years on Imperial tours to get to know his elites better and show himself to the masses, spending winter 770–1 at Antioch after a grand tour of the East from Alexandria via Egypt, Palestine, Syria, Mesopotamia, Media, and Persia and most of 769 in Greece, the Aegean and Asia Minor,772 in Illyria and the Danube provinces, and 773 in Gaul, Spain, and North Africa from Tingis to Carthage, in 774 he made the most of the overthrow of the weak son and successor of his ally Liutprand the Langobard by his cousin 'Duke' Desiderius (OTL figures) to declare war on the Langobards.

His plans had encompassed annexation of the war-torn and collapsing Langobard realm for year and Probus had already drawn up a campaign plan to carry this out in 766. Now as Desiderius started to round up and execute his rebel provincial barons and replace those who did not surrender with his own toadies Justinian gave sanctuary to those who fled across the Carpathians in winter 773–4 and noisily demanded their restoration plus full compensation and a grovelling apology from their 'tyrant'. As he was already summoning his troops for a campaign in 774 and getting his strategists to 'war-game' an invasion he clearly did not expect or probably want Desiderius to give in and a successful invasion and annexation was more politically useful. With the new leaders of the 'Carolingian' dynasty that now ruled the Frankish realm, Pepin's sons Carolus (normally a Roman officer commanding a frontier cavalry unit on the Oder as he found this more suited to his restless talents than tamely administering a Roman vassal province) and Carloman supplying Frankish troops and the Khazars sending in a cavalry force of nomads to cross the Dnieper and occupy the eastern Langobard lands around the upper Bug in early 774 the Emperor led his troops North. A huge army of over 50,000 Romans in five columns of mixed cavalry and infantry used the existing trade-roads to occupy the main fortresses and small towns of Langobardia and the Church headquarters at Cracovium welcomed the Romans as 'liberators' as they were resisting Desiderius' tax-demands. As the Langobards could not meet the well-armed Roman armies in battle with any hope of success Desiderius burnt or hid all the food-supplies and retired to his main fortress of Varsavia, its wooden walls covered in earth to stop 'Greek Fire' burning them down, and withstood a siege. His plan was to wait for the Romans to run out of supplies and have to retreat while his men launched guerilla attacks from the forests, but Justinian had a large force of civilian and military 'volunteers' accompanying his army cut down the forests around all the roads so the Langobards could not creep up on his land-convoys. Other supplies were brought up the River Vistula to the Roman camps by ship from the Baltic and in the meantime less well protected Langobard forts were besieged and taken one by one and turned into Roman strongholds.

Eventually Desiderius and his cooped-up army and the civilians sheltering in Varsavia ran out of food and had to surrender, the obstinate king reportedly being forced to do so at sword-point by worried barons who had their own lands to protect and were aware that Justinian was offering an amnesty and full possession of their property to all who gave in quickly. For once the Emperor was merciful and did not burn down Varsavia as he had threatened to do but had it quickly turned into a Roman fortress for 10,000 soldiers who were used to life in northern climes, erected a new Roman-style stone-walled fortress there, and resettled the distrusted populace out in unfortified wooden towns in the countryside that they could not defend if they revolted. Varsavia was kept as a major trading and agricultural centre but was settled by imported Romano-Germans and Danes and was cleared of Langobards. In the next couple of years the Empire slowly replaced most of the local barons by veteran Roman or Frankish officers and deported the majority of the Langobard rural populace to Marcomannia or Dacia with the more peaceful and leaderless Slavs being left alone provided that they converted to Christianity and supplied tribute (mostly in animals and corn plus timber) and troops to the Empire. Cracovia, another royal fortresses, and other strongpoints became Roma fortresses and before the Emperor left for Rome in September 774 he inaugurated a new Roman citadel with a small Imperial and military 'HQ' on the Wawel Hill there as the centre of administration of the new province of 'Langobardia'. But given the poor soil and harsh winters plus the reputed hordes of roaming bears and bison there were few volunteers among the army veterans that Justinian sought to settle in the region and even with a degree of enforced settlement for veterans in the late 770s and 780s it still remained a Slavic rather than Roman area for decades to come and outside the towns and fortresses Roman control was lax.

The military frontier now advanced to the River Bug and a chain of fortresses were set up along it, defended by a mixture of farming 'limitanei', a rota of infantry regiments from across the Empire, and cavalry patrols plus local Slav mercenaries. In 776 the Emperor returned to the region after a spring – early summer tour of Rhaetia and the Rhineland to see that the work of Romanization was proceeding smoothly and founded a new port of 'Justiniana' at the mouth of the River Vistula so that exports could be sent more easily by sea across the Baltic to Claudiana and on to Rome's North–Western provinces. The Empire also now controlled the amber trade on the southern shores of the Baltic but as the swamps and forests of Prussia and Lithuania were too dense and unhealthy for settlement by Roman farmers left this region to the local tribes provided that they assisted Roman trade and paid tribute. As the work of integrating the Slavs and the remaining Langboards into the Empire was going to be a long one even with the majority of the autonomist barons deported Justinian took no notice of those eager military strategists who wanted him now to extend his power East to the Dnieper. They wanted to have the new network of Roman roads across Langobardia developed so that they crossed the Bug and reached over the forested plains North of the Pripyat Marshes to the lands of the upper Dnieper – now mostly settled by Slavs but with a few adventurous Swedes moving in from the Gulf of Riga/Livonia to acquire furs and timber inland and trade as far as the river. The Swedish 'Rus' (believed to come from the local word for 'rowers' as they rowed their longships up the rivers if there was no wind) were by now starting to settle the lands East of the upper Baltic and by 800 had founded a trading-centre inland of Lake Ladoga at 'Novgorod' ('New City'). Justinian was to be advised by businessmen who were trading up the Dnieper and dealing with the local 'Rus' in the 780s that this could be a boom area and invaluable to Rome in terms of furs and timber, not least for wood for the use of the navy. But with the finance ministry already complaining about the cost of Romanizing 'Langobardia' and building new major Roman urban centres at Cracovia and Varsavia the Emperor did not wish to bother with fighting 'irregular' and unprestigious bands of Slavs and 'Rus'. The only major result of his annexation of the lands West of the Bug for this region was that bands of Roman officers hunting for wild animals to export as trophies to the Empire (not least for aristocrats' private parks) began to explore the plains East of the Tatra Mountains in the 790s and 800s. Small, unofficial 'roads' (earth not the usual Roman stone) were built to help them transport their animal quarries and were able to facilitate local trade with devolved groups of Slavs as far as the upper Dnieper.

Having shown his ability as a general and will to annex new lands to the Empire and extend Rome's 'mission' in Langobardia, Justinian pressed on with new confidence. In 778 he took the action – suggested by more imaginative military bureaucrats on and off for decades, and backed by finance ministry 'cost-cutters' – of cutting back the number of senior commands on frontiers that had been in need of military co-ordination and roving mobile armies in the 4th to 6th centuries but did not now really need them. The role of 'Count/ Master of Soldiers of the Rhineland'/Upper and Lower Germany, as senior to the regional 'duces' and in charge of his own regional 'comitatus', was no longer really needed and the end of the Oder frontier confirmed that. The same applied to the 'Count' of the 'East/Oriens' in Mesopotamia with the Eastern frontier shifted as far as the Indus/Beas and Jaxartes and the Arab lands to the South either allies or too weak to be a danger. The less north-centric of the military strategists had also wanted the Countship of Britain' to be abolished once the Picts had had their realm sliced in two and its SE half annexed as far as the Dornoch Firth, Great Glen, and 'Orca Promontory' (John O'Groats). But Justinian did not accept that as there could still be trouble with Ireland or (so far a minor problem) the Norse pirates around Orkney and Shetland and so his reforms of 778 abolished the 'Countships' of the Rhine and the East alone and abolished their 'comitati' and their bureaucracies but retained military depots and arsenals plus training-camps for recruits on the middle Rhine (around Moguntiacum and Colonia Agrippinensis) and around Ctesiphon.

The 'North German' command was now shifted to the small Lower Elbe trading-port of 'Augusta Germanicorum'/'Hamburgium' (Hamburg), as an entrepot at the riverine end of several major roads across the Westphalian plain and up the river and also within close reach of the Danevirke frontier-dyke and Jutland should the latter be attacked. The ducal command of Transrhenus was given enhanced authority over the Danish and Lower Baltic military regions to co-ordinate defence there – with the first commander, 'Count of the North', being the Emperor's trusted colleague the Frankish commander Count Carolus, known to his people as 'Carolus the Great' (OTL: Charlemagne, Frankish king and 'Holy Roman Emperor') and backed by the regional Church as a devout and pagan-hating Catholic who was helping to fund conversion and new monasteries in Langobardia. (He held the Countship from 778 to 786 and again from 790 to 798.) The Mesopotamian command was broken up and part of its mobile 'comitatus' was moved to the Oxus and Jaxartes under a new 'Count of Transoxiana and Khorasan' (the Persian name for the region) who led a force of 12–15,000 cavalry to keep back the raiding Turks and train recruits from the latter as Roman mercenaries, this office being the superior of the 'duces' of Bactria and Sogdiana. A separate 'Count of the Desert Frontier' was set up with a smaller roving cavalry command based at Hira, a desert town South of the Euphrates some way from Babylon that had once been the 'HQ' of the Sassanids' Lakhimid tribal allies. This watched the north Arabian deserts.

The old 'Countship' and 'Masterships of the Infantry and Cavalry' (sometimes three separate commands, some time with one man holding two of the three) on the lower Danube with their infantry and cavalry 'comitati' were maintained in order to have a flexible and war-ready force that could counter any trouble on the steppes, though as of 778 the Khazars were firm Roman allies and their vassal tribes (eg the Magyars) under their control. The 'Countship of the Caucasus' was also kept on in order to guard the passes of the Caucasus range into Colchis, Iberia, and North Adiabene against raids from the steppe while the 'Countship of the Indus' guarded the Indus and kept down the tribes around Kabul. These restless and bold looters were difficult to relocate to the controllable plains nearby although the Emperors kept on trying this through the C8th and into the C9th, as whenever they were rounded up and moved out of the hills at sword-point by Roman soldiers they drifted back again a few years later and killed anyone who had been planted in their lands. Justinian did not venture east again to observe the situation there at first-hand after his 'one-off' visit to Antioch, Edessa, Nisibis, Ctesiphon, Charax, Susa, and (for a rally of the Persian nobility) Istakr in spring-autumn 782 and after his Dacian and Marcomannian tour of 783 he did not venture beyond the Mediterranean. As he kept up his love of athletics and his belief in toughening up the Empire's young men to revive the self-discipline of the old Roman Republican heroes he attended the Olympic Games in person in 780 and 784 to present the prizes and made long speeches there in favour of the Ancient Greek athletic ideal, even reviving a modified version of the extra-tough 'agoge' youth training system at Sparta in 780 on his Imperial visit to the Peloponnese as a way to provide many tough and muscular – and obedient – young Greeks for his army in an attempt to bring back the values of Lycurgus. (The latter, the great 'founding father' of Spartan institutions, was a favourite hero of his and he erected a gold statue of him on the Capitol in Rome.) To Hellenists he was 'Lycurgus Revived' – to Christians, 'the Athlete of Christ'.

Justinian was also more confident of long-term dynastic stability after his twin sons Rillanus and Septimius were born in September 780 just after his return from the Olympics to Rome. He made sure that the identity of the elder child was verified by a panel of attending nobles and priests at the time and no mischievous politicians would be able to stir up the 'younger' child to revolt by telling him that he was really the elder but had been 'cheated out of the throne at birth by a mistake or a plot'. The younger son was duly destined for the Church to invalidate him from the succession and prevent any plots and was given a religious-led education and was made a deacon at the age of 16 (September 796) whereas Rillanus received a rigorous education in secular subjects, governance in particular, and also had to do military training as an 'ephebe'. But in the event Septimius was the tougher and the more suited to army life and had to make do with riding and athletics, chafing at his hours spent studying the Bible and the Church Fathers or at religious services with his devout mother Maria Eucheria, while Rillanus was lazy and feckless and did not like his harsh programme of study or his hours of learning to fight and studying military tactics. There was also a rumour that in fact the Empress had given birth to triplets and as a mix-up at birth meant that nobody was sure who the second-born child was the Emperor had had the existence of the third child 'airbrushed' out of the official records and had forced the doctors and servants in attendance to sign pledges of secrecy. The attendant nobles had left the birth-chamber at the Marble Palace, the 'Porphyry/Purple Chamber', after the second baby had been born – and the birth of a third child was never proved. But by the 820s rumours were spreading that the Emperor had had the third child handed over to a midwife, the wife of one of his top doctors, and she had had it adopted under an assumed name by a travelling pedlar as the illegitimate son of a court lady. (Evidently no noble or courtier could be trusted to know the secret and bring the boy up in greater comfort.)

The unpopularity of the harsh and boorish Emperor Justin and after him the dubious legitimacy of his successor Constantine V as Emperor may have sparked off the apparent search by dissident courtiers and military officers for the 'missing baby' as the figurehead for a coup and there was certainly some plot of this nature underway in 822–3. But if so the 'secret Prince' was either never found or if he was found was not keen to reclaim 'his' throne and the case became one of the enduring mysteries of Imperial history, with later pretenders emerging in the later 9th century to claim the throne as 'sons' or 'grandsons' of the 'missing Prince' but never dislodging the line of Constantine V and most ending up in gaol as 'subversives' after secret trials where the judge and lawyers were sworn to secrecy. For the moment in the 780s and early 790s the only problem for the Imperial Family was the – carefully hidden except from senior courtiers – laziness and lack of commitment to his destiny of Prince Rillanus. He preferred partying, drinking, gambling, and swimming with his friends to study and he preferred to watch horse – and chariot-racing and gamble on the results to riding, and as 'Princeps Iuventutis' and a member of the 'Ephebes' from 794 he had to take part in the latter's camps and take a lead in their athletics and military training as ordered by his father but only did so under protest. He was not stupid and he did understand philosophy and the ethics of Roman governance and he was to show his support for these and for his tutors as an untrammeled Emperor by continuing his father's funding of philosophic institutions, not to mention scientific experiment, but it was clear by his mid-teens that he would be a self-indulgent socialite Emperor who let his ministers govern in his name not one who devised and directed policies. As with the previous generation, many observers wished the Imperial sons 'birth-order' had been the other way round.

In that vein the Emperor, doing his best to bully his son into acting more responsibly and instructing his tutors to remind him in gory detail what had happened to Caligula and Nero the self-indulgent Julio-Claudian despots, began to prepare his ministers and advisers for rule by a 'non-active' Emperor. He nudged the Council to start to debate about and come to conclusions on policies and senior appointments without always waiting for his 'lead'. He also used the fact that Rillanus had a degree of respect for the Church and its self-sacrificing philanthropic moral leaders – if not for its attitude to free sex and gambling – to get the Prince to know and appreciate the socially agreeable and cultured Pope Hadrian. The new Western Church leader (OTL) was Latin nobleman and former teacher at a top monastic school who thanks to his well-placed episcopal relatives and an egregious ability to impress important appointment-makers rose through the Church administration to be elected as Pope to succeed Stephen – to whom he was by then secretary and letter-writer – in 772. Ruling the Church deftly and keeping out of controversy with his own 'flock' by unequivocally backing the Iconodules and giving generously to shrines of the Virgin Mary, Hadrian ruled the Western Church until 795 as a dutiful partner of the Emperor and made no objection to the latter's Constantinian assumption of doctrinal leadership and direction, or to the killings and deportations underway in Langobardia to 'Romanise' it after 774. The Emperor was duly able to press ahead with his theologically risky act of giving the Imperial office the ecclesiastical ranks necessary to enable an Emperor to receive priestly legal inviolability and to lead Church services if needed in 779. The Emperor was now in effect to be a priest and was entitled to wear priestly vestments once he reached the age legally needed for priestly rank (i.e. 30). This was more to do with sidelining any radical priests' or monks' objections to the religious nature of certain ceremonies in the annual round participated in and/or featuring the Emperor at the Imperial, i.e. 'Sacred', Palace, in which Justinian was reviving the ideas of his grandfather Leo IV, than with the Emperor directing theology and outflanking his Patriarchs if they tried to obstruct him. It was political not theological in its rationale, but some 'Iconoclasts' feared the latter at the time due to the controversial attempts by the new Patriarch Arcadius of Antioch to moderate religious policy on icons and bring their faction back into the mainstream Church.

The Churches at Constantinople and Alexandria were opposed to what Arcadius was trying to do. Given the known sympathetic views of the Emperor and Pope Hadrian on icons the Antiochene and other Syrian 'Iconoclasts' feared that Arcadius and his supportive local Praefect Diodorus, nephew of a deceased 'Iconoclast' bishop who had ended up in gaol after a decade in a slave-mine, would be purged and Justinian was assuming extra priestly powers in order to secure this by 'fiat' if needed. But in fact Justinian was reluctant to act as Diodorus had friends at court and they were assuring him that the Praefect and Patriarch were saving him a lot of money and embarrassment by calming the 'Iconoclasts' down and decreasing the number of attacks on 'idolatrous' churches and churchmen in Syria. But in the event the leniency shown by the authorities only encouraged another extremist leader called Abbot Peter of the St Simeon monastery near Emesa to rouse his followers with violent speeches to 'purge sin' by wrecking all the churches containing icons or murals – or any other portrayals of religious subjects – in Emesa in April 782. The police had to be sent in by Diodorus to rescue attacked clergy and restore order, and as the Patriarch did not order the ruined pictures to be restored over the next year the number of attacks on similar 'dens of Belial' in inland Syria multiplied and 'Iconoclast' groups with weapons began to spill over into Palestine and ransack churches and monasteries that did not meet their exacting standards in Galilee and Samaria. For once the usually venerated Emperor was not trusted but attacked by clergy, for presuming to act as a priest.

Both the 'corrector' (under-governor) of Damascus sub-province and the governor of Palestine I (i.e. North Palestine, governed from Caesarea Philippi) protested to the Emperor that the feeble Diodorus was responsible for all this by giving the 'go-ahead' to vandals and the Patriarch was colluding with the violence. As a result an Imperial commission of enquiry was sent out to investigate while a special detachment of troops and police sent from Rome attacked the rioters head-on and started to kill and arrest them, their commander having full powers to ignore the Praefect. Once order had returned the Praefect was told to surround Abbot Peter's monastery and drag him out, refused in order to avoid bloodshed and just wrote to him asking him to go on retreat in the wilderness for a while, and was sacked by Justinian. Troops surrounded and stormed the monastery and killed a number of monks as they arrested Peter and the latter ended up executed for rioting, arson, and vandalism and most of his captured monks sent to the mines. As 'Iconodules' protected by troops took over and 'cleansed' the monastery of St Simeon the Patriarch refused to go along with this and ended up tried by a special Church tribunal on Imperial orders, sacked, and deported to a desert monastery himself.

The purge of 'Iconoclasts' and those who would tolerate them from the Syrian Church that followed in 784–5 led to more disorder and an exodus of fleeing suspects to hide in the deserts and Syria was to spend the next five years under martial law, every pro-'Iconoclast' monastery being closed as the Emperor now turned on Iconoclasts as rebel fanatics who defied the Law. As the new Patriarch Constantius proclaimed that those monks and nuns who followed the 'blasphemous' doctrine were not even in religious orders as they had violated the Church's disciplinary canons they were dismissed from their monasteries en masse. The Emperor showed a warped sense of humour by having a large group of the more obstreperous of them assembled in the public theatre at Ephesus (to which they had been banished) and forced to marry each other so they were ineligible to be monks and nuns thereafter. (In OTL it was the Byzantine emperor Constantine V who did this.)

In 786 a Council of the Eastern Church met at largely pro-'Iconodule' Constantinople, presided over by its Patriarch Tarasius (OTL Patriarch then) (an Imperially-selected Church civil servant), and declared that icon-'veneration' (not 'worship') was not only theologically allowable but was to be praised and promoted as it encouraged the non-literate to understand the divine and human drama of the Bible better. After that the 'Iconoclasts' were driven out into the wilderness – often literally, as many of them ended up hiding in Arabia Petraea or even making the long journey to the strictly austere Arab trading-cities of Mecca and Medina. The 'Iconodules' ruled not only the clerical 'establishment' of all the East but the monasteries and nunneries too. The 'Iconodule' tone was set by and much pro-icons writing commissioned by the greatest learned Christian thinker and bibliophile in Church office of the era, the hard-line 'Iconodule' Abbot Plato of the 'Sakkudion' monastery in Bithynia (OTL figure). The Emperor was able to claim that the 'deviants' had been totally defeated and the West and East of the Christian community were back in total ecclesiological harmony, as witnessed by his wife Maria Eucheria on her devout pilgrimage to Jerusalem, Bethlehem, Mount Sinai, Galilee, and the shrines of the great 'stylite' saints in Syria in summer 792. Justinian himself remained in the West apart from his occasional visits to Greece and his brother Justin acted as a roving military inspector for him and also served as 'Count' of the Caucasus region in 788–91 and of Transoxiana in 792–6 to keep an eye on the most potentially dangerous frontiers. When Pope Hadrian died in 795 Justinian appointed an even more politically obsequious but rather less popular successor, the devious if talented Papal chancery finance-director Leo III (OTL Pope), to succeed him and passed over various more respected theologians and philanthropic bishops in the interests of 'control' and obedience.

This showed that the Emperor, who ignored advice to appoint a more learned and respected theologian instead of a 'political' figure, was succumbing to an increasing obsession with creating an obedient political structure to govern the Empire smoothly. He had hardened not mellowed with age, though he could still relax on his hunting-trips with his trusted ex-army colleagues and horse-mad nobles and his interest in finding new and challenging species to hunt led, unintentionally, to his importing and helping scientific studies of exotic African wildlife as he had his traders in East Africa who were visiting the ports of Kilwa and Mombasa buy and bring back animals such as giraffe and zebras for him to put in his large hunting-parks across central Italy and hunt. (Some of these also appeared on mosaics and murals of religious, usually Old Testament events in the era's churches.) Justinian also brought in a number of rare tigers and leopards from India to hunt and was known to use a pet elephant sent by the rajah of Varanasi on the Ganges for military parades (infantry only as it was scared of horses). Typically Rillanus was too inept or scared a rider to dare to take part in his father's elaborate hunts for exotic beasts that might fight back or alarm his horse but his twin Septimius did so and hunted with rather more enthusiasm and success than was seeming for a future bishop. There were gossipy rumours that after one excessive drunken party left a disguised Rillanus, who had sneaked out of the Marble Palace with some friends, unconscious and naked in a brothel in a seedy quarter of Rome the police raided it and his friends fled – just as the Emperor was making an address to a reception for top nobles about the necessity for Cato-style moralistic Romans to defeat the 'wiles of Bacchic temptation' After this apparent incident, in May 797, Justinian was thinking of disinheriting his heir and making him a bishop instead and might 'de-frock' Septimius to be his new successor, but if so this was forestalled as on 21 July 797 he died of a sudden seizure, aged 55, after an impressive 30-year reign that was the longest period of Imperial office since Titus II's .

Chapter 8

Rillanus II 797–812: An Unworthy Heir and Important Tasks Neglected?

Son of Justinian

Justin 812–820: The Military Martinet. War in the North – Teaching The Norsemen a Lesson.

Younger Brother of Justinian

The late Emperor had made his dispositions for a stable political succession and avoidance of any turbulence caused by an underage heir, and as Rillanus succeeded at the age of seventeen the Council proclaimed the Empress Maria Eucheria as regent as laid out in her husband's arrangements. Justinian had no intention of letting the brusque and narrow-minded philistine Justin near power given his capacity for making enemies. Rillanus had been told by his father at an earlier and happier stage of their relationship that he did not have to rule, only reign, and as long as he avoided doing harm and making important judgements on inadequate evidence and without taking his experts' advice he did not have to work as hard as Justinian had done. Rillanus accordingly did not challenge his mother's right to govern for him until he was eighteen and apparently refused suggestions from ambitious young courtier friends of his that he should push her into a nunnery as she was so fond of good works and take full power himself.

For this lazy and greedy but not bad-hearted young man, the archetypal spoilt and extravagant 'golden lad' of court life, the Imperial role was there to be acted out like an actor and to be enjoyed and his main concern was to get his hands on as much money, good food, and rare wines as possible, together with being able to gamble what he liked without being told off. Accordingly he sacked his tutors, while remaining on good terms with those who he liked, and gave senior court posts to his own coterie of young officers and ex-schoolfellows at his private 'classes' in the Palace, with a twenty-year-old rake from a multi-millionaire noble Italian dynasty of five hundred years' standing in the Senate becoming his chamberlain and another half-dozen young officers aged under twenty-five his 'Gentlemen of the Bedchamber'. But apart from these appointments and the creation of a new troupe of Imperial dancing-girls (mostly from his favourite brothels or the households of his richer friends) he did not make many changes to court life and he did his best to attend what events in the annual round of ceremonies did not clash with his parties and race-meetings, performing with grace and charm and winning the public over at the Games with his interest in the races and gifts to the winners. The Empress and her favourite clerics tut-tutted at his lack of morals and open consorting with 'loose women', including a number of well-endowed young ex-wives of prominent courtiers. But the flattering and ambitious Pope Leo did not object and even cut the coronation Mass in October 797 by half so the Emperor did not become bored. As Rillanus was a keen Iconodule and liked portraits of the Holy Family and saints on artistic and aesthetic grounds, commissioning many from the era's greatest icon-painters to keep the Church happy, that dominant faction hailed him as a great and holy patron and ignored the stories of his debauchery and extravagance.

The 'Master of Offices' Leo Parcellius (in office since 795), 'Count of Sacred Largesses' Honorius Iacellianus (in office since 793), 'Count of the Privy Purse' Justus Trocandrus (in office since 790), Postal 'Logothete' Tiberius Raupellius (in office since 788), Public Works minister Julianus Anicetianus (in office since 794), and secretary for correspondence Antonius Batravellius (in office since 790) had been set up in the mid-790s by Justinian as his unofficial 'inner Council' of six. They, along with the more frequently changed holders of the ranks of Praetorian Praefect and 'Quaestor', would govern Rome with him and if he died would replace him and rein in his ineffective and lazy son. As Rillanus had no quarrels with any of them and they did not seek to interfere in his private life or extravagance he kept all six of them in office well into the 800s and the direction of Roman state policy hardly changed in July 797. Even when the rampant Imperial spending got further out of control and Rillanus started to build expensive new holiday villas with huge swimming-pools, reception-halls, and garden terraces on Sicily (mostly around Syracuse) and on Corcyra in the Ionian Sea for his summer retreats after 800 it was only the cost-cutting finance minister Iacellianus who risked quarrelling with him over his 'unwise' behaviour.

He was sacked and then Rillanus appointed an equally competent but more emollient successor from within the bureaucracy's senior ranks, Camillus Castronius, to succeed him and he 'tweaked' spending to save on other departments' provincial spending (mostly on junior ranks' salaries) to keep up the outflow of money that the Emperor demanded without affecting important projects. As Rillanus celebrated his majority with grand tours of the Empire to show himself to his subjects – northern Italy and Gaul in 799, Britain and the Rhineland to Rhaetia in 800, Greece and the Balkans in 801, Asia Minor and Syria in 802, Carthage and Tripolitania to Alexandria in 803, and Dacia and the lower Danube plus Cherson and Colchis in 804 – he was still hugely popular with the public as a handsome and charismatic if by now slightly overweight young man who knew how to make a speech and make a show at the right time. There was unease about him in the Council, but no sense of anyone willing to plot.

The Emperor continued to support philosophy and scientific experimentation, partly as one of his more eclectic tutors in the early 790s (Domitius Alexianophilus from Alexandria University) had been an expert on and enthusiast for the work of Archimedes and was recalled to court in 798 to advise the Emperor and the ministers on how to progress beyond the 3rd century BC-scientist's mechanical contraptions for the Syracusan army and navy to benefit the Roman armed forces. The decision was apparently pressed on the Emperor as showing his commitment to the military – seen as his weak spot, with intelligence reports of frontier generals' grumbling. This duly led to Alexianophilus and his group of assistants being recruited to the 'high command' HQ to work on adaptations of Archimedes' machines for use by the Roman army in sieges and on 'ship-lifting' haulage cranes with hooks that could be put on huge 'quinquereme' galleys and used at sea to attack and sink enemy ships. By the late 800s enough naval contraptions had been built to enable tests to go ahead at sea in the central Mediterranean with replica Arabo-Somali pirate galleys and Indian Ocean (Arab and southern Indian) sailed 'dhows'. The intention was to make Rome's navy in the Indian Ocean, based at Aden and Socotra, and the squadron that patrolled the lower Persian Gulf and approaches to the Indus invincible and so create full regional security for merchants. Rillanus was generous in his pumping funds into this project even if it was more due to a fondness for exotic Indian trade-goods (which he displayed at his summer retreats in Sicily and on Corcyra and to a lesser extent at the Marble Palace) than imperial and expansionist military ideals – unlike his generals' and admirals' enthusiasm. The project was played up on his coins to show his continuing his father's devotion to Roman power.

Tests were also carried out on the new Archimedes-style artillery and siege-engines at the lower Danube armies' training-grounds and barracks around Nicopolis and Silistria. Once they had been modified by experience some were used in the recapture of some forts in allied Daghestan, overrun by rebel nomad vassals of the Khazars who had overrun the area en route to a planned attack on North Adiabene, in 807. Also long-range 'flame-throwers' were developed for use in throwing 'Greek Fire' over the walls of enemy cities and towns and were tested on abandoned towns (left useless to residents by the adjacent River Jaxartes shifting its course after landslides and floods) in Sogdiana in 808. All this was designed to reconcile the ever-critical military leadership to the Emperor's lack of interest in offensive warfare and his increasingly dubious interference from c. 804 in the business of military promotions to aid the careers of his friends among high-living young officers, especially in the 'Scholae' and other fashionable non-'front line' regiments. By 808 this had cost him the services of two successive Praetorian Praefects who resigned in disgust. Though the military commanders away from Rome were not much affected as Rillanus' debauched and gambling-mad friends preferred 'safe' jobs in Italy to life on the frontiers. But the more moral and less loose-living officers of 'smart' regiments, in Rome in particular, grumbled at the number of lazy and spendthrift juniors being promoted over their heads just because they had been at Imperial parties and won the Emperor's goodwill and/or were spendthrift patrons of racing-teams at the Circus Maximus. The Emperor ignored his uncle Justin's demands for a war against the increasingly bold and assertive Turks beyond the Jaxartes frontier, who were now raiding across the Kara Kum desert into eastern Hyrcania as the Jaxartes had too strong a line of forts and patrolling cavalry units to be worth tackling. But all that happened was that in 806 he was moved from his current post as a 'special consultant commissioner' and 'Frontier Cavalry Count' in Bactria-Sogdiana and sent off to a 'rear' post running procurement and training at the Arab frontier 'HQ' at Hira in Mesopotamia.

Rillanus preferred to avoid the prospect of having to send a costly and potentially dangerous expedition to meddle in the affairs of the feuding Turkish warlords on the Turkestan steppes and instead just ordered his revamped command on the Jaxartes to bribe the restive chiefs and/or hire some of their best cavalry commanders to work for not against Rome. As the rural citizens of plundered eastern Hyrcania rioted against their useless 'dux' (father of one of the Emperor's cronies) and complacent governor and set fire to the latter's palace in the provincial capital, Rayy, the Emperor sent in more troops but only to punish them. These carried out exemplary executions but did not rebuild the sacked or undermanned frontier forts around (often besieged but not taken) Zadracarta at the south-east corner of the Caspian Sea. The situation in Hyrcania continued to deteriorate and there was a flight of panicking or ruined peasant-farmers to the hills and forests of the Zagros range and collapse of agriculture in the later 800s and early-mid 810s as a result of the Emperor's neglect. The same nonchalance and protection of well-connected but useless commanders hit the situation in Britain and Caledonia as the 'Classis Britannia' fleet, based at Dubris, Othona, and Gariannonum plus a newer (8th century) northern naval base on the Firth of Forth, were unable to catch fast and cunning Norse raiders in their adaptable longships.

The Norse 'Viking' ('Men of the Viks' i.e. fjords), short of land in mountainous Norwegia and in need of prestige and loot from successful raids, were too cautious to alert and arouse the wrath of the well-led and flexible Roman squadrons that were now sent to the Skaggerak or to raid Jutland after the past Roman attacks on the Vestfold plains. But after a successful 'hit and run' looting raid on the prestigious north-east British monastery of Lindisfarne in July 793 (OTL event) they began to attack the north-east coast of Britain from the Humber up to the Dornoch Firth regularly and the small Roman naval squadron in the Firth of Forth rarely caught their ships in time. The commanders there and at the Roman bases at the mouths of the Spey and the Ness continually asked for support and extra ships and men and were given a few of both by Justinian in 795 but were ignored as the Norse were seen as a 'minor irritant' after the regency ended in September 798.

With more Norse settling on the Orkneys and now raiding the under-manned Pictish lands in north-west Caledonia the 800s saw the incomers 'ethnically cleansing' the Outer Hebrides and settling in considerable numbers on bleak, infertile but strategic Lewis – and from 808 on Skye, the main islands still under Pictish control until then. Indeed, some (many?) landless local younger sons were rumoured to be running away to join the Norse as scouts and suppliers.

A Norse slave-market developed at Dunvegan and from the mid-800s the settlers and annual expeditions of raiders from Norwegia were raiding disordered Ulster in Ireland and carrying off its inhabitants as slaves and its livestock for Norse farms. As the invasions and raids did not affect the Empire directly beyond a few 'irritating' attacks each year on coastal farms and villages in eastern Caledonia and NE Britain (Votadini territory) the 'high command' in Rome did not bother to interfere as it was clear that the Emperor was not interested and would only get angry if reminded of this problem. It was left to the enterprising and worried *'dux'* of Caledonia, Asprenius Nonianus – usefully from a senior senatorial dynasty in Rome with relatives and friends in the Senate to back him up and read out his dispatches to his superiors – to intervene with the limited amount of military support at his disposal in his period in office there, in 798–806. He assisted the weakened and outnumbered local Picts in the western Highlands and the allied kingdom of Dalriada to fight off Viking raiders, and though he and his supportive naval commanders on the east coast caught and punished some raiders they were unable to halt the takeover of the Hebrides by incoming Vikings. In 805 the army of allied Dalriada was ambushed and mauled in a glen near Loch Fyne by two combined forces of Norsemen while Nonianus was absent retaking a Norse-occupied fortress in bleak north-west Caithness and driving Norse slave-traders back to the coast.

Nonianus acquired heroic status as a traditional Roman warrior fighting off axe-swinging Northern 'barbarians' in his Caledonian campaigns and was celebrated in poetry by patriots in Rome. But the annoyed Emperor arranged for his recall to Rome to take up an advisory post at the 'Military Strategy Centre' in late 806, effectively to shut him up. Though the brilliant young general was able to revitalize Roman 'anti-insurgent' tactics at handling fast-moving land and sea raiders – and won the support of Justin when the latter visited the capital in 807 – he would not shut up about the Empire's failing north-western strategy and he was increasingly backed up by angry and humiliated generals. Senators too alleged that Rome was letting its citizens down, and hinted at Court complacency. This then led to the Emperor sacking him from his post and exiling him to Epirus for alleged subversive remarks at drinking-parties for senior generals, late in 809. Rillanus appointed one of his 'flashy' young officer friends, brother of the current leading Imperial mistress, to take over in Caledonia late in 806 and he proved a disaster who lacked ideas or flexibility. After he was ambushed with an over-confident cavalry force while riding across the Atholl hills to support the latest (fifth in a decade) king of Dalriada by a fast-moving force of Norsemen with local scouts in summer 808 he had to flee on foot with a few survivors and hide in the local bogs while most of his men were killed or taken off as slaves by the raiders. The sight of the *'dux'* of Caledonia hiding in a bog and then limping back to the nearest Roman base disguised as a local peasant while his abandoned captive officers were paraded in loincloths and chains in a Viking slave-market in Trondelag and sent off to work on local farms as 'thralls' (serfs) humiliated the Empire. It led to attacks on Rillanus in the Senate, with comparisons of him to Nero who had looked like him (he was now both overweight and in possession of a beard) and his current mistress, a Syrian prostitute who lived in the Marble Palace with a large entourage of girls as her maids, to Nero's wife Poppaea. But Rillanus did not alter his military dispositions and was more interested in the current arrival of an embassy from T'ang China, whose ambassadors were entertained with regal displays of luxury and huge banquets plus a month of races to show them that the Emperor was a 'Son of Heaven' like their sovereign, worthy of respect. The Northern frontier was of little interest to him compared to his fellow- 'world rulers' – and their impressive displays of power.

While Rillanus, a great showman and amateur choreographer, was arranging firework – and dance-displays plus a massive athletics tournament by the 'Ephebes' in Rome to overawe the ambassadors the Norsemen proceeded to overrun all of coastal Dalriada in successive landings by armed immigrant bands in 808–11. In the latter year they sacked the kingdom's main town and fortress of Dunadd and created a new Viking 'jarldom' there, and as the Dalriadan ex-king Custennin (Constantine) Mac Fergus (OTL) fled to the Empire to try to get help Rillanus had him detained in Gaul so he did not turn up in Rome and embarrass him. The survival of any of the Dalriadan nobility and their refugee coastal farmers and villagers was left to a minor but brave and ingenious local noble trained as a Roman officer, Cinaed mac Alpin (OTL king Kenneth mac Alpine), who took leave of absence from his command to return home and evacuate a column of his people from the Firth of Lorn to settle in Roman-allied northern Strathclyde around Loch Lomond. As the NW of Caledonia fell to the Norse and the latter then moved on to start to settle in more fertile Ulster too the alarmed Irish Church leadership at Armagh, who were relying on a hastily hired force of Roman soldiers to prevent the cathedral and monastery there being sacked, appealed in autumn 811 to the Church in Rome for help. This made even the bland, 'Imperial lackey' Pope Leo – who was already facing the fury of moralist clergy and monks for not objecting to the Emperor's lurid private life and many mistresses – agree to make strong representations to the Emperor that he was letting Christians be persecuted by the pagan Norsemen and had neglected his duty. The Emperor and the Pope had jointly ignored 'lobbying' by the most distinguished of many contemporary British monastic scholars, the theologian and 'Church Fathers' expert and long-standing monastic school teacher Alcuinus of Eburacum (OTL :Alcuin), on behalf of the sacked monastery of Lindisfarne and its worried neighbours at Iarovium on the Tyne as early as 798. Pope Leo had then passed on the monastic request for help in getting captured monks rescue from slavery and assorted looted treasure from the monastery redeemed from Norse warlords' treasuries to the Church and 'dux' in Dania and they had paid up ransom-demands (haggled down to a lower level by threats of naval attacks on Vestfold if the Vikings were not more reasonable) and had their men and property returned some months later. As the British and Gallic Churches were scared of more attacks the Emperor had had the coastal patrols in both regions increased and smaller and faster vessels hired for the 'Classis Britannica' – equipped with 'Greek Fire' to destroy Viking ships, though usually the latter had carefully evaded them. The Gallic Church, which had close links with Rome via the inter-connections of noble dynasties that supplied bishops to both regions, had been bought off too. The education ministry had agreed to help fund a plan for a new theological and monastic training school – upgraded in the 820s to a full university – at the shrine and monastery of St Martin at Turones on the River Loire, where Alcuinus was the main senior teacher and C2nd to C5th 'Church Fathers' expert hired to head the teaching when the academy opened in 804 and in 808–12 he was then the abbot of the Turones monastery.

But giving generous grants to educational projects in the intellectually confident Iconodule Church of the West was not going to fob off complaints about the Emperor indefinitely. The same applied in the East where the carefully non-combative careerist Patriarch Tarasius of Constantinople (OTL) and his counterparts in Antioch and Alexandria kept their mouths shut and their clerics and monks 'gagged' with prosecutions and deportations of anyone who attacked Rillanus' laziness and immorality. But Abbot Plato of Sakkudion, in Bithynia, the stern guardian of public morals, was barely kept in check by the wily finance-expert Praefect of Constantinople in 801–11, the Imperial ally Nicephorus the Phrygian. (OTL: the then Byzantine Emperor.) By now Rillanus had also been damaged by his fractious relationship with his ambitious and maverick brother Septimius, a reluctant Bishop of Tarentum (802) who his brother virtually forced to take up a major see by threats to put him in prison for illegal homosexual affairs with teenage boys and who then spent more time hunting and partying. Septimius was not appealing to the Church moralists as a replacement Emperor but was still the target of assorted courtiers annoyed at missing out on promotion or lucrative Imperial grants. The mercurial Septimius was as selfish and hedonistic as his twin and after Empress Maria Drusilla died in 804 his conduct deteriorated further as he began to conduct homosexual affairs openly and promoted his lovers in junior Church offices. The supine Pope Leo and his equally careful careerist senior bishops began to be openly condemned for setting a bad example by their toleration of this sort of behaviour by writers and preachers across the Empire, some radicals (including ex-'Iconoclasts' in Syria and Palestine(implying that the Italian Church as a whole was corrupt and worldly and needed to be purged. Meanwhile secular nobles and retired ministers in the Senate and senior generals looked on disgusted.

After Pope Leo (OTL figure) barely survived an attempt by 'grass-roots' pressure, backed discreetly by moralist Gallic and Spanish bishops, to have a commission set up to investigate him for taking bribes and promoting incompetent and over-young relatives of Imperial allies at the 808 Western Church Council even he had to show that he was a protector of justice and the poor. He duly had a commission set up to purge 'unworthy' junior (not senior) Italian clerics, and the devious and by now rather worried Emperor, alerted by the police to plotters gathering around Septimius, did not intervene as his brother was investigated for corruption and in early 809 was hauled before a court for alleged public indecency with his male lovers. The usual backroom deals were arranged by courtiers who did not want a Prince, albeit a maverick and scandalous one, humiliated and Septimius was found innocent amidst public rejoicing in Rome and (due to his lavish public festivals) in Tarentum, but he was eventually sacked in 810 for embezzlement after a 'sting' arranged by the police at the Emperor's request. He was required to leave Italy and go into exile at a remote monastery on Crete, supposedly to pursue his 'monastic vocation' but in fact to get him away from plotters and keep him under surveillance as a security risk while his current lovers were investigated and most were exiled too. The scandals were not over yet and possibly the plots were not either as in May 811 the Prince disappeared from his monastery and was apparently found dead at the foot of a steep cliff a few miles away, aged 31. Although he was supposed to have had a mental breakdown due to the after-effects of 'withdrawal symptoms' from some drugs that he had used to take at his parties, run away from his monastery, and fallen down a cliff stories soon spread that he had in fact escaped with the collusion of some of his guards who had been bribed by a secret group of army plotters. Septimius may have been intended as a 'front-man' for a new regime – but if so was he 'silenced' by his brother's men?

The disgraceful behaviour and increasing disregard for the law or the social conventions of Rome by Rillanus had led to a revival in interest in the republican political views of those stern moralists who Justinian had hailed and had had paraded as examples of 'Roman virtue' to the young, e.g. the two Catos and Cicero though he had always insisted that it be stressed a republic led to power-struggles and chaos.

In that vein some young university intellectuals in Rome had gone beyond studying Republican Roman virtues to discussing the assassination of Julius Caesar and vowing to emulate Brutus and Cassius and rid Rome of the 'tyrant'. They had linked up with dissident officers who had failed to interest Prince Justin in their own plot and who were turning to the idea of Septimius as a controllable 'puppet emperor' despite his failings, who in turn were reportedly linked to the disgraced general Nonianus. Though Rillanus and his new police-chief, 'state security secretary' Paulus Posidosianus (a post created by Justinian in 790), kept the whole affair under wraps and exiled all who dared to say publicly that the Prince's 'death' was more than a tragic accident he was soon being called a fratricide and though the 'late' Septimius had been too spoilt, greedy and immoral to be hailed as a martyr the Church was up in arms too. Pope Leo was faced with increasing anger and contempt from within his junior and even his senior ranks. In fact it was later alleged by 16th-century investigative historians that Septimius was not killed in the fall at all but that he vanished from the scene and was the subject of a frantic police hunt while a 'lookalike' was found – probably a man who had been used before to impersonate the Emperor at state ceremonies if he was too hung-over or too busy with prostitutes to attend them. This man was killed off and given a state funeral so that if Septimius did 'surface' he could be written off as a pretender.

Nonianus was said to have been involved in the 'rescue' via friendly Aegean Island fishermen who knew the cliffside paths in that part of Crete and to have hidden the Prince at his 'exile' estate in Epirus. The fact that a few months later Nonianus was arrested for a supposed plot to return from exile and kill the Emperor, tried before a 'maiestas' (treason) court behind closed doors, and sent to a slave-mine in the Illyrian mountains for life was explained as a punishment for the 'rescue' and for his failure to say where Septimius was hiding. Had he betrayed the Prince he would have been allowed an easier punishment of exile on an Indian Ocean island off Aden and it was not clear exactly why Rillanus' successor Justin had not pardoned him – had he wanted Septimius killed too, as a potential rival? But in 815 Nonianus was allowed to exchange his slavery in a mine for agricultural labour on a 'latifundia' farm in Dacia and in 820 he was pardoned after Justin died but never allowed back to Italy and presumably he had no idea by that time of where Septimius was. Some later claimed that an anonymous Aegean sea-captain of mysterious origins who ended up trading with and settling in India was Septimius and others that he repented his wild life and ended up as a holy hermit in rocky Caria who received Imperial funding for his hermitage from the 820s to the 850s. But in any case he never reappeared in public. The stories did undeniably testify to both murky goings-on in the Imperial Family and widespread cynicism about official explanations – which alarmed monarchists saw as damaging their favoured institution. Meanwhile the Emperor was now booed in the streets of Rome and had to call off the ex-'Saturnalia' chariot-races in December 811 as he was pelted with refuse in the Circus Maximus as he presented prizes and had to flee to the old Imperial Palace nearby for safety while his troops cleared the stadium, killing over fifty people in the 'crush'. After this he left Rome in a hurry and his ministers persuaded him to agree to a new Church synod of the Italian bishops being called to set up a formal legal investigation into charges of corruption and crooked appointments for cash made against Pope Leo. The enquiry found that there was a case to answer and so the Pope went on trial and was eventually forced to agree to abdicate in return for a pardon, the determination of the stern moralist Bishops of the Gallic and Spanish Churches to see him disgraced and ruined having caused them to spend a lot of effort and cash on finding the evidence against him. They, not the Emperor's allies on the reluctant legal commission, were hailed by the public and the Eastern Churches as heroes.

An impeccably honest and philanthropic junior bishop from a noble local Sabine dynasty called Stephen, who had spent a lot of time personally educating poor boys and girls and washing the feet of the poor as a bishop in Calabria in the 800s and had sold off his see's gold plate to pay for a hospital, was made Pope instead and soon restored the dignity and reputation of the see, fortunately for Rillanus being too forgiving and congenial to blame the Emperor or his Italian colleagues for the recent scandals. But if 'St Stephen the Second' was very popular with rich and poor alike the bishops who had excused the Emperor of consorting with prostitutes, 'killing' his brother, and sending a popular hero to the slave-mines were still hated and the next local synod, in 814, saw them pelted with mud on their way to the meeting in Rome. The current 'wave' of younger and (if in office) junior ecclesiastical 'reformers' and Christian 'purists', who outside intellectual observers such as the shrewd semi-pagan antiquarian noble 'wit' and bibliophile Armandus Arastadorus commented would have been rowdy 'iconoclasts' smashing up 'idols' if this had been legally tolerated, were turning on a 'conformist' and careerist hierarchy. The Church leadership had to show that they were willing to act more idealistically. Prompted by his alarmed Catholic lay advisers and some fellow-generals who had idealistic Christian beliefs (and in some cases were using their family money to found monasteries or schools), Rillanus' by then successor Emperor Justin had to set up a new commission to decide who else should be sacked to save the Church's reputation and this time put moralist Spanish and Gallic – and North African – bishops on it with 'full powers'. A third of the Italian bishops and almost all those appointed by Leo since 800 were sacked and he himself was despite his pardon required to hand extra money and possessions back to the Church and then sent off to a cell in a strict monastery in Dalmatia to repent at leisure. By that time Rillanus was in disgrace and exile too, as he had followed up his attack on Nonianus by travelling to Constantinople to hold a vindictive Church Council of the Patriarchate's bishops to try Abbot Plato of the Sakkudion monastery for his latest libels against him, this time implying that the Emperor had committed fratricide. The Emperor and his Syrian mistress, who he now married in the Eastern ex-capital in January 812 well away from the furore in Rome (but only got a parish priest to conduct the ceremony in his Sacred Palace chapel there as Patriarch Nicephorus would not let him use the cathedral of Hagia Sophia), were less at risk from angry crowds in Constantinople than in Rome as his affairs were less well known there. He had also lavished patronage on the city and its Church, especially 'Iconodule' churches and monasteries, but even so the sight of Abbot Plato being condemned for treasonous libel and dragged out of court to prison calling the Emperor 'Nebuchadnezzar' to his face stirred up anger and Rillanus now closed down the famous Sakkudion monastery and sent all its monks into exile, most to harsh Syrian and Palestinian monasteries. The monastery's treasures were seized by the treasury to pay for extra resources for the defence of Turk-raided Hyrcania and the new Empress, who was devoutly wearing white and simple robes and doing good works but convinced nobody of her holiness, was sent to present rich gifts to other leading local monasteries to win the Church round. But weeks later the Emperor made the fatal mistake of summoning Justin to court to explain why he had been illegally paying a visit in disguise to the troops and local Count on the lower Danube – was he involved in a plot?

But if Justin had been up to no good he had prepared his ground well and contacted many senior officers in the 'comitatus' and the 'Scholae' as well or else the disgusted senior officers of both would not put up with Rillanus any longer, and on 12 April 812 the arrival of Justin in Constantinople with his escort of lower Danube officers – meant to be bringing him as a prisoner but in fact treating him with honour – was greeted by huge and welcoming crowds. Simultaneously a large group of 'Scholae' officers, led by their commanders, surrounded the Sacred Palace and demanded that the guards on duty let them in. What exactly happened as the group of generals and their juniors, accompanied by priests sent by the Patriarch, confronted the Emperor is not clear and the official line had it that he was presented with a long list of his 'crimes' and was persuaded that he was an incompetent and corrupt ruler who was bringing disgrace on Rome and had to abdicate. But within hours he had handed over his regalia to the arriving Justin and signed a document of abdication, aged thirty-one, and the Patriarch gave his blessing to the new Emperor Justin (aged sixty-seven) before the transfer of power was announced to the city's Senate and in the cathedral. The Senate in Rome apparently taken by surprise, acquiesced – and was accused by moralist thinkers of having failed to do its duty and put Rome first earlier.

Next day the coup was confirmed to the city's crowds in the Hippodrome to loud cheers while a message by carrier-pigeon was sent to Rome where a similar military coup took place there as the Marble Palace was seized and the abdication was announced to the Senate, and though Justin had never been popular he was regarded by all except a group of Rillanus' toadies and assorted crooked or hedonistic court nobles and officers as much preferable to his predecessor. Despite a torrent of abuse in the Senate and in the Church Rillanus was never put on trial for his crimes but was exiled quietly to one of his holiday homes on Corcyra and later in 812 was transferred to a monastery in the Peloponnese as 'Brother Marcus' to live out his life as a humble monk, living in poverty and chastity (presumably) for the next fifty years. But the Empress was declared to have been married to one of her rakish admirers in Antioch before and not been divorced properly so she was not even legally Empress and she had to hand back all her wealth and was exiled to remote Iberia where she was locked up in a nunnery in the Caucasus mountains and was not allowed out for years to come and then only on pilgrimage. The new Emperor sacked nearly all of his predecessor's ministers for not standing up to the 'tyrant' and those who had been involved in corrupt practices ended up having to pay back all their gains though Justin was too canny to disgrace the entire 'government machine' with open trials and gaol-sentences and even most of the ex-ruler's dodgy court appointees escaped prosecution provided that they paid back al that they had been given and left Italy. As the rule of law and public honesty was restored and the monks and abbot of the Sakkudion monastery were returned to their residence with honour and a public apology Justin found himself unusually popular and even his cancellation of most of the new race-days that Rillanus had introduced to Rome and his refusal of a full or early pardon to Nonianus did not dent his early good reputation. Despite his fears the institution of the monarchy was not much damaged once he had got the Imperial 'spin' machine in action to write off his predecessor's reign as a 'one-off' aberration. The new Emperor, an abrupt and autocratic ex-general with no cultural interests and few friends except a group of his trusted long-term military colleagues and men he had been educated with at the Palace in the 740s and early 760s, was inexperienced in politics and inclined to distrust all of Rillanus' 'inner circle' of bureaucrats who had sanctioned his amoral and maverick rule, not least on moral grounds. His own ultra-Catholic wife Drusilla Julania had died in 807 so he was a widower with no close religious-minded 'stalwart' to back him unlike his father, but the Palace and capital's administrative classes 'closed ranks' around him to protect the role and status of the Emperor from any questioning of its usefulness and offered him their support. He accepted this, albeit with grumpy suspicion and an immediate suspending of many of his brother Justinian's and nephew's grand ceremonies and parties as unnecessary.

The role of Emperor as protector of justice and unity was revived and a series of special commissions in 812–16 purged 'unworthy' senior administrators and punished aristocratic friends of Rillanus who had used his influence to achieve unwise grants of money, gifts, and land or had had legal cases swayed their way, and the ruthless and efficient new 'Master of Offices' Agrippinus Agatianus, brought in from a role as head of the administration in Ctesiphon in 808–11, proceeded to winkle assorted corrupt incompetents out of the state administration and bring in many new provincial 'self-made' men, mostly winners of the state service examinations in the 780s to 800s. 'Count of the Sacred Largesses' Xenon of Tyre, son of a successful self-made Phoenician 'merchant prince' exporter of Levantine goods to Italy who had hundreds of ships at his beck and call, purged the Imperial finances of waste and made it clear that all expenditure had to be accounted for and 'double-book-keeping' or 'under-the-counter' pay-offs would be ferreted out and end in the culprits being sent to the mines. The Emperor kept on more of the aristocracy who Rillanus had given court sinecures or undemanding roles in the Imperial service in their home provinces than his early boasts suggested would be the case. This was due to a cautious desire not to create enemies and plots rather than a lack of reformist zeal, and the Church was allowed virtual free rein to enforce the veneration of icons on the dubious or hostile citizenry and its own officials in the East and to set up pious and theologically restrictive schools in the West and East alike. The education ministry made sure that hostile bishops did not interfere in university studies of the scientific and other analytical works of Aristotle or dare to suggest that Plato was an unworthy and 'sinful' pagan subject unworthy of study by the proper Christian. (Plato's C3rd AD anti-Christian follower Plotinus was another matter, but the banning of students and tutors who studied him from Church schools or offices was partial even in the strongest times of orthodox zeal in the reign of Justin and was not enforced by many liberal officials; it was most strict in Gaul, Spain and Italy plus parts of Asia Minor.)

Justin posed as a pious Christian of impeccable orthodoxy and went on pilgrimages in his early years in power, eg to the monastery of St Benedict in 821 and Greek and Thracian shrines plus Ephesus in 822, while he also kept up Imperial attendance of Church services and religious processions on holy days more than Rillanus had done. But his main interests were military and he quickly carried out his pledges to put the army first by increasing the military budget by 15 per cent in 821–2 and promoting a new wave of capable middle-ranking officers who he had come across as a 'count' and as an inspector to senior rank as 'duces' and at the 'general staff' HQ in Rome. The development of military technology carried out under Rillanus was kept up and its budget doubled and the Emperor now arranged for the army to liaise with the education ministry about luring bright young men with good academic records into the 'military engineering' sections of army bases and the Military Strategy Centre. As the amount of cash spent on and the capability of the officers supervising the fortification of the most dangerous outer frontiers was stepped up even in 812 the frontiers of Hyrcania were repaired and new forts erected there at a fast rate by a dynamic new 'dux' with a keen and forceful staff of engineers. The wrecked agriculture of the province took years to recover and was not helped by an ongoing drought in the 810s that led to a need to spend huge sums on repairing and adding to irrigation all over the high Persian plateau and in the Bactrian plains too. Indeed it was taking so much money to keep corn-growing and feeding cattle viable the local governors and some wiser nobles ended up suggesting that a greater emphasis on pastoral farming – sheep in particular – might be cheaper and easier and in 818 the government's local advisers approved this and recommended it to Rome. As a result small farming in the region, the backbone of the Roman way of agriculture but more suited to a more fertile region like the plains of fertile Mesopotamia, was to be eclipsed by roaming tribesmen or noble-hired shepherds with flocks of sheep in decades to come. With a lack of nomad used to this sort of farming in the plateau –the Roman state had deported the old Sassanid tribes to be kept an eye on in the Arab desert fringes in the C7th as a security hazard – the Empire was to call in an increasing number of Turkish tribesmen from Turkestan, men with huge flocks of sheep and who were used to moving around an arid area in their tents and not settling in one place.

Given the security risk of looting-prone and bored young Turk warriors attacking settled farmers or turning brigand this had to be carefully managed and most of those hired by the local governors ended up being either Turkish 'civilian' chieftains who were already sheep-rearing entrepreneurs who wanted to get away from the threat of brigands and civil war in unruly Turkestan or else pro-Roman chiefs who had already served in the Roman army and were trustworthy. As a result the Turkish population of the Iranian plateau was to rise significantly in the 820s to 870s and a greater number of young men from this background ended up in the Roman armies in the East, either with Turkish or with Roman names and cultural affiliations, and some even started to head to Ctesiphon and Constantinople or to Rome to join the Imperial regiments there. The influx of Turks gave a 'career path' to restive Turks beyond the frontier and this and the firm repression of raiding in Hyrcania restored peace to the NE frontier. But in the NW it was a different story as firm repression of raids by an augmented and better-led 'Classis Britanniae' and a doubled-in-size Hibernian Sea fleet was not enough to keep the restive and risk-seeking Norsemen back. The latter had overrun the Hebrides and most of Dalriada and as of 812–15 were now settling in Ulster and evicting or enslaving the locals, though for fear of Rome they steered clear of the monastic HQ at Armagh, and from the start of his reign Justin was planning to punish the Norsemen where it mattered by taking over the fertile plains of southern Norwegia and having his men trained for this war while he had many new ships built and fitted with 'Greek Fire'-throwing artillery and in Caledonia armed patrols of up to 5000 new troops kept an eye on the coasts with fast cavalry and small war-galleys and had more success than previously in catching and defeating Norse raiders. The Emperor was too cautious to leave Rome and take charge of the war himself given his fear of a coup, notably by the reviving if small group of intellectual republican fans of the Catos and Cicero. So he appointed one of his close friends and old military cronies with decades of experience (including as 'dux' of Dania), Claudius Camillianus, to take command instead, and in spring 815 a huge flotilla of ships armed with 'Greek Fire' loaded up with troops assembled from all over the Empire and headed from Gesoriacum across the North Sea to land on one of the fjords east of Vestfold. More ships took part of the garrisons and 'limitanei' of the Danish provinces plus more troops from Germany and the Rhineland across the Skaggerak from Claudiana to land nearby and the allied Swedes sent in a force by land.

Most of the 'Classis Britanniae' was involved with the invasion while most of the troops in Britain proceeded North to invade Dalriada from the Clyde to link up with refugee prince Cinaed and the Hibernian Sea fleet landed troops in Argyll. The choppy seas and treacherous tides meant that the usual large and heavy galleys – 'dromones' – of the Imperial navy, which the North Sea commanders preferred to use (and to order from the Empire's dockyards) as they were not affected by sudden drops or shifts in the wind and could be rowed steadily at a known pace, were supplemented by more than usual light sailing-ships commanded by locally expert captains. Some of these were the sons of Danish, Frisian, and British fishermen or maritime traders who the meritocrat Justin had had recruited into the navy as knowing the seas better than the usual aristocratic young Mediterranean landowning elite officers. Where the latter had been kept on, usually at a senior level, they were told firmly to taken on local pilots and listen to their local sailors too. With a squadron of Hibernian Sea warships (from a fleet which had always had more local and lower-class recruits who knew the seas better, as few elite Mediterranean officers wanted to serve somewhere so 'backward' and isolated) lurking off the Dalriadan coast ready to blast any interfering Viking ships from the Hebrides or Ulster with 'Greek Fire', the reconquest of Dalriada proceeded relatively smoothly. Cinead and his exiles, who knew the countryside, helped to hunt down the fleeing Norsemen in the hills and bogs. Most of the latter gave up after the killing of those who stayed to fight and the burning of their 'steadings' and the Romans moved on by sea to land on and reconquer the Inner Hebrides one by one, ending up in spring 816 by retaking Skye and selling off the captive Norse women and children to Roman slave-traders at the Vikings' own slave-mart of Dunvegan. But the infertile islands were no use to ambitious Roman farmers and it would be too costly to have a fleet patrolling all the seas from Kintyre to Cape Hraf ('turning-point' in Norse) in Caithness with all their many inlets and small islands so the region was turned over to Cinaed and his Gaels from Dalriada as semi-autonomous chieftains. They duly ruled as Roman anti-piracy naval allies.

The Roman navy went on north to retake the Orkneys in summer 816 and set up a new Roman anti-piracy base there at Scapa Flow harbour, backed up by a network of forts on Mainland and a body of Gaelic 'limitanei' farmer – soldiers who were to be joined later by defecting and land-hungry Norse mercenaries who found it more profitable to join Rome than emigrate to Ulster and scrabble for lands there. Meanwhile the main invasion of Norwegia proceeded with systematic efficiency to take or starve out all the fortresses and palisaded settlements, from farms to small towns, that the Norse of Vestfold lived in unless they surrendered promptly and the survivors were marched off as slaves or fled to the forests inland. As a network of Roman forts were set up on each of the lowland fjords in the region and new roads were built between them the farms were handed over to incoming army veterans and/or younger sons of farmers in Dania and Germany who had no land of their own and were eager to set up new homes elsewhere. The inland forests were slowly cleared of refugees and guerillas in 816 and 817 and a new Roman provincial capital of 'Justiniana' (Oslo) was set up on a strategic point on one of the major fjords close to the coast. But with the countryside still full of armed and desperate refugees launching attacks on Roman bases and convoys and a seemingly endless area of inland forests for them to hide in, linked by passes over the mountains to the Norsemen of Trondelag to the North, the war continued to flare up for another decade and the completion of the new Roman roads up the fjords to the higher passes and the building of wooden forts to shut the latter did not stop small groups of 'rebels' sneaking through the mountains to attack the invaders. The countryside was to be unsafe for the incoming Roman farmers for decades and the Roman entrepreneurs who moved in to set up new businesses felling and exporting timber needed armed guards and even so suffered frequent losses to attacks, and even the well-protected and soon quite large town of Justiniana and the cleared agricultural lands around it were not altogether secure for another half-century.

But as far as the Emperor and the Imperial propaganda machine were concerned the new province of 'Norwegia' was secure and Justin was duly declared 'Norwegicus' and issued coins showing a captive Norseman grovelling before him in 817, and a network of new forts on the fjords at the western end of Vestfold, where the mountains came down to the sea, plus their own separate 'mini-fleets' of fast ships armed with 'Greek Fire' prevented the Norsemen to the west around Bergen from attacking the new Roman lands by sea except in 'hit and run' raids (often in winter and/or fogs). The current Jarl of Bergen, Erik 'the Bloodthirsty', and his senior nobles were killed in a major naval battle as the Romans defeated their attempt to invade Vestfold by sea in spring 817 and after that there was no major attack on the new province while a cousin of Erik's agreed to sign up as a Roman ally and take over the smouldering ruins of Roman-sacked Bergen as a loyal vassal who would keep the peace and see off local attackers. But the majority of the many independent lords that governed separate fjords or larger territories from Bergen to Trondjheim remained hostile and in 819 the current leader of the Frankish kingdom/province, of Transrhenus, Pepin the son of the late Franco-Roman general Carolus (d 814), led a force of land-hungry Franks to set up a new 'buffer state' of Frankish warriors in part of the jarldom of Bergen which could keep the more restive local Norsemen on the defensive with constant raids and make agriculture so difficult that sensible warlords would sign up as Roman allies and keep the peace. (Only a few did so long-term.)

The 'Viking problem' was not solved unlike what Justin claimed in his speeches to the Senate after the war and in fact many exiled Norsemen and their families from Vestfold now emigrated to Ireland as did the evicted settlers from the Hebrides. Indeed the lack of land for them to hold independent of Rome proved a crucial stimulus in a substantial emigration taking place in the 830s and 840s from Ireland onwards to Iceland far to the north-west, rediscovered by their traders in the 820s, although this also reduced the pressure from the Viking settlements in Ulster (based around Strangford Lough) on the monastery-rich midlands where Roman mercenaries were protecting the great 'treasure-houses' such as Clonmacnois, Clonfert, Durrow, and Seir Kieran from attack but the Ui Niall 'High Kings' were not so successful in their own wars against the attackers. But the Norse pirates had been given a sharp lesson and scared off raids in the North Sea, and trade between Britain, northern Gaul, Frisia, and Dania was kept safe so although the threat of piracy and general regional instability was already affecting mercantile confidence and some ports were in decline Justin had prevented a slump – which would have affected Imperial revenue and possibly finished off newer ports such as Dorestadium. This was his legacy to the north-west of the Empire which he never visited as Emperor, along with the preservation of the small client-kingdoms of Strathclyde and Dalriada, and the Norse as well as the Turks beyond the Jaxartes now pulled back from open confrontation with the Empire though wars and settlement by exiled Norsemen continued in Ireland. The local Church continued to appeal to the Empire for open and permanent military aid as the incapable 'High Kingly' army of infantry volunteers from five separate kingdom continued to be defeated by fierce hordes of axe-wielding Vikings into the 840s.

Justin held a 'Triumph' for his success – as planner rather than as the direct leader, but with all the participating generals invited to take part and to be crowned with laurel wreaths by him on the Capitol and to receive a Senate seat for life at the end of the parade – in September 817. The war cemented his position as Emperor after a shaky start when some senators as well as intellectuals had been asking openly if the follies of Rillanus had shown that the idea of a hereditary Emperor was a disaster and could not be repeated. As Justin had no close heir – assuming that Prince Septimius and the elusive 'third Imperial triplet' were really dead – he was urged to declare the Empire elective and put a proper election-system in place like Nerva had done in theory in AD 97 or organise a system for nomination of an heir as Diocletian had done in AD 293.

But he hesitated as his dynasty had been built on the notion of family inheritance not election and Justinian, like Leo IV, had always backed the idea of a 'sacred' Imperial family with the Emperor as God's chosen and anointed candidate to hold the 'Oikoumene' ('World Empire) together. In the end, after considering re-marrying and begetting an heir who would presumably have to be governed by a regency council if Justin did not live to his eighties, he arranged a new law in 818 that the Senate would elect a successor if the Emperor did not choose one. He would make his choice clear by public declaration and hopefully the grant of the office of 'Caesar' if he had time to do this – leaving it to a private, written will raised the risk of forgery by dodgy courtiers or secretaries and Justin was a suspicious man. His own choice was delayed and during 818–19 he consulted various distant relatives and senior generals as potential heirs, but by early 820 he had settled on a descendant of the dynastic founder Constantine III in the female line, the distinguished judge and veteran Bithynian lawyer Constantine Monachorus who was then forty-six (born 774) and had a record for energetic dedication to duty, incorruptibility, an encyclopedic knowledge of the law, and not least an unflappable ability to judge people and situations with shrewd ruthlessness but honesty.

The former teenage athlete and wrestling-champion Constantine might not have any military connections but he was a pious orthodox 'lay preacher' with time spent on 'retreat' in harsh Cappadocian wilderness monasteries on his 'holidays' and a reputation for fasting and talking theology with holy men so the Church approved of him, he was a firm but not fanatical 'Iconodule' who had a large collection of icons and took part – barefoot at times – in processions on saints' feast-days, and he had apparently wanted to be a monk and had allegedly been told that his duty was to be a lawyer and defend the poor in a vision. As a lawyer he had taken on many cases on behalf of the poor – e.g. against corrupt and rack-renting landlord and illegal property developers – without charging a fee but he had no truck with the republican 'bring back Cicero's Rome' demands of young radical lawyers and law-lecturers who had been alienated from the Imperial role by Rillanus. He had even at one point defended the arrested popular general Nonianus only to have his candidature as his defence barrister ruled out on a legal technicality by a judge 'leaned on' by the law ministry on Rillanus' orders, and as he had noble and Italian ancestors he was acceptable to the Senate in Rome. His late first wife had been a member of a prominent Constantinopolitan noble family and his eldest child and only son by her, Marcus, was a Protectores' cadet married to another (Thracian) heiress so their nobility were in favour of him too. The only dubious mark against him as far as the Roman elite was concerned was his second wife, the formidably learned but somewhat outspoken former Alexandria University star female philosophy pupil Irene of

Nicomedia (Bithynia) whose father had been a humble village schoolmaster but who was both acquisitive and ambitious, and her own 'take' on her husband's studies in the law had been published in Constantinople and caused scandal as she wanted women to enter the senate and all reasonable professions (i.e. not the army) and believed in a 'long-term male plot' to deny them their rights led by St Paul(who had banned them from serving as clerics). But even Irene was a formidable and learned character who could hold her own in intellectual debates in Rome as she had done since her husband had been appointed as an adviser to and commissioner at the law ministry in 817, and Justin duly appointed Constantine as his 'Caesar' and chosen heir in January 820 and commended him to the Senate as an outstanding example of Roman aristocratic virtue as well as his most suitable relative to succeed him. As Constantine had one son and no fewer than six nephews, the sons of his late younger brother Domitius (d 814), the succession seemed secure, and when the Emperor died suddenly on a visit to Dalmatia after being taken ill with stale fish at a banquet on 25 September 820, aged 75, Constantine succeeded as Emperor and was hailed by the Senate the next day when a message reached Rome.

Chapter 9

New Dynasty: Monachorus Constantine V 820–838 Not Up To The Rising Challenge? Irene 838–846 And Civil War Dangerous Innovator or Victim? Constantine's Widow.

After the military priorities of Justin's reign and the aftermath of the scandals of Rillanus' reign, the stern and moralist Constantine was determined to present a scandal-free regime and also to tighten up on court 'insider' promotions and perquisites, beginning in his own staff from his former legal jobs and the current law ministry team to take on senior court and secretariat roles. The actual team of ministers were kept on from Justin's reign well into 822 and the first sign of a major change was the appointment of a Galatian (north-west Asia Minor) bureaucrat formerly in the Constantinople praefectural secretariat, Justus Trogontius, as 'Master of Offices' in June 822 followed by his replacement of almost all the under-secretaries in that office who assisted him, but behind the scenes the Emperor relied more on his secretariat and les on the official senior ministers for advice. He also quietly sidelined the senior offices usually held by nobles, e.g. the Praefecture of Rome and the Rome 'aedileships', in favour of listening to the holders of more junior offices who were usually self-made provincial careerists risen through the ranks from success in the regional civil service examinations. These and his own personal associates in the more 'activist' and 'moral justice'– seeking ranks of the Italian and Constantinopolitan legal professionals had more 'clout' than great nobles. The ex-generals who had held sway with Justin were quietly ignored though flattered with continuing honorary ranks and gifts, and in the words of a later Rome University professor of government in the 16th century Constantine divided the personnel of governance into the 'serious' and the 'dignified' and sidelined the latter from real influence. His speeches to the Senate and to the meetings of the ruling bodies of major professions in Rome in the early 820s – which he assiduously attended, the first Emperor to do so since Constantine IV – laid great emphasis on the Imperial role as 'keystone of the arch of government' and the setter of the moral tone of governance, but unlike with the ceremonial-loving Leo IV (and to a lesser extent Justinian) this was based on bureaucratic supervision and assessment of the ruling 'machine' by paperwork and meetings, plus regular investigations of personnel and policy-implementation by palace-chosen commissioners, not on establishing a mystique of rule by grand and physically impressive ceremonial. The Emperor was now to be seen as hard-working and above moral reproach, as suitable for the 'Heir of the Apostles' (Constantine the Great's term which Constantine V revived).

The Emperor kept up most of Justinian's ceremonial, to greater levels than done by Rillanus or Justin, and as a devout Christian made much of his attending religious services in Rome and at other top churches and shrines across Italy. In in winter 821–2 he was resident at the Sacred Palace in Constantinople and in winter 824–5 at the imperial palace in Antioch to do likewise at their leading religious sites while in spring 826 he went on an Easter pilgrimage to Palestine and attended services and visited monasteries in Jerusalem, Bethlehem, Galilee, and Mount Sinai. (The monastery of St Catherine at the presumed site of the miracle of the 'Burning Bush' was by now a major shrine there, as developed in the 6th century.) He also promoted the veneration of icons as a means to make it easier for the illiterate to understand Bible stories, participate fully in worship, and become more holy and his gifts of Imperial gold and silver from spendthrift Rillanus' collection to decorate icons and shrines was a major boost to the Church in the Mediterranean provinces and its splendour. He formed a close partnership with the equally hard-working and devout Pope Paschal (in office from 823 to 841) (OTL figure) who was equally dedicated to the use of icons and to 'cleaning up' the granting and use of senior office in the Church to ensure that serious-minded and philanthropic candidates not just well-connected ones acquired office.

The Italian Church was 'cleaned up' fully under this pairing as capable junior clerics, earnest youngish nobles with a reputable history of religious devotion and spending, and outsiders from Gaul and Spain were brought in to take over senior offices. Constantine was also the first Emperor to lead a major, elite mass-pilgrimage to the shrine of St James at Compostellanum in Gallaecia, Spain (at Easter 827). He used his Greek tour of 824 for the Olympic Games to attend ceremonies at major shrines and other monasteries and give lands in remote mountain regions, e.g. the Phocis region around Delphi and the Mount Athos peninsula near Thessalonica, to hermits for them to study and fast in peace and set up cave or wooden hut hermitages. In his own Bithynia he lavished gifts on the great monastery of Sakkudion, whose reputation had spread far across the Empire after its defiance of the now reviled Rillanus, and when Abbot Plato died in 826 helped to secure the election as abbot of his equally learned theologian nephew Theodore (OTL figure) who also became a major religious figure. His patronage extended to the rising 'female religious institution' 'star' nunnery outside Mytilene on the island of Lesbos that was led by the venerated Abbess Irene (d 836, OTL Eastern Empress from 797–802), later beatified, who had inherited a fortune and much land in Attica in the 770s from her businessman father and spent it on the 'Iconodule' cause as a lay patron of this before setting up her own nunnery as its abbess in 800.

The feminist views and leadership of a major girls' school at the Lesbos nunnery by Irene was not to the liking of all clerics and the usually conservative Constantine received criticism, e.g. in Gaul, Spain, and Britain, from moralist preachers and monk writers for associating with a woman who would not stay silent as commanded by St Paul but offered her own opinions to men and women alike at Church councils and was said to intimidate landowners into giving land to her nunnery. But he ignored this resentment and even visited the nunnery himself on his 824 Greek tour, en route to the shrine of St John at Ephesus. This was probably due to the enthusiasm for Irene of his wife, her namesake, who formed a connection with her and used her backing to improve her own reputation as a devout and generous patroness of nunneries and Church girls' schools. Most of the latter were for middle-class or wealthy girls, as a 'trade-off' with their parents who would then give generously to the school and its parent monastic institution, but Abbess Irene educated farm-girls of talent from across the Aegean and western Asia Minor too and thanks to her a number of these ended up as abbesses in the early-mid-9th century.

The Emperor relied to an unclear degree on his wife as an adviser in matters of religious and also intellectual policy and it is clear from her later policies as Empress that she fully understood and valued the use of ceremonial and presenting a dazzling and over-aweing appearance as the 'anointed one of God' to the public. This also coincided with the opinions of ceremonial-approving officials in the palace administration from the body recruited by Justinian pre-797 and their heirs. But in military policy he had his own clear priorities and these did not encompass further wars which he regarded as a waste of money and lives (and so a sin) and at best as a 'last resort'. There was no more talk of extending Roman control over North-West of the fjord-mouth fortresses set up at the Southernmost part of the Norwegian coast overlooking the Skaggerak and any idea of augmenting the fleet in the Dornoch Firth and at Scapa Flow to take the Shetlands from their Norse pirate settlers was quietly shelved. But Constantine did not listen either to cost-cutting bureaucrats in the finance ministry who wanted the 'Classis Britanniae' scaled back and who argued that the North Sea crisis was now over and keeping hundreds of warships with their crews on 'standby' was a waste of resources. The 'cheese-paring' veteran cost-cutter Artemius Araestophanius, a Cilician accountant and former inspector of regional tax-collecting who became finance minister in 822 and lasted until the end of the reign, had great sway over the Emperor in such matters as making sure that public works contracts were properly valued and were not 'rigged' in favour of over-expenditure and 'kickbacks' to contractors. These habitual problems were tackled even in traditionally lax provinces such as Egypt and upper and lower Mesopotamia, but Constantine would not have the military budget touched – probably out of fear of a coup by angry generals who were still brooding over one of them not being chosen to succeed Justin – and the building of new forts on the Jaxartes in Sogdiana and in eastern Hyrcania to hold back the raiding Turks continued. Nor did he interfere with glory-seeking frontier 'preventive' raids on the Turks there.

From 822 Constantine relied heavily in determining military policy on the slightly controversial but ruthlessly efficient and blunt figure of a physically imposing 'self-made' general from Phrygia who had made his name as a commander in Transoxiana in the 810s, Leo the Armenian (OTL Byzantine emperor), as Praetorian Praefect. As the latter had been an 'Iconoclast' enthusiast and a local icon-smasher and cleric-intimidator as a farm-hand teenager in the 790s before he joined the army he was not popular with devout senior (often noble) generals or the Church and was rumoured to be semi-literate and was regularly sniped at in the Senate. The restored-to-favour Nonianus, now put in the Senate in the mid-820s as a personal favour by the Emperor on account of his work for justice and proud to show off the scars on his back from his time as a mine-slave and to promote working-class juniors in his new role as a 'comitatus' advisor, was also influential in deciding what to do about continuing Norse attacks in Ireland and occasionally in Caledonia and about tribal raids on Daghestan and North Adiabene. But in view of the attitude he had long taken to Imperial autocracy Constantine apparently had him watched closely by the police and his young acolytes (republicans in particular) quite often got taken in for questioning or offered a choice between a trip to the police's torture-cells in Rome or spying on their patron. The Empress was distrustful of Nonianus as a threat and her circle of devout and pro-autocracy noblemen and their wives were supposed to be trying to blacken his name and get him gaoled. Though Constantine left this hugely popular public figure alone and let him run his own racing-club and teams in the Circus Maximus in the 830s to distract him from politics it was later claimed that it was no coincidence that Nonianus ended up dead of a supposed overdose of medicine weeks after Irene became Empress in 838.

The reign of Constantine saw him prioritise trade over war – not least as a means of adding to income from customs-duties – and he was particularly interested in the East on that account, paying a personal visit to the huge and flourishing port of Charax on his Mesopotamian-Median-Persian tour of April to August 828 (after his second stay at Antioch). As the Roman Persian Gulf and Red Sea/Aden/Socotra fleets kept the Indian Ocean relatively free of pirates to assist the free flow of goods to and from India and Taprobane Constantine sent a major embassy with rich gifts to the great trading state of Anuradhapura in Ceylon (and its king Dhappura II) in 822–4 that went on to visit the major states of southern India and signed treaties with most of them. The embassy took along gifts for all the rulers involved, whose names had been collected beforehand from Romano-Mesopotamian merchants who traded with their ports, and made invitations to them to send embassies to Rome. As a Ceylonese embassy led by a junior prince of the royal family of Anuradhapura visited Rome in 827–8 (coming and going via the Red Sea and Egypt) this was made the most of by Imperial propaganda. It was also used by the Church to have a Catholic embassy invited to Ceylon to set up a mission there – and the Ceylonese visitors' gifts of rare animals were displayed in the Imperial hunting parks or were given to favoured nobles but on Imperial orders were not hunted and killed. The Ceylonese embassy also brought along a small and aristocratic Buddhist monastic delegation who set up Rome's first Buddhist monastery, much to the scandal of the Catholic Church which regarded them as 'heathens' and ensured that as soon as possible they were moved to Sicily and that anyone who converted to Buddhism was sent packing from court.

The Emperor did take on a minor military action in defence of trade as the increasing tribal-led chaos and decline of towns and farming alike in northern Abyssinia in the early 9th–century, where drought was causing famine This led nomads to move their herds of animals east from the Sudan deserts into Eritrea, and resettle on Abyssinian lands there, and on routes leading to the main Roman port of direct trade-access to Abyssinia, Massawa (Adulis was further north) tribal raids meant it now took longer to travel from there to the nearest Abyssinian-held towns around Massawa fell in a coalition of pillaging tribesmen in 822, and its inhabitants were driven out or enslaved, cutting the route South to Axum. The *'dux'* of Arabia Felix and the port naval force commander at Jeddah both wrote to the current king of Abyssinia requesting him to intervene as a few Roman merchants escaped across the Red Sea to safety. But nothing happened so in 824 Constantine agreed to let a Roman naval force from Aden intervene and added troops with 'Greek Fire' and artillery were sent down the sea from Egypt. The resulting expedition, small by Roman standards but well-armed, retook Massawa from its brigand new rulers and set up a permanent Roman base there which repaired the walls, rebuilt the sacked town, and thereafter protected the mercantile residents and a small number of local farmers who chose to return. But this did not amount to annexing all of the former Red Sea coastal province of northern Axum as Praetorian Praefect Leo and the military commanders in Arabia Felix had recommended and it took the cautious Emperor a decade to be reassured that the port would not be an unnecessary drain on the Roman budget and was paying for itself in terms of customs-dues from merchants travelling to and from the new heartland of truncated and somewhat 'devolved' Abyssinia, a weaker state than the old Axumite one, in Gojjam to the south.

The hard work and enterprise of a corps of 3,000 or so Roman troops, some of them Arab camel-riders hired from the mercantile princes of the Abbasid dynasty at Mecca (now led by the famously wealthy Harun 'the Magnificent' (OTL Caliph Harun ar-Raschid), in protecting the mercantile convoys that travelled from Massawa to the Abyssinian capital in the later 820s and 830s was rewarded by the route becoming safer thereafter as their success in repelling ambushes put the tribal brigands off. There were ideas raised in intellectual and Council circles in Rome of bringing in lots of new farmer-warriors to settle in the north of Abyssinia to make the area more productive and secure for travellers – and more urban – with the new landed 'stakeholders' having good reason to help the Empire keep the roads secure and so saving on the need to pay for regular troops there.

This had worked in the forests and swampy heaths of northern Germany for three or so centuries and to a degree was now working with prosperous farmer-soldiers in Vestfold in Norwegia, both of these regions having been 'civilised' in this manner, and roaming nomad brigands and bands of 'hit and run' robbers had been marginalized there – why not try it out in East Africa? But the land was less fertile and there were few rivers and more deserts in Abyssinia and its neighbouring lands, as Imperial geographers and surveyors reported after a major landed survey (set up by Justin, who had been asked to investigate the feasibility of settlement-expansion there in 818) reported in 824. Constantine was immune to mercantile claims that annexing all of the coast would bring in more wealth, not least in slaves, and Church requests from Alexandria to help the Abyssinian Christians repel their 'heathen' nomad attackers. Instead his naval efforts in Africa went on sending enterprising young officers who wanted to make a name for themselves to sail down the Eastern African coast to trade with and extort favourable treaties from the coastal town 'partners' of the southern Indian (Tamil) and Ceylonese states and to explore as far as the mouth of the Zambezi, which a Roman expedition reached in 836. From the late 820s onwards some shrewd merchants in Aden and other Arabia Felix ports were even sending regular annual ships to the Kenyan coast to collect local wildlife and ship it to Egypt and on to Rome as exotic pets for the Roman nobility, following on from C8th voyages there but now better-protected by Roman warships.

This and the start of Roman mercantile expeditions via a 'stopping-off point' at the ports of the now friendly Ceylonese kingdom of Anuradhapura to the Bay of Bengal in the 830s added to Constantine's income. His role as 'Lord of East and West' was played up in his official propaganda, but with constant petty wars going on in India the extra insight gained by his traders into the state of the peninsula only led to ambitious generals starting to grumble that his predecessor Justin would have had the nerve and imagination to plan a proper extension of Roman power by armed attack on this fabulously rich but hopelessly divided land. Itcould be a new 'jewel in the Imperial crown' (as one playwright in the pay of expansionist generals called India in his 835 winning play at the annual Rome drama festival on the subject of the ancient Greco-Indian kingdom of 2nd-century BC warlord Menander). The complaints by generals and ultra-expansionist intellectuals, some of the latter university-educated romantic worshippers of the 'glory days' of Pompey and Julius Caesar's Eastern exploits and some Church militants interested in Christianizing the 'pagan' Indians, may also have been behind the Emperor's decision to distance the creation and direction of foreign policy from the army 'high command'. The latter had an inbuilt advantage as possessing experts who had served on the frontiers and in some cases had been commanding there themselves. The Rome 'HQ' and Military Strategy Centre often hired former garrison-commanders or cavalry and infantry patrol leaders from the Indus and Beas garrisons or from Kabul and Sogdiana. Constantine distrusted them as having a stake in backing frontier aggression – glory and loot for their relatives and friends. Accordingly, from 826 Constantine delegated the role of advising him on and compiling information on foreign policy to a new, civilian ministry, that of the 'Logothete of the Drome' or foreign minister – the Greek name reflecting his own NW Asia Minor background and the number of 'logothetes' in the Constantinopolitan administration. The first man to hold the office was the skilled and multi-talented Marinus 'the patrician', a nobly-born bureaucrat from Constantinople, from 826 to 833 (OTL figure). The second was the Armenian (but mostly employed in Antioch) noble Arsaber (OTL), married to the heiress of a Mesopotamian trading dynasty with Indian and Ceylonese/Taprobane connections. Both these men were antagonistic to military priorities and brought in their own, Eastern secretariat staff to help run the department. Fortunately the Praetorian Praefect Leo (OTL Eastern Emperor 813–20) did not make a fuss, though some generals asked him to do so and not to assist the new minister by letting him use military intelligence – and someone important was probably behind a failed attempt to get rid of Leo in 829 by having him attacked by assassins at a Christmas church service near his Rome mansion. (He famously fought the attackers off with a candelabra until his bodyguards arrived and this was then played up as showing that God was on his and his employer's side.) (In OTL this was how Leo, as Emperor, died in 820.) Leo's high reputation with the ordinary soldiers may well have scared angry pro-war generals in Rome off planning coups using the Guards.

The idea of invading India and extending the Empire – and gaining fabulous riches – certainly appealed to Constantine's heir, his vain and showy son and Irene's stepson Prince Carus (born 807). But despite his success as a 'Protectores' cadet and then a junior officer in Bactria and Sogdiana in the mid-late 820s he was lacking in commonsense and stability and inclined to live wildly with his cronies and Constantine was by 830 in despair that he would end up like Rillanus, a drunken and spendthrift wastrel and a poor judge of men. He had had the boy brought up by expert tutors and then given a strict military training and Carus was a good horseman, a congenial character who made many friends among young officers, and not short of bravery on the frontier. But to exacting Constantine he was not of the stuff of good rulers and as Emperor would be open to disastrous advice. Rather than hedge him in by a body of ministers who would do the real governing as Justinian had planned to do with Rillanus, he was driven by his belief in government by the just and the capable to plan to exclude Carus from the succession – in which his wife Irene who despised the young man, was presumed to be his eager accomplice if not indeed behind much of his hostility. Already there were wildly different attitudes to the clever and ambitious Irene among the elite, the Senate in particular, and also among writers – as was to be reflected in historians' accounts of her rise to power and her reign (and her fall in 845–6, which led to a lot of 'back-dated' explanations of how the latter had been 'inevitable'). Was she a valiant and forward-looking 'reformer' and the brains behind her husband, who despised Carus as he was useless and would be a bad Emperor, or was she a power-hungry adventuress who wanted him out of the way to put herself on the throne and so encouraged him to misbehave? Carus was not totally incompetent but he refused to marry the distinguished and beautiful if rather boring young heiress who his father selected as his bride in 831. He married a low-born market-girl from Naples instead in a major scandal, and when he refused to divorce her as his father ordered he was locked up in a remote villa while the Church declared the marriage invalid. He was then sent off to Langobardia as a deputy commander of a roaming cavalry unit in the remote Bielowice forests who were protecting the Bug frontier and the nearby timber-concession 'logging camps' from raids by Slav and nomad tribesmen from the East.

The idea was to toughen up and test the Prince and turn him into a suitable successor and in the meantime the Emperor had a law passed by the Senate requiring any new ruler to be adult (i.e. over eighteen) and approved by both his predecessor and the Senate or else an election by the latter would follow. The Church passed a law to declare any usurper excommunicated 'per se' and any soldiers who took part in rebellion liable to severe legal penalties and eternal damnation. While Carus was away the focus of ambitious courtiers turned to his eldest cousin, the Emperor's late brother's eldest son Marcus, who was also a trainee officer but was rather less scandalous. Married to a respectable noble bride of the Mucianus dynasty of Latium landed aristocrats with dozens of consuls in her extended family's past and links to eight major senatorial dynasties, the dutiful and dashing cavalry officer Marcus was currently in the 'Protectores' and was kept in staff posts in Italy by the Emperor while his cousin was away, logically as a 'stand-in' heir if Carus proved useless and incorrigible and/or the Emperor died while Carus was nowhere near Rome. But in the early-mid 830s Irene began to be spoken about as a potential successor too and despite her new public façade of devout modesty and loyalty to the (usually conservative) senior Western Church archbishops and the Pope she was undoubtably ambitious and was up to various manoeuvres behind the scenes.

A number of plays and poems about the great female Roman political leaders of the past appeared in the early-mid 830s, written by figures linked to supporters of Irene in the nobility or the Church. The careers of the venerated 'Augusta' Livia, Emperor Trajan's wife Plotina, Septimius Severus' wife Julia Domna, Constantine 'the Great's mother (St) Helena, the C5th 'Augusta' Pulcheria, and the 5th-century Western Empress Galla Placidia were duly praised and were brought before the eyes of the elite with the 'message' that a woman was quite capable of governing wisely or at least running affairs from behind the scenes. Attempts to 'whitewash' or at least improve the reputation of Nero's intensely 'political' mother Agrippina the Younger were more controversial and some conservative figures at court were implacably opposed to Irene, but in the Emperor's words in a speech on her birthday in 833 she was 'the cleverest woman in the Empire'. She was shrewd and ruthless and had no qualms about pretending to be a devout and humble wife who only sought to help her husband and to protect him from greedy careerist administrators, ministers and courtiers who wanted to see Carus succeed to the throne in order to exploit him and use him to loot the Empire's coffers. The increasingly frail and querulous but still hard-working Emperor, his old wrestling injuries catching up with him as his back gave him trouble, believed that Carus the 'rake' would be a new

Rillanus – i.e. an incompetent rake – and sought to save the Empire from him. As Marcus loyally refused to step over his cousin into the heirship Constantine ended up sending him off to a remote garrison in the steppes of the Crimean peninsula near Cherson in 835 in an outbreak of temper and then had Carus summoned back to Rome in disgrace for marrying a tavern-keeper's daughter in Cracovia and having an 'illegitimate' son (as the Church quickly ruled him) by her. The disgraced heir was told off at a stormy interview with his father at Ravenna, well away from the gossips of Rome, and sent off to a remote Alpine monastery near Lake Garda to 'repent' and do some dedicated studying in the arts of governance with a squad of hand-picked tutors and university experts ahead of being married off to a woman selected by his father. He was told that if he resisted any of this programme he would be sent to a monastery for life, and a few months later he escaped from this unofficial 'custody' and turned up in Rome in disguise to hide out with an aristocratic ex-cadet friend of his. Presumably the later story that he was planning on a dramatic appeal to either the Senate or the 'high command' of the army was correct. The new 'Master of Infantry' Gordianus Gesticianus, a former commander of his as a junior trainee who had always favoured him, and other officers were probably involved with the plan – and the recent death of Praetorian Praefect Leo had elevated a lacklustre military administrator bureaucrat, Lucius Lollianus, to the latter's office so his juniors were less likely to follow him in staying loyal to Constantine and Irene than they would have done to 'veteran hero' Leo.

The shadow of a coup lurked in Rome for the first time since Leo IV's final months in 749–50, but this time the Emperor had more support where it mattered than his presumed heir, not least as he was a just and hard-working ruler and a devout Catholic, and the secret/intelligence police were tipped off and hunted Carus down in time. The Prince was arrested and removed in secrecy to a remote villa in Apulia and subsequently to a fortress in Epirus in disgrace and it was given out that he was suffering from alcoholic delusions and had become violent. Although he probably did end up as a drunkard railing against the Emperor rumour had it that Irene or her favourite minister and secret ally, the 'postal logothete' and elite-letter-interceptor Theoctistus (another of the north-west Asia Minor group around the Imperial couple), had deliberately 'hooked' Carus on addictive brands of alcohol or poisoned him. Carus died of apparent delirium from alcohol early in 837, with the Emperor criticized openly in the Senate for his harshness and banning a play that presented him as Constantine 'the Great', Carus as the latter's purged and killed son Crispus, and Irene as the ruler's lying and power-crazed second wife Fausta. The rude references to scandal in the Emperor's favourite predecessor's family enraged him – and he defended Irene and blamed Marcus for encouraging her critics.

Though Marcus was the presumed next heir he was never proclaimed as such and Constantine did not recall him to Rome but required him to keep away. After his service in the Crimea ended later that year transferred him to North Adiabene to serve as a lowly patrol commander against raiding nomads.

Officially Marcus was loyally learning to serve the Empire and would be recalled after a few more years' service, but in effect he had been sidelined too. The Emperor made his wife 'Augusta' in December 837 and gave her a seat in the Senate a couple of months later, citing the position of Emperor Alexander Severus' mother Julia Mamaea. But all of Irene's increasingly extravagant and public philanthropic acts and her attendance at major pilgrimages in Italy, made much of by the Church, could not halt alarm among the elite that she was angling for the throne and needed to be stopped. The Empress had her husband's support and during his back-related illness that kept him bedridden in early 838 she sat in for him at Council meetings with his written permission and portrayed herself as a modest and dutiful wife who had not sought to be thrust into the limelight but was carrying out his wishes as his nephews were all useless and a public danger to the stability of the Empire. Certainly the rakish partying and chasing of prostitutes by his third and fourth nephews, Julius and Patroclus, in the mid-830s as they did their 'Protectores' training did them no favours and the latter was also mixed-up in a race-rigging 'scam' by a friend's chariot-racing team at the Circus Maximus in 836. Neither of them was a plausible alternative heir.

The second of the Emperor's nephews, Basilicus, was a less athletic or military-minded and more studious character but was also not too hard-working and had an antagonism to the military and to Roman imperial expansion (arising from his romantic devotion to pre-Alexandrian Greece as a student at Athens in the mid-820s). That meant that Constantine feared to have him as heir lest he cause a military coup once he was Emperor, but at least he had agreed to marry and to choose a respectable wife and his bride of 827, the aristocratic Thracian amateur poet and devout Iconodule enthusiast Cassia, was a major asset for him in the political 'stakes'. Cassia (OTL Byzantine woman poet and abbess, nearly Empress), a clever and idealistic young woman who had originally wanted to be an abbess and had studied under the famous Iconodule abbess/headmistress Irene the Athenian at her Mytilene nunnery school, was a devotional poet of considerable talent. She had entered top provincial poetry competitions under an assumed, male name (no women were allowed to compete except in Athens and Alexandria) and she had much in common with the Empress who had helped her husband to choose her as a bride for Basilicus at a time when Irene was seeking to undermine Marcus by promoting Basilicus as heir in his place. But that did not mean that Irene was prepared to see the vague and rather indecisive young man rule with herself as his guide behind the scenes and her own restless and increasingly unscrupulous ambition got the better of her as Constantine's heath declined. Most of the ministers seem either to have backed Marcus as heir or to prefer to set him aside and put Basilicus, who had three boys by 838, in as the 'front man' for a ministerial council advised by the 'Augusta'.

But events overtook them, and a backlash among conservative senators against the idea of having Irene in the Senate led to the latter persuading her husband that the objectors were secret allies of Marcus who would stage a coup and have her thrown in a nunnery if they were not stopped. The just and idealistic Constantine was also irritated at the idea of a talented woman with gifts of governance being stopped in her tracks by a group of greedy and arrogant men who would not let a woman govern on principle whereas in past history Pulcheria and the C3rd AD empresses Julia Maesa and Julia Mammea had governed wisely and well. In late summer 838 a series of arrests of leading conservative senators for alleged (and probably true claims of) embezzlement of public funds and tax-evasion occurred, all targeting enemies of Irene. The new finance minister Honorius Honoratianus, a self-made administrative manipulator and tax-evasion-hunter from a humble and ultra-religious Catholic background in Belgica who had risen through the bureaucracy after his public examination success, was the man behind the purge. But he was supposed to have been prompted by Irene to target 'decadent' and 'parasitic' noblemen as his duty to God, and with him and the equally brilliant and manipulative Theoctistus behind Irene she was able to have herself proclaimed as 'Caesarissa' and potential co-heir with Marcus in October 838. A month later, on 21 November, Constantine V died suddenly of a seizure apparently induced by the strain of his back-problems, during a visit to Campania to supervise the closure of all casinos in Baiae and Naples on charges of public immorality (which the Church had been angling for for decades but which Irene had now arranged for them), aged sixty-four. The Senate duly proclaimed Irene as Empress the next day as required by the late ruler's will – read out by Theoctistus, who was later accused of forging it. A squad of loyal Guardsmen attended the minister to scare off protests – which Irene's rivals soon played up.

Technically Marcus was co-emperor but in view of his inexperience was required to accept Irene as his partner and marry a woman of her choice and accept the advice of his ministers' majority opinion for a trial period of a year, but in the event he suffered a 'fatal accident' on board his ship en route back from Colchis to Constantinople a few weeks later in a storm. He was declared by the Imperial officials from Constantinople who had gone by sea to Colchis to collect him as having fallen overboard when the ship lurched as he was being seasick, aged thirty-one. Rumour had it that the officials, chosen by Irene months ahead of the event for this duty, had thrown him overboard on her orders, but this was never proved despite the late prince's brother Basilicus, as Emperor, setting up an enquiry in 847 and it might have been an accident. The Senate lacked the nerve or the unity to declare Basilicus as the new co-emperor as Constantine had not made any provision for this and the Church under Pope Paschal backed the idea of Irene as sole ruler. With the Church proposing to excommunicate anyone who defied the late Emperor's wishes the elite in Rome backed away from any plans for a coup, not least as the army 'high command' disliked Basilicus almost as much as the Church did and would not defend his rights. The military leadership in Dacia, Marcomannia, Britain, Norwegia/Dania, and on the lower Danube, the only commands with substantial numbers of troops at hand and within a shortish distance of Rome, grumbled but did not act against the new regime in case the other Northern commands backed Irene and they were defeated.

As Irene had gambled, the loyalty or at any rate inertia of the European commands then scared the Eastern ones off a rebellion and in any case the popular ex-soldier Marcus and the reputedly pacifist and anti-expansion 'student' Basilicus were different propositions as candidates to be acclaimed by a rebellion. With the Church in Constantinople, Antioch, Alexandria, and Ctesiphon backing her unequivocally as an Iconodule and a proven devout, orthodox philanthropist she was safe for the moment and could modestly assure the Senate that her model would be the holy and hard-working Pulcheria not the powerful Livia. She portrayed herself as the 'Mother of the Empire' and the 'Handmaid of the Lord' and had coins issued as such, and as she now stopped attending the Senate out of respect for conservative senators' feelings (or so she claimed) and chose to govern through her ministers, led by Theoctistus as 'Master of Offices', Honoratianus in charge of finances. The new Praetorian Praefect was the famous Bardas (800–876), another Anatolian and a distinguished general who had served successfully as 'Count' of the North Adiabene/Caucasus command in the early 830s. He was also a skilful politician and the brother of a leading super-rich abbess, Iconodule, and philanthropic founder of schools, hospitals, and orphanages in Greece, the orthodox-supported (later St) Theodora of the Deceleia nunnery in Attica. The Church thus backed his family. Theodora (805–867) (OTL: Eastern Roman Empress 830s), daughter of a north-west Asia Minor landowner from Paphlagonia, and the slightly older Irene had worked together already for a decade to found elite schools for well-off girls in Greece and western Asia Minor and to organize pilgrimages to major local shrines. She probably acted as the Empress' link to the crucial pro-Irene military figures of Bardas and his equally popular and distinguished brother Petronas (OTL figures), a leading commander on the Indus frontier who now in 839 became the 'Count' of this frontier. With these two and other generals who disliked Basilicus and wanted a war of expansion against India launched coming round to back Irene her regime survived its shaky first few months and the Empress avoided any controversial measures and kept on reassuring the elite in Rome that she would continue all her late husband's policies apart from his lack of interest in eastern wars. Even there the grandiose new Imperial rhetoric from the 'new Deborah', as her Church fans called her after the Old Testament prophetess, was nor reflected in outright action to annex any kingdoms. With the trustable Petronas in charge of the large new army of 40,000 men that was built up for war on the River Beas in 828–9 the Empress used this to invade the nearest rajahdom at Amritsar in support of an exiled younger brother of a man who was charging Roman traders extortionate customs-duties. The capital was besieged and taken in spring 839 and the pretender was installed in power and promptly cut customs-duties by a half so Roman traders were pleased. Although the Empire annexed some crucial border fortresses East of the river, built a road from the largest of them back to a new bridge over the Beas so it could be rescued quickly in case of an attack, and installed a mercenary bodyguard at the new rajah's capital to keep him in power the effect in terms of a major shift of military power in the region was less than Irene boasted to the Senate. Petronas had to send his deputy to Rome to lead the parade at the resultant Triumph as Irene needed him to stay on the frontier and keep his troops loyal.

All round the reign of Irene was marked by a careful commitment to benefiting traders and businessmen rather than great nobles, as the sort of self-made men open to new ideas and taking risks who ought to appreciate an unusual and risk-taking female ruler who had overturned centuries of tradition. Thanks to the equally unusual and risk-taking ideas of Honoratianus and his staff of 'jumped-up' (as older bureaucrats at the finance ministry called them) young or youngish provincials the old government concentration on taxing the rich indiscriminately – except for those who managed to hide their real assets, usually devious businessmen and/or nobles owning hoards of jewellery and passing off their lands as their wives' or children's – was downgraded in favour of rewarding enterprise. Investing money in new business ventures or in Imperially-sponsored philanthropic projects, eg schools, orphanages, and hospitals, was rewarded by tax-breaks for the first three years of such projects. Investors who helped an Imperial project were associated with these by being named as co-founders in the official records and on public plaques, and special ranks of honour (within the Nobilissimus grades) naming the recipient as a public benefactor were also granted out to these people which gratified their vanity and enabled them – and their families – to show off. Irene thus shrewdly appealed to the vanity and ambition of wives as much as to the menfolk who actually did the investing and received the honours. A new 'Imperial Investment Bank', created using money taken from the tax-revenues and in particular the eastern trade-customs and the northern (Langobardia/Swedia/Norwegia/the upper Dnieper and Don valleys) fur trade, was set up in 840 by Honoratianus to co-ordinate investment and channel it to the most deserving projects. Prosperity, the Empress hoped, would reward the Empire's elites and scare off plotters.

Nobles and businessmen were encouraged to invest in the IIB too and in return received share certificates that they could keep as proof of their holding in the bank and use to claim profits from it every year in proportion to their investment. This idea was apparently brought from China by a merchant relative of one of Honoratianus' assistants in the 820s, and this made the bank a long-term success and vastly boosted the input of successful or socially ambitious businessmen into the government's finances –voluntarily. The business community, mostly in the capital and major Mediterranean cities plus an arc curving across Mesopotamia to Persia and increasingly the 'Silk Route' cities of Bactria, was won over to the unusual and controversial but innovative Empress. She was as much regarded as a reliable patron and representative of their interests as Constantine V had been of honest lawyers and jurists, though in fact it was Honoratianus who deserved the credit. As trade boomed and the crucial new 'low customs' channel into the Punjab, en route to the Ganges valley, caused many new traders to get involved in the Indian trade or existing ones to make even greater profits from it the reign of Irene saw the prosperity and size of bleak, mountain-surrounded Kabul and the ancient cities of the Bactrian plain, led by Balkh, Bukhara, and Merv, increase rapidly and in due course successful citizens there have the money and confidence to pay for a boom in private and public building. The domed Persian style of architecture was usually used rather than the rectangular 'hall and columns', Greek-derived styles more usual in Rome. The locals kept to Persian robes (and even turbans) and slippers rather than the Roman togas and sandals as a confidence in Iranian culture was revived in the middle decades of the 9th century the local elites. In due course this spread into Persia 'proper' too to the ancient cities of Istakr and Susa, and to the new coastal port of Ahwaz (known to the Romans as 'Claudiopolis' after its re-planner Claudius III) and the mercantile oasis city of Shiraz, later a famous home of Persian-language poets such as the later 9th-century Phirdausius Firdawzi (OTL), author of the regional national epic the 'Shahnameh' ('Book of Kings', i.e. the Achaemenids, Alexander, the Seleucids, the Parthians and the first Sassanids). The new wealth and confidence there gave the Empress' regime fierce local elite loyalty – and scared grumbling European frontier generals off daring to risk a rebellion, which their troops would not back.

All this revived confidence and prosperity in Persia and its satellite regions was underway before the 830s and was not entirely down to Irene and Honoratianus, but their boost to trade and investment undoubtably provided a major bonus and speeded the process up and probably the war in India which the generals wanted would have done the opposite. The Empress was also appealing to the Church as the candidate of piety and increased her rate of founding schools – particularly for girls – and orphanages across the Empire, especially in the cities of the poorer West, after 839. So she deserved her accolade of 'The Children's Augusta' though its bestowal by the Senate in 842 after she had opened a major new school for the capital's poor girls – educating some 500 in each 'year class', a huge number for a contemporary school, with a friend of Abbess Theodora as the headmaster – was a typical piece of fawning opportunism by the nobles and careerist bureaucrat members. Legislation was implemented banning the physical chastisement of girls under the age of twelve by teachers – fathers still had rights to do so as the 'paterfamilias' of each household – and was enforced by a board of jurists and government inspectors, though in practice a lot of the flogging was carried on privately and covered up. Irene also encouraged women who were not married to teach and opened a college in the capital to teach them in 842, assuring the dubious ministers and clergy that this was only to free male teachers to tackle the most difficult or needy male pupils and help the women to be better and more informed mothers as they later taught their own children at home. The senior clergy were reluctant to accept this but with the relatively liberal (though anti-Iconoclast) new Pope Gregory and the fanatically moralistic but fair-minded new Patriarch Ignatius of Constantinople (OTL) (son of one of Justin's generals, Michael Rangabe) 'on side' with the Empress they had to give in. The plans were promoted by 'on-message' Church loyalists in sermons as following Christ's approval of useful Martha and Mary.

But this was still a rare initiative and had little effects outside Italy and the 'downside' of Irene's deal with the Pope and his senior bishops over this was that she appointed a veteran and anti-pagan Spanish religious lawyer, Dalmatius of Cordoba, as her new education minister in 841. He tightened up the amount of Bible teaching and studies of the Church Fathers in state-backed schools and orphanages. The Empress' enthusiasm for 'hard-line' (doctrinally speaking)-style Catholicism coupled with a commitment to appointing 'moral' and philanthropic ecclesiastics to high rank rather than the usual predominance of more 'relaxed' socialite upper-class careerists spoke for her idealism and Christian values. She was duly praised by earnest moralist Catholic – and a few non-Catholic – writers and preachers as the 'new Pulcheria', in emulation of the great 5th century-Eastern Empire ruling 'Augusta'. (Her doctrinal strictness was also seen as like that which Pulcheria had showed to the Monophysites and other 'heretics' at the 451 Church Council of Chalcedon.) She and her religious bureaucrats duly made the most of this and she hired skilled organisers of 'saints' days' religious ceremonial from the Church to help create a new 'calendar' of religiously orientated Court ceremonies to appeal to the faithful and added on public distributions of food on great saints' days in Rome. This emulated the ritual of Emperor Leo IV's grand and 'holy' Court in the mid-8th century – but to her annoyance a substantial body of both Church and lay Catholic elite members always held aloof from her as a woman and a 'usurper' and as the number of her genuine and rumoured political crimes rose this escalated.

There was also a degree of 'exclusivist' Italian aristocratic and hereditary 'civil service families' resentment at the number of 'outsider' and 'provincial' personnel who she had given 'fast track' appointments in the Church in Italy and in her civil service bureaucracy, with a large number of the beneficiaries being devout if not very 'learned' (in terms of Greco-Roman literary culture) Iberian and Gallic Catholics. Indeed Irene had distant relatives herself among the Baetican landed gentry in the Iberian peninsula, some of whom she invited to Rome with high rank or promoted in the bureaucracy there and in the Spanish provinces in the early 840s as a way to add to her already wavering 'support base'. Two of her distant cousins became governors of Baetica, two more of Lusitania, and one of Narbonensis in southern Gaul with very little previous experience while younger relatives of hers were 'fast-tracked' in the Imperial guards-regiments. This added to her support as a 'good Catholic' in the Iberian region, with probable results in terms of the support that she still had there when she was overthrown in 846, but it was to be used against her elsewhere.

The stern and highly moral but well-educated Gallic and Spanish bishops who backed Irene as the 'chosen one of the Lord' as Empress had firm views on education being used to raise a generation of pious and obedient Catholics across the Empire and that meant much more religious teaching in schools and a purge of 'pagan'-allied intellectuals from being teachers. The Empress even agreed to close down the chairs in Plotinus' philosophy at Rome and Syracuse universities and deport all tutors there who objected – a controversial measure quickly reversed by Basilicus in 847. At least the study of Plato and Aristotle continued as they could be portrayed as 'groping towards' an enlightened Christian theology and understanding a little of the workings and majesty of God's Universe. Indeed Irene even posed as a patron of learning and certainly encouraged 'useful' scientific experimentation into medicine and anatomy by doctors at her and her friends' hospitals in her reign as benefiting the public. The great medical theorist and discoverer of the circulation of the blood through the body, Hermodorus of Tralles, started his career as a junior doctor in a medical school attached to a hospital which she had founded as Empress consort in Miletus in 835 and later worked under her proteges at a hospital in Brundisium although his major discoveries were not made until the 850s. Similarly the experiments on the anatomical workings of small animals and insects made by the naturalist Gessius Propertianus in the 840s and 850s were done at a private zoological park in Mutina, northern Italy, owned by one of the Empress' ministers and where she allowed local pupils at her schools to go to see wildlife – as she did schoolchildren across the Mediterranean world at parks owned by allies or proteges of hers who she ordered to open them occasionally.

Irene was an odd mixture of the philanthropic and far-sighted (to be ranked with Michael I), the shrewdly businesslike, and the cold-bloodedly ruthless. Even the largely hostile Senate came to accept her good points eventually, not least as no more was heard of her threat to put women in the Senate, but her treatment of her husband's relatives was a reason for the more scrupulous of the elite to be wary of her. Even if she had not killed Princes Carus and Marcus – as was widely believed – she had no hesitation in public mistreatment of the latter's brothers, the most obvious threat to her. Prince Basilicus, too pacifist and unworldly to attract military support and too fond of the ancient Athenian democracy to appeal to the pro-autocracy bureaucrats around the throne, was nevertheless required to retire to a remote part of northern Italy with 'ill health' under 'medical supervision' early in 839. He had to live at a guarded villa, and months later he was implicated – or framed? – in a botched plan to take him to the Dacian army and start a revolt and was removed to a fortress in the Alps near the Great St Bernard Pass where he was kept as a state prisoner. Having 'confessed' to his crimes, probably after torture, he was not even tried but was declared to have repented and announced that he wanted to become a monk, and from then on 'Brother Basil' lived in a guarded monastery deep in the mountains of Helvetia as a humble 'brother' doing menial labour, kept an eye on by the secret police, until late 845 when rebellion threatened again and Irene had him moved in secret to a monastery nearer Rome within reach of her hired thugs. His wife Cassia was forced to divorce him once he became a monk and was then made a nun, though Irene did permit her to live in a respectable and not too harsh Dalmatian convent in decent conditions and to continue writing her devotional poetry and her younger children were allowed to live with her. But Prince Zeno, her eldest (born 832), could be the focus of a plot so Irene kept him as a hostage in the household of one of her junior ministers under an assumed name as a humble page-boy with the police watching him and vetting all visitors. Basilicus' younger brother Julius the over-ambitious, glamorous, and potentially dangerous rake was castrated – supposedly at his own wishes but this is unlikely – to invalidate him for the throne as a eunuch and was then sent to a monastery in a remote area of Greece under an assumed name. His less dangerous brothers were also made monks and were put in very difficult-to-access monasteries in a remote area of pro-Irene Gallaecia in Spain but were physically unharmed.

Apart from her treatment of her husband's relatives and various plotters – who almost all ended up either executed or in the Marcomannian slave-mines – Irene was by and large merciful and her efficient police kept her abreast of almost all plots before they became serious. But though she had done a lot for trade and business and her philanthropy was legendary her reputation was to stand higher in later generations, when women were an accepted part of the elite and involved in many professions. At the time even the Church was by and large uneasy about her and some stern moralist clerics and preachers would not support her, despite her philanthropy and her patronage of shrines and icons, on account of her 'unnatural' views on and help for women and girls. They could not forget her harsh words about St Paul and her theoretical defence of women deacons before she had gained power and made the most of stories about her vanity and the amount of money that she spent on dresses and cosmetics. Indeed her use of the Imperial ceremonial was grand and costly enough to rival Rillanus II's or Leo IV's though she was far more active and shrewd politically than either of them and she consciously used 'show' as a means of propaganda to stress to the uneducated and the pious that her court was the reflection of Heaven and herself the chosen of the Lord so rebellion was a sin.

The enthusiastic popular demonstrations in her favour on mass-pilgrimage 'events' at major shrines in Italy, Gaul, and Spain (usually on saints' feast-days), which her supportive ecclesiastical affairs department bureaucrats and local governors prompted and aided with public banquets and distributions of money, acted to put potential rebels off acting in fear of causing mass riots if they took over towns or garrisons. Her supportive Praefects in Constantinople, Antioch, Alexandria, and Ctesiphon were careful to hold these sorts of public rallies on saints' days (complete with supportive sermons by tame clergy) on her orders. Her publicly-announced funding for new baths, schools, homes for the aged poor, and orphanages in their cities – and the building-projects that these entailed – also kept the public there docile, though they alarmed cost-conscious finance experts in the Rome bureaucracy and she sacked three of her treasurers in a row in 839–40 for not being enthusiastic enough over her high spending. Irene was lucky that she had no obvious alternative who the more traditionalist Catholic nobles and Church leaders could support verbally or in plots, as the moral standards of her late husband's nephews were suspect except for Basilicus and the latter was seen as a weak character and not necessarily honest in his new 'holy monk' role. As it was mostly 'Hellenist' and 'Ciceronian revivalist' senators and academics who attacked her openly the Catholics would never ally to these 'pagans'. She was too insecure to leave Italy throughout her reign as she did not trust her ministers and top commanders not to stage a coup in her absence, and she did not even attend the Olympics though she continued her husband's patronage of the 'Ephebes' and of Greek-style physical fitness in general and liked attending athletics competitions in Rome and Naples. She also patronized music and was unusual for a ruler in having her own choir and taking an interest in the contemporary development of chant-singing from the 'plainsong' (all the participants singing the same words in tune) of the Benedictine monasteries in Italy, dateable back to the 6th century, to more daring multi-layered chanting of different melodies and words at the same time by different rows of singers. Her interest in and 'propaganda' use of music was another testimony to her unique capabilities.

The great polyphonic composer and choreographer Decimus of Aniane, a former Gallic monk turned musical experimenter attached to the Papal household who had run the Pope's choir since the 820s, worked for her and ran her Palace choir. She had an unusual boys' choir of several dozen elite boys from schools in Rome who performed for her at state ceremonies, but in typical fashion her detractors turned this innovation against her. They claimed that she really liked them to perform naked for her in her private apartments and that their choirmaster was one of her supposedly many lovers and that the boys were in effect hostages for their well-connected fathers remaining loyal. Her 'behaviour enabled critics, often nobles, to present her as a 'Messalina'. The lack of an obvious heir to the Empress was one major problem for the regime and it is unlikely that despite lurid rumours her penchant for wearing long, ornamented robes hiding her plump figure was in order to conceal a secret pregnancy in 839–40 and that a young boy who she made much of at court in the following few years and talked of adopting was really her illegitimate child. But she used the uncertainty to dangle the prospect of selecting an heir from among the ministers or their proteges to keep them loyal and also apparently suggested to the senior clergy and administrators around Pope Gregory that the only way to ensure a safe, Catholic succession and the continued triumph of 'hard-line' orthodox doctrine was to establish a joint religious-lay commission to oversee an election of her successor. Given her cunning and her habit of playing one faction off against another she might have been serious or just trying to keep all potential threats loyal by suggesting that if they supported her she could choose an heir connected to their own grouping. But her manoeuvrings certainly extended to offering the potential of the succession to her military 'strongman', Bardas, either for himself or for his good-looking and talented teenage son Antigonus (OTL) who from 843 was a leading member of the 'Ephebes' and was also a successful athlete and boxer at their annual games. The contortions of palace intrigue also led to part of the group of 'Republican Rome revivalist' intellectuals at Rome University and among the literary-minded and amateur philosophers in the capital's aristocratic 'salons' being lured by pro-Irene Catholic intellectuals in the Rome Church 'establishment' to link up with them in the cause of an elected 'best man' with learned credentials being chosen as Irene's heir in 844–5. This would be either a learned theologian with sympathy for Platonic studies or a nobleman with Church links, but this approach failed to secure definite results as the literary and philosophical 'salonistes' could neither agree on a candidate or trust the devious Empress.

In the end time ran out for her regime despite its achievements after another plot within the unreconciled aristocrats in the capital, possibly aided behind the scenes by the recently sacked public works minister Julius Januarius (who had been replaced by a Papal nominee who was diverting money from provincial road-repairs to new Church schools and seminaries in Gaul and the Rhineland run by his friends), in June 845 led to mass-arrests. As the purge netted over two dozen leading nobles. Irene lost her usual nerve and had them all tried and most of them executed with their families being beggared and their property seized for Church purposes. The fact that, as her propagandists trumpeted, the mansions and estates were used to help and house the poor did not alter widespread disaffection thereafter. Nobles antagonistic to Irene or her ministers or the Papacy were afraid that they were next and that as some of the accused had been convicted on dubious evidence Irene was using informers who were preying on the rich and inventing evidence while several of the treason trials' judges had resigned sooner than convict everyone so the legal profession was furious and the'Quaestor' resigned too. In November 845 the city's police-chief was assassinated in a night-club in a professional 'hit' followed by the poisoning of the Empress' chief of intelligence and a major fire at the latter's offices destroyed piles of evidence (real or invented) against other suspects. With the evidence lost the Empress and her allies could not find convincing details of any more plots and the promotion of a second-rate career administrator to take over the intelligence department probably led to poor decision-making and a lack of shrewd guesswork or 'hunches' by the leadership there in the next months. In March 846 the regime was taken by surprise as the 'Count' of the Marcomannian frontier, John 'the Scythian'(a Romanised, Dacia-resident officer of Avar descent but with a well-connected Italian noble wife from his time at the 'comitatus' HQ in Rome), and the commanders in Marcomannia, Dacia and Langobardia held a secret meeting in a remote hunting-lodge near Augusta Prahavorum. Then they gathered their men at a nearby army base to declare that Irene was deposed for murdering Princes Carus and Marcus and they recognized Basilicus as Emperor. Her real or suspected assassinations and political trials were loudly cited to stir up fear.

The plot had been arranged in association with the military commands in Dania and Norwegia and they duly backed it while John's personal allies in the command on the lower Danube murdered their loyalist 'Count' a few days later and started a revolt too. As the more pious Catholic troops were told that the evil Empress was a murderous whore who had conned the Pope and his clerics into backing her and God would punish the Empire if she was not removed a number of local clerics blessed the rebels and reassured those who were dubious about the 'sin' of rebellion. As they started to march on Rome the Empress ordered Bardas to prepare the 'comitatus' for action and the British and Caledonian armies to intervene and head for the Rhine to intercept the rebels in Rhaetia. But the latter army was suspiciously slow in gathering its troops and crossing the North Sea to the mouth of the Rhine though this was probably due to hesitation over what to do about a simultaneous mass-assault by a coalition of Viking warlords on the 'High Kingly' army in Ireland. There in 845 the local Norse pirates and settlers in Ulster had moved South into Midhe to blockade Tara and set up a new riverine base on the Liffey at Dubh Linn ('Dark Pool'), a small Romano-Irish trading-town. The lack of any Roman expedition to help the desperate Irish ruler and Church led to the Vikings under robber warlord Olaf 'the White' (OTL) defeating the 'High King' and sacking Tara. The victors then proceeded to spread out over the midlands and sack major monasteries, causing the monks to flee with their treasures if they had time into the SW Munster hills of Kerry. But the civil war in the Empire had to take priority and the hesitant British-Caledonian army, led by 'Count' Aufidius Proscellianus, eventually reached the upper Rhine to find that the Marcomannian-led rebels were already across the Danube in Noricum. Possibly bribed, they entered into secret talks with their envoys that resulted in them evading a confrontation and in effect abandoning Irene by only slowly heading on towards the Brenner Pass – which Irene's later apologists insisted was either a 'plot' by male generals to remove an unwelcome female ruler or else a 'fit-up' by aristocratic Proscellianus to stop Irene from her probable post-victory purge of Italian nobles hostile to her rule.

The Empress now had Bardas and his troops, joined by garrison troops summoned from the Numidia and Mauretanian deserts and mountains and by the best of the 'Scholae' regiments and the 'Protectores' from Rome, set out from the capital to northern Italy to block the invasion-routes. Basilicus was brought from his monastery by an intelligence department unit and lodged in the dungeons under the old Imperial Palace on the Palatine as a hostage with several dozen sons of leading senators. Though the abbess Cassia was rescued from her nunnery by rebel emissaries before Irene's men arrived to capture her too her eldest son Prince Zeno was snatched from his ministerial 'guardian' – who the Empress feared was about to defect – and ended up in the Palace dungeons with the hostage boys. (Apparently his guardian had recently made him 'marry' his nubile daughter and have sexual relations with her in the hope that if the Prince was killed there would be an heir ready to be put on the throne later as the nearest male heir of Constantine V, but this marriage was later declared invalid by Basilicus' orders in 847 as forced.) The East stood by the Empress in nominal terms and had a lot to thank her for but its commanders, even the loyal Petronas, did not hurry to intervene. They probably realised that any expedition would take too long to reach Rome and if the rebels won would end up fighting them, and in the end Irene's fate was settled by the rebels' cavalry dashing South. They occupied the 'gap' between the Julian Alps and the new lagoon port of Venice (a rising mercantile town which was the latest, 9th century entrepot for Eastern trade to central Europe and which was unusually built on piles on marshland in the middle of a lagoon near the declining Aquileia) before Irene's men arrived and local troops from the loyalists' military bases around Mediolanum defected to them. Bardas did his best with his troops, but the capital's regiments had not fought in combat for centuries, the 'Protectores' were novices, and the Africans were used to guerilla war and ambushes not 'hand to hand' and head-on mass-battles. In the crucial battle near Padua on 18 May 846 the 25,000 or so loyalists were outnumbered and outfought by around 60,000 frontier troops who were used to fighting and their Slav, Swedish, and Khazar allies.

The rebel lower Danube troops were approaching so if Bardas won he would have to fight them within days and this may have disheartened his troops, and after a five-hour combat the rebels won and the 'Irenists' managed to disengage and withdraw reasonably intact to their camp thanks to Bardas' skill but ended up either besieged there or slipping away to avoid the Danubian troops' arrival. Possibly Bardas had been in touch with old colleagues in the main rebel army or the Danubian one and been promised his life and fortune if he saw sense or perhaps he was revolted by the just-arrived news that Irene's 'hit-men' had murdered Prince Patroclus and his next brother Prince Anastasius in their monastic prisons in Epirus. Three days after the battle he surrendered in return for an amnesty and proclaimed Basilicus as Emperor and John 'the Scythian', as 'Consul of Liberty', and the rebels marched on towards Rome. The Empress' men were promised their lives if they surrendered and most did so and the wise Pope Gregorius and most of his senior clergy fled Rome and went in to hiding, but even so the Empress had the courage or foolhardiness to shower money on the 'Vigiles' and the poor of Rome in return for their fighting on as a 'holy army' in the supposed cause of Catholicism. It was as well, considering her ruthlessness when cornered, that a senatorial 'snatch squad' of armed relatives and servants of senators (and even a few younger senators) stormed the old Imperial Palace on the night of 18–19 June as the rebel army approached and rescued the hostages. The emaciated, starved, rag-clad Basilicus and several other hostage nobles were in no condition to be involved in the battle that followed but were still paraded in the Forum Romanum at dawn next day and the untouched Prince Zeno (aged fourteen) and the hostage boys assisted the Roman rebel forces by climbing on roofs and pelting the loyalists with tiles. For the first time since the battle of the Milvian Bridge in 312 the capital was the centre of fighting. The Empress' remaining guards and 'Vigiles' attacked the Forum and were driven back, and then a large and armed crowd attacked the Marble Palace where Irene was still holding out. Advance parties of the rebel army then arrived and the 'Battle of Rome' on 19 June 846 saw the loyalists being driven out of the Palace and off the Capitol and fleeing to Ostia. Though Irene escaped too and took ship for Spain she was driven into a harbour in Sardinia by a storm and was killed there in early July, aged 48, probably by 'rebels' (or rather Basilican regime loyalists) after she had been arrested and her loyal sailors tried to rescue her. In the aftermath of her flight her reputation was denounced in ever wilder terms in the Senate and by anti-Catholic university and socialite 'literati' while none of her previous allies dared to speak up for her or her early achievements. But given the number of her high-profile crimes, especially against her husband's family, this worst fate for a fallen ruler since the pagan emperors defeated by Constantine in the C4th was inevitable.

Chapter 10

Basilicus 846–860: The Restorer. Nephew of Constantine V.

The Aftermath of Civil War – Crises in Spain and on the Upper Indus, Plus Disruption on the 'Viking' – Threatened Coasts

The Palace was not badly damaged but the sight of an eager mob looting the Imperial treasury and the Empress' collections of clothes and jewels did nothing for the reputation of the Empire, and as the Senate proclaimed Basilicus, aged forty-four, as Emperor on 22 June but he was too weak to govern for weeks after being starved by his captors a council of current and ex-ministers and rebel generals governed in his name. They were assisted by the returned new Empress Cassia who insisted that her divorce had been forced and so was illegal which the Church duly ruled. The latter was in an embarrassing position as having defended Irene almost to the last and the generals, led by the sceptical and only vaguely Christian John 'the Scythian', insisted on all Irene's pro-Church legislation and intellectual repression being cancelled. But her philanthropic work was continued and none of those projects were cancelled and the main religious casualties of the revolt were Pope Gregorius, who was suspended from office, had to do penance, and never recovered his authority, and assorted Catholic ministers who were sacked and told to return all the money that they had made out of Irene's regime. Theoctistus was sacked too and was put in a monastery minus his fortune, Petronas was able to negotiate his pardon as were all the other Eastern commanders – the new regime was too glad to avoid a prolonged civil war to object to this – and Bardas shamelessly toadied to the new government and stayed in office. The same applied to many ex-Irene supporting 'new men' frontier generals and civilian city Praefects who had sat out the civil war.

Although conservative demands to abolish the right of women to teach and to close Irene's women's teaching college were halted – largely by pressure from the now triumphant foes of Catholic conservatism in the Senate and in the intelligentsia – the Empress was roundly condemned in many speeches in the Senate and by assorted liberal nobles in the next year or two. She only just escaped a vote being passed in the Senate to inflict the *'damnatio memoriae'* on her, last seen for the anti-Christian persecutor Maximinus in 313. Doing that would have meant cancelling all her legislation and there was much, eg her investment bank, that was uncontroversial and was widely supported as was her philanthropy. But her reputation remained very poor for centuries to come and the Church excused its support for her by alleging that she had tricked its leadership. In terms of intellectual appeal for younger elite idealists in the more 'advanced' (in terms of material civilization and levels of education) Mediterranean/Levantine worlds, the orthodox Church had suffered a major blow to its credibility by enthusiastically backing a ruler – and the first politically dominant 'Augusta' since the much less controversial Pulcheria at that – who had quickly proved to be a tyrant and was associated with high-profile murders, which it had brushed aside. (A few university or monastic writers had expressed disquiet at her actions in public and so had junior clerics in sermons, but no senior bishops had done so.)

The long series of government-approved appointments of 'careerists' as senior bishops, men who were accustomed to 'keeping their heads down' in politics if they wanted promotion, in the western, 'Catholic' half of the 'Church of the Oikoumene' had averted the risk of senior clergy daring to get involved in internal Imperial Family or governmental feuds, or in 'heresy' – but it had led to a lack of moral leadership which now disillusioned idealists, Christians and non-Christians alike. Nor had the leadership of the 'Orthodox' Eastern half of this Christian world been notable for its early attacks on the Empress or indignation at the sidelining of the 'rightful heirs'. But there had been some open criticism in the pulpits and in university theologians' writings of the very idea of a female ruler and a few comments about 'the new Jezebel' or 'the new Herodias' – with the daring challengers to the State ending up sacked or thrown in gaol on Irene's orders (or allowed to flee into exile quietly by disillusioned or dissident officials and judges). The unofficial, traditionally 'risk-taking' non-orthodox sects and the 'pro-pagan' intellectual Hellenists – except for those who admired the idea of a woman ruler more than they hated her Catholic beliefs – had been quicker to condemn the 'tyrant'. So they reaped the rewards in public and intellectual kudos and attracted more recruits in the coming decades. Hostility to the 'pro-tyrant' Church also rose in the ranks of the less socially and religiously orthodox Senate families in both Rome and Constantinople and among the more idealistic members of the Mediterranean provinces' urban and landed elites. There was a degree of criticism by a 'Hellenist' strand of thinkers that in the 'good old days' of the – pagan – Early Empire great moral leaders such as Seneca had stood up to Nero but no such challenges had met Christian tyrants such as Constantius II or (as far as his detractors were concerned) Theodosius I. By definition, complacent or 'State-worshipping' Christian elites were 'incapable' of such bravery or honesty; and the concept of blaming the Church for Irene's untrammelled 'rampage' became popular in liberal political circles (small in size but 'high profile') in the next half-century. This became focused, approvingly, on the non-Catholic cultural and intellectual priorities of the new Emperor Basilicus' son and successor Zeno II after 860. This notably spread among the capital's and various Mediterranean cities' urban 'literati', who staffed both the civil service and the universities and who wrote most 'serious' books (histories and political commentaries included). Though in reality the 'reformer' and 'Christian moralist' Irene had been far from a puppet of the Church's most reactionary circles – and had been disliked by many of them as a woman – she was focused on in the imagination of the 'literati', those with nostalgic feelings towards the more intellectually liberal times of the Hellenistic and Early Empire periods in particular. Indirectly, the official Church's moral reputation as a champion of 'justice' was damaged – at least for future elite employees.

The murders of Princes Carus and Marcus, though never proved, were generally assumed to be Irene's work while the success of her Eastern mercantile policy was put down to her following the wise advice of finance minister Honoratianus – who escaped the dismissals of her ministers as being invaluable to the Empire and stayed in office until 851 though his influence at court had now ended. The main Irene supporter to keep up a degree of influence and patronage was Bardas (who in 852 even married off his son Antigonus to a daughter of Basilicus' and Cassia's). Having negotiated the surrender and pardon of assorted commanders loyal to Irene and to her firm (or belligerent) orthodoxy in summer 846 and so saved the Empire from a prolonged civil war, Bardas now assumed the role of loyal lieutenant and military organizer to the unmilitary and fearful Basilicus. The new ruler had not altered his views on the undesirability of aggressive military philistines running the Empire as a result of his sufferings and who had indeed been bolstered in his monastery by finding ideals in common with Christian pacifists there. As a result, despite being 'rescued' by the army Basilicus disliked and tended to marginalise their leaders.

There was also an initial danger of a major rebellion by either one of Irene's ultra-Christian, Catholic loyalists (presumably in their own name as she had left no heir) or of an opportunist military commander trying to break away from the Empire. But the very speed of the Empress' overthrow and the time that it took news to travel from Italy to the furthest provinces meant that news of the Northern rebellion only reached Nubia, Abyssinia, Arabia Felix, the Indus valley, the Sogdian frontier, and the furthest reaches of Garamantia shortly ahead of news of its success and of Irene's fall. Thereafter, the fact that all the Mediterranean armies except for a few Catholic provincial 'duces' in the Iberian peninsula had quickly pledged allegiance to Basilicus meant that any rebel in the outer provinces would have to face the united forces of the Mediterranean armies – so was a rising worth the risk? Luckily the loyal *'dux'* of Hispania Tarraconensis, Decimus Sabirius (a former military academy classmate of John the Scythian) managed to take his light anti-brigand cavalry and tough irregular Vascones (Basque) archers, normally used to patrol the Pyrenees and the Cantabrian mountains against robbers, in a swift ride down the Ebrus valley to catch the local would-be allies of the Baetican 'pro-Irene' forces among the coastal garrisons unawares. These were heading for Valencia to join Irene's men but the attackers routed them in a surprise attack, a few days after news had reached the area that Irene had been killed so they had no figurehead to rally round. Survivors plus pro-Irene coastal naval squadron commanders in Baetica and Tarraconensis, all hard-line Catholics and enemies of the 'un-Christian rebels' who had dared to attack the 'Chosen Daughter of Holy Church', managed to get away by sea to Lusitania as Sabirius' men and local volunteers secured Valencia. The aid of pro-Irene Catholic officers in Mauretania who sailed into Gades with reinforcements enabled the rebellion to hold out in Lusitania until spring 847 despite the loss of Olisipa and most of the south to Basilicus' troops (some of the latter sent from Italy to help Sabirius).

The war was more a matter of skirmishes in the bleak inland Lusitanian hills as the rebels shunned a direct fight against large Imperial forces. After their main army was finally caught by central 'comitatus' cavalry and Numidian scouts and routed in camp in May 847 it turned into a lingering 'brigand' (or ultra-Catholic 'patriot', for its supporters) insurrection in which fanatical Catholic monks and hermits helped to inspire loot-hungry peasants to attack the estates of the rich and passing merchants on the inland plains. It was seen as a messianic 'war of Christian equality' in the name of the late Empress, who assumed a mythical quality, or of various swashbuckling and devout local peasant leaders. At the lower social level, the Church and its champion Irene were seen as the defenders of social justice and of the 'godly' way of life blessed by the saints, whose local cults had a strong core of defenders. But though the local cults of Christian 'martyrs' and past great bishops and hermits were strong in rural Gaul, Britain, and the Rhineland too no 'peasant rebellion' disturbances or pro-Irene myths proliferated, there possibly due to the local landed elites not having been so opposed to the overthrow of a 'devout and divinely-blessed' sovereign in 846. A number of important young landed nobles in central and northern Gaul who had been at military college with or had served with one or other of the nephews of Constantine V, Irene's foes, were hostile to her and had largely been passed over for promotion or sacked from the army in 838–45 and were instrumental in stirring up feeling against her in their home areas.

The result of Imperial victory in Spain over a weak and not very co-ordinated resistance, the latter with minimal support from the urban elites who feared for the safety of trade and their assets, was never in doubt. The war was written off as a local peasant brigand one not a political challenge by the government long before order was fully restored in 855–6 by methodical new Imperial commanders. Most of the Empire was unaware it was going on – and certainly it was never, even in 846–7, dangerous enough to inspire imitators elsewhere. Its main result was to embarrass and politically marginalize the 'old' Catholic nobility of Baetica and Lusitania, families who had run the region unofficially since the 4th or 5th centuries for which they now suffered exile and confiscation of lands by the suspicious new government. A new elite of incomers, often rich urbanite merchants or self-made military men with personal loyalty to the new regime which had given them offices and tax-remissions, took over. A number of ambitious younger sons of major landowners in drought-hit, increasingly unprofitable inland Numidia and Mauretania – who had their eye on 'safer' estates that would make more money in the Iberian peninsula and so signed up to fight for the government in Spain in 847 – secured large, confiscated estates. As they brought along their tenants and workers too there were sneers from horrified local 'old families' that a horde of half-civilised Africans and 'desert Berber nomads' who spoke poor Latin and usually used the Berber or Punic tongues (an exaggeration) had taken over south-western Iberia. The demography of the ruling landed classes certainly changed – and indeed a few useful Arab commanders from Garamantia and Tripolitania, who were used with their tough horses to track down rebels, secured huge estates and in due course local offices too. Some of them also brought in their North African large-scale cattle – and sheep-ranching farming methods to the uplands of the Iberian peninsula, where there were more rain and all-year-round streams to keep their stock alive than in drought-hit north-west Africa in the 840s and 850s, after they were given large estates there confiscated from allegedly 'suspect' long-term landed dynasties. There had always been more 'ranching' in this area than corn-growing as the soil was not as fertile as in the river-valleys, but the shift to raising huge herds of stock now accelerated. So did the importation of the new owners' non-local, often Berber stockmen – and a degree of 'North African' cultural influence also crept into upland south-central Lusitania and Baetica in the next century too, including the dissemination of Berber oral epic poetry and music.

The North African culture of incoming landowners was also an important new development, and was in contrast with the old-style 'Celtic' culture of the longer-established ex-tribal landed dynasties of Gallaecia to the north-west and western Tarraconensis (to which many evicted 'rebel associate' landed gentry relocated) in the north-east. The 'mystic brotherhood' Christian associations, often with a harsh and austere semi-'Iconoclast' tinge, of the Mauretanian and Numidian interior also now influenced Christian spiritualty in the area where the incomers settled. The evicted 'hard-line' Catholic landowners who had supported Irene were to keep up their own militant faith as a form of defensive 'identity' and nostalgia, including in the central and southern Iberian regions' towns.

One of the most notable, later governor of Baetica in the 860s and builder of a new public baths and cathedral in Sevillanum and a large new Arabic-style mansion with gardens full of desert oasis plants at Cranaderia (OTL : Granada) in the mountains above the southern coasts, was the super-rich former army captain and cavalry commander Abdullah (in Roman 'Adullaphius') al-Ummaya from the ancient mercantile presiding dynasty of Mecca in Arabia.(OTL: the Ummayad dynasty of Caliphs in the Levant and Al-Andalus). He and his large family, already engaged in regional trade from their commercial offices in Alexandria and Carthage, had brought desert troops from Tripolitania to aid the 'Basilican' regime's troops to hunt down 'rebel' bandits in Baetica in the late 840s. They were granted large estates there – and members of the 'clannish' family were to appear as local sub-governors and leading city councillors and cultural patrons in Spain and Lusitania for many decades. Similarly, they patronized new local monasteries and hermitages and favoured 'austere' and 'simple life' reformist abbots who shared desert-style hostility to 'soft' living, praying and fasting regularly and abstaining from alcohol. His equally rich and high-spending grandson Ramanius (OTL: Caliph Abd-ar-Rahman, d 961) was to be governor of Baetica in the 920s and 930s and creator of a huge new library and public baths in Cordoba. The family indeed brought in much written cultural material from their Levantine homeland for the new libraries plus Middle Eastern protégé scholars to work for them as personal secretaries and librarians – including even a few Persian and Mesopotamian mathematicians, doctors, and astronomers in the 10th century. (This is how the family's own sponsored 'Academy of the Physical Sciences', the 'Jewel of Learning', grew up as a sort of private university outside Cordoba in the mid-10th century, free from local Church disquiet at its promotion of 'pagan origin' Babylonian and Sassanid mathematics and astronomy.) Ironically, the Basilican regime thus relied on 'new men' here as heavily as Irene had in Rome.

A similar politico-social upheaval with local landowners who backed a 'rebel' commander in his attempt to fight for the cause of Irene, in this case a more quixotic gesture given the distance from Rome, was caused by *'dux'* Attalus Arauntiacus in Gandhara, on the upper Indus. He was backed by about two-thirds of his province's army as he rallied support for the Catholic cause and the Empress in 846 (indeed proclaiming his rebellion in her name when she had already been killed). The other troops were rallied to the cause of Basilicus by one of the late Prince Carus' army friends who was now commander of the garrison at the famous 'Rock' of Attock. This meant that they could block the Indus crossings and stop the rebels advancing west to Kabul; most of Gandhara was held by the rebels and their local Indian mercenaries into spring 847 but then Petronas arrived up the Indus with troops from the Mesopotamian armies and fleet plus a 'pincer movement' force that advanced South-east from Sogdiana once the passes were clear of snow. The rebels were defeated in battle on the banks of the Beas, with more Roman troops from Arabia and Egypt having sailed from Aden up the Indus to land on the Eastern side of the Beas to the rebels' rear. The rebel army command was decimated by purges of the officers and transfers of the troops in the course of a five-year occupation by 40,000 new troops from Europe and Africa which also removed most of the Catholic nobility and civil service elites who had backed the rebels (a lot of them out of fear or prudence). The mixture of 'hit and run' raids by fleeing rebels from the hills and forests and resistance by evicted landowners caused chaos and near-famine in Gandhara for several years and the aftermath of the rebellion was long remembered as the end of the post-conquest prosperity of the region. Most of the main cities escaped serious damage – but the lesson of not backing rebellion against the central government's larger army was learnt by the frontier regions of the East. Prudent commanders saw that a local revolt would be overwhelmed.

The defeat and socio-political marginalization of the (mostly Catholic) elite who had been loyal to the Empress and Catholic doctrine also left their local Nestorian, Buddhist, Zoroastrian, and even Hindu foes in a strong position as they offered their services to the new Emperor's regime. The Indus region's Catholic Church and its lay backers became much weaker forces for the next century or so. The acquisition of monastic estates and building of new Buddhist monasteries by the leaders of their resurgent faith was notable in Gandhara in the decades after 850 where the Catholic faith and its leadership languished in semi-disgrace, the Buddhist community (as well as the Nestorians) having rallied to Petronas' arriving army and offered them cash and volunteers in the late 840s. Though the pious Basilicus was not a man to honour 'pagans' with high office and kept loyal Catholics in the most senior civilian positions Zeno after 860 had no such scruple. Also benefiting from backing the right side and funding the new regime in 846–7 was the family of the then Praefect Isaac Barmecidius of Ctesiphon (in OTL a prominent then destroyed Abbasid Caliphal civil service dynasty), who had held the civilian administration in Mesopotamia together for Irene in the early 840s but in 846 deftly switched sides and enabled the new regime to offer all troops who defected from Irene a large pay-rise. His, ex-Hyrcanian tribal noble family was to hold the city's Praefecture and the provincial governorship on and off well into the C10th as regime stalwarts, to the irritation of many of their local rivals, though their Christianity was of dubious orthodoxy and the Catholic Church detested them. There were allegations then and later that the new post-846 regime had deliberately 'targeted' major Catholic aristocratic office-holding families that had backed Irene – or at least had eagerly carried out her government's orders and had not abandoned her quickly enough once the news of the 846 revolt reached them – in the eastern provinces in general, citing the lists of sackings of governors and deputy governors of provinces, magistrates, and senior provincial and major city administration bureaucrats in the late 840s and early 850s. (Notably, this 'purge' was gradual and did not get underway until after the last rebellions had been put down, so there was no 'groundswell' of panic by or co-ordinated resistance by the victims – probably a deliberate policy set out by the Imperial Council in Rome.) The number of senior officials replaced in 848–58 was certainly over twice that of a normal decade and most of these men were Catholics and had held some high office in the early 840s, and most of their replacements were – though not necessarily non-Catholic – not noted for their patronage of State Church institutions. More minority Christian sect members and Zoroastrians achieved high office in the 'Persian' provinces, Mesopotamia and Bactria included, in the decade 850 to 860 than at any time since the reign of the equally 'non-Catholic' Caracalla pre-709. There were more literary 'Hellenists' in office too – but whether this was a result of a definite policy or just due to a search for reliable 'non-Irene supporters' elite members to promote was unclear. The antagonism to 'conventional' Catholics and other allies of a disciplinarian State Church on the part of the Council, and now of the Emperor too, was however clear after 860, with Zeno II in charge. His own promotion of the intellectual 'cults' of the pagan early Emperors at the expense of those of Constantine 'the Great' and Theodosius I was apparent – as was his approval of Emperor Julian.

As the cautious Emperor Basilicus would not trust Bardas to run military matters on his own one of the leading commanders of the 846 invasion of Italy, *'dux'* Julius Marcellinus of Dacia, now became 'Master of Infantry' to counter Bardas' influence and see that the 'rebel' leadership also gained major military offices. Balancing out jobs for the rebels and the loyalists of 846 was a difficult process and did sometimes lead to incompetent *'duces'* or regimental or garrison commanders who had taken the right side at the right moment or were too well-connected to be sacked keeping their jobs and so causing minor disasters. This occurred on the volatile Bactrian/Sogdian/Indus and Beas frontiers where once Petronas had left to take over an augmented Eastern 'rear base' command

and administrative HQ at Ctesiphon in 848 the removal of the peasant-abusing, girl-kidnapping, trader-blackmailing orthodox enthusiast ex-'Irenist' cavalry patrol commander Andriscus Arsamaticus on the Jaxartes led to him rebelling. He held his local forts for two years, even besieging and extorting ransom-money from Maracanda, until a Roman loyalist expedition under Marcellinus' nephew drove him out to flee to the Oghuz Turks. The chaos and the rebel's extortion of taxes from the landed elite and traders caused them to rally to the government once its armies arrived.

In the British 'sector' the new regime quickly let the 'Count' who had assisted its Marcomannian/Dacian/Langobardian forces in 846 by not attacking them stay on in 846–50. He proved equally cautious and rather more disastrous from not meeting the Vikings in Ireland head-on but letting a (too small) mercenary force go to Leinster to help the refugee 'High King' return to Tara and only sending a small naval force to try to keep Vikings in Shetland from coming by sea to assist their allies in Ulster. The latter squadron was sunk after losing its way in a channel in the Hebrides while chasing a Viking squadron that had arrived from Iceland and sailing into a whirlpool. The Vikings not only landed over 5,000 reinforcements and retook Tara but then overran Leinster too and sacrificed the 'High King' to their god Odin, and as Basilicus and Honoratianus the finance-minister were agreed that money should not be 'wasted' on this 'small' pirate problem that was most dangerous for the non-Roman Irish the Vikings ended up settling the east coast of Ireland. They sunk the small Roman squadron based on the island of Manannan (Isle of Man) and took their bases and the entire island too in 849, and went on to start raiding Venedotia (Gwynedd) and Carvetia (Cumbria). The under-funded Roman Hibernian Sea fleet had its work cut out to keep piracy within reasonable limits despite their advantage of 'Greek Fire' – they could not usually catch fast Viking longships to open fire on and sink them. Though the Roman shore patrols on the British west coast kept the enemy from being too bold isolated farms and villages were sacked for decades. Possibly the wary Rome high command feared a naval defeat by nimbler Norse ships would spark off a revolt so ignored the 'minor piracy.'

With the Church in Ireland ignored as an old ally of Irene (they had shared 'hard-line' Catholic theological views and one bishop had compared her to their saintly nunnery-founder and educator St Brigid of Kildare) the see of Armagh had to hide its treasures in the Mountains of Mourne as St Patrick's cathedral and monastery were burnt and the area settled by Scandinavians. The situation in Ireland was so bad that in the 850s Olaf 'the White' of Dubh Linn and his ally Ivarr 'the Boneless', the hugely overweight pirate son of the legendary 830s-40s pirate Ragnar 'Hairy-Breeches' (all OTL figures), were the rulers of much of eastern Ireland. All that the new and more effective Roman commanders in

Britain, led by Rhodricus (OTL: king Rhodri of Gwynedd) the current head of the long-established noble kindred of Cunedda in Venedotia who was 'Count of Britain' from 852–60 by the (wise) choice of Bardas, could do was to protect their own coasts with new forts and patrols. They gradually trained local fishermen and enterprising young nobles to man small squadrons of fast Roman ships that could actually catch up with and sink Viking ships. The Vikings had the sense to stay clear of the North Sea south of an approximate line running from the Firth of Forth to the top of Jutland and the relative prosperity of the coasts facing this area continued. The now reasonably secure Roman province of Norwegia (Vestfold and around Oslo) exported timber and furs to the Continent and Britain, and created a pro-Rome trader elite, 'hit and run' raids by Irish Vikings began on western Gaul. As the inlets of the Armorican coast became infested with Vikings each summer from the civil war of 846 and their ships sailed up the Loire to sack Nantium in 852 the Emperor had very reluctantly to pay for instituting the first naval command in the Bay of Biscay and set up a force of vessels to drive them out. NW Britain was remote and marginal; Gaul was not.

Between the Viking threat to the extreme north-west of the Empire and the rebellion in and subsequent Turkish raids on the Jaxartes region in the north-east the reign of Basilicus was not exactly one of military glory. But avoiding a major civil war was more important to the government in Rome and the Emperor himself, a timid man who had been not that discontented to live in a monastery once he had got used to the discipline as he had always been austere and reflective, was firm on the need to avoid military adventures and deferred to Bardas and Marcellinus. He was indeed not that dedicated to administrative work either and was too insecure and unsure of himself to enjoy ceremonial. But he took part in a full round of it in Rome – and in Constantinople when he was residing at the Sacred Palace there from September 848 to April 849 after a tour of his beloved Greece and attending the Olympic Games – as his duty to show his people the role of the Emperor as the 'reflection of Heaven' and inspire loyalty and unity. Cassia was equally withdrawn, though more from her scholarly priorities as she was not as insecure as her husband, and her main role was to continue the public philanthropic work of Irene and transfer the loyalty of her clients to the new (or rather old) dynasty, which she managed successfully. Indeed like Irene she attracted some moralist and conservative Church criticism for her views on women's education where she continued the pioneering work of her predecessor and even allowed a few talented women students to attend the new medical school that was opened in Rome in 851, saying that the needs of medicine meant that anyone with brains and skill should be enlisted to give their best to the Christian people of Rome and that Jesus Christ would have approved. Women – unmarried – doctors were 'sold' to the Senate as 'heirs of Martha' and virtuous semi-nuns.

Cassia also instituted an annual poetry prize for women poets which was judged by the capital's poetry school and which she presented herself and she enrolled not only the usual daughters of rich nobles but talented daughters of rising civil servants and businesspeople as her ladies-in-waiting and duly. More were later appointed to attend on her daughter-in-law Thermantia, a Cisalpine Gallic beauty of noted pious views who she arranged to marry her sexually restless and promiscuous guards-officer eldest son Zeno in 851. The new Empress had her religious vision for a pious and Christian future for the Empire as much as Irene had done but in a more tolerant and 'flexible' manner. She had no hesitation about enrolling people of mixed religious views to serve her or seeing that intolerant bigots who would only promote those of hard-line doctrine did not get appointed as bishops or as senior Church administrators. As the Emperor was uninterested in matters of religious policy or personnel she ended up as the main selector of new bishops and Church school and university senior personnel in the West with the new (849) Pope Leo, a former bishop of Venusia in Apulia and before that 'confessor' to Basilicus and his brothers as boys, Leo (OTL) was as convinced as her of the need for reconciliation after the civil war and also realised that after enthusiastically backing Irene right up until her fall the Church had a poor reputation with many as a toadying department of state and 'persecuted' Platonic intellectuals and liberal-minded nobles alike wanted to rein it in forcefully. Leo's reply was to select only morally upright and hard-working men with a reputation for philanthropy and for dealing fairly with the poor for Church offices and to put 'control' of views and theological aggression against 'heretics' to one side. In his years of office to 858 he was to be generally effective though the 'ultra' Catholic bishops and intellectuals in Spain who had venerated Irene, rallying around the works of St Augustine of Hippo which were under attack in Rome's University again for alleged excessive demands for theological correctness for the clergy, distrusted him. In Constantinople the moral but politically compromised Patriarch Ignatius, a 'man of the elite' despite his hairshirt-wearing austerity who as the son of a top general had always followed official orders and who had stood by Irene until she lost control of Rome, was as resented by and intrigued against by much of the nobility as Pope Gregorius had been in Rome. In 853 he was finally evicted by a synod on – probably rigged – charges of doctrinal mistakes and ignoring charges laid against politically useful and well-connected clerics, and he was replaced with Cassia's support by a learned and far more theologically subtle intellectual from a court background called Photius (OTL : Patriarch of Constantinople) who was currently a lecturer in theology at the city's university.

Photius was a Platonic expert who had corresponded with the Emperor as a young man and also the compiler of a rare encyclopedia of Romano-Greek learning which ran to seven volumes and had taken in (summaries of) all the major and most of the minor Greek and Roman philosophers and scientists from the C6th BC to the C6th AD. He could speak nine languages, had been on a trading-voyage to India as a young man and collected Hindu and Buddhist manuscripts, and was tolerant and keen on many different cultures, and as he was impeccably orthodox in his views and good at charming important people even the austere bishops and abbots who resented Ignatius being driven from office eventually came round to support Photius as an outstanding if too self-important Patriarch. The new Patriarch was a major supporter of the right of tutors at the universities of Constantinople and Ephesus to teach what they liked provided that it was not too outrageous and he duly stimulated a new 'surge' of interest in and work on Aristotle, creating new chairs of study on him in both universities. He also encouraged work on the half-forgotten ancient scientists such as Thales and Aristarchus who he had covered in his encyclopedia and scoured the Empire to find and give teaching –posts on them to fellow-enthusiasts.

The prime duty of the Church was to teach and to make God's Universe more understandable in Photius' opinion not to insist on right doctrine, and with this agreeing with the opinions of both Emperor and Empress he became the leading intellectual figure of the Church in the Empire in Basilicus' reign. He was often invited to come and give theological lectures in Rome – neglecting his pastoral duties, his enemies sniffed. He was thus able in the 850s to teach and influence the equally syncretic and tolerant, if rather more worldly, Prince Zeno who regarded him with affection. Under him the Church in Constantinople worked with not against the acquisition of knowledge and he was able to influence Pope Leo too as the latter respected his scholarship, though he was not liked by all his clergy and some regarded him as too 'soft' on pagans. Extending his influence, he arranged for another tolerant and learned scholar, Arsames Ardaburius, to be chosen as Patriarch of Ctesiphon in 857 to see that the local Church in Mespotamia included skilled and devout but theologically dubious teachers and junior clergy in their lists of new bishops and abbots, including men who had originally been and/or still hankered after Monophysitism or Nestorianism. This annoyed assorted 'hard-liners' promoted under Irene who ended up attempting to have him sacked by manufacturing fake charges and then left the Church when a tribunal in 862 acquitted him.

Photius was an expert on Nestorian doctrine and philosophy as well as on Plato and Aristotle and had included Nestorian thinkers and teachers in his encyclopedia to the horror of extremist Catholics. As his allies proceeded to open up the Mesopotamian Church and its Persian daughter-Church to men who had Nestorian leanings and were less than completely orthodox in their opinions this led to the 'hard-line' orthodox leaving the Church. But the majority of senior and junior clergy alike were 'Imperialists' or 'Melkites' (to use the Egyptian phraseology) who put the state's unity and the Emperor's wishes above defending precise words and views. The new opening to the less orthodox maintained majority support and also provided a more tolerant local Church atmosphere where intellectuals, mostly based at towns with a tradition of local schools for the over-sixteens like Merv and Nishapur, could talk and write about how to reconcile logic and observation with what was said in the Bible or by the Church Fathers. This fed into the current interest in Aristotle and his experiments and a new 'Persian Aristotleianism' arose in these schools and in the higher education institutions (e.g. Church seminaries) of Ctesiphon and Istakr that was to lead to new scientific experimentation there from the 860s onwards and to the foundation of a University of Ctesiphon in 892, and this could all be traced back to the patient work of Photius under both Basilicus and Zeno.

Although the Emperor was a keen follower of Plato of old and had picked up added learning on the Church Fathers in his monastery so he valued education and intellectual experimentation highly he was not an organizer or even much of a man of vision. It was his learned wife and his sexually promiscuous but intellectually enquiring eldest son Zeno who grasped what Photius was aiming for and so made an effort to provide him with resources. In a similar manner the Emperor presided over his council and urged it to prioritise stability and reconciliation but he was too weak a character to enforce this. It was his new 'Master of Offices' Atticus Ascletianus, a Sicilian bureaucrat who was in office from 847 to 858, who was the mastermind of who to select for what post and how to balance the demands of often contradictory and competing senior figures and factions in the elite. He was aided by a group of former second-tier administrators under Irene who replaced the 'compromised' men of the early 840s in governance. Also involved were a new grouping of a dozen or so senior Italian nobles with some civilian administrative service who joined the new council in 847 and were replenished every few years by new figures who like them could speak for the Senate majority. The Emperor and his wife and senior advisers were in agreement that the most essential task of the new regime was to restore confidence in and within the Empire and in that cause political turmoil had to be avoided. A policy of replacing ministers only by consensus among the existing body of ministers and senior administrators, the Senate included, was followed for all of the fourteen years of Basilicus' reign, with the result that some well-connected or popular figures who were lacking in 'grasp' or initiatives kept their offices longer than they should have done. Personnel under attack could often manoeuvre to stay in power by mobilizing their supporters in the administration or the Senate. There was also a degree of 'provincial balance' that meant that at least one of the dozen or so top office-holders had to be from Gaul, one from Spain, one from Greece, one from the Balkans, one from Asia Minor or Syria, and one from Egypt in order for them to 'represent' the elites of their home region by keeping in touch with opinion there and receiving information and requests from it.

This did 'short circuit' potential dissent and highlight local problems and difficulties with the irrigation-systems in Egypt or with roads and bridges not being maintained properly in the mountains of the Balkans, Asia Minor, or remote areas of Spain were quickly reported to the Imperial Council via these 'back-channels' to the locally-originated minister and acted upon. A similar system operated unofficially in the 'high command' of the military as local regions' regiments and garrisons were almost all 'represented' by a close connection of a current or by a former senior officer from them and these could then receive information and alerts from their 'home base' and pass these on to Praefect Bardas and his council of advisers. This was adapted in the late 840s from finance minister Honoratianus' long-standing practice of having local tax-collecting and resource-distributing officials in the provinces able to report problems via their contacts (usually from their own regions) to him at the finance ministry, and was highly successful. It was to be kept up under Basilicus' successors, but in their case the idea of the ministers themselves coming from these regions – as opposed to them just having senior aides who did – was soon dropped under Zeno II as too restrictive of who he could appoint. There were complaints, eg from honest and 'reformist' lawyers and intellectuals versed in the governance of Rome under the Late Republic and Julio-Claudians, that the desire to avoid controversy or hunts for culprits from the reign of Irene (which could lead to dodgy inventions of charges by grudge-driven foes of government figures) had led to criminals in high places escaping justice. The 'pagan' – or 'heretic'-purging Church officials and Catholic ministers of 838–46 were allegedly let off their crimes under this policy. But Basilicus and his new 'Quaestor' Justus Julianus did go after police officials and the department of secret intelligence and several dozen of the latter's senior officials were quietly removed and/or 'retired early' on half-pensions in 847–50 though open trials were usually avoided.

The Rome police and the 'Vigiles', who had led the attempt to drive the June 846 'rebels' out of the Forum Romanum on behalf of Irene and had killed hundreds of Romans in their own capital and had then looted rich people's homes in the south-east suburbs as they pulled back to Ostia, were purged more openly and more thoroughly as early as autumn 846. Some trials and executions did take place with a police official who had ill-treated and starved Basilicus and other top hostages in the final weeks of Irene's reign being thrown off the Tarpeian Rock on the Capitol for treason, the new regime having declared that Basilicus' reign had begun when he was proclaimed Emperor by the rebels in Marcomannia so that any action against his supporters after that amounted to treason. All who fought against 'his' army in Italy in May-June 846 were at risk of prosecution if they did not obey the new regime and hand over all their ill-gotten gains. (Technically that made Bardas and his senior officers at the battle outside Padua liable for prosecution, but they were given a pardon in a simultaneous law as were all the provincial garrisons and regiments plus senior civil and military officials loyal to Irene then.) After that purge the hunt for the 'tyrant's collaborators' was scaled down and even the castrated and forcibly tonsured Prince Julius had to accept that he would not get justice and agree to the return of his property and a seat on the Council plus assorted honorific ranks and perquisites. Basilicus was subject to a lot of criticism for buying off both opponents and the victims of Irene by this sort of measure but was able to defend this as avoiding internecine strife between 'victims' and 'oppressors' of Irene's reign.

The supremacy of the Law and a ban on religious discrimination by the lay authorities against either minority 'heretic' Christian sects or pagans followed the early legal measures against Irene's police and intelligence associates in 846–7. Thereafter the era's politics calmed down as the Council bought off Senate criticism by appointing lots of disgruntled senators to new and lucrative advisory councils and committees to 'assist' various ministries. Though Basilicus was too humble and austere a person to have much interest in ceremonial and from the mid-850s his rheumatic problems (possibly caused by Irene having him kept in a waterlogged cell on his initial arrest to intimidate him) restricted his mobility or ease in standing for long periods for ceremonies. But the apparatus of dignified and visually splendid ceremonial continued in Rome as much as possible and was usually only halted when the Emperor went off for his August holidays at one of the Imperial villas on Corcyra or, most often from 850, in the Aegean on Naxos or Samos. The splendour-loving Zeno, a connoisseur of rich robes and jewels, was more than happy to make up for his father's ill-health and to take the lead role in ceremonies where necessary in the mid-late 850s, once his military training and a series of tours of the Mediterranean provinces had ended. As 'Caesar' from spring 858 he took over most ceremonial and also presided at most of the public Games, taking a keen interest in chariot-racing and knowing a lot about horses but steering clear of the open partisanship or association with extravagant and womanizing young rakes that had damaged Princes Carus and Marcus in the 830s. This was in contrast to the race-faction-sponsoring, stud-owning Prince Julius who was one of Rome's leading racing patrons and also ran his own polo-club for ex-military officers and raffish aristocrats. (Rumour had it that Julius was allowed to bend legal rules on financing racing-clubs and evade paying tax in order to keep him happy and out of politics.)

The ailing and ineffective Basilicus was withdrawing from anything but a part-time and formal role in governing a good two years before he died on 16 February 860, aged fifty-seven, and was generally only brought into making decisions once his advisers had decided what to do among themselves. But though his eldest son was a more forceful character and had decided views on some issues, especially religious toleration and a Hadrian-style reverence for Ancient Greek culture, Zeno was fitful in his interest in the minutiae of administration. He tended to rely heavily on the advice of his secretaries (e.g. in who to promote) and on those ministers who he trusted, led by 'Master of Offices' Ascletianus and by Bardas, although a few intriguing courtiers and Catholic nobles did try to stir up his brother Honorius against him to secure the latter a share of power and perquisites to pass on to them. But the Prince was a dilettante more interested in plays and poetry than in power and he was encouraged by his fellow-patron Antigonus, the super-rich playboy ex-officer son of the watchful Bardas, to spend his time on his private pursuits not seek political advancement. Indeed some said that Bardas was using Antigonus to keep the intelligent and potentially dangerous Honorius from taking an interest in power and that the two of them supplied the bisexual Prince with lovers of both sexes to distract him. Eyebrows were also raised at the alleged financial patronage of Bardas for a successful but humbly-born professional wrestler from a remote Macedonian village (near one of Bardas' estates) called Basil 'the Macedonian' a six-foot-six 'he-man' with rippling muscles, who rose from being Antigonus' stable-boy to an Olympic-standard wrestler in the 850s then moved into Honorius' household as his professional horse-breaker and his personal wrestling trainer. The ambitious and acquisitive but uncouth Basil (OTL : Byzantine Emperor from 867) became the Prince's closest friend and adviser on sporting matters despite his lack of knowledge of culture and was reputed to help to find him new lovers from his raffish sporting circles. By 860 he had the Prince too tied up in an endless round of socializing, sports-training, and running a stud (to add to his poetic patronage) to have time to challenge his elder brother. Thus the unease of devout Catholics or Platonic and 'Ciceronian' moralists over how easily Zeno was able to get rid of his unwanted wife Thermantia once she had given him an heir (Probianus, born in 857) and have her 'dumped' in a convent for wealthy women with a religious 'mission' run by the Benedictines near Mantua was not exploited to undermine him as it could have been. By the time of Basilicus' death Zeno had set up house in a villa at the elite holiday resort of Antium with his new mistress, the beautiful but venal Cypriot ex-hotelier's daughter Serena, who he was to marry in 861 and make his Empress. Zeno was clearly going to be a more forceful and active ruler than his father – but would he be a great statesman or a luxury-loving showman run by his shrewder ministers?

Chapter 11

Zeno II (I): 860–883. The Hellenist Revival, The Emperor's Passion for the Classical Age – and the 'Viking Showdown' Conquest of Northern Norway. Son of Basilicus

On Basilicus' death in February 860 Zeno II became formal Emperor, though he had been exercising power as 'Caesar' for the previous couple of years and the senior ranks of government hardly changed. The first of those ministers appointed in a 'regional balance' but lacking much capability or initiative, as seen above, were not removed until 862 so Zeno did not see it as a priority to restore dynamism to government. Ascletianus was to stay in power and continue to arrange most administrative and a good number of ministerial appointments until 865, and Bardas and his wary ally Marcellinus were also trusted by Zeno and were more devoted to the details of policy and supervising personnel than he was so they continued to run military affairs. The 'Master of Cavalry' in Rome was replaced early on by a racing-stud-owning ex-cavalry officer former mentor of Zeno's but he was competent if owing his appointment to 'cronyism' not an outstanding military record. Only in 867 was Zeno to take a step into leadership of military policy and personnel by arranging for Bardas to retire and appointing a new Praetorian Praefect but also a new and more powerful deputy to him, known in Greek terminology as the 'Great Domestic(us)', to supervise the running of the provincial armies and their commissariats more closely. (The Praefect would now run strategy and the deputy would run personnel and resources.)

Zeno was however more conscious of the need to restore Rome's military reputation and teach its 'insolent' enemies a lesson than his father. He had hankerings after the role and legacy of Alexander the Great and the more successful Seleucid kings, and though his own interests were more in the East than the West he saw that the main current threat was that of the Vikings. He listened more than Basilicus – or Bardas – had done to the complaints of merchants that British-Irish trade was being wrecked and British trade with western Gaul and Spain was being damaged by Norse pirates operating from Ireland, the Isle of Manannan, and the western Hebrides. This might be small-scale compared to grand strategy in the East, but it mattered and accordingly Zeno ordered the Hibernian Sea fleet to be doubled in size and augmented by new ships with extra-strong 'Greek Fire' tubes that could hit enemy shipping at a greater distance and a new commander used to rough northern seas, Adelricus Atrambatinus (of Saxon origin but from family long resident in Britain), took over the fleet.

More Danish farmers and their sons, who made extra cash out of the harvest season from fishing or trading and so were expert sailors, were moved in the 860s from their farms in Jutland or the Danish islands to eastern Britain, principally Icenia and around Lindum (Lincoln) and Eburacum (York), to settle and to serve in the 'Classis Britanniae'. The men who they replaced were moved to the Hibernian Sea or the Firth of Forth and Dornoch Firth commands, and indeed as a result of the influx of several thousand Danes to take over farms in the Eburacum region – and start to set up new pastoral 'ranches' on the high moors and in the steep valleys to the north-west – there was to be a notable rise in the use of Danish names and terminology in the region. What had once been a 'Brigantian' Romano-British region became seen as what locals nicknamed 'New Dania' or 'British Dania'. Already by 864–5 there were many new Danish sailors in the British North Sea and Channel fleets who were more used to the tidal and wind problems of the region and to tackling mobile Norse pirates than the more conventional (and often from different regions) local Roman officers, meaning more success in catching Viking pirates. While they kept the eastern and southern seas quieter and even helped in the summers to keep Viking pirates off Armorica the Roman military supplied troops and artillery to the embattled new Irish 'High King' Mael Sechnaill (OTL figure) in Midhe from 862. Zeno did not want the expense of a major war but he did want the Vikings defeated and an opportunity to claim glory for the victory. So in 862–4 a large force of 20,000 Roman infantry and 5,000 cavalry aided Mael Sechnaill to regain his dynasty's ancient headquarters of Tara and all of Midhe. Then they joined a Roman naval blockade of Dubh Linn (which had to surrender and was made a Roman port/garrison base) and in due course the Romano-Irish force drove the Vikings all the way back to Ulster and killed Olaf 'the White' in battle.

Ivarr 'the Boneless' and his brothers Halfdan and Ubbe (OTL figures), who had joined him from Iceland with more Vikings for the war, survived as rulers of Ulster but had to surrender control of Armagh (where the Church was restored to control and the sacked cathedral rebuilt but a new Roman garrison was needed to protect the see's headquarters). The Vikings had to put up with a chain of Roman fortresses cutting Ulster off from Midhe, and with a permanent garrison of some 7000 or so Romans now on the Ulster-Midhe border and 3000 or so more stationed at Dubh Linn the 'High Kingdom' of Ireland became a Roman client-state. The Church hailed Zeno as a hero of Christianity in sharp contrast to its recent objections to recognizing Serena as Empress and the new Pope Nicholas (OTL), a cultivated and tolerant man like his predecessor Leo, put down all subsequent moralist protests against Zeno with more decisiveness and kept him happy that way so that he would continue to take an interest in Ireland. But once Zeno had celebrated his Triumph as 'Hibernicus' in 864 he lost interest in the region and he ignored military appeals to finish off the Vikings in Norwegia, by annexing the Bergen region and its petty jarldoms and then taking Trondelag to the north, as too expensive – and pointless as the Vikings would only head off to Ireland and re-start the war there.

Zeno's main interests apart from Greek culture lay in the East, and in that region he was equally wary of war but was determined to increase Rome's presence albeit by trade and expeditions of exploration not invasions. He summoned assorted captains who had explored the east African coast and the Bay of Bengal to Rome to meet him early in 861 and drew up a plan of action to make Rome the dominant force in Indian Ocean trade. Geographers from the 'Museion' in Alexandria, an institution which Zeno treated with reverence and in 862 ordered to be rebuilt on the basis of its early Ptolemaic floor-plans and re-staffed with a full complement of scholars, and from the city's university were also summoned to this Imperial planning-meeting. Experts on the 2nd century AD geographer Ptolemy submitted surviving manuscripts of his and copies of his lost works and notes to the Emperor and his new 'Eastern Geographical Committee', and thereafter the Eastern/Oriental trade ministry was mandated to work in collaboration with these geographers and the relevant experienced captains, naval and mercantile alike, to plan expeditions. As T'ang China was descending into anarchy with a weak and bureaucrat-hobbled central government, ineffective emperors who were prisoners of their ministers or their feuding courtiers, frequent coups or child emperors, and breakaway provinces it would be no help to Rome in clearing the great sea-routes or land-routes along which trade passed of bandits and pirates. Zeno quickly realized this from the reports which he received from traders who had been there since c.830 or had met Chinese traders and diplomatic missions in the Hindu states of Bengal or in the emerging kingdom centred in Burma's central Irrawaddy plains. Instead of a grand Romano-Chinese alliance to make the 'Silk Road' and sea-route trouble-free arteries of trade, Zeno sent out new naval and mercantile expeditions from Aden and the Persian Gulf ports in the years after 863 to travel to the Indian sub-continent and Ceylon and exchange gifts with and sign trade-treaties with the rulers there before escorting convoys of trading-ships back to Aden and the Gulf once goods had been exchanged. As a result it became the routine each year for a Roman naval convoy from Aden and a separate one from Charax to each escort a large group of mercantile ships to India and Ceylon with the trade-winds and then escort them back a few months later. Zeno hoped to use the role of Rome as guarantor of safe trade to assert 'soft power' as far as Ceylon, the ancient Taprobane.

Zeno was also interested in exploiting the disaster that had struck the large Buddhist religious and lay community in T'ang China in the mid-840s – at a time of Roman politico-military preoccupation with the collapse of Irene's regime so it had not been exploited then despite appeals in 845–7 from the alarmed Buddhist abbots and lay aristocratic/merchant leadership in Gandhara to the successive rulers in Rome, Irene and then Basilicus, for help. (The devout Irene had taken no notice of the appeals as she had disapproved of 'sinful and pagan' Buddhism, though Basilicus had issued orders for tax-relief and food aid for all Buddhists fleeing China who crossed the Karakorum Range mountains to Gandhara). The devout and pugilistically nationalist – and insecure – Chinese emperor Xuanzong II (ruled 840–46), a man who had ironically shared some traits with Irene though in his case his religious zeal was directed towards promoting 'native' Chinese neo-Daoist religion, had regarded Buddhism – and also Christianity – as an intrusive and 'subversive' foreign doctrine that unpatriotically lured his subjects away from their traditional religion and culture and aroused the gods' wrath. He had been prompted to act by bureaucrats who wanted the State to get its hands on the riches and the lands of the many Buddhist monasteries. After firstly driving 'superstitious' and 'exploitative' extremist or minority sect Buddhist monks and nuns out of their monasteries and secularizing them in 842–3, in 845 he had banned Buddhism altogether. He had closed down the monasteries and nunneries, secularized their occupants and made them take up secular occupations (and pay taxes), and had banned all Buddhist worship – though it continued in private and in isolated rural locations.

This massive purge, which had been promoted as a patriotic 'strike' against foreign influence and had been followed by a ban on Christian worship (most of which in China was Nestorian not orthodox so the Church in Rome had not complained about it via the regular Imperial trade embassies to China), had not lasted long. It had been reversed when the autocratic and somewhat maverick emperor had died in 846, still in his early thirties, and his more consensual brother had succeeded him. But in 845–6 several thousand monks and nuns plus a smaller number of lay Buddhists had fled to India across the Himalayas to live in religious freedom, most to the large Buddhist community in the sympathetic local states of Bengal but a smaller number along the 'Silk Roads' to Gandhara. About a third of the Nestorian community (including most of its 'ex-patriate' Persian and Gandharan merchants and priests and their families) in

China had fled too, to Gandhara. Once Irene had fallen the refugees had been able to get a more sympathetic hearing and greater financial help from the lay authorities in Rome as the humanitarian ex-prisoner Basilicus and his religiously syncretic Council had more interest in them than the harshly Catholic Irene and her Council had done. Also the new governor of Gandhara in 847–52, Julius Cassianactius, and his successor in 852–9, Probus Proterianus, had both been local Gandharans of doctrinally 'relaxed' not Catholic beliefs with some Nestorians and Buddhists on their councils of advisers plus Nestorian relatives. These men and their local merchant allies in Taxila, keen to restore stability and Roman 'pride' and to build up their income from rich taxable subjects after the recent demoralizing civil war, had encouraged the refugee Buddhists and Nestorians to stay in Gandhara even when the T'ang regime was trying to invite them back home. They had warned the non-Taoist and non-Confucian communities in China and its western subject ally regions in Zinjiang that they could not rely on the 'corrupt and viciously nationalist' T'ang regime, run by a mixture of weak and unstable emperors and feuding courtiers, to guarantee their safety or their possessions. There was neither stability nor a guaranteed rule of Law in T'ang China – but there was both in the Roman Empire, which once the 'evil usurper' Irene was dead was tolerant of all religions and would protect all its subjects provided that they paid their taxes and stayed loyal. This policy by Emperor Basilicus and his Council and his north-west Indian governors duly attracted growing numbers of worried lay Buddhists (many of them merchants and intellectuals) as well as resentful or nervous secularised Buddhist monks and nuns from China to join the 'safer' Buddhist community in Gandhara in the 850s. This also helped the regional government and its military by enlarging the community of those rich and politically active subjects who were not Catholics and so were unlikely to hanker after a regime like Irene's – and as local inter-state wars hit the Buddhist communities of the middle-lower Ganges many of their lay and religious elite also ended up settling in the 'safe haven' of Gandhara.

As a result the prosperity and cultural syncretism of the region revived in the mid-late 850s and so did its tax-revenues, and the number of Chinese as well as Bengali Buddhist scholars at the university of Taxila increased substantially and it became a major centre of 'Mahayana' Buddhist thought by around 855, eclipsing the now steeply declining Buddhist intellectual centres of China around the capital of Chang'an. Indeed, since 845 assorted worried Buddhist thinkers had been bringing large quantities of Chinese Buddhist scriptures to safety in Gandhara. A number of closed Buddhist monasteries in China never reopened after 846 but the most determined and/or devout of their personnel moved over the next decade to Gandhara and set up new institutions there. All of this was to continue and have greater Imperial patronage after 860 from

Zeno, who unlike his father Basilicus was interested in Buddhist thought and appreciated the religion's lack of Catholic-style obsession with doctrine. Zeno also now promoted the role of Rome as a guarantor of religious liberty and syncretic thought to attract scholars from Buddhist northern and central India (plus minority Christian and Hindu sects) to settle in Gandhara and the lower and middle Indus valley. As a man who knew his history, he argued via official propaganda that the Emperor was the heir of the tolerant 2nd century Greek ruler 'Milinda' (i.e. Menander), king of the Indus and Ganges regions, and brought peace and justice to his peoples unlike the feuding Hindu kings and the tyrannical T'ang emperors.

Pirates were now put off attacking as the 'Greek Fire' on the Roman naval vessels could destroy their ships at a distance. The extra confidence given to the 'India merchants' by this boosted investment, and as money flooded into the trading-companies (smaller family ones and larger groups of collaborating merchants) from people who now saw the India trade as a worthwhile investment trade boomed. Eastern luxuries flooded into the Empire, initially to the east as far as Antioch and Alexandria and gradually and to a lesser extent to the Mediterranean lands. In return the Empire exported its own trade-goods and as India was short of sturdy materials for clothing in the winter and relied on flimsy cotton Rome could export woollen clothes there along with new (to India) types of timber and in years of Indian famine grain and other foods. Rome exported its own artwork – including icons, which came to have a minor influence on more realistic portraiture in Indian painting, and statues which revived the C2nd BC Greco-Bactrian influence on statues of Indian gods and kings. In return a mass of Indian statuary and ornaments were brought to the Empire and became objects of value to the rich. The more syncretic, usually Greek 'paganism' – influenced learned men of the Empire, especially in the universities and upper classes of the eastern Mediterranean and Mesopotamia/Persia, picked up ideas from Indian culture and learning that were brought by Indian merchants or by Romans who had lived in India for years trading, though the Church frowned on such 'heathen' ideas as a 'threat' to devout Christians. Thus the ideas of Indian mathematics that had already brought the 'Indian numerals' (the zero included) to the Empire a couple of centuries earlier became important to and had a considerable impact on Roman mathematicians though this was to take decades from c. 865 to work though into writers' treatises and into teaching. A few daring Roman – often Mesopotamian – mathematicians had already visited India and attended on major scholars there to pick up ideas in the 7th and 8th centuries and a few books had been written bringing in Indian ideas and relating them to the work of Pythagoras and the mathematicians of Ptolemaic Egypt (e.g. Eratosthenes). But the amount of pirate attacks on shipping had made the journeys to India – except in large convoys – dangerous so few scholars had dared take the risk and now the greater security led to a comparative 'flood' of these travelling to India, the Ganges valley schools and Maharashtra in particular, in the later 9th century and within a decade or two these ideas were filtering through to Roman universities.

The more advanced astronomical observations and, crucially, understanding of and work on constructing glass lenses for telescopes in India now also began to filter through to the Empire, notably to Persia and Mesopotamia first not Alexandria though the latter had been full of distinguished astronomers under the Ptolemies and their works were still read. Probably the concentration of the current university leadership in Alexandria – and their funding – on philosophy and, in science, on 'useful' medicine and on military engineering was to blame for this. The State directed funding – to proven useful – science in Egypt; Iranians were more 'self-starters'. Certainly by 860 some energetic younger astronomers in Egypt who had studied the star-catalogues of the 2nd century AD – scientist Ptolemy and the primitive telescopes of Ptolemaic Egypt had moved on to Mesopotamia to work at schools there, and possibly the survival of the records of the ancient 'Magian' astronomer-priests of Sassanian Iran who had studied the stars and promoted astrology there also attracted them – and astronomy had a professorial chair at the new university of Ctesiphon, The leading later 9th century-Romano-Mesopotamian astronomer Callicrates of Seleucia, connected to a leading local trading dynasty and with relatives who had traded in India and could teach him the relevant languages, spent a decade in India learning advanced astronomy and mathematical calculation after the start of Zeno's naval-escourted trading convoys. On his return home he constructed his own new telescopes at Seleucia and studied the stars to discover new constellations and to create his own 'star maps' – and to assess and back the Indian theory that the stars were not all set on a fixed background by the gods but were balls of fire like the Sun, dim or bright depending on how far away they were from the Earth. This theory was duly put out in his writings in the 880s and 890s and gained support from the more enlightened members of the academic community and, crucially, from Zeno himself (then no longer Emperor and in 'retirement' but hugely influential with his sons the then Emperors Probianus II and Aurelianus II).

Although the Church was furious as there was no mention of other worlds in the Bible so theologians and preachers alike called this 'blasphemy' the State backed Callicrates up. His work was never condemned though many conservative scholars, especially Catholic and orthodox ones, boycotted his work and managed to get the education ministry to keep him out of a professorial chair as likely to cause riots. The study of astronomy only spread slowly compared to that of mathematics, not least as the latter could be used to help military engineering calculations and so improve siege-weapons and was taken up by the Praetorian Praefecture and Military Strategy Centre. The first new chair of astronomy in the Empire's universities had to wait until the mid-C10th (at Alexandria, with one at Athens soon following but the Papacy keeping them banned from Rome and the Gallic and Spanish universities), but chairs of mathematics began to proliferate in the later C9th, boosted in Zeno's second reign in 902–12, and from the 870s new chairs of medicine were also created. In this case the 'New Galen', the pioneering surgeon and analyst of a long list of diseases (and potential remedies) Isidore Iamblichianus of Mediolanum (d 918), did not pick up his ideas from India but from personal observation in three decades as an army surgeon before he went into private practice. He was also an expert on Galen who acquired access to his notes through contacts in Rome, but his work was backed up and then taken further by traders and their proteges who had visited India and acquired medical knowledge there and the military 'high command' were also prepared to put money into his research so they could stop soldiers succumbing to epidemics in camp and so ruining campaigns. (Iamblichianus was particularly useful to them in linking dirty water to typhoid epidemics.)

While the added Indian connections boosted Roman science in the later 9th century and 10th century and so could be linked to Zeno's initiatives the Emperor also revived Imperial patronage of the drama. He led a major revival of the plays of Plautus (the main, 2nd century BC-Roman comedy playwright) with a special 'Plautus Festival' planned, sponsored, and attended by the Emperor in Syracuse in 863. But his fondness for and revival of the 5th century BC – comedy writer Aristophanes' work was more controversial as the latter could be – and was – called vulgar and crude. His plays, seen on the public stage at Epidaurus in 864 for the first time for centuries in a new Aristophanes Festival set up by his intellectual admirers among the local nobles and literati but backed by Zeno, led to the Church picketing them and staging rowdy demonstrations by 'spontaneous' groups of 'outraged citizens' led by clergy in Corinth and Athens. (The Emperor had had the Epidaurus site guarded by troops in case of trouble.) Quite apart from the sexual references and the crudity the plays included attacks on the revered philosopher Socrates as a publicity-seeking fraud who was exploiting the gullible and the would-be trendy and causing young men to sneer at their elders. Though the Emperor as a 'relaxed' expert on Greek culture accepted that comedy had to be uninhibited and offend people there were many earnest Platonists as well as Christians who regarded Aristophanes as going too far – was he not partly responsible for Socrates being executed as a socially disruptive troublemaker? The Aristophanes festival had to be hastily re-examined after large numbers of bishops complained to the Emperor and even the ultra-cultured and liberal-minded Patriarch Photius of Constantinople called his plays 'obscene'. The issue set liberal-minded and cultured fans of C5th BC Greek culture against each other as well as against the Church and Zeno eventually agreed to have the festival restricted to once a decade. But his concurrent plans for an annual 'Aeschylus Festival' at Epidaurus, stimulated by the discovery of nearly a dozen of that playwright's lost works in an Alexandria archive by the Emperor's theatrical history expert friend Xenocrates Sosibellius in 861, went ahead as Aeschylus was a respectable tragedian who had plenty to say about the human condition and even his musings on divine 'behind the scenes' manoeuvres and settings of lessons for imperfect humanity could be called a 'groping by a thoughtful and learned thinker after the real Christian truths'.

Aeschylus and his fellow-dramatists Sophocles and Euripides could be called thoughtful explorers and illustrators of the human condition and Divine providence and to a degree 'pre-Christian intellectual forerunners', as Plato had been seen for centuries. Hence Sosibellius was not attacked so violently by the Church over his Aeschylus festival and this duly became an annual event, was attended by Zeno on his Greek tour of 866, and from 869 included an annual competition in writing plays in the style of Aeschylus which was to attract new, young dramatists well into the C10th. It was to lead to new plays being written about themes of and people in Roman history – including the Early Empire but mostly on the great figures of the Late Republic. In this vein Sosibellius set up an annual Sophocles Festival at the old theatre next to the Acropolis in Athens in 868 and an annual Euripides Festival at the old theatre at Delphi in 877. The latter led to a major revival of the old town there which had declined to a village since the Temple of Apollo was shut as anything more than a minor tourist centre. Zeno not only gave Sosibellius an annual treasury grant to pursue his great work on reviving Greek and stimulating Roman drama but made him 'Consul of Drama' in 872 and then set up a new sub-ministry of the education ministry in 874 to funnel funds to drama festivals, dramatists, and theatrical troupes all over the Empire. (He did hope to revive the widespread Mediterranean drama 'culture' of the last few centuries BC, but in practice with the Church hostile the project only got off the ground in Italy, Greece, parts of liberal urban coastal Asia Minor and Syria, and Egypt.)

Zeno's passion for the ancient Greek arts was well-known and was to a degree exploited by ambitious and funds-hungry entrepreneurs who coaxed large sums of money out of him for dubious projects, though as he built new churches too and funded a school for teaching icon-painting in Constantinople the Church's objections were muted except in ultra-conservative areas. He played a major role in the revival of the old Early Empire tradition of realistic sculpture too as he wanted to revive the era of the great sculptors like Pheidias and Praxiteles and in 866 founded a new 'School of Sculpture' in Rome, calling in the best sculptors in the Empire to staff it and paying grants to young men to study there. He ran his own schemes to add new statues and friezes in the antique style to the Marble Palace in Rome, the Sacred Palace in Constantinople, the Imperial holiday villas at Syracuse and on Corcyra, Naxos, and Samos, and the palaces of Caracalla at Antioch and hundreds of sculptors and their assistants were to be employed there from the late 860s so the young trainees at the Rome sculpture school had a career guaranteed. But his greatest project was to restore the 'Colossus of Rhodes' – though out of deference to the Church as a giant statue of St John not as one of the pagan sun-god Helios – and this plan, as drawn up by one of his top sculptors called Domitius of Tyre (Phoenicia) and commenced in 878, continued to be hit by delays and was widely ridiculed. The ancient skills of the Rhodians in the 280s BC had been lost though their surviving diagrams and other useful clues were found in Alexandria by a crack team of the Emperor 'scholars before the work commenced and were used by Domitius. But the statue (with legs close together and not straddling the harbour, which concept it turned out had not been used in the original either) kept on collapsing and had to be rebuilt several times, and as wits joked that it was really meant to be a 'Colussus of Zeno' and reflected his conceit the bearded, robe-clad 'St John' certainly had a resemblance to the Emperor and had to be guarded from attack by Christian zealots who regarded it as idolatry.

The statue, two-thirds of the size of the original was finally complete in 885 after Zeno had abdicated and was ignored and denied repair-funds by his sons as an embarrassment and when it collapsed in the mid-10th century it was left to rot. But at least it showed Zeno's commitment to the achievements of Ancient World culture and when he decided to reconstruct the 'Hanging Gardens of Babylon' too, now as an exotic tiered garden of some 300 acres at the suburban town of Lanuvium in the Alban Hills near Rome, this was more successful. This collection of terraces of exotic Eastern plants and trees, some brought from India and Ceylon, was a masterpiece of Roman garden design and well within the capabilities of current horticulturalists as was the work of constructing an aqueduct to bring water to it from the Sabine Hills. With a large workforce of Imperial employees busy on it this project, commenced in 880, was finished in 889 and was then opened by the ex-Emperor in person – and became a major tourist attraction and a source of income for the treasury as when the Emperor or his family did not want to use it the site was opened to the public for a fee.

The Emperor had ideas to restore the other missing 'Seven Wonders of the World' too but the finance ministry managed to talk him out of it, and as the greatest Imperial patron of the ancient cultural arts for centuries – even out-matching Caracalla – he managed to fund the training of what was to prove to be generations of young artists, sculptors, garden-designers, dramatists, and architects as well as scientists. Equally importantly, he built up a supportive network of leading nobles who were able and willing to help with all this funding and to see that the capital's elite all played their part. (His supporters crucially included his sons as well, so that most of the projects would be kept up by the next generation.) The amount of money spent on the 'Colossus' was difficult to defend and caused unnecessary budgetary problems for the Empire and publicity problems for the spendthrift Emperor as it coincided with locust-plagues and famine in Nubia and the southern Arabian provinces that needed urgent relief-work. It was as well that the philanthropic relief-programmes put in place in previous such famines by the Church in Egypt and its daughter-Churches in Dongola and Alwa were (barely) adequate to the task of feeding the starving rural populace as they thronged the cities demanding food. But at least it did lead to useful experiments in constructing huge edifices that were useful for buildings as well as statues and the military engineers 'on site' as well as sculptors learnt useful facts for future reference. (On a different level, awe at the sheer capabilities of the 3rd century BC Rhodian sculptors and their teams of workers by the Roman work-crew and their supervisors 'fed into' a revival of enthusiasm by architects and sculptors in the capital's and other schools of art and architecture for finding out and re-using the lost skills of the past, with complementary disdain for post-3rd century Roman cultural 'ignorance'.)

The ongoing crisis in the Yemen as harvest after harvest was eaten up by locusts and the rural population fled the farms hit tax-revenues there and it was as well that customs-revenues at Aden and the Red Sea ports were flourishing in the Indian trade-boom despite the cutting of customs duties back by Irene to aid trade. Indeed the collapse of agriculture and the forced selling-up of unviable farms by ruined farmers to their creditors and/or the 'financially cushioned' owners of 'latifundiae' estates meant that the rural part of 'Arabia Felix' more or less collapsed in the 870s and 880s. The bankrupt countryside was in sharp contrast to the booming port-towns with their 'new rich' merchants and bankers. (New banks to invest in the eastern trade as a 'surefire success' emerged in Arabian ports as well as Egypt and Mesopotamia in these decades.) The ever-watchful and land-hungry Arab nomads from the desert moved into inland 'Arabai Felix' to grab the empty farmland for their herds of camels, sheep, and goats and had their own 'boom', which helped to add to the prosperity of Mecca and Medina (and in the Yemen, Sana'a and Taiz) from their elite's spending. But rich and fractious tribal chiefs also started to fight over land and water-holes so the long-established security of the 'Pax Romana' collapsed inland. With the Empire's local troops and civilian officials too short of staff and money to intervene and having enough to do to feed the fleeing rural peasantry the Yemen became a very different place by c. 930 from what it had been in the 860s. A similar long-term drought and locust plague hit Darfur in the west of Nubia and caused more tribal squabbles over land and water and an emigration of the area's few farmers to Nubia to seek work in the Nile valley towns. But as long as none of the assorted rival chiefs or petty village headmen with their own militias actually challenged the government the Roman administrators and troop-commanders tended to keep out of the rising chaos and probably very little of it was ever reported to Rome – or taken any notice of by an Emperor and group of ministers who regarded the local Africans as primitive 'barbarians' who barely spoke Latin and had no culture.

The drought, locust-plague, and resulting collapse of central governance (in so far as there was any) in Abyssinia also went unnoticed and the only alteration of affairs in that region South of the Red Sea was that hundreds of ruined farmers or their children sought jobs in the local coastal trading-ports of Eritrea, led by Adulis and Massawa. These had a mini-boom in the 870s to 900s as they benefited from the Indian trade-expansion too, and Zeno's own interest in the region was limited to his restless and ever-eager quest for lost geographical knowledge that led him to send out captains from the Red Sea and Yemeni ports down the coast South from the 'Horn of Africa' to Mombasa, Kilwa, and on to the mouth of the Zambesi. Zeno had read that a Persian naval expedition had circumnavigated Africa and sailed South down the coast well into the lower hemisphere and then back up the western coast to Mauretania in the time of 'Great King' Xerxes (c 480 BC), as originally stated by Herodotus. He wanted Romans to do the same and in 868 instituted a prize for any Roman captain who did so, but in the event most of those who took up his challenge in the 870s ended up being sunk or shipwrecked and were never heard of again. Storms blew others off course to Madagascar and the smaller islands of the Maldives which were thus discovered and explored in the 870s and were put on new maps. Large quantities of tropical fruit from these islands, as from Ceylon and the southern part of India, made their way to the Empire after this and were added to the menus of expensive Roman banquets – and were thundered about as a 'sin' by the Church.

As Zeno fantasized about the Romans taking over the entire trade of the Indian Ocean and urged his captains on he did not bother with the rather more pressing fact that back in the humdrum world of north-west Europe the Vikings, thwarted in western Britain and hemmed in in Ulster, had now landed their hordes of land-grabbing pirates and 'smash and grab' raiders on the shores of the Shannon estuary in Munster in the west of Ireland and in 872 Halfdan Ragnarrson set up a new headquarters there at Limerick. The Scandinavians poured into western Ireland to settle and set up new farms during the 870s and the recently liberated monks and farmers of the midlands, having been saved from the threat of Vikings in Ulstar and Dubh Linn by the help of the Roman armies, now faced a new threat from the west. With another restless and land-hungry migration of Vikings heading off to the wilds of Iceland (largely beyond the knowledge of the Romans) and more small 'probes' of the coasts of north-west Spain by pirate captains it was merely luck that the flamboyant and recklessly bold Roman deputy naval commander at the Biscay squadron's island HQ of Regianum (Rhe, off La Rochelle) caught a major Viking pirate expedition straggling back from sacking the Gallaecian town of Corunna after a storm in autumn 876. He launched a quick attack to sink their commander's longship with 'Greek Fire' and rescue most of the hostages, and the government was quick to play this up as thanks to their vigilance not luck.

The information that a hostage, who spoke Norse, had acquired by overhearing his captors boasting during a banquet enabled the Roman 'Classis Britanniae' to send ships to intercept a planned surprise attack on the shrine of St David at Menevia in Demetia (Pembrokeshire). The Empire could then launch an attack on the main southern Irish Viking pirate base at Cork while its 'jarl' Ivarr was away and rescue more prisoners and retrieve piles of loot from Spain, sinking all the local Viking ships that were not away on raids. But though the complacent new Praetorian Praefect Arcadius Autricanius, a cultured administrator appointed by his fellow-drama-patron Zeno who had run a private drama troupe as *'dux'* of Marcomannia in the 860s and had a poetess wife, proclaimed that the Vikings had learnt their lesson a growing group of 'Young Caesareans' at the 'comitatus' HQ (so-called as they were students of the military commentaries of Julius Caesar) dissented and managed to win over the Emperor's eldest son and heir, Probianus. The latter, an imaginative and talented young officer of nineteen who the Emperor had just married off to one of the leading young ladies of the huge and super-rich landed Anicii dynasty (leading senatorial stalwarts since the 4th century) and the equally venerable and more anti-Catholic Symmachi, had his own links via the relatives of his fellow-'Protectores' officers to militant anti-Viking generals and military administrators and set them to work. It was probably mainly due to this unofficial alliance that the usually anti-war Zeno eventually agreed to a major campaign to punish the Vikings in their Norwegian homeland and drive them out into the seas towards Iceland in a series of naval 'sweeps'. In 876 the Emperor had divorced from his talented and beautiful but vain and greedy second wife Serena, a spoilt and party-mad socialite who encouraged her pet poets to hail her as 'Queen Selene' (i.e. the ancient Romano-Greek moon goddess) to the fury of the Church. This had improved his relations with Probianus and ended the threat that he would disinherit the latter in favour of his son by Serena,

Aurelianus (born 868 so a decade younger than his half-brother). In addition the fact that Probianus was personally modest and devoted to philanthropy and had sponsored a number of schools and orphanages himself had won round the Papal administrative machine in Rome to back him against the 'son of the whore' (i.e. Aurelianus) despite his sharing his father's enthusiasm for Greek drama and art. The Church in the Irish midlands was pressing for Roman intervention to stop their monasteries being attacked from the Shannon valley. As a result of intensive 'pro-war' lobbying and internal manoveures at the 'war ministry' (the Praetorian Praefecture offices in Rome) Autricanius was sacked in spring 878 and war was planned on the Vikings with troops and ships being summoned from all over the Empire. A Romano-British mercenary expedition was sent out to Ireland in summer 878 under a senior (in rank) but young and innovative commander from the army in Britain recommended by its 'Count', the local Romano-Saxon noble Alfredius Ceaulinus (OTL: 'Alfred the Great'). They duly defeated the Viking thrust East from Limerick intended at pillaging the great monastery of Sier Kieran by ambushing the invading commander Guthrum (OTL figure and Alfred's principal foe) in boggy farmland and cut his over-confident force of semi-drunken pirates to pieces. Then they pressed on as the Norse fled to take Limerick by surprise with the gates open and storm it. Guthrum had to hide in the mountains of Clare and sign a treaty promising to hand back his prisoners and loot and turn Christian to keep his truncated kingdom, with Limerick being taken as a Roman fortress and the Vikings relocating to Galway. As the Vikings preferred to keep their section of the island to risking losing it all to a full Roman invasion the treaty held and the 'kingdom of Galway' became a successful trading-base for the more peaceful Norsemen to trade with the Romans in the coming decades (albeit at times selling them Irish loot and slaves). Alfredius became a 'Hero of Rome', honoured by the Emperor with medals and monetary prizes at a ceremony in Rome to celebrate his victory, and as a devout Catholic he used the money to found a new British monastery at Atelnium (Athelney) in the marshes of Dobunnia where as a boy he had learnt in books the guerilla tactics that had enabled him to defeat Guthrum.

In spring 879 the main war followed in Norwegia as rising general Aulus Condidarus and 50,000 troops – mostly infantry as it was too mountainous for cavalry – were landed from the sea in the Bergen region by the 'Classis Britanniae' . They overran it fort by fort, village by village, and fjord by fjord, and as the Roman navy kept the local Viking s at bay from rescuing the attacked area by attacking their shipping with 'Greek Fire' whenever it ventured out to sea the Romans methodically occupied the entire region of 'Rogaland' that spring and summer and then cleared the local mountain valleys where the surviving

Vikings were hiding. The occupation of 'Hordaland' to the North followed in similar vein in 880 and then in 881 the Romans landed a huge amphibious force in the plains of Trondelag while another army marched north over the mountain passes from Constantinia (Oslo) to take the retreating Norse in the rear. Once the wooden-walled town of Trondjheim had been set afire and stormed, its walls falling to Roman flame-throwing engines, the Norse had to realise that they were finished as a force on the Scandinavian mainland and the more prudent jarls surrendered to keep some of their lands. A large fleet of refugees led by their main commander Harald Finehair (OTL) fled to Iceland and more jarls held out in the far north. But most of those left on the mainland gave up in late summer 881 and handed in their weaponry and once they had sworn homage to the Emperor on their sacred arm-rings most kept their word out of a practical realisation that they stood no chance of success in a rebellion but if they kept quiet and obedient they could make money out of trade with the Empire, especially in furs and timber. The Roman 'high command' did not trust the thirty-five or so senior jarls out of a hundred or so in Norwegia who surrendered and most had to hand over their sons as hostages to be taken to Rome and educated as Romans – many of these ended up in the Roman army as successful officers in the 890s and 900s. About a third of the Trondelag was confiscated for settlement by Roman farmers (often Danes and Germans) while a network of forts was set up to guard all the conquered fjords and Roman roads were constructed across the Trondelag and linked it to the Constantinia region and Trondjheim became a Roman fortress and trading-town, with no Norsemen except those on lists of approved 'trusties' allowed into the Roman-redesigned town for a decade though after that a Norse 'quarter' was built.

But the outcome to the war did enable those Norse who 'Romanised' and remained loyal to prosper as farming and trade slowly revived and by 900 a major 'industry' in exporting timber to the Empire was underway in the Trondelag while the Church slowly Christianised the locals. Zeno had considerately insisted that nobody be forced to convert as he feared land-seizure and bullying by the Catholics and it was not until the 920s that the slow moves towards conversion to Christianity by incoming missionaries really became successful. The Emperor was not over-keen on the stark and Germanic-style warrior culture and belief-system of the Norse. But he recognized its similarities to that of early Greece and its 'Heroic Age' and wanted to align the Norse warrior elite to Rome so they would fight for not against it. Accordingly he stood up to Pope John (in office from 872 to 884) who wanted the new province of 'Norwegia Ultima' (Bergen to the Trondelag) to be converted en masse to Catholicism and insisted that the surviving Norsemen be able to keep their own beliefs and religious and cultural practices for a generation or two. So assorted local headmen and priests were co-opted with grants of confiscated land or trading-opportunities to export their farms' crops and stock to the Empire and even the local Norse administrative/judicial council-meetings, or 'Things', were retained. (This was meant to be temporary but eventually became permanent.) The Norse had to abandon certain of their cultural practices and laws that were explicitly contrary to Roman practice but most were retained and were confirmed by the first civil governor of the province, a German by origin called Carolus Cassianus and related to the royal house of the Franks, in a special 'Law-Thing' meeting of the Norse elite in an encampment outside Trondjheim in spring 883. Subsequently local Norse law and customary practice was codified by Roman officials sent by the 'Quaestor' in Rome (in Probianus II's reign but by a man appointed by and in a plan arranged by Zeno) and was incorporated into the Roman law-code as that of a 'Special Administrative Zone' like the ex-Merovingian kingdom of Transrhenus in Germany. As there were plenty of opportunities for warlike young Norsemen in the Roman army many of the restless sort of young warriors who had previously been involved in piracy or land-stealing in Ireland now headed for the Continent and military careers. Although about a fifth of the next generation of warriors illegally went over to the Shetland and/or Faroes and/or Iceland to join the exiles enough remained to keep the northern parts of Norwegia largely Norse in ethnic makeup and cultural orientation – aided by the harsh climate that led to many Romano-German incomers going home after a few years. The war restored Zeno's standing with the armed forces and also acted for the benefit of Probianus who had lobbied hard for it and built up a group of supportive generals to back him at court. In the next few years the Emperor became more obsessed with restoring and experimenting with Greek culture to the neglect of his administrative role and indeed spent most of 880–2 in Greece or Constantinople, wintering in the latter in 880–1 (where he built a large new modern but Hellenistic-style summer palace on the East shore of the Bosphorus just upstream from Constantinople, at Bryas) and in Ephesus in 881–2.

The latest project that Zeno spent large amounts of cash and time on was his plan for an 'Academy of the Muses' with branches in both Rome and the Empire's 'cultural heart'(as he called it) Athens, with schools of learning for each of the nine arts or educational disciplines which had a tutelary 'Muse' and chairs of studies and junior lecturerships in each. The nine 'schools' were to be the subjects for the nine departments in each Academy, and each was to have a student body who would be recruited from all over the Empire and be coaxed to take part and then to become experts in and contribute to their fields (e.g. by teaching the next generation) by Imperial grants of cash and honours. Despite Zeno's typically claiming the credit for it all and his toadying court poets calling him the 'New Father of the Muses' – in which guise he had statues put up to himself in Rome and Athens – the idea had been evolved by his circle of supportive young or youngish, well-educated, Hellenophile cultured nobles in Rome in the early years of his reign. The originator of the plan for the 'Academy' was his friend Hostilius Herennianus, from 882 his 'Consul of the Art of Epic Poetry' and later his chair of that art in the Rome Academy, but Zeno was the person who provided the cash and the resources of the education ministry to support it, appointed its supporter Julius Epigeniarus as minister of education to see it through (he was in office from 882 to 907 as both of Zeno's sons kept him on), and brought in the architects to design the Academy buildings. In April 883 the Academy in Rome was founded and building it and recruiting staff commenced, the one in Athens following in 884 with Zeno going there to supervise it. But by this point he was no longer Emperor, as his ministers were becoming concerned at his neglect of business and his lack of concern for matters that were not involved with the arts or sciences. The military leadership had been expecting him to follow up his over-running of central Norwegia by either taking over the north too, as far as the Lofoten Islands, or else drive the Vikings out of Ulster where Halfdan had been succeeded in 881 by his son Eystein. Probably bored with governing and being nagged by his civil servants and Pope John about his duty to his people, Zeno surprised the Empire by abdicating in a speech to the Senate to celebrate Christmas on 19 December 883, aged fifty-one, and announcing that Probianus would take over immediately at the age of twenty-six, and the following spring he left Rome to supervise the establishment of his new 'Academy of the Muses' in Athens and encourage students and teachers to sign up for it and so boost the Empire's Hellenic cultural activities.

Backed by Patriarch Photius to reassure Christians that it did not involve 'pagan' thought to the detriment of Christianity, Zeno – now honoured as the 'Basileopator', 'Father of the Sovereign', and second in rank to Probianus – went on to Alexandria in 885 to do some research on the work of Ptolemaic scientists in the 'Museion' and chivvy young scientists to us this resource and develop Roman engineering, medicine, and the natural sciences further. But his activities were to take an even more unusual turn as next year he poured money from his generous allowance from his successor into building a squadron of ships for a geographical voyage into the Indian Ocean and in 887, having recruited a body of scientists and retired naval personnel for his expedition, he set out via the Canal of Necho for Aden, Socotra, and Mombasa. The ex-Emperor than vanished off the radar of the Roman world for a couple of years and only reappeared in autumn 889. Apparently he had been trying to find a way south round Africa like the legendary expedition sent by Xerxes but had been prevented by storms and adverse currents, but he had definitely reached the Zambezi and then the land of the Basuto people as he brought back some delegates of the latter's king to Rome in 890. He established an occasional Romano-Basuto trading link that exchanged European goods for local African wildlife and exotic plants and fruits. The Basuto kingdom which he had reached was from now on known by the Romans as 'Rhapta', the name used by Zeno, after the ancient trading-port and kingdom in that region known by that name in literary sources. He had also spent a winter on Madagascar, where Roman merchants were thereafter to occasionally intermingle with Hindu Indonesian immigrants and merchants from the emerging kingdom of Srivijaya. The 'Navigator Emperor' might not have circumnavigated Africa as intended, but his exploits entered the Empire's records and imagination and helped to keep him in the public eye and counteract the disgruntlement of the administrative elite with his lackadaisical attitude to work and his reckless spending of public money.

Chapter 12

Probianus II 883–892; Aurelianus II 892–902; Zeno II (2) 902–912

The Sons of Zeno. Two Very Different Offspring by Two Very Different Women – And Their Father's Return

Probianus was as much of an enthusiast for Greek culture as his father and kept up the latter's projects apart from the 'Colossus of Rhodes' restoration, disappointing cost-cutters in the administration. But he was far harder-working and a skilled political operator who managed to conciliate rival factions and lobbyists for rival projects and campaigns, balancing out the awarding of senior offices skilfully with a view to both social and geographical origins and holding expensive but useful receptions for the noble and cultural elites when in Rome and other major cities. Whereas Zeno had had few interests in visiting regions except Greece and its cultural 'offshoots' Probianus made a bold first Imperial visit to recently conquered Norwegia Ultima in 884 and held a grand reception for the Norse and the incoming settler elites at Trondelag. In this he made a speech in Norse and argued that the warrior ethics and spirit of adventure of the Norsemen was best served as part of the 'World Empire', taking the oaths of allegiance of leading jarls and rising young swordsmen in the local Norse style. Indeed he was to organise his military leaders to recruit the Norse – also those from long-conquered Vestfold and the Constantinia region – into the Roman navy as well as the army and send out the first Norse Roman officers in command of their own ships on voyages to 'show the flag' to and extort allegiance from settlers in the Shetlands and Faroes in the early 890s.

In keeping with the idea of a Romano-Norse alliance, he also let a leading Norse noble of royal ancestry in Vestfold whose father had surrendered their landholdings in Rogaland as the Romans invaded and so kept the family estates (minus a few strategic points that were fortified s garrisons), Jarl Rognvald or Ragnald (OTL), act as the local Roman civilian viceroy on the Faroes and set up a large sheep-breeding estate there. But Roman troops set up local forts too and a Roman naval base was created at the main harbour, and in the years to come restless Norse farmers who were short of land in the Trondelag, Hordaland, or Rogaland due to Roman settlers moving in there were licensed by the authorities in Trondjheim by agreement with those in Britain to move to the similar 'sheep-farming hill country' of Carvetia (Cumbria) in hilly and rainy north-west Britain. There they were to set up sheep-farms and join in a booming agricultural economy with closer contact to major urban markets than in isolated Norwegia.

The independent Norse in Ulster remained intact and free from Roman interference as they were keeping the peace and trading with not pillaging the lands and traders of Rome and the Roman expansionists were thwarted of their desire for a 'short victorious war'. But instead the watchful and shrewd Probianus – a man with close military contacts who understood how soldiers and generals thought and valued aggressive patriotism more than Zeno did – arranged for a time-consuming but not that expensive or risky steppes campaign in the Ukraine in 885 to back up the new Khagan of the Khazars against a rebellion by his Magyar vassals. This latest influx of restless and glory – and loot-seeking nomads to the Don steppes who had been growing restive at the demands of tribute and troops made by their Khazar masters for decades. But under a weak and ageing Khagan in the late 870s they had finally risked a revolt and had been successful and seized lands east of the lower Dnieper, and though Zeno had typically ignored this potential danger to Rome, even when Roman fur-traders and timber-contractors were attacked. Probianus now sent in 12,000 Roman cavalry and 8,000 infantry to aid the new Khagan in restoring order and this well-armed expedition helped the Khazars to force their rebellious vassals to sue for peace and hand over hostages. The upshot led to the Khazars preferring to move the Magyars across the Dnieper westwards out of range of their heartland and as a result the latter posed a greater threat to Rome and were closer to and able to raid Roman-allied tribes between the Dniester and lower Danube. But for the moment the war resulted in a useful victory and a propaganda bonus for the Emperor, and the Magyars were left too wary to attack Roman traders and contractors again, so the enterprising timber – and fur-traders in the Crimea recovered in confidence and with renewed investment. They were able in the 890s to get a new entrepot for the local trade set up at Kievum on the middle Dnieper, within reach of and protected by patrols sent from the Roman frontier forts in the Pripyat region. (They were also now joined by Swedish 'Rus' shipborne traders from the Dvina river-basin to the north-west.)

Meanwhile, the new Emperor ensured that money and competent personnel were poured into the 'comitatus' HQ and the Military Strategy Centre in Italy and that the elite 'Scholae' regiments were opened up more to the sons of provincials rather than being kept for Italians (and a few sons of elite nobles and bureaucrats in the Mediterranean region). After the difficulties in finding enough serving senior naval personnel who had expert knowledge of the difficult waters and changeable weather of the northern North Sea and the Hibernian Sea for the Viking wars he also set up a new naval training academy at Rutupiae near Dubris in Britain to train 'local' sailors in these waters and 'fast-track' them to suitable ranks in 886. They were to work hard to restore the adaptability of the Romans' local fleets' personnel as well as shipping to combat the quick and fast Viking raiders without having to bring in as many non-naval fishermen as had had to be done recently – which in due course came to mean recruiting Norsemen who were now Roman subjects too. The well-off and 'Latinate culture'-orientated Roman naval officers from long-Romanised provinces, even Dania, still looked down on (sometimes still pagan) Norse officers and it would be a long time before Rome had any 'Viking' admirals. But it was a start and the Emperor took some young Norsemen who he had met and liked on his Norwegian visit into the 'Scholae' too in the late 880s and enabled them to rise to senior ranks.

The Church under new Pope Marinus (OTL) (in office 884–94) was not happy at the Emperor allowing Norse citizens of Rome to remain pagan and although some missionary work was allowed in Norwegia Ultima this was low-key. The new Bishop of Nidaros who was installed to take charge of it was a German who had long experience of dealing with and a sympathy for the Scandinavians back to his time as a priest in Vestfold, but the Emperor was able to manage the resulting criticism of his lacklustre attitude to Christianization in the far north better than Zeno would have done due to his emollient attitude to and skill at handling promotions of personnel. He deliberately backed away from defending the rights of Nestorians and Monophysites to their legally established rights to Church property in Mesopotamia in the face of a legal offensive to repossess this by an aggressive new orthodox Patriarch of Ctesiphon in the mid-880s to win orthodox backing where his father would have defended the minority Christian community.

Probianus could protect the rights of the small local incoming Buddhist and Hindu Indian trader communities better on account of their usefulness to trade and the offence that their sovereigns back in the East would take if they were persecuted and deprived of their temples and lands as the Church now wanted and he did this. But he did take a greater risk in allowing his mother, the divorced first ex-wife of Zeno, back to Rome as the 'Dowager Empress Thermantia' given that she had enemies among the elite, including courtier partisans of her exiled successor Serena. The latter would have been recalled too – she was now living in luxurious but petulant exile in Crete – had she not shown Probianus unremitting hostility and implied to his envoys to her that he was not the rightful Emperor and her son Aurelianus should be ruling instead. The bland and rather unimpressive Aurelianus, a competent junior officer and cavalryman with interests in Greek and Greek-influenced drama and poetry and a rather more inspiring fiancé (a former star female student and distinguished Christian devotional poetess from Antioch called Xenia Landacia, daughter of a leading lawyer there), was not going to be the first choice for Emperor of anyone who wanted more than a 'front man' who would do what he was told. Several plots against Probianus as a 'pagan sympathiser and ally of the heathen Vikings' by courtiers allied to Serena in the mid-late 880s failed miserably, but Probianus and his wife only had one child, a daughter called Proba, and as she failed to conceive again it looked as if Aurelianus might succeed to the throne eventually.

In the meantime Probianus made conscientious efforts to get to know that part of the Empire which had not seen him and where he had not served as an officer and he paid state visits to the North African provinces from Tingis to Leptis Magna in 885, Egypt and Palestine followed by Phoenicia in 886, Asia Minor, the Caucasus and Mesopotamia in 887, the Balkans and Rhaetia in 888, Britain and Gaul in 889, and Spain in 890. As he acquired more knowledge of senior personnel he took less advice and time in making appointments and chose less on the grounds of balancing groups and factions and more on the grounds of proven capability and energy. He left the running of the finance ministry to his chosen candidate of 884, expert and veteran tax-dodging-hunter Gallus Galicianerus whose job was now to concentrate on seeing that the ingenious ways that the rich used to evade paying their fair share of taxes (especially in provinces with long-entrenched landed nobilities used to having their way and the local bureaucrats deferring to them). The minister was to avoid any need to put up taxes on the income-generating traders and investment bankers to pay for the expensive projects launched by Zeno. But most other ministries were reshuffled several times in the mid-late 880s and ended up with stern, hard-working and energetic provincial 'new men' in charge and those nobles who kept their roles on the Council had to have shown that they were up to managing a complex bureaucracy and delivering results. The Eastern trade ministers were allowed to experiment with offering financial 'tax break' incentives to new investors (often landed aristocrats) to get them to prop up ever more trading-ventures to the Orient with their cash and the finance ministry then had to cover the cost of this by extorting more money from tax-dodging nobles who were squirreling their cash and other assets away and not helping the economy by investing. Probianus made it clear that he would not cut spending on public works projects to recoup the lost money as these benefited the ordinary citizens and also showed the Emperor's generosity and so boosted his reputation.

Galicianerus was also allowed to come up with ways of taxing the Church – indirectly so as not to arouse preachers' wrath – and settled on new taxes on estates owned and new mansions built by the high clergy and over-large ecclesiastical households. This initiative of 887–9 was declared as a move to boost 'holy austerity' and 'clergy living like the early Apostles and so becoming more holy' and did not affect spending by the state on churches and monasteries or philanthropic projects. Accordingly a current movement among the more austere and devout lower clergy in both rich Western provinces like Gaul and Spain and ones in the East subject to periodic religious 'grass-roots' campaigns (e.g. Iconoclasm) took up this call by the Emperor's chosen clerical preachers in Easter sermons in 887 to bring back Apostolic poverty and commitment to living like the poor Zealous monks were particularly fond of it, so the angry aristocratic senior clergy who found their estates and households or their private building-projects pored over by the taxmen were unable to muster much support for complaints at synods. Pope Marinus, a loyal and carefully-selected clerical bureaucrat who wanted to be on good terms with the court, did not listen either. The Emperor looked set to be in for a comfortably long reign and began to talk about restoring the idea of the next ruler being chosen by the Senate on his recommendation not being his dynastic next heir and so passing over Aurelianus in favour of one of his uncle Honorius' sons. But as events turned out the appearance of a defeat for the scheming Serena and her court allies – high-spending opponents of the new taxes – was deceptive. On 12 May 893 Probianus, aged only thirty-five, was killed in a freak accident as his carriage overturned while he was on his way to a banquet in Lugdunum from a remote hunting-lodge in the Cevennes where he was on a holiday 'retreat' with some fellow-ex-officers and other military strategist associates planning the next stage in Roman imperial expansion.

This was a move to forcibly enrol the Magyars as Roman subjects and open up the Dnieper valley to Roman agricultural settlement to meet the pressure on fully-occupied lands in the lower Danube valley. This would protect the mélange of Germanic and former steppe nomad (e.g. Avar, Bulgar, and Alan) ex'barbarian' farmers and pastoral nomads in 'Scythia' (Wallachia) and the lower Pruth valley from raids by the Magyars without needing a long and expensive line of Roman forts on the Dniester. It would enable Roman soldiers and traders to advance directly on good roads from the lower Danube and the Carpathian passes to the Dnieper to trade and patrol, but the Emperor's plan for a major campaign to do this in the course of 894–5 were cancelled as he was unexpectedly crushed by his overturning carriage. Though his death was to the advantage of the manipulative, ruthless, and increasingly indebted Serena nobody could prove that she or her scheming if competent courtier nephew, Carus Posidonius (a former Guards rake and now master of the Emperor's private stables), were involved or that the 'accidental' dislodging of rocks up a hillside above the road from the hunting-lodge had been due to human action. The Emperor, like Michael I with his 'running into bandits', may just have been unlucky. In both cases, the lack of a large escort meant few witnesses.

Once the news reached Rome the Senate and ministers met and agreed that as the legal next heir Aurelianus, aged twenty-five, should be named as Emperor and oaths of allegiance were duly taken to him. But with the Church as well as the ministers dubious about his mother's capacity for mischief and seeking revenge on her old foes Aurelianus had to promise to keep her out of Italy and though she was allowed free movement in the East – and soon decamped to Antioch to 'live it up' at Caracalla's palace there after she was banned from the coronation – she was paid large sums of money and given an impressive 'court' as 'Empress Mother' to stay away from Italy. She did not break this promise until 898, her interests being looked after and her salary secured by Carus who now became his cousin's head chamberlain as someone who he could trust. Aurelianus had been belittled by his mother's Court foes and his late brother's men as a hopeless puppet of his friends and of the socialite aristocratic allies of his disgraced mother who hung around him looking for patronage. A lot of senators and ministers would have preferred one of his more dynamic cousins who had proved themselves as military officers. His uncle Honorius, their rakish stud-owner and chariot-racing club organizer father, hated Serena and wanted her family to be ruined for good, not least as Carus had once raped a niece of his wife's at a 'Protectores' officers' orgy and had the affairs hushed up. But Aurelianus was now taken in hand by expert manipulator 'Master of Offices' Domitianus Dexterianus and was persuaded that he had the backing of God as he had unexpectedly come to the throne and owed it to Him to be a good ruler. The impressed Prince/Emperor obligingly agreed that he should do his duty and seek to set an example of virtue and cool, shrewd leadership. Probianus had always awed his less confident half-brother as he was better-looking and better at making decisions but Aurelianus had his own virtues and he was not so devoted to military expansion and more inclined to think about the victims of Roman aggression and thoughtless army campaigns across civilian lands. Accordingly the new Emperor gravitated more towards the philanthropic and pacifist 'moderate' Church leaders and the liberal-minded, Hellenophile intellectual philosophers plus the earnest and justice-seeking 'Ciceronian' fans of a rigorously moral and truth-seeking legal profession. He proved to be not such a fool as his critics had alleged.

Under his leadership, mediated and coaxed by Dexterianus and the coterie of earnest young intellectuals from Rome University who were Aurelianus' personal dinner-party guest 'regulars', the careerist and competent but none too scrupulous 'Quaestor' Justus Jovanerius was replaced by a moralist youngish fan of the career and work of Cicero, Syracuse university legal lecturer Caius Mariscellius, in 894. A new system of legal commissions' full of experienced inspectors was set up to investigate how justice was functioning across the Empire and prosecute defaulters and trial-riggers as well as to suggest improvements in the conduct of trials. This clever revival of Titus II's idea of the Emperor as a wise legalist was to deal within a number of habitual current unjust and dodgy practices and highlight ways of bending or ignoring the technicalities of the law which were then revised by a new 'addendum' list to the legal code written by an Imperial Commission set up in 897 and issued in 902. The learned and religiously 'intense' Empress Xenia, was a modest woman who wore simple linen, wove her own and her husband's clothes, had helped out scrubbing floors and cooking meals at orphanages under an assumed name before her husband's accession to get to know the people and their problems. She had a large coterie of pious upper-class lady friends and allies who invested in deserving projects with her and joined her to fast and debate the Bible, and was a practical rather than a virulently intolerant 'heretic'-hating Catholic and a devout 'student' of Pope Marinus' successor Stephen IV. She duly backed up her husband's determination to use their luck to do good and rein in the proud. Though the fashionable nobility mocked the young couple as middle-class 'prigs' full of fake religious sentiment who lacked the wits to understand culture or the grace to enjoy the 'high life' the poor of Rome adored the Empress and admired her husband for being a humble man doing his best. The philanthropic Pope, elected in a backlash against the careerism and the toadying of the higher clergy to morally dubious and high-spending Emperors like Zeno, had an admiration for the work and morals of the great – and outspoken – 5th-century philanthropist Patriarch/ St John 'Chrysostom'. He encouraged the Imperial couple to continue to carry out good works in person and attend almsgiving at soup-kitchens rather than keeping up Zeno's old round of ceremonial. But the Emperor was too nervous of offending the already scornful great nobles to entirely drop the annual rotas of grand appearances at ceremonies by the Emperor though now he usually dressed in simple white robes not in rich silks and jewellery. He was only really 'committed' to the ceremonies that involved Church services and visits to shrines, not enjoying the Games at all and ordering the chariot-drivers to take more care not to crash and injure their horses.

As the Emperor had no interest in the minutiae of court life and offices the latter were largely left to the arrangements of his cunning and publicly devout but secretly corrupt and office-selling cousin Carus. The latter came to amass a fortune and build a new palace for himself in Rome out of the proceeds, telling the gullible Emperor that it was funded by his private family banking 'foundation' that had helped to build lots of orphanages in Syria and Asia Minor. But Aurelianus himself restricted his public works spending on new public buildings – as opposed to schools, hospitals and orphanages. He only spent much money on a new public Baths in eastern Rome, designed to provide free massages and hairdressing for the poor and free public access to all facilities, and on a new 'Forum of Zeno' (a tribute to his father's public works spending and his explorations) where imported goods from the areas of Africa and the Indian Ocean islands discovered by Zeno could be sold and Imperial finance ministry agents sold off – cheap – the confiscated possession of tax-fraudsters.

The Emperor shared his father's and brother's interest in poetry and, provided it set a good moral example, in drama but attended fewer competitions than they did, avoided raffish cultural figures as 'immoral', and never personally chose a winner of a prize that was not explicitly Christian. Many new plays on themes connected to the struggles of and within the early Church were written in his reign and figures who he admired like the devout Emperor Theodosius I or the 'Augusta' Pulcheria were celebrated. He also avoided theological controversy as a waste of time and so a 'sin', which meant that when Pope Stephen unexpectedly died in 901 he refused to endorse the 'best man' candidate of the Papal bureaucracy and most of his own ministers, the Bishop of Bononia, as a virulent if pertinent critic of the Monophysites as heretics. He colluded with a faction of careerist administrators in selecting the bishop's far from distinguished and secretly faction-manipulating bureaucrat rival Formosus (OTL figure, and a controversial one.) This job-distributing, favour-selling, careerist 'insider' of the Papal bureaucracy was probably the worst Pope in terms of moral leadership for a century or more and he ended up secretly using money that was meant for running and improving Papal philanthropic institutions to buy off rivals and critics with sinecures not to mention using the late Pope Marinus' well-meant Papal 'Eastern trade investment fund' as a Papal bank which squirreled away his own fortune safe from the taxman. But at the time his spending on well-designed new churches and cathedrals across the West, usually built by architects from the Imperially-sponsored Rome school of architecture and proteges of ex-Emperor Zeno, was seen as a bonus and he was hailed as keen to improve the shabby fabric of Church buildings. The Pope and his board of architects caused a major works-programme to improve cathedrals to carry out new building in Italy, Gaul, Spain and Britain in the 900s. Under Aurelianus and his father Zeno this led to major new buildings emerging like the cathedrals of the Holy Virgin in Lutetia (Paris), Colonia Agrippinensis (Cologne), Burdigala (Bordeaux), Toledum in Spain, and Venta Belgarum (Winchester) and Aquae Sulis (Bath) in Britain, replacing modest old buildings with larger ones in the new style with long naves and aisles and at the East end square towers, and indeed this style and this Papal-led spending initiative was to continue for decades to come in one form or another. The Church's public fabric was improved immensely.

As Pope Formosus claimed to Aurelianus in defence of his 902 request for a doubled Imperial subsidy to the Papacy, it also inspired devotion from the ordinary citizenry and provided space for new devotional artworks. But moralist 'grass-roots' preachers and monks claimed that it was too worldly and encouraged 'show' not devotion to God and nobody at the time had any idea that the Pope was selling contracts for the designing and building to those who could pay him for the opportunity and was putting the money in secret accounts in his Papal bank. This dodgy practice continued after 902 under Zeno who was keener on architectural 'renewal' and opportunities for young architects than on morals or strict accounting. He was as much to blame as his son, as he was careless about money, but the latter was later to be blamed once information on the Papal financial frauds emerged. Aurelianus was also negligent in reining in his spendthrift mother Serena who was allowed to return to Rome in 898 – or, rather, returned illegally and defied the police and Praefect of Rome to send her away again. Although she was not allowed to interfere in politics and was loathed by most of the ministers she resumed her social life as leader of a high-spending faction of greedy and selfish nobles and their wives and in private made fun of the dowdy and 'over-moral' Empress and the cost-conscious ministers. The vindictive and intriguing Serena did her best to have Aurelianus' male-line cousins ruined as his wife seemed to be infertile and they would presumably succeed him. Once their ally Praetorian Praefect Marcus Musonius, a capable and level-headed hero of the annexation war in Trondelag, had retired in 900 she managed to get his successor Hostilius Honestinius (cousin of one of her noble socialite hostess allies) on her side by loaning him one of her ladies-in-waiting as a mistress to feed his fantasies and lending his debauched son prostitutes from an establishment run by one of her low-class Ostian associates. As a result early in 901 Aurelianus' younger cousin Leo was framed for a drunken orgy, being arrested by the police after being kidnapped by Serena's friends and drugged and dumped in a brothel, and put on trial as the Emperor refused to do him any special favours in his disgust at how the prince had let the Imperial Family down. Probably Serena intended to remove him as a potential successor to her son.

Leo's ally Zeno the 'Basileopator' (Greek for 'Emperor's Father') was away exploring to Ceylon on his latest expedition and Leo was convicted for immorality and sent to a remote monastery in Dalmatia for a five-year sentence as a lay brother to do hard labour and repent. He had to divorce his wife – who was a tavern-keeper's daughter who he had married while on military service to stop his parents forcing him to marry an unwanted heiress instead so she was considered beneath him by them and most of the Roman aristocracy. (His son Constantine was declared illegitimate and sent off to live with his mother and her family at their tavern.) With his father Honorius boycotting the court in disgust and one faction of liberal-minded nobles, mostly young and Hellenophile, as well as the majority of 'Protectores' officers believing that Leo had been framed the Emperor and his sternly virtuous 'Ciceronian' 'Quaestor' Aurelius Julianus were the subject of vicious libels.

Serena was accused of being a pimp and was forced to resort to demanding the use of the police to secure convictions of her traducers for libel. When Zeno returned from the Far East he was appalled at what had happened and defended Leo's innocence, but the Emperor for once refused to listen to his father. He made it a trial case of moral vigilance against favouritism for the rich and with the support of the Church he proceeded to insist that Julianus set up a legal commission to investigate other apparent cases of drunken misbehaviour and abuse of penniless young women – and teenage boys – by debauched young Guards officers in recent years that the legal profession in Italy had apparently covered up.

The highly moral and more shrewd Empress was busy with the latest of her philanthropic initiatives, a pioneering girls' choir for orphans in the great cities of Italy. This was bringing together the pupils at various orphanage schools run by the Church to add the harmony of girls' voices to those of boys who had already been singing 'plainsong' and 'part-chanting' in harmony in Papal choirs for some decades after the musical Pope John set up a children's choir. Serena seemed to be triumphant as she planned to move in on Leo's elder brother Honorius and arranged a 'sting' to catch him at his rumoured pastime of illegal gaming. Serena was so confident that she did not care that Zeno disgustedly turned down her appeal for a reconciliation and remarriage between them late in 901 and married a Ceylonese dancing-girl (30 years her junior) who he had brought back from his eastern trip instead. But then all changed as on 2 February 902 the Emperor fell ill of food-poisoning on a trip to open the new cathedral at Mantua in northern Italy and died within hours, aged thirty-three. The cause of his death was probably polluted water that had seeped into his host's kitchens from a nearby river and it was unlikely that some foe of Serena or ally of Leo's poisoned him to enable the Empire to be rid of her influence. But for whatever reason the throne was vacant again and when the Senate and ministers met next day they decided that the rumours already circulating about Honorius' gambling and womanizing – spread by Serena and her cousin the chamberlain Carus – meant that he was an unwise choice to be Emperor. The widowed Empress Xenia might be in shock but she was determined to keep the 'debauched' Honorius off the throne, not least as he would no doubt pardon Leo. So after an appeal from her to the Senate via one of her court officials on 4 February the Senate agreed to a ministerial proposal to re-acclaim Zeno and he became the second Emperor – and the second Zeno – to regain his throne.

Now aged seventy, Zeno had not lessened his tendency for overspending and his Hellenophile cultural instincts but he was a more stable character than Honorius or Leo. He was ambitious enough to agree that his 'unsuitable ' wife Jahanara, aged 33, should not become Empress but be his morganatic wife as 'The Lady Janhanara' and her children should have no right to the throne as they would be half-Ceylonese not fully Roman. Thus Zeno was re-crowned in St Peter's Basilica on 25 April with a grand ceremony and then a month of Games and public banquets, starting his second reign with the generosity to the public which he intended to keep up. The Empress Xenia retired to a suburban palace – not a nunnery as she was committed to continue her public work. She spent her time initially running her new girls' choir (which was initially controversial but soon became a valued part of Imperial ceremonial occasions and Church festivals and services) plus her many schools, hospitals and orphanages. But in 905 she left Rome to join her fellow-patron of devout Catholic schools for provincial girls, the wealthy British (Saxon) abbess Adelfleda of Glevum (Gloucester) who was daughter of the great general Alfredius (OTL: Aethelfleda, 'Lady of Mercia', d. 918) – now retired as abbot of his monastic foundation at Adelneium (Athelney). They set up a pioneering undergraduate college to teach brainy girls who aspired to be abbesses and headmistresses theology, at the Gallic religious centre of Remigianum (Rheims). The Emperor was left without a hostess as his wife was judged socially too inferior to lead Roman society by its snobbish matrons and all his daughters by Serena had married and left Italy. But by this stage he was losing interest in leading court life and presiding over social events in the winter 'season' in Rome anyway as he was into his seventies and preoccupied with his cultural interests. He was writing (usually undistinguished) plays about the great dramas of past Imperial dynasties in the 4th century to 7th century AD in particular, so 'high society' was left to run itself. Serena, who had been banished again to Syria on his accession amidst suspicion of her involvement in Leo's disgrace, was never recalled despite her ex-husband receiving many appeals on her behalf from her friends.

Zeno was also too cautious of moralist opinion and the poor attitudes that many of the ministers and senators had of his own past record – and of his latest wife, who received most of Serena's property in Italy in 904 and mostly lived in her Rome palace not directly at court at the Marble Palace with the Emperor – to pardon Leo at once. It was 905 before he was cleared by a review tribunal and allowed back to Rome amidst popular rejoicing, but at least the debauched and foolish rake had learnt his lesson and he stayed as a monk dressed in sackcloth, 'Brother Leo'. He continued to attend many Church services and to spend much time studying the Bible and working as a helper in charity soup kitchens in the capital to add an element of virtuous self-denial to a family that was still tainted by the stories of its debauched private lives, and the dislike of the current Emperor's current wife with her dubious past. The supposedly reformed and certainly more conscientious Zeno still overspent on his 'Academies of the Muses' in Rome and Athens and his drama-competitions. Zeno had the ruthlessness to purge the dodgy chamberlain Carus, who his younger brother Honorius (d 905) as well as the latter's sons and their friends blamed for the framing of Leo, and sending him off to exile in Armenia and all of Carus' wealth was seized. Assorted courtier friends of Serena who had urged her to remarry Zeno were frustrated in their endeavours to return to favour with the new Emperor, but Zeno did not bother to remove the hastily effusive and helpful Pope Formosus who kept his post and his wealth. The state of the rather too worldly, careerist 'Lateran' (the Papal administration, centred at the Lateran Palace) remained a major publicity problem through his second reign though all he was concerned about was to secure its loyalty and see that the current drive to rebuild churches and cathedrals continued.

The veteran Patriarch Photius of Constantinople, a learned and tolerant ally of Zeno's, had finally died in 900 and been succeeded by a more narrow-minded and culturally ignorant moralist abbot and doctrinal 'hard-line' anti-Monophysite called Nicholas Mysticus (OTL figure) in order to appease the 'hard-line' wing of the Constantinopolitan clerical elite. Equally moralist and doctrinally aggressive orthodox clerics were in charge in Antioch and Alexandria too, but the government insisted on the need to keep the local Nestorian and Monophysite lay merchants and administrators 'on side'. To avoid offending the small resident Indian and Ceylonese merchant communities in Mesopotamia (hardly any of whom were Christian) the Patriarchate of Ctesiphon had remained in the hands of tolerant, careerist clerics who did not bother with enforcing doctrinal rules in the 890s – on orders from the government in Rome. Zeno kept this up and saw that the 'hard-liners' were kept away from senior Church posts in Mesopotamia and Persia, a line also followed after his death by his nephews. The most prestigious figures in the Church in this era were not the careerist and court-approved senior clerics in the Church administrations but 'reformist' thinkers. These were usually middle-ranking bishops or abbots or theology professors with more time on their hands and less of a governing role, who argued and wrote in favour of a new 'mission' for the Church. It should be leading and setting an example in honest and conscientious administration on the basis of what Christ and the Church Fathers had taught, as was exemplified by the revival of interest in the career and works of the leading 'honest and just administrator of high birth and high morals' of the later 6th and early 7th centuries, Pope Gregorius I.

To the suspicious Formosus (d 907) and the equally careerist and bank-organizing administrator Popes who Zeno and then his son Honorius appointed to succeed him, the veneration for Gregorius was a coded attack on them and on the overstaffed and intrigue-riven Papal Lateran bureaucracy of the 900s and 910s. The Lateran was virtually as department of state and it kept on seeing that 'safe' careerists not maverick holy men won senior sees. But as the papacy had been playing up Gregorius as an example to follow for centuries it could not object though clerical writers did. The principal current commentary on and written extension of the sense of mission of Gregorius' works was indeed by a learned and famous theologian who was an 'untouchable' Imperial favourite and not even a cleric in origin, the former 870s Romano-Saxon general Alfredius, abbot of Adelneium in Britain, whose ten-volume commentaries on Gregorius' works came out between 890 and 910. The other major initiative of the era was also connected to the lay nobility in origin rather than the careerist senior Western clergy, as in 910 a major new abbey was founded by, and on the estates in southern Gaul (West of Lugdunum) of the former noble landowner turned holy man and abbot Odolarius Justinarius of Clunium (d 932) (OTL figure). The monastery's first abbot and chief funder and organizer, was to revive and re-energise the 'Order' of the 6th century St Benedict of Nursia, re-creating the late saint's ideals of combined hard labour, prayer, study of the Bible and Church Fathers, and all-day-round religious services. The 'Way' of St Benedict had been copied, either fully or partly, by new monasteries across the Empire (mostly in Europe) for centuries but had lost some of its appeal in recent decades. But now its leading new 'fan' Odolarius sought to copy it exactly in a fully regulated system, with the same rules for each 'Benedictine' abbey, that would also set up a 'community' of identical abbeys with identical ideals and practices helping out and inspiring each other. This plan of his duly caught on and was to be a major cause of re-energising the monastic community in the West in the mid-10th century but at the time passed more or less unnoticed and was ignored as the work of an eccentric 'loner' by the Papacy.

The latter's worldliness and priorities of working with the government suited Zeno who had never liked religious fanaticism or the whole idea of doctrine-obsessed holy men ordering the laity about. But craftily he endorsed current 'grass-roots' enthusiasm, including a movement of abbots and monks in the fairly isolated inland mountains of the Balkans. This was an area open to incoming Slav farmers in the later 9th century as they fled turmoil between the Khazars and Magyars on the steppes. The reformers planned to teach eager young monks to learn Slavic languages and go out to Langobardia and the Dnieper plains to convert the Slavs there to orthodox Christianity and thus to pacifism. The learned and ingenious linguist Balkan abbot (St) Methodius of Thessalonica and his brother (St) Cyril (OTL figures) had created the first written Slav/Slavonic script in the 870s and 880s, and Zeno regarded this movement as worthwhile as it helped to Romanise and 'civilize' the pagan, animist Slavs and so aid their transformation into useful Roman farmers.

Zeno's own interests in moral philosophy lay in the world of the Hellenist 'Stoics' and other Greek philosophic traditions not in Christianity. In his second reign he inaugurated several new chairs of this form of philosophy in universities across the Empire and in 905 held a grand philosophic conference for the Empire's top experts on Plato, Aristotle, the Hellenistic era's thinkers, and Plotinus in Rome which the Pope did not dare to attack despite being egged on by militant preachers. With the current leading Eastern (e.g. Mesopotamian) university enthusiasts for and developers of the thought of Aristotle at this conference Zeno too an interest in their work for the first time and encouraged them to systematize it, write it all down, and teach it to others and provided education ministry subsidies for this.

As a result of his enthusiasm a new 'Philosophical Academy', centred around the work of Aristotle, was founded at Nishapur in Bactria in 908 and the university of Ctesiphon had a major expansion in the next decade which Zeno's nephew and successor Honorius continued to fund as prompted by him. Indeed Zeno's appointing of a senior administrator from Ctesiphon, Bassianus Bactrinaus, as his education minister in 909 was a crucial systemic boost to these projects. The minister had colleagues and relations involved in the academy at Nishapur and he was to remain in office and directing funding there until 928. Zeno also boosted schools and the recruitment of teachers to teach Oriental languages (especially Indian and Ceylonese) ones across the east to future traders and Imperial envoys during his second reign, having learnt Sinhalese and Tamil for his own pre-accession expedition to Ceylon. He set up a languages school affiliated to the department of the 'Logothete of the Drome' (foreign minister) in Rome as early as 903, and under him there were no fewer than four official embassies to the kingdom of Anuradhapura in Ceylon and three to the emerging Chola kingdom of the Tamils in southern India which he had identified on his own expedition as a useful Roman trading-partner. The southern Indian Hindu kingdom of the Chalukyas at Vengi was also sought out as a trading-partner and potential ally with an embassy there in 908. The fact that Zeno had a wife from the region with her own connections there was a major bonus for him and for his ability to establish good relations there though both the Church and snobbish Roman nobles loathed and boycotted her.

The only criticism that could be made of his world-wide interests and 'wide horizons' was that his own priorities in the east led him – and a succession of military planners in Rome – to neglect the Far West. He ignored the potential implications of intelligence stories from spies in the world of Atlantic trading that the Norse in Iceland had now discovered a whole and huge new island in the distant Atlantic, beyond Iceland which the Romans had always referred to as the end of the world – 'Ultima Thule'. Traders of Danish and Norse origin who worked for the Roman government and travelling fishermen and explorers from Jarl Rognvald's Roman-allied lands of the Faroes had been reporting since c.890 that the exiled jarl Harald 'Finehair' (OTL figure, first king of Norway) of Trondelag and his men had not been content with living on the egalitarian, farmer-led island of Iceland. They had been venturing further to the north-west across the fishermen – and whale-hunter-travelled seas and had found a large land full of wide and bleak but useable green plains which they had called 'Greenland'. But this was now confirmed as Roman traders disguised as Danes visited the new Viking settlements in the 'East colony' of Greenland soon after 900. Before long the Vikings, bringing in their flocks of sheep and goats to raise them on Greenland's southern plains, had moved on up the sound to the west of the island to set up a 'West colony' . By 915 they had also found a new and even larger 'island' – in fact, the American mainland – beyond to the south-west, which was called 'Markland' by them. But Zeno and his planners were not interested in bleak Arctic plains and moorland when they had rich East Asia to trade with. The only Roman interest in the continuing Viking exploration there was in the fact that as the Norse expanded their colony many of their farmers in Ulster and Galway in Ireland who preferred warfare or exploration/trade to peaceful farming started to leave the region after c.915 and so reduced the risk of new wars there endangering the precarious, Rome-allied 'High Kingship' and the Church which was based at Armagh.

With the Norse now busy with their new exploration and settlements in Greenland and exploiting the fisheries and the growing whaling capacity of the North Atlantic the threat of a resumption of war in Ireland dissipated. The Empire did not have to bother with keeping a large army force on the western coasts of Britain, based at Deva (Chester) on the Dee estuary with its large and improved harbour and to a lesser extent at Maridunum (Carmarthen) and Glevum (Gloucester), ready to be sent to rescue the Irish 'High Kings' from immanent disaster. Due to the inadequate and haphazard governance of a succession of squabbling petty dynasts of the Ui Niall family as 'High Kings', usually alternating between the lines ruling in western Midhe and at Ailech in western Ulster, a 'modernising' movement was growing up in the Irish Church. This was demanding that the island be taken under the wing of the Empire as a permanent protectorate with its feuding kings replaced by meritocratically chosen Roman civil governors and ancestral Irish laws augmented by the Roman legal code. But the self-interests of the lay elite continued to stymie that though ecclesiastical delegations on pilgrimages to Rome raised the issue every few years after the 870s. Probianus the warrior-Emperor had been interested but the timid and cautious Aurelianus had not been, and Zeno had other priorities and did not rate the Irish highly anyway. But ironically one of his closest literary aides and favourite experts on Homer, the poet and linguistic anthropologist Marcus Musicianus (his 'Consul for Epic Poetry' and chair of the epic poetry department at the Academy of the Muses in Rome from 879 to 907), was a fan and a translator into Latin of the Irish literary epic 'The Cattle Raid of Cooley' ('Tain Bo Cualnage') and regarded the Irish epics of their 2nd century to 4th century AD 'Heroic Age' as being worthy of Homer.

The only war that Zeno countenanced in his reign was one in 903–4, a combined military and naval attack on the coasts of Somalia to punish pirates who had been raiding Roman civilian shipping en route to and from Mombasa and Kilwa. This was led on land by Andronicus Ducas (OTL figure) from Cappadocia, the latest cultured aristocrat with an expertise in Hellenistic literature as well as military tactics to attract Zeno's patronage but a skilled cavalry commander and siege-warfare expert too. He and his band of dashing young ex-'Protectores' officers were sneered at as 'parade-ground popinjays' by tough, risen-from-the-ranks working-class meritocrat provincial generals at HQ in Rome who had made their names in the harsh Viking wars in Norwegia in the early 880s. The blunt-spoken ex-sailor admiral who commanded the naval contingent that landed them to attack the pirate bases and fired 'Greek Fire' rockets from their warships at the latter, Himerius of Tyre (OTL figure), expected them to be repulsed by the cunning and ruthless Somali Arab brigands. But the general and his officers surprised many by being effective in tactics as well as in 'chivalrous' hand-to-hand combat like Homeric heroes. The pirates were lured into traps outside their bases, including feigned retreats and Ducas himself pretending to be injured on one occasion so the enemy leaders rushed at and tried to kidnap him, and the enemy were efficiently dealt with for a minimum of casualties. Ducas then used his charm to persuade one leading pirate to guide the Romans into an 'impregnable' fortress on a rocky 'stack' on the coast in return for a promise of a job in the Roman navy and his daughter marrying a Roman officer who she had looked after when he was a hostage earlier. Ducas led the attack himself to overpower the surprised guards, catch the enemy commander in bed with his mistress, and throw his brutal lieutenant off a cliff at which the others holding out in a tower gave in. This war was later celebrated in Roman epic poetry in the manner of a Homeric combat with Ducas as the hero and duly cemented his reputation. On a practical level it did not exactly do his career any harm. With Zeno impressed and his elder nephew and heir Honorius, a former colleague of Ducas' equally dashing but more vain and reckless son Constantine (OTL figure) as a 'Protectores' cadet, even more so. Ducas ended up as Praetorian Praefect to Honorius when the latter was Emperor, in 916, in effect as his military supremo.

The occupied pirate strongholds became the nerve-centres of a permanent Roman coastal command in Somalia and the officers stationed there were instructed to be careful to keep the inland tribes, who had far-flung desert oases to retreat to out of reach of all but the toughest Roman camel-borne patrols, as friends by judicious bribery and a system of regular presents. With the coast secured Zeno was to press on to get his Alexandria University geographer allies to mount expeditions inland from Mombasa into the vast plains of Kenya after 911 with a view to seeing if any were fertile enough to be turned into plantations that could grow food-supplies for the South-East of the Empire, the drought-hit and agriculturally crumbling Yemen in particular. Zeno even had plans to set up a regular Roman colonial presence in East Africa and see if Rome could grow the plants that provided the popular southern Indian drink of tea – introduced to the Empire after his pre-accession expedition there, when he brought tea-plants back to be tried out in botanical gardens in Egypt. But in the event this was over-ambitious and the plan did not outlive him as his ministers and his heirs were not interested. Zeno died on 24 April 912 aged eighty, after a reign in two parts of thirty-three years, and his elder nephew Honorius, aged thirty-eight, succeeded him. But despite being by then a more respectable and harder-working figure than the lackadaisical rake of two decades earlier he was soon seen as a feeble ruler who lacked his uncle's vision and 'drive' if also lacking his tendency to spend vast amounts of money on whimsical projects.

Chapter 13

Honorius II 912–920. Leo V 920–927. Evening of a Dynasty.

Zeno's Nephews

By the point of his accession in 912 Honorius, Zeno's elder nephew and senior surviving male relative, was a fairly respectable figure who had been doing his best to rehabilitate himself as a reliable and socially responsible aristocrat for a decade. He had been mostly living in Rome and been coaxed and unofficially mentored in who was who in the administration and what Imperial duties involved by the current 'Master of Offices' and by assorted conservative courtiers who did not want to see Zeno, always a maverick, adopting another heir or even proclaiming that one of his three daughters by Jahanara would succeed him as 'Augusta'. Honorius had been persuaded to marry a respectable aristocratic bride, Agathocleia, from a leading eastern Asia Minor landed dynasty (Argyrus) in 903 in the hope that she would give him sons and so his current son Leo would be cut out of the succession. But in the event they only had daughters too and the conservative senators and Catholic Church leaders would not countenance a female ruler. Once Zeno was dead and Honorius was Emperor he cancelled the late ruler's plans to set up a new farming colony in the plains of East Africa and the Roman interest in the region was cut back so that the military/naval trading missions there concentrated on bribing the usually nomad, flock-raising rural African chiefs with gifts in exchange for wildlife for Roman nobles' parks and exotic plants for botanical gardens. But trade with the southern Indian realms and Anuradhapura continued, with Romano-Arab merchants in Aden as well as Romano-Mesopotamian merchants in Charax and Ctesiphon having invested money in and sent personnel to the region in a large scale and having fleets of ships travelling to and from it every year. Luxury goods were flooding into Mesopotamia and up the Red Sea to Egypt as a result, and the buyers had a vested interest in keeping the trade going and lobbied the Roman government accordingly. Though coin was flowing to India and Ceylon to pay for the imports the Empire was both exporting its own goods (such as Mesopotamian and Arab region metalwork and sculpture for the local elites) and was acquiring naval expertise in the Indian Ocean navigation routes that helped to train its sailors and develop better ships and the use of the Indian-style compass. In return the small but eager Buddhist 'mission' in Ctesiphon and Charax continued to seek out recruits in the Empire and won over assorted idealists who disliked the intolerance of the rival Christian sects, whose feuding in Mesopotamian cities and aggressive attitude to the Zoroastrian elite of inland Persia was annoying the less zealous Romano-Greek-Iranian administrative elites there .

Honorius took no greater interest in the 'heathen' Vikings and their discoveries in the North Atlantic than Zeno had done, but at least the latter's enthusiasm for Greek-inspired scientific discoveries continued and a new Geographical Academy to draw up and improve maps and train geographers was set up in Rome in 915 as a scientific counterpart to the Academies of the Muses. The most famous of their early lecturers was the widely-travelled and mostly self-taught explorer of the Central Asian steppes, Gandhara in the upper Indus valley, southern India, and the East African coasts (all while accompanying trading missions), Harunus Massudiantus (OTL: al-Mas'udi) (died 957). He was an insatiably curious investigator of both historical and geographical knowledge from a mercantile family in Mesopotamia. This master linguist and amateur philosopher and astronomer had been educated in the 900s at Ctesiphon university, and had also studied for a couple of years at Antioch – so he was familiar with both the Greco-Roman and the pre-conquest Sassanian Mesopotamian academic worlds. During his voyages he compiled extensive notes on the sights that he saw and the tales that he heard and where possible consulted local books while on over twenty years of journeyings across the eastern world. Then he wrote it all up as an exhaustive compendium of knowledge, the 'Meadows and Mines of Exploration', in the 940s while lecturing on his experiences at the university of Beyrutus. He ended up thanks to the fame of his work as a guest professor at the university of Alexandria, and built up an extensive circle of students and admiring colleagues there who helped to disseminate his discoveries.

Known as the 'Persian Herodotus' and responsible for bringing a reasonably detailed account of the history of India since the time of the Greco-Bactrian kingdom of Menander in the 2nd century BC and of the kingdoms of Ceylon and Burma to the Romans, Massudiantus stimulated a whole new 'school' of Eastern studies in the Empire's Eastern Mediterranean universities. He 're-balanced' the thrust of eclectic philosophical studies towards the Indian works that he brought to Beyrutus and Alexandria universities and later left to them as his 'heirs'. To a lesser extent he spread Indian astronomical and medical knowledge too, acquitted from the region's top schools and universities, though this was already being spread westwards by a limited number of travelling scholars and some of what was later ascribed to his findings was already being taught in Mesopotamia by the later

9th century. (The famous medical and mathematical schools of Ctesiphon were founded in the 850s, as stimulated by earlier scholars who had been to India on trading missions, and he may have used their publications to add to his own discoveries in his published compendia of these sciences.)

His researches into and collection of books of 'pagan' Hindu, Buddhist, and Jain philosophy were less important in stimulating western interest and research, as the Church and its allied scholars denounced all this as 'sin' and 'heresy' and were less amenable to the world of Hinduism with its multitude of gods or to the radically non-Christian Buddhist 'mindset' than they were to 'pagan' Neoplatonism. The latter did have a concept of the 'One' supreme being and had been seen as semi-compatible with Christianity by distinguished thinkers such as Origen. But the sheer breadth and depth of his intellectual discoveries and collection of important writings reminded the more open-minded Roman thinkers that there was a whole non-European intellectual world beyond the Roman frontiers that was not composed solely of tribal 'barbarians', in Asia if not in Africa. His geographical and ethnographical data about the peoples of the Indian Ocean region was to be used by Roman travellers, traders included, and later by military planners too for centuries. The importance of his collections of South Asian books, which he himself used his earnings to recruit linguists to start translating into Greek and Latin, only filtered through to the intellectual world of Rome later in the century via Rome academics who had been to Alexandria to study or work. They duly alerted the Great Library management in Rome who arranged for State-run translation projects to be set up to acquire copies of the books for the use of Rome scholars; but translating all of his works took the best part of a century.

Medical schools also continued to spread through the early-mid-10th century, mostly in the Mediterranean world and the Persian lands, with 'input' from Eastern doctors who moved from the Persian lands (and even a few from as far away as India) to the Mediterranean world to treat the local elites. In 918 the future most 'go-ahead' medical school of the Mediterranean world was founded at Salernum in southern Italy by the Emperor's personal doctor Aulus Gessilicus, younger son of a noble dynasty in Apulia and 'bankrolled' by his family and his heiress wife's dynasty (mostly as a means of benefiting from Zeno's 'tax-breaks' legislation. The Emperor himself was not particularly bright or expert in cultural matters but had been brought up by his father and the late Zeno to regard culture as an appropriate destination for princely patronage and surrounding yourself with a coterie of cultural figures as a sign of good taste and judgement. This continued under him as ruler in 912–20 with appropriately learned and artistic figures being invited to his 'salons' and Honorius giving out the prizes at assorted drama and poetry festivals plus occasionally the Academies of the Muses. He was also meticulous in reviving the old tradition of more active

Emperors in taking the lead as a patron of and participant in hunting the wild boars in Italy and on various overseas tours. His expertise in the 'field' won his praise from his large list of noble guests at his elaborate hunts, and unlike Zeno and Aurelianus he also bothered to attend and take the salute – on horseback – at military parades and to present the medals at the Empire-wide 'Ephebes' corps games and at military athletics competitions.

He and his wife made regular tours from April to September (or sometimes a month or so later) most years and so visited most of Italy plus Sicily in 913, Gaul and Spain in 914, the Rhineland and Britain plus Caledonia in 915, Dania, Germany, and Marcomannia plus Rhaetia in 916, Greece and the Balkans in 917, and Asia Minor, Syria and Palestine in 919. He took along a large entourage and got to know the local nobility with large hunting-expeditions at Imperial estates in the relevant provinces, and his absence from Rome for five months or so most years added to the emergence of the 'Master of Offices' as the effective 'leader' of the Council and the main determinant of policy in his absence. The office changed hands every year or so until 917 to give various talented administrators a chance to show what they could do – and wits alleged that other ministers encouraged the Emperor to change its occupant more often so that they stood a better chance of securing this well-paid role with its accompanying court honorary ranks, estates, and seat in the Senate plus large pension. But from spring 918 the devious and manipulative if effective 'ultimate insider' Caius Musonicianus, a Tripolitanian (Libya) administrator with a talent for wheeler-dealing in influence and 'buying' support by promises of perquisites and more interested in making the most of his position than in creating useful new policies, was 'Master of Offices'. The stream of eye-catching initiatives that had marked the reigns of Zeno (and been kept up since 912 to a lesser degree) dried up. The new chief minister was more interested in building up his own power and buying off or undermining enemies at court and he was also later proved to have built up a semi-legal private fortune and used a network of financial trusts to acquire estates and shares in trading-companies. With the current 'Quaestor' and his senior teams of inspectors unimpressive and chary of alienating someone with the Imperial ear he got away with his devious fortune-building. He was soon infiltrating his clients into other top offices – and making himself useful to the son-less Emperor's presumed heir, the 'pardoned' but still distrusted Prince Leo who was allowed to come to court but was not given any formal office or role.

Honorius' brother Leo at least had a son, Constantine, so if he could get the snobbish and status-conscious Senate to cancel the bastardization of the boy (or allow him to be proclaimed legitimate by a special license that did not entail having to recognize Leo's 'insulting' and 'disgraceful' marriage to an innkeeper's daughter, who he had long since abandoned) the Imperial line would be secured.

But the current Empress' Argyrus relatives preferred to have one of Honorius' daughters succeed him so they, as her cousins, could reap the benefits and were intriguing in the Senate to secure that. The self-confident and well-connected Court noble Andronicus Ducas and his vain son Constantine also had hopes of the throne, at least for the latter, if the current Emperor did not have a son, did not allow any of his daughters to succeed him, and wanted to 'cut out' the controversial Leo and his son. Accordingly there were subterranean currents behind the current political debates in Rome in the later 910s over whether the role of Emperor should be that of a 'front man' for a smoothly operating oligarchy rather than an active 'chief executive' if he was a boy, a female, or politically inadequate. It was also queried if the succession should be by election and if so by whom, but nobody was expecting the question to arise soon and Honorius and his wife could still have a son and render the 'threat' of Leo or 'innkeeper's son' Constantine on the throne as irrelevant.

However on 25 April 920 Honorius died unexpectedly of an allergic reaction after a banquet in the northern Italian town of Verona on his way to his latest Imperial summer tour (to Dacia and the lower Danube), aged only forty-eight – in itself a reminder that the health of the current crop of princes was dubious, with Leo 's health undermined by a mixture of drink and drugs that he had taken as a young officer and fasting as a monk. The Senate and ministers held a two-day 'crisis' meeting that eventually agreed that the easiest and safest option was to allow Leo to succeed but pass a law cancelling his monastic status so he could remarry. Leo, aged forty-two, had never expected to come to the throne and had been believing that his brother and the latter's 'in-laws' would arrange for Honorius' eldest daughter Maria to succeed him. Indeed it was later alleged that the conniving Musiconianus had arranged for Leo's succession by 'calling in favours' and using secret police records of assorted senators' private misdemeanours to blackmail them so he could play Emperor-maker' and earn Leo's gratitude. Once Leo was Emperor he indeed deferred to his 'Master of Offices' and let the latter appoint other new ministers and oversee the selection of the next finance – and legal ministers too. Leo also had Musiconianus' help in having his son Constantine, now aged twenty-one, recalled from his impoverished life helping to run by grandfather's inn in inland Asia Minor. The youth became a Prince and had a hasty education in the arts of government arranged, but though Leo was called a 'puppet' of the widely disliked 'Master of Offices' the two of them swiftly had Andronicus Ducas arrested for suspected peculation and bank fraud in his family financial trusts and exiled to a remote area of Pontus so he could not start a coup. Constantine Ducas was bribed with a senior role at the Military Strategy centre to keep quiet and was then 'picked off' and exiled too in 922. There were no military revolts and most of the senior commanders across the Empire seem to have felt that Leo had been hard done by to end up in a monastery thanks to court intrigue by the late Empress Serena and deserved his chance to show what he could do as Emperor.

In fact Leo was not that much of a puppet and it was merely that he was both inexperienced and lazy and it suited him to have Musiconianus running the administration while he presided at ceremonies and receptions and gained confidence from being flattered and made up to by his subjects. Though Leo did not leave Italy at all for three years and then only went to ultra-loyal Constantinople (where he was welcome to the orthodox laity and clergy as an ex-monk) for winter 923–4, probably due to fears of a coup, he did veto assorted proposed appointments by his chief minister and keep the latter from giving out too many honorific ranks and perquisites to his relatives and clients. In spring 924 Leo proceeded to Antioch by sea and there picked up another first-rate organizer and 'reshuffler of top jobs' with a talent for balancing and paying off potential factions, the senior Antiochene administrator and recent deputy City Praefect Ausonius Autracellius. The latter was given a major court role to reorganize and cut costs in the bloated ranks of the Imperial Court that saw him show his effectiveness. As a result that autumn Leo surprised all who had written him off as a hopeless and dithering 'yes-man' to his crafty chief minister by suddenly sacking Musiconianus, ordering an enquiry into his financial dealings that blackmailed him into handing back most of his fortune in return for an honourable retirement with the rest of it, and appointing Autracellius as 'Master of Offices'. Though the latter was to prove as able at securing posts for his own allies as his predecessor had been he was less obvious about it, made fewer enemies, and only enriched himself and his sons to a moderate degree so they were less hated and even had some Senate backing (based on the sons' marriages to top Italian nobles). The Autracellius 'regime' was to amount to 'jobbery' and secret deals as much as the Musiconianus one had done and it was to be kept on by Leo's equally insecure and inexperienced son Constantine well into the 930s. But in this case the chief minister did share power with other top civilian officials and he also helped Leo to gain in confidence and build bridges to various important 'interest groups', including the still rather too worldly Lateran Papal bureaucracy. The criticism of ineffective and careerist Popes led to the Emperor and his 'Master of Offices' selecting a more popular and higher-rated theologian, Bishop John of Mutina, as Pope in 926 (OTL figure), and he restored a degree of moral purpose and theological expertise to the Papacy. In the case of religion, Leo took his position as the successor of Constantine and the major lay actor in the business of episcopal appointments and revising theological/disciplinary canons seriously. He was at first anxious that he would be thought a fraud for abandoning the life of a monk, having it carefully re-stated in the new 921 canons that if someone had been forced to become a monk against their wishes it could legally be declared invalid. He assured all in his speeches to religious audiences (e.g. the 921 Western Church Council at Ravenna) that he had been privileged to be a monk and learn abstinence, discipline, and the value of hard labour and prayer, and he was grateful to his mentors at his 'unwelcome' monastic residence. He also attended religious services, fasted regularly on holy days, wore a hairshirt and/or a monastic robe on fast-days, and went on pilgrimages to Italian shrines every year. He also debated theology with visiting experts at his palaces, and he seems to have been accepted as a genuinely devout character not a fraud by most clerics. This even applied to the more demanding religious reformers who, like abbot Odilarius of Clunium the leader of Gallic monastic reform, were demanding that the 'lax' abbots and their supervising bishops cleaned up the lazy and comfortable lives indulged in by many monks at semi-secularised monasteries (at some of which the abbots acted more as great landowners than austere men of God and even went out hunting).

When it came to his old, pre-monastic life as a wild-living young officer who had cared more for wining, dining, and womanizing than military tactics and had fought shy of going off to the rigours of a frontier fortress Leo did invite his old 'Protectores' and 'Scholae' regimental colleagues to private social occasions at his palaces and to hunts across Italy. He proved to be as good a rider at hunts and military reviews as he had been before he was made a monk. But he lacked expertise in strategy or knowledge of much of the Empire's military personnel and he relied heavily on the current Praetorian Praefects, the 'Grand Domestics' under them, the leadership of the 'comitatus' in Italy, and the senior personnel of the Military Strategy Centre to know what to do and who to appoint to what post. Increasing influence came to be exerted by the new (919) head of the MSC, the self-made Anatolian admiral (Red Sea command from 912–18) Romanus Lecapenus (OTL: Eastern Roman Emperor 919–44). This self-made officer was a shrewd commander and a skilled sailor but most successful at coaxing and intriguing his way into senior command at 'headquarters' and impressing both senators and civil service administrators as a reliable man who listened to advice and got things done. In Romanus' case his rise to power was aided by the fact that his somewhat lazy and arrogant but good-looking, charismatic and expert swordsman officer second son Constantine (born 899), was an aide to the new Emperor's son Constantine. He duly introduced the Prince not only to his equally raffish younger brothers Stephen and Theophylact but his beautiful and shrewd sister Helena (901 – 961). The latter, who had the brains that her younger brothers lacked – her elder brother Christophorus (born 896) (all of the Lecapeni family are OTL figures) was a successful and energetic young lawyer rising through the ranks as an Imperial prosecutor and inspector but was not as keen on power as his younger brothers were – ended up as the smitten Prince Constantine's wife in 926. From that point the family's hold on a senior position in the Imperial Palace was guaranteed. Romanus Lecapenus himself, the 'self-made' son of a Galatian peasant whose talents had led to his uncle bringing him to Constantinople to be educated as a naval cadet acted as the Emperor's reliable 'resident expert' on all matters naval and most matters military. Renowned for his breadth of knowledge, commonsense, and unflappability and able to impress and help out his superiors as a brilliant sailor and tactician, he played an important role, helped by his own naval experience, in guiding the Emperor through the crisis of a rebel Arab sheikh with delusions of independent power taking over Rome's Persian Gulf entrance vassal trading-town ally of Sharjah in 926 and staging pirate attacks on Roman shipping. The main Gulf fleet was at that point absent protecting a large mercantile convoy and diplomatic embassy to the Chola kingdom in southern India, which secured a valuable new trade deal and lower export-rates for Eastern sandalwood, spices, and carvings to the Roman Empire, and it was Romanus who calmed Leo's panic that he would be accused of letting Rome be insulted and its merchants held hostage and would be deposed by a military coup. He gathered a collection of 'ad hoc' squadrons from the Red Sea and the Indus' mouth without affecting local defences too much, appointed an experienced admiral in Zeno's former expedition to command, and arranged for the latter to swiftly attack and retake Sharjah and seize the pirate usurper for public execution, driving his tribal brigands back into the inland deserts and oases. The crisis' dramatic and effective resolution was put down to wise advice from Leo in a self-effacing speech in the Senate by Lecapenus and the relieved Emperor was sure of his indispensability form that point. Known to all as just 'The Admiral' Romanus was technically the first Roman naval commander to actually use that, originally Arab title ('Amir al Bahr', 'commander of the sea') for a supreme naval commander as he had been nicknamed this by his Arab sailors during his Red Sea command in the early 910s.

Romanus also set up a new chain of anti-pirate bases along the Gulf coast as far as Oman, closing the small ports and fishing-towns there to pirates and forcing their semi-brigand lords (often refugee tribal chiefs from Hadramaut who had found life in that province under Roman law to be short on opportunities for plunder) to sign up to supply sailors to the Roman fleets. In his shrewd opinion, the restless and success-hungry young Arab fishing/trading/pirate captains of the minor Gulf ports had talent that should not be wasted and needed to be lured into Romans service by pay and promotion – and as daring venturers they could then help to spread Roman influence in the Indian Ocean and to suppress the sporadic attacks on Roman ships by Indian and Ceylonese coastal pirates. This venture secured the entire line of the Arabian coasts from Kuwayt round to Hadramaut for the Empire and gave new careers for the restless young warriors of the more feud-prone tribes there as Roman naval recruits and, if good enough, as officers. A 'stratum' of swaggering but highly brave and capable Arab naval officers ended up in the Roman navy and mercantile marine as this came to dominate the waters of the western Indian Ocean under Emperor Leo and his son Constantine and increased regular trading links to the 'Swahili' coast of East Africa (as desired earlier by Zeno).

Romanus, a master of grand strategy but cautious and not one for risks, also made sure that the most successful local Arab trading 'bosses' in Arabia Felix who made fortunes out of the Indian trade were not tempted to put their cash into schemes for autonomy or rebellion. He invited them to go into partnership with Roman Mediterranean merchants to export their stockpiles of goods direct and cheaper to Europe, offering eye-watering tax-breaks – but once they were tied up in legal contracts with these 'partners' they were too reliant on the latter to keep up their earnings to risk any breakaway plots. Extra (European) Roman troops in the booming Red Sea ports kept the locals under watch. Ambitious younger elite Arab warriors who were not busy at sea in the Roman navy were enrolled in new Roman regiments by the shrewd and expert bandit-suppressor John Curcuas (OTL figure), the 'dux' of Arabia Felix in the 930s and an old Cappadocian aristocracy connection (of semi-royal Armenian descent) of the courtier Argyrus family, and were packed off to fight for Rome up the Nile or against Berber brigands in southern Numidia. Curcuas, who shared Romanus' skill at picking and making the most of talent and not caring about capable volunteers' social or ethnic backgrounds, later moved to Rome under Lecapenid patronage to 'shake up' training at the main Italian cadet-schools that trained officers for the army. While Romanus ran the grand strategy of military and naval power his officer younger sons assisted with talent-spotting promising young officers in their 'Scholae' Guards units and later in their 930s frontier commands in the East where they proved their bravery and other martial skills, and Romanus' son Christophorus came to be a reliable source of information on the legal profession and its rising stars, commencing his rise to become 'Quaestor' to Constantine VI in 935–42. The only other person who the Emperor trusted as much as this family was the equally Anatolian but in this case aristocratic general Bardas Phocas (OTL figure), one of his own ex-colleagues as a young officer in the late 890s, who was now *'dux'* of North Adiabene (Baku) and in 924 was recalled to Rome to act as the Emperor's personal aide-de-camp. As a major stud-owner in Cappadocia, Bardas provided a personal link to the world of elite cavalry horse-breeding and its socialite offshoots. His role – and that of his Cappadocian horse-breeding aristocratic friends and relations – in raising and training horses for the Imperial cavalry was important in the long term in improving the quality of the latter with their horses being supplied to much of the Empire's European and Levantine regiments and garrisons. It was matched in the lands to the east by the Transoxiana landowner and stud 'supremo' Bahram Samanius (OTL: emir Ismail the Samanid), principal supplier of steppe-bred horses to the regiments and garrisons of Sogdiana and the Jaxartes frontier in the 900s – 920s.

The drought-affected valleys of the Oxus and Jaxartes had suffered an agricultural decline in the later 9th century added to by brigandage by expelled money-strapped tenant-farmers ruined and sacked workers, and arable farms and orchards there had largely been replaced by pastoral farming. This also aided the growth of huge stud-farms in this region in the decades from c. 880 to 920, and the army was a reliable source of income. Bahram Samanius was one of the most successful and also reputedly the most ruthless of a number of 'stud magnates', some of them self-made retired army men of Turkish extraction, who cashed in on this boom. They and the local administration turned a blind eye to the evictions of indebted small farmers to make way for their large horse-herds. This was the 'downside' of the improvement in breeding and stamina of the army's 'North-Eastern frontier' horses, which was to aid the success of the Roman invasion of north-west India later in the century. As the military advantages and the work and money it gave to local landowners impressed the authorities in Rome the civil authorities ignored the injustice and social tensions even if the law was being blatantly ignored. More 'outlaws' turned bandit in the mountains of Badakshan or the Hindu Kush, while the biting satires of the corrupt and biased judicial system and 'rich-favouring' governors by a circle of talented young poets (usually writing in Persian not Greek or Latin as a 'protest gesture') in the local commercial and cultural 'hub' of Balkh in the 930s led to complaints of 'subversion' to Rome. A number of trials and exiles for alleged 'libel' and 'undermining the State' followed as the Justice Ministry sent in a team of lawyers to see that the 'ungrateful young wastrel' poets were dealt with, and most of the victims ended up living under police 'watch' in Mesopotamia or Syria. The lower ranks of the Church in Sogdiana also stood up for the accused in vain though their seniors kept quiet, and this duly attracted more recruits to a 'rebirth' of spiritually zealous new monasteries by disillusioned charismatic monks in the region. This caused the founding of new and austere monasteries and hermitages in the nearer reaches of the Pamirs away from the 'sinful' and authority-toadying behaviour of the urban elite. The local bishops, seeking in vain to impose central authority and theological 'test' on them, accused them of Nestorianism but this was probably slander in most (though not all) cases. But the general urban public of the great Oxus cities like Balkh, Buckhara, and Urgenj, benefiting from the improved and more secure trading-links to China overland as the pro-Roman Turkish warlords of the steppe were bribed or intimidated into protecting trading 'caravans' better in the 920s, were uninvolved in these controversies.

Chapter 14

Constantine VI 927–950: Finale of a Dynasty. Son of Leo V

The sudden and unexpected death of Leo V of a heart-attack on 19 September 927 during a Marble Palace reception, aged forty-nine, after only a seven-year reign precipitated his son Constantine onto the throne aged twenty-eight, the ministers (led by Autracellius and Lecapenus) having decided that it was too risky to put the late Emperor's eldest daughter on the throne as this could cause a provincial military revolt. Elements in the Senate and the Church would have preferred an election to choose a more 'worthy' and moral candidate who was not under a taint of illegitimacy, but the mechanism for doing this was not in place. In addition it would have offended those conservatives who believed in the principle of hereditary succession, as used for inheriting land and other property. The new Emperor had had a steep 'learning curve' to discover how to rule the Empire and who the elite were as he had been brought up in a low-class tavern in the provinces and in addition he had not done any but basic military service. Unlike Leo V or Honorius II he did not even have fellow ex-trainee officers to rely on as a group of friends, but this also made him a suitable 'front-man' for his more ambitious and power-seeking ministers although he was duly seen as their puppet and was widely derided in private in Rome elite social circles.

As the son-in-law of Lecapenus he was most open to the latter's influence and the military supremo was treated unofficially as an effective 'Basileopator' like Zeno II had been to his sons. But the crafty minister avoided being awarded this official rank or any other major new honorific in order to decrease jealousy and he also made sure that his three eldest sons all married into the upper ranks of the Roman nobility so that they had 'in-law' connections who had a stake in keeping the family at the centre of power. Constantine, his confidence bolstered by his far more clever and socially-attuned wife Helena, was cautious at first and made no major moves on policy or even appointments in order not to create criticism and well into the 930s he was relying on Autracellius to check and/or recommend all senior appointments in the civilian sphere. The Pope checked those in the Western Church and the army and navy appointments were either initiated or 'run past' Lecapenus. But thanks to his wife and a top team of speechwriters which he inherited from Leo he was able to present a coherent vision of honest and hard-working governance to the Senate and the public in his speeches, and he was a good 'actor' in public and could combine a mixture of masterful confidence and apparent sincerity.

Constantine kept to Leo's programme of public appearances and ceremonies if not to his full, rigorous religious programme of church and monastic visits and pilgrimages, seeming to be a devout and pious Christian of orthodox views to reassure the more wary or anti-'immorality' Churchmen and intellectuals who had at first looked askance at him for his dubious background. His own feelings of resentment at the Church for refusing communion to his mother or her relatives for 'immorality' and calling on him in the past to renounce them probably remained. He had a number of dubiously Christian and rather raffish young officers and 'Hellenophile' enthusiasts for Ancient Greek moral codes among his personal Court elite and in his Household. He was personally an enthusiast for the – pagan – 'Hellenic' heritage of Roman civilization and introduced a number of Hellenistic-style names for Court and Household appointments, as well as attending a lot of revived Ancient Greek plays at annual festivals in Rome and Sicily. Constantine was a fan of Euripides and as a cynical writer paid for a new and 'definitive' edition of his works, and indeed it was thanks to Constantine's personal interest in 'lost' Classical works that a team of scholars hired and paid by him tracked down a number of missing plays by Sophocles and poems by the 6th-century BC master-poets Anacreon and Simonides in libraries in Ionia and had them copied and brought to Rome. He doubled the size of the 'Poetry' section of the Great Library in Rome and saw to it that all sorts of venerable – and sometimes quite sexually explicit – poems were recited in public at his cultural dinners, and in 933 he created the first 'Professorship of Poetry' at Rome University, followed in 935 by a second one at Syracuse. (The more philosophy-orientated or puritanical 'Hellenists' however sniffed that the Empire was supposed to be preserving the more useful 'high culture' and scientific works of the Ancients, not lewd drinking-poems. His tastes were seen as suitable for a 'tavern boy'.)

But in public he was discreet and moral and he mouthed all the reassuring speeches given to him to read out on official occasions as the usual fulcrum and top symbol of a Catholic Court which followed the annual round of Christian feast-days with the Emperor attending religious services daily and treating the Pope and visiting senior clergy with respect. The Emperor remained at the centre of the well-established 'image of Heaven' rituals of the Imperial Court, venerated by the less sophisticated of his subjects as an intermediary with the Divine. He was portrayed in religious mosaics in the same way as the saints or the Divine court of angels, and he made the most of his opportunities to look majestic in rich silk robes and shimmering jewels – a long way from the life of a humble inn, as his critics sneered. He had the appearance of a courtly noble, if not the background. He gradually built up a personal clientele of younger nobles who he could trust at his Court though due to his dubious legitimacy some stiffer Italian 'old nobility' families, mainly devout Catholics, boycotted his court so there were more flexible 'service nobles' and their sons among his allies and in due course his court appointments. He also did more to take part in cultural events with a Christian as well as a 'Hellenist' context, as prompted by his advisers and a clique of young 'literati' nobles connected to Christophorus Lecapenus in particular. One of the latter, the 'neo-Theocritan' (i.e. follower and imitator of the 6th-century BC Greek poet of rural life and rustic idealism, Theocritus) poet and commentator Diocles Deciderianus, became his principal cultural adviser and 'Consul for the Arts' and provided most of the recommendations for Imperial patronage which the Emperor acted upon throughout the late 920s, 930s and early 940s. The Emperor also acted as a major patron of architecture, as Zeno had done but this time not as extravagantly and more as a co-ordinator of private patronage and also not as an amateur architect himself. In this case Demetrius Antrigonarius, the Constantinopolitan architect of recent private baths, chapels, racetracks, athletics-tracks, dining-halls, and bedroom-suites for the nobility in their summer homes on the Bosphorus shores and the nearby Princes' Islands, acted as his main adviser. This man's most well-connected rich patrons, cousins of the Lecapenid relative (and Romanus Lecapenus' aide) Romanus Argyrus, recommended him to Empress Helena in 929 to build at her husband's planned summer retreat near Capua in Campania.

This bolstered the influence of the 'dome and hall' Oriental styles from Persia in elite circles' building-projects and State buildings in Italy in the mid-10th century. The Imperial and Papal patronage of icons continued to follow the current artistic trends in the East but with a greater degree of realism and less stylization. The 'nave and aisles in a rectangular hall plus a tower at the east end' form of Church architecture continued to develop in the West but with less Imperial 'input' and spending on it than Zeno had patronised. The Emperor and his money-conscious Lecapeni 'in-laws' were careful not to seem too extravagant and though Constantine was a heavy drinker, not least from his youth serving in a tavern as well as out of stress and fear of assassination by snobbish nobles, he did not let this lead him into making rash promises of money while drunk as his great-uncle Zeno and cousins Probianus and uncle Honorius had done. A series of careful and 'detail-commanding' finance ministers served him and ensured that spending did not get out of control or the palace budget expanded too much. They were also themselves reined in politically and replaced every couple of years by Autracellius who did not want them emerging as rivals. Constantine was also cautious in the military field, and with budgets to look after and a need not to risk ventures that might go wrong and lead to criticism he quietly shelved all over-ambitious calls by 'experts' to strengthen the Empire's position in Africa (by extending Roman power south in the Sudan to the marshlands of the upper Nile or west towards Lake Chad) or in Asia (by interfering in the internecine wars between the Turkish tribes north of the Jaxartes and installing one or other of their branches as a formal vassal of the Empire with a regular tribute of men and horses). Embassies did however travel in his reign to the desert kingdom of Kanem on the shores of Lake Chad, returning with gifts of African elephants and gazelle to breed at Imperial wildlife parks in Italy and with exotic precious stones that whetted the appetite of Roman merchants, and to the southern Sudan desert tribes of Darfur. In both cases the links continued in later decades and the Roman military ended up recruiting a regiment of African javelineers from Darfur to station on the Red Sea coast of Eritrea and secure slaves and cash tribute from the inland tribes between the Sea and the upper Nile.

However, Constantine was prepared to back more commercial ventures by merchants by sea to the southern Indian peninsula and to Ceylon as less risky than a war, and in that cause kept up Zeno's plan of regular Roman naval escorts for the larger trading convoys to and from this region. In order to avoid any more Arab tribal attacks on and piratical use of the independent port towns on the south side of the Persian Gulf (mostly makeshift Arab settlements run by local chiefs or a small merchant oligarchy that traded with the Empire and India) he agreed to a 928 plan by Romanus Lecapenus and the Roman naval authorities in the Gulf, based at Charax. They advised him to secure formal treaties with all the main ports there, e.g. Bahrayn, Qatar, and Dubai, requiring them to admit small Roman garrisons and a Roman administrative staff to collect new customs-duties in the manner in which Rome had recently subdued the warlike tribes of Oman and eastern Hadramaut. In return, their menfolk would have job opportunities in new Roman army regiments, and as most of the volunteers were cavalry they were enrolled in existing Roman regiments in inland Persia and Bactria and sent off to garrison the frontier there against 'hit and run' Turkish raids. (Conveniently, the more restless and potentially uncontrollable Arab officers were settled there and were not allowed to return home.) This form of 'protectorate', enforced by regular naval visits, would keep the towns loyal and warn off any attacks from inland and new outbreaks of piracy. Although this was only agreed by the Emperor as a cheap means of securing an 'easy' diplomatic victory that could be played up as him safeguarding commerce and peace in a Vergilian scenario (i.e. as heir to Augustus in bringing stability and a 'golden age') in practice it served the Empire well. It cut the manpower available to the Gulf tribal chiefs, and warned them off any alliance with the emerging anti-Roman 'brigand state' of the 'Qarmatians', i.e. 'Seceders' (in Arabic) (OTL), a coalition of émigré 'losers' in the inter-Arab tribal struggles in northern Arabia after the later C9th droughts. They had lost out in battles for scarce water-resources for their herds and had had to move to the north-east of the peninsular, inland south of Charax, in the 890s and 900s.

This grouping of a mixture from assorted earlier tribes had then set up a new 'state' of brigand rebels who attacked other tribes and settled lands in southern Mesopotamia. They were continually being joined by runaway agricultural workers and irrigation-slaves from lower Mesopotamia, adopting a fierce 'Iconoclast' version of Christianity that portrayed the Empire as a land of icon-worshipping 'sin' which it was their duty to attack and loot. Though this movement barely registered with the authorities in Ctesiphon as more than a minor irritant they were sacking minor towns and farms around Hira and ancient Babylon and ambushing travellers South of the Euphrates by c. 900 in 915 a local Roman military expedition had had to be launched to drive them out of their main oasis settlements South of Hira and push them further East into the lands south of the Gulf near Bahrayn. The 'Qarmatian' coalition existed by pillaging their neighbours and attracting ambitious and impoverished local working-class men and others of low social rank of financial status to join them and by 928 they were casting their eyes on Bahrayn with its growing wealth from the Roman Persian Gulf trade to India. Thus Constantine's approval of the military action to bring the coastal sheikhdoms and merchant oligarchies under the closer control of the Empire staved off this threat and in the 930s the brigands moved on east to tackle the inland tribal chiefdoms of Oman instead.

Meanwhile in the West Constantine also authorized a slightly more risky but essentially small and local 'mopping-up operation' in a similar vein in 930 to annex the Norse fjords North of the Trondelag. This was no threat to the Empire or its central Norse trade entrepot of Trondjheim (yet) due to local fear of the devastating potential of 'Greek Fire' to sink attacking ships but still independent of Rome and a source for restive Vikings to sail off to Ireland or Iceland/Greenland. The local Norse merchants and seaborne traders in the Trondelag had been lured to set up trading associations on the Romano-Greek model and export local timber to the provinces of north-west continental Europe and /or built ships to the region's Roman traders.

This was seen as a way of keeping them busy and weaning them off piracy, and some were by now trading as far as Britain and Ireland which their ancestors had once pillaged. The lack of farmland in the narrow, steep valleys was also causing substantial numbers of landless younger sons to join the Roman army or move to farm in Roman eastern Caledonia, where the local *'dux'* wanted loyal outsiders to keep an eye on the region's restive locals. But some restive young Trondelagers were still sneaking off illegally to join their 'free' kinsmen in Iceland and Greenland, and the Roman authorities feared that plots to rebel in the region might result and were lobbying for the Empire to deal with the nearest likely 'rebel' allies in northern Norwegia first. As a result the Roman navy in the North Sea took a landing-force of around 12,000 men from Bergen up to the Arctic Circle in late spring 930 to take the region fjord by fjord and force the local farmers and occasional remaining lords to either surrender or flee. This 'land of fishermen and timber-cutters' was no major asset in trading terms and was more valuable in terms of long-term strategy in forcing bold and adventurous local commanders – often both farmers/fishermen and part-time warriors – to sign up to accept the 'Pax Romana' and work for Rome or to leave for exile. But as most of the menfolk in this region surrendered after a 'showpiece' demonstration of their will to resist there was not much fighting and compared to the Trondelag campaign earlier there were only a few short sieges and there was very little confiscation of lands. The main results were that a lack of opportunities for farming or trading in the region under the 'Pax Romana' led to an exodus of those with ambitions to indulge in these pursuits across the Roman North Sea world. This was mainly in Britain and Caledonia as the Romano-Danes of Dania and the Skaggerak coasts did not welcome Norse 'interlopers' into their well-established trading networks and the Continental elites to the south regarded them as semi-heathen barbarians. The watchful Roman military and naval commanders in the Trondelag wanted to 'thin out' the local manpower. Other Vikings departed secretly for Iceland to join those already in exile there, and some tried to illegally settle on isolated islands in the Orkneys and Shetlands well away from any Roman outposts and killed or evicted the locals during the 930s. This led to complaints by refugees to the Roman naval base at 'Portus Orcadius' in Scapa Flow and the troublemakers either having to leave or paying large bribes to be allowed to stay. There were only a small number of Roman naval patrols in the region with most of the available naval shipping busy protecting trade to the more important Cluta (OTL: Clyde) estuary in western Caledonia and to the river-mouths of Ulster in Ireland, so most of the scattered groups of Viking incomers managed to buy their way out of prosecution or violent suppression as the 'easy option' for the Roman commanders to take. They were after all good sailors and more useful as naval recruits than the evicted farming and fishing 'Picts'. Some of these new settlers were able to win good reputations with the Roman anti-piracy patrols in the Hibernian Sea as 'poachers turned gamekeepers' in the mid-10th century and even preyed on their (anti-Roman) fellow-Vikings in the Faroes with Roman naval backing to keep the Faroes' jarls on the defensive.

Some of the more successful self-made Viking chiefs-cum-captains settled in the Hebrides duly set up new jarldoms of their own there and built large and prestigious wooden halls to which Romano-Caledonian as well as Scandinavian associates came as visitors for their family feasts and assorted festivals. These included Arailt (Harald) Ivarrson from the 'House of Ragnar Lothbrok', Einar 'the One-Eyed' of the ex-ruling dynasty of Vestfold in Norwegia, and Thorfinn 'the Stout' who had reputedly made a fortune out of blackmailing isolated western Irish monasteries into paying his band of pirates off in the 900s–920s. (All OTL figures.)

The fishing-grounds off the Lofoten Islands were now opened to Romano-Norse fishermen from further South and Romano-Danish fishermen from Jutland and a new Roman market for fish and timber was set up at Tromso. In the long term there were also bonuses for the Empire in terms of added military recruitment to the Roman army and navy – many of the northern Norse seamen were skilled in handling the dangerous North Atlantic seas and now brought this advantage to the Roman navy – and in the extra timber (and later furs from Lapland) that could be brought south to be traded in Britain, Dania and Germany. The campaign was as usual presented to the Senate and public as a triumphant vindication of the Emperor's wise judgement and a sign of Divine approval for the extension of the 'Pax Romana'. Indeed the Emperor proved more open to the strange but compelling heroic and magical sagas that the incoming Norse army recruits to the 'comitatus' (and to a lesser extent the Guards) brought to Italy, as he heard them at army personnel social occasions, than most of the snobbish Roman elite. Unlike them he did not dismiss Norse culture as inferior to Mediterranean Romano-Greek 'civilized' ways. There was also to be some literary enthusiasm for and investigation of Norse legends by the more open-minded Roman scholars with an interest in non-Roman legends and oral poetry later in the 10th century that was stimulated by this arrival of new Norse military recruits (and to a lesser extent traders) from the remote north of Norwegia. But this was frowned on by the Church in Rome and in more conservative, doctrinally-obsessed regions such as Gaul, Spain, and North Africa as 'pagan' and thus 'sinful'. It was accordingly more common among scholars in Greece and Asia Minor who were already open to non-Mediterranean legends and poetry. The veteran Alexandria University literary investigator and linguist Basilius Bardanacius (d. 969), who by the 930s was already a leading expert on ancient Egyptian and Babylonian myths and had been writing them up for some years, was also to move onto Norse and Germanic myths and write a volume on them. He was active in this field at the end of Constantine's reign when there were a number of pioneering Norse timber-exporters from both Trondjheim and Tromso resident in Rome and in pursuit of contracts to supply timber to state building-projects in the western Mediterranean.

In Germany, whose ancestral religion and legends were closely kin to those of Scandinavia but lacked the advantage of a local university or much other 'post-16' education, what literary culture there was centred on either the Church or on heavily Romanised landed aristocrats. But in Britain (also short of non-Church education outside the south-east) there was already an extant, local corpus of 'Celtic' legends centred on an entirely different pantheon of gods and heroes and an imagined pre-Roman kingship. All of this went unnoticed by the self-consciously Latinate and Hellenic literary elite around the Court and university and the Academy of the Muses in Rome. The latter's idea of 'epic poetry' for their teaching – and research-programme was Romano-Greek and left out the 'barbarian' cultural world of the north. As Constantine – who did his best to be a literary patron, albeit one directed by more expert friends and clients – lacked the cultural skills and enthusiasm of Zeno he was content to follow the established trends of patronage and development not strike out with his own ideas. Indeed, his concern to appear as a conventional and acceptable Emperor and to live down his unusual and lower-class past led him to increasingly rely on the good opinions of conservative administrators and noble courtiers, the majority of whom were attuned to Catholic 'mores'. In line with this he fell back into a routine of Palace ceremonial and a regular round of annual visits to institutions across Italy (increasingly Church ones to seem pious like his father Leo) though he did attend the 932 Olympics during a tour of Greece and the Balkans, *en route* to winter 932–3 in Constantinople, and he also visited Syria and Egypt in 934 and Gaul and Spain in 936. Thereafter, he hardly left Italy at all except for occasional summer holidays in Syracuse in the late 930s and early 940s and two summer visits by specially commissioned 'luxury' five-tiered galley to the Aegean and the coast of Ionia (941 and 944). This reliance on a structured and and hierarchical world saw a deferential court as the 'reflection of Heaven'. This bolstered his often wavering sense of confidence, and his fondness for promoting the current trend in the highly structured and uninspiringly bureaucratic Church to praise the Imperial office as the 'defender of the True Faith' did not stop him from continuing to have a circle of hard-drinking and congenial cronies for his private parties with whom he could relax. Indeed the return of his less respectable brothers-in-law Constantine and Stephen Lecapenus to administrative roles at 'military HQ' in Rome in 938, with Constantine becoming 'Grand Domestic' i.e. deputy Praetorian Praefect in 940, saw this dubious pair actively using the Emperor's reliance on them to inform him of military opinion to see that he promoted their own friends and blocked their detractors. The wiser and more honest Christophorus as 'Quaestor' was a more admirable adviser and their father Romanus probably aimed to present him as the next Emperor given his accession to assorted honorific ranks and senior role as a court adviser in the late 930s and early 940s. When Autracellius retired in 942 the old Admiral even had his eldest son made 'Master of Offices' amidst angry claims of insufferable 'jobbery' and monopoly of senior offices in the senate. In fact Christophorus was honest and just and made a series of good appointments of senior ranked administrators in his department and of assorted legal commissioners and inspectors across the Empire after 942, cleaning up not creating corruption unlike his family's enemies claimed. If he did exercise a degree of control over ministerial appointments his choices were competent and the fault in letting him make decisions was that of an Emperor who by this point was growing lazy and increasingly alcoholic. (In OTL Christophorus died young.)

The veteran admiral and his military allies rather than Constantine were the deciding factor in agreeing in 938 to intervene in the current civil war between rival factions of the Magyar tribal leadership in the Ukraine to try to stabilize this potential threat and arrange for a pro-Roman leader to take over, the Khazars' power now being in sharp decline as their regional vassals broke away from them. This civil war also brought in the new Swedish-origin 'Rus' warlord ruling in Kievum near the Magyar region, Igor grandson of Rurik (the latter having been a 900s-910s timber-trader and mercenary-supplier chief magistrate of Novgorod on Lake Ladoga to the north), (OTL) to seek Roman help as one of the rival Magyar contenders turned on his trading-town for its help to his enemies and besieged it. The Roman expeditionary force under 'Count of the Euxine and Crimea' Justin Hauterius' deputy commander Titus Javanerius relieved the Magyar siege of Kievum later in 938. After a winter consolidating its position there they moved on to the Don valley to link up with the Khazars and attack the triumphant Magyar pretender Arakindas. But this expedition went wrong as the cautious government in Rome had not given Javanerius as many troops as he and Hauterius wanted – rumour had it that Lecapenus was afraid that if the commander won a decisive victory he could use the public euphoria to turn on his long-time rivals the younger Lecapenids and stage a revolt or a coup, so a stalemate was politically preferable. A surprise reinforcement of nomad Magyar-allied cavalry fell on Javanerius' camp as he chased the enemy back up the Don and caused chaos.

Flaming nomad arrows set fire to the Roman tents, their artillery depot was captured and dismantled to be dragged off on Magyar wagons, and hundreds of Roman soldiers were killed. Though Javanerius managed to extricate what was left of his army and get back to the Sea of Azov for a naval evacuation the triumphant Arakindas took over the Magyars' entire realm and expelled his rivals, then blocking the Dnieper to Roman shipping and capturing assorted Roman merchants there for ransom. Igor tried to rescue the Romans with his Slav/'Rus' forces but was ambushed and killed and 939 ended with the Magyars besieging Kievum again. Although its Roman-built stone walls and artillery protected it successfully and Igor's widow Helga (OTL) rallied the state successfully in the name of her young son Sviatoslav (OTL), a Roman army from Langobardia arriving to the rescue in spring 940, the Magyars blocked the Dnieper by preying on Roman and 'Rus' shipping at the rapids (where the sailors had to land and carry their vessels round the midstream rocks) until in 947 the Emperor paid them to desist and the defeat was the cause of militant patriotic rioting by the lower classes in Rome and other cities. The enemies of the Lecapeni blamed them for incompetence and 'jobbery' and the Church had to crack down on preachers and monkish writers who started to attack 'sin' in high places or even to suggest that God was punishing the Empire for making a bastard Emperor. When Christophorus Lecapenus, the best of the younger male generation of his dynasty, died suddenly in spring 947 aged fifty-two that ended his father's hopes of him succeeding his brother-in-law.

The old Roman nobility now rallied against the Lecapeni and their success in getting the Emperor to appoint a friend of theirs as the new 'Master of Offices' and another as 'Quaestor' so they could cover up their influence and corrupt practices led to a mass-resignation of other ministers in reply in July 947. With Romanus Lecapenus ill and off work it was the Empress, who to her credit was morally concerned at her brothers' behaviour, who persuaded Constantine VI to back down and appoint some acceptable new ministers who were not connected to her family. The ageing and sick Romanus Lecapenus had to retire to avoid an investigation by legal department commissioners of his finances. The competent new 'Master of Offices' Philostratus Pauntercius exercised a ruthless and totally honest 'clean-up' of the government in 947–9, restoring public and senatorial confidence in it, and the mystery assassination of the obnoxious Constantine Lecapenus in May 948 while he was under legal investigation for embezzlement and selling offices was said to be either due to a 'hit' by officers who he had cheated or a grudge by the family of a discarded mistress (one of many). It was even said that he had been killed to stop him turning State's evidence and betraying the Emperor's part in covering up his crimes. Though his equally unsavoury and extravagant brother Stephen was put on trial for corruption he was allowed to go free after pleading guilty and handing back all the money which he had taken illegally plus two-thirds of his estates and he was able to retire to Galatia in peace; the other brother, Theophylact, fled to Egypt and was not prosecuted but his estates were seized too. (The sudden fall of the younger Lecapeni is OTL.)

The Emperor's reputation was ruined by association with them and the remainder of his reign was to see him reduced to a querulous alcoholic who was only sporadically fit enough to take part in official ceremonies or appear in public. But the new ministers and army leaders did not pursue him for his past mistakes or let too much criticism of him appear in public and the Church hierarchy continued to praise the Imperial office. Even its present incumbent, the shameless careerist Pope Theophilus (a cousin of a leading senator and very much a bureaucrat more suited to a lay than an ecclesiastical role, who had virtually inherited the bishopric of Padua from his uncle in 928) blamed all the recent military disasters and lay corruption on anonymous figures who had conned the noble Lecapeni. The grass-roots and provincial disgust at the part that the Papacy and the central bureaucracy in the Church in Rome was playing in a 'cover-up' and the prosecution and exiles of anyone who dared to object damaged the reputation of the Papacy for decades. This led to calls for the next Emperor to conduct a 'clean-up' and choose more moral and independent figures for high Church office. But in the short term the 'cover-up' had its way and even in the more sternly 'Ciceronian' wing of the Senate, a group of aristocrats of old family who wanted the Senate to take a greater role in governing and rein in corrupt bureaucrats, the Empress was not criticized. It was accepted that she had done her best to rein in and then to expose her unsavoury three brothers – Christophorus was praised as having been above criticism and of high morals. The latter's judicial work as kept up by the legal department under its new 'quaestor' and a team of inspectors who the late minister had largely chosen himself. When the disgraced Constantine VI finally died of an alcoholic fit on 22 July 950, aged fifty-one, and the dynasty was extinct in the male line it was 'Master of Offices' Pauntercius' younger brother Romanus, a strictly moral senior judge in the Roman city law-courts of exemplary reputation, aged 54, who was chosen as Emperor by the Senate on the fourth vote on 24 July. This was on account of his good work in judging and sentencing the young Lecapeni's cronies in the 947–8 trials, which had brought him into the public eye as a man of 'virtus' and reliability. A man of high reputation and integrity had been chosen not a puppet of a faction of nobles or state bureaucrats – albeit only as various higher-profile candidates all had enough enemies to block their accession. But would this prevent ambitious generals, in the 'high command' in Rome or on frontiers, deciding to challenge the civilians' unexpected choice?